IF YOU BELIEVE IN WHANGDOODLES[1] AND GILLYGALOOS,[2] YOU'LL BE THE TOPIC OF MUCH CUGGERMUGGER![3]

"THERE IS NO COMPARABLE WORK. I UNRESERVEDLY RECOMMEND IT."

—*Chicago Daily News*

"You can dip in anywhere and come up with pay dirt...hundreds of words to stand your hair on end."

—*Newsday*

1 a mythical bird that grieves continually
2 a mythical bird that lays square eggs
3 whispered gosipping

Josefa Heifetz Byrne, daughter of the famed violinist Jascha Heifetz, has had a flourishing career as a concert pianist and composer. Before making her debut as a pianist in 1957, she studied for two years at the Paris Conservatory of Music, and later won composition prizes. She has performed in scores of American cities. Now, her hobby of collecting odd and unique words has resulted in this one-of-a-kind and wonderful dictionary.

Mrs. Byrne's Dictionary

of Unusual, Obscure, and Preposterous Words

Gathered from numerous and diverse
Authoritative Sources

By Josefa Heifetz Byrne

Edited, with an introduction by
Mr. Robert Byrne

WASHINGTON SQUARE PRESS
PUBLISHED BY POCKET BOOKS NEW YORK

WSP

A Washington Square Press Publication of
POCKET BOOKS, a division of Simon & Schuster, Inc.
1230 Avenue of the Americas, New York, N.Y. 10020

ISBN: 0-671-49782-0

First Pocket Books printing January, 1984

10 9 8 7 6 5 4 3 2 1

WASHINGTON SQUARE PRESS, WSP and colophon are
registered trademarks of Simon & Schuster, Inc.

Printed in the U.S.A.

Editor's Introduction

Incredible as it may seem, every entry in this book, even the most ludicrous, has been accepted as a formal or legitimate English word by at least one major dictionary. The dignity that goes with endorsement by lexicographers of trusted sobriety, however, was not enough for inclusion here—subjective criteria were applied as well. The words had to strike the author as unusual, obscure, difficult, unfamiliar, amusing, or preposterous. Thus Mrs. Byrne has created a new kind of dictionary: one based entirely on her own tastes.

A language like English, rich in synonyms and near-synonyms, leaves an enormous slag-heap behind it as it advances and evolves. Some nations appoint commissions to root through the ash pile and dispose of the worst clinkers.

The problem, of course, is that one man's clinker is another man's nugget. Applying the label is often a matter of personal preference. Mrs. Byrne made the choice several hundred thousand times during the ten years she spent researching this book. Working alone and without government support (or even comprehension) she managed to assemble the six thousand weirdest words in the English language. Nobody asked her to do it because nobody thought such a thing was possible. In fact, I asked her *not* to do it. Completed, the book stands as one of the most remarkable and peculiar feats of compulsive lexicography since Cawdrey's *A Table Alphabeticall . . . Of Hard Usual English Words* in 1604.

Mrs. Byrne's Dictionary brings into view thousands of little-known curiosities that lie buried in specialized dictionaries and unabridged works too bulky for browsing. Mrs. Byrne exhumed many words from the boneyards of the obsolete and the nearly forgotten because in her judgment they deserved another chance to live. Words like *hieromachy—a fight between men or women of the cloth,* and *minimifidianism—having almost no faith or belief.* Words like *furfuraceous—covered with dandruff; kakistocracy—government by the worst citizens; omphaloskepsis—meditation while gazing at one's navel;* and *gardyloo!—a warning cry made before ejecting slops from the windows of old Edinburgh.*

For years anthropologists have been describing certain Hottentots with the help of the word *steatopygia—having too much fat in the buttocks*. It is far too useful to be restricted in its application to the African bush. The American people need this word.

Medicine and law have many terms that merit wider currency. In these pages you'll find *deraign—to settle a dispute by combat between the litigants*, and *dharna—an attempt to collect a debt by camping on the debtor's doorstep until he either pays you or you starve to death*. Political analysts should find a use for *palilalia—involuntarily repeating a phrase faster and faster*.

Some words are included because of their odd mixture of meanings. For example, several dictionaries define *bismer* as *1. shame; 2. a disgraceful person; 3. a steelyard; 4. the fifteen-spined stickleback*. My favorite in this group is *merkin—1. female genitalia; 2. false pubic hair; 3. a mop for swabbing cannons*.

In writing definitions, the goals were clarity and directness. *Edentate* is defined by one word: *toothless*. In contrast, the sixth edition of Merriam-Webster's Collegiate offers *destitute of teeth*. In addition to pomposity, most dictionaries are afflicted with an unfitting evasiveness when it comes to certain words relating to the human body. You'll find no frustrating delicacy or cowardice in Mrs. Byrne. When faced with words like *rectalgia* and *proctalgia* she comes right out and calls them a pain in the ass.

Some readers may complain that more than a sprinkling of slang should have been included. Others will claim that words are in that should be out, and vice versa. Such readers can only be invited to write their own dictionaries.

Although *Mrs. Byrne's Dictionary* has enough comedy in it to reward casual browsers, it is intended to serve as a supplement to a desk dictionary. A word not listed in either place is not worth having at your fingertips, unless, of course, you are an institution, a library, or a governmental body at the federal, state, or municipal level.

The author and editor apologize for the ammunition this book provides to bad writers.

ROBERT BYRNE

In the good old days when *Webster's New International Dictionary* (2nd edition) was considered the undisputed authority, one had merely to consult it in order to settle an argument concerning the pronunciation, say, of the word *contumely*. It offers one: *kŏn'tū-mē"lĭ*. End of argument. But suppose that same argument arose today? *Webster's New International* (3rd edition) heads its list with kən-tū'mə-lē, followed by nine more for comparison shoppers. Thirteen other dictionaries add to the disagreement by disgorging twenty additional pronunciations and bringing the grand total to thirty-one.

First syllable accented with secondary stress on penultimate:

     kŏn'tū-mē"lē
     kŏn'tū-mē"lĭ
     kŏn'tōō-mē"lĭ
     kŏn'tōō-mē"lĭ
     kŏn'tə-mē"lē
     kŏn'tyə-mē"lē
     kŏn'tyōō-mē"lē
     kŏn'tyōō-mē"lĭ
     kŏn'chə-mē"lē

First syllable accented with secondary stress on antepenultimate:

     kŏn'tū"mə-lē
     kŏn'tū"mə-lĭ

First syllable accented without secondary stress:

     kŏn'tū-mə-lē
     kŏn'tū-mə-lĭ
     kŏn'tū-mē-lĭ
     kŏn'tū-mē-lə
     kŏn'tōō-mə-lē
     kŏn'tōō-mə-lĭ
     kŏn'tōō-mə-lē
     kŏn'tōō-mə-lĭ
     kŏn'tyōō-mə-lē

kŏn′tyŏŏ-mə-lĭ
kŏn′chə-mə-lē

First syllable accented in three-syllable version:

kŏn′tūm-lē
kŏn′tyəm-lē
kŏn′təm-lē
kŏn′chəm-lē

Second syllable accented:

kən-tū′mə-lē
kən-tū′mə-lĭ
kən-tū′mē-lē
kən-tŏŏ′mə-lē
kən-tŏŏ′mə-lĭ

My own favorite pronunciation, *kŏn′tŏŏm-lē*, is not yet among the accepted ones, but the way things have been going I'm sure some day it will be.

Most dictionaries do not confront the browser with such a variety of conflicting pronunciations. *Charientism* (a gracefully veiled insult), a word I finally tracked down in the august pages of the *Oxford English Dictionary*, was bereft of pronunciation even in that grand panjandrum of lexicons. "If you don't know how to pronounce a word, say it loud!"[1] hence, *kăr′-ĭ-ən-tĭz″əm*, based on Greek roots and cold logic.

Mrs. Byrne's pronunciation guide is self-explanatory with the following exceptions: the long u (ū) resolutely maintained by the British is shortened whenever I think I can get away with it. The vowel sound in *care, fair*, etc., I do not consider to be significantly different from that of the short e in *lĕt, mĕt*, etc., *when followed by an r*. The act of sounding the r is enough to slightly alter the pronunciation. Therefore, I have not used a different symbol. (Care=kĕr; fair=fĕr, etc.) Like everything else in this dictionary, the pronunciation, though not necessarily authoritative, is decidedly authoritarian.

I wish to state plainly that this is not a book in which one may find romantic stories about word origins. Etymological books abound and proliferate like drosophilae. There is surely no need to add to that swollen list. I do include the etymology when it seems necessary for a complete understanding of the word, or when it is uncommonly interesting. As for definitions, I have written them after comparing those of the leading authorities. Any errors, however, are my own, and behind them I stand nervously.

JOSEFA HEIFETZ
(Mrs. Byrne)

[1] William Strunk: *The Elements of Style*, edited by E.B. White; The Macmillan Company, New York, 1959.

Pronunciation Guide

main stress'   secondary stress"

hallucination (hə-lōō"sĭn-ā'shən)
paleontology   (pā"lē-ŏn-tŏl'ə-jē)

Stressed Vowels

a	man	(măn)
a	made	(mād)
e	let	(lĕt)
e	be	(bē)
i	sip	(sĭp)
i	wine	(wīn)
o	hot	(hŏt)
o	cold	(kōld)
o	sore	(sôr)
u	dull	(dŭl)
u	fugue	(fūg)
u	burp	(bûrp)
oo	good	(gŏŏd)
oo	food	(fōōd)
ou	out	(out)

Unstressed Vowels

The *schwa* (ə) sounds like a cross between the u in dŭll and the u in bûrp.

balloon	(bə-lōōn')
omen	(ō'mən)
gallon	(găl'ən)
Saturday	(săt'ər-dā)

The short i (ĭ) usually retains its stressed sound in unstressed syllables, though the lack of stress will soften it somewhat.

Consonants

c	cat	(kăt)	th	thin	(thĭn)
c	cent	(sĕnt)	th	this	(thĭs)
g	gender	(jĕn'dər)	x	ax	(ăks)
g	get	(gĕt)	x	exhibit	(ĕgz-ĭb'ĭt)
q	quay	(kā)	y	year	(yĭr)
q	quick	(kwĭk)	z	zebra	(zē'brə)
s	so	(sō)	z	azure	(ă'źər)
s	is	(ĭz)

FOREIGN

1. The French nasal sounds: ent, in, on, un, are indicated by N as, *lent* (lŏN); *vin* (văN); *mon* (môN); *un* (ŭN). 2. The heavily aspirated h, as the ch in Bach; is indicated by ĥ as, *Bach* (bŏĥ). 3. The french u in *dur* and the German u in *für* are indicated by umlauts as, *dur* (dür); *für* (für).

---

măn; māde; lĕt; bē; sĭp; wīne; hŏt; cōld; sôre; dŭll; fūgue; bûrp; gŏŏd; fōōd; out; gĕt; thin; this; year; ażure; ō'mən"; viN; für; Bacĥ

aa (ä'ä) *n.* rough, crumbling lava (Hawaiian).

aasvogel (äs'fō"gəl) *n.* the South African vulture.

abacinate (ä-bäs'ĭ-nāt) *v.t.* to blind by putting a red-hot copper basin near the eyes.

abaction (ä-băk'shən) *n.* cattle-stealing.

abasia (ä-bā'žĭ-ə) *n.* inability to walk because of lack of muscular coordination.

abattoir (äb'ə-twôr) *n.* a slaughter-house.

abatvoix (ö-bö-vwö') *n.* a sounding board or canopy over the speaker's platform (French *abbatre* = to throw down + *voix* = voice).

abbey-lubber (äb'ē-lŭb"ər) *n.* a lazy monk pretending to be ascetic; any loafer.

abbozzo (ö-bôt'sö) *n.* a rough draft or sketch.

Abderian (äb-dĭr'ĭ-ən) *adj.* pertaining to foolish or excessive laughter (from *Abdero*, the birthplace of Democritus, the "laughing philosopher").

abditive (äb'dĭ-tĭv) *adj.* able to hide; hidden.

abducent (äb-dōō'sənt) *adj.* carrying or drawing away; abducting.

abecedarian (ā"bē-sē-dèr'ĭ-ən) *n.* a person learning the alphabet; a beginner; one teaching the alphabet or fundamentals of a subject. *-adj.* pertaining to the alphabet; elementary.

abecedism (ä-bē-sē'dĭz"əm) *n.* a word created from the initials of words in a phrase; an acronym (slang).

abigeus (äb-ĭg'ē-əs) *n.* a cattle rustler.

abiogenesis (ā"bĭ-ō-jèn'-ə-sĭs) *n.* spontaneous generation.

abishag (ä'bĭ-shàg) *n.* the child of a woman and married man not her husband (from Hebrew = the mother's error).

ablactation (äb-läk-tā'shən) *n.* weaning.

ablation (ä-blā'shən) *n.* surgical removal; wearing or wasting away.

ablepsia (ä-blèp'sĭ-ə) *n.* blindness.

abligurition (ä-blĭg"yər-ĭsh'ən) *n.* extravagance in cooking and serving (obs.).

ablutomania (ä-blōō"tə-mā'nĭ-ə) *n.* a mania for washing oneself.

abra (ŏ'brŏ) *n.* a narrow mountain pass (Spanish).

abraxas (à-bràk'səs) *n.* a god worshiped by the Gnostics until the thirteenth century; the word carved on gems, which were used as charms or amulets.

abreaction (ăb-rē-ăk'shən) *n.* release of repressed ideas or emotions during psychoanalysis.

abrosia (à-brō'zĭ-ə) *n.* fasting.

abscotchalater (ăb-skŏch'ə-lā"tər) *n.* one in hiding from the police (slang).

absinthism (ăb'sĭn-thĭ"zəm) *n.* a nervous or mental illness resulting from overimbibing absinthe.

absquatulate (ăb-skwŏt'yə-lāt) *v.i.* to leave hurriedly, suddenly, or secretly.

absterge (ăb-stûrj') *v.t.* to wipe clean; to purge.

abuccinate (à-bŭk'sĭn-āt) *v.t.* to proclaim, like a fanfare.

abulic (à-boo'lĭk) *adj.* pertaining to a lack of will power. also *aboulic*.

acalculia (à-kăl-kū'lĭ-ə) *n.* the inability to work with numbers; a mental block against arithmetic.

acanaceous (à-kən-ā'shəs) *adj.* prickly.

acapnotic (à-kăp-nŏt'ĭk) *n.* a nonsmoker.

acarophobia (ă"kər-ə-fō'bĭ-ə) *n.* fear of itching or of those insects that cause it.

acarpous (à-kŏrp'əs) *adj.* fruitless, sterile. -syn. *agennesic, apogenous, anandrious*.

acataleptic (à-kăt"ə-lĕp'tĭk) *adj.* incomprehensible.

acceptilation (ăk-sĕp"tĭl-ā'shən) *n.* the settlement of a debt without payment.

accessit (ăk-sĕs'ĭt) *n.* a prize for students in second place (British).

accidence (ăk'sĭ-dĕns) *n.* 1. a grammar book. 2. the fundamentals of just about anything.

accismus (ăk-sĭz'məs) *n.* a phony refusal (rhetoric).

accolent (ak'ō-lənt) *adj.* living nearby; neighboring. –*n.* a neighbor.

accubation (ak-ū-bā'shən) *n.* reclining at meals.

accubitum (à-kū'bĭ-tūm) *n.* a crescent-shaped couch for five people used by ancient Roman diners.

acedia (à-sē'dĭ-ə) *n.* apathy, boredom, sloth.

aceldama (à-sĕl'də-mə) *n.* a battlefield (referring to the alleged "potter's field" near Jerusalem bought with Judas's filthy lucre. Acts 1:19. Matt. 27:8).

acervuline (à-sûr'vū-lĭn) *adj.* resembling small heaps.

acescent (à-sĕs'ənt) *adj.* slightly sour; turning sour.

acetarious (à-sə-tĕr'ĭ-əs) *adj.* pertaining to plants used in salads.

acetylseryltyrosylserylisoleucylthreonylserylprolylserylglutaminylphenylalanylvalylphenylalanylleucylserylserylvalyltryptophylalanylaspartylprolylisoleucylglutamylleucylleucylasparaginylvalylcysteinylthreonylserylserylleucylglycylasparaginylglutaminylphenylalanylglutaminylthreonylglutaminylglutaminylalanylarginylthreonylthreonylglutaminylvalylglutaminylglutaminylphenylalanylserylglutaminylvalyltryptophyllysylprolylphenylalanylprolylglutaminylserylthreonylvalylarginylphenylalanylprolylglycylaspartylvalyltyrosyllysylvalyltyrosylarginyltyrosylasparaginylalanylvalylleucylaspartylprolylleucylisoleucylthreonylalanyl-

leucylleucylglycylthreonylphen-
ylalanylaspartylthreonylarginyl-
asparaginylarginylisoleucyliso-
leucylglutamylvalylglutamylas-
paraginylglutaminylglutaminyl-
serylprolylthreonylthreonyl-
anylglutamylthreonylleucylas-
partylalanylthreonylarginylar-
ginylvalylaspartylaspartylalan-
ylthreonylvalylalanylisoleucyl-
arginylserylaspraginyl-
isoleucylasparaginylleucylvalyl-
asparaginylglutamylleucylvalyl-
arginylglycylthreonylglycylleu-
cyltyrosylasparaginylglutam-
inylasparaginylthreonylphenyl-
alanylglutamylserylmethionyl-
serylglycylleucylvalyltrypto-
phylthreonylserylalanylprolylal-
anylserine (ă-sē″tĭl-ĕt-sĕt′ər-ə) n.
(1185 letters) the protein part of
the tobacco mosaic virus
($C_{785}H_{1220}N_{212}O_{248}S_2$). for the
longest word, see *methionylglu-
taminyl*... (1,913 letters).

achaetous (ə-kāt′əs) adj. hairless.

acherontic (ăk-ər-ŏn′tĭk) adj. dark,
gloomy, forbidding (from Hades'
river, *Acheron*).

achlorophyllaceous (ə-klôr″ə-fĭl-
ă′shəs) adj. colorless.

acicular (ə-sĭk′ū-lər) adj. with
sharp points like a needle; needle-
shaped.

aciniform (ə-sĭn′ĭ-fôrm) adj.
formed like a grape cluster.

acology (ə-kŏl′ə-jē) n. the science
or study of medical remedies.

acomia (ə-kō′mĭ-ə) n. baldness;
-syn. *atrichia, calvities, phalacrosis, alopecia*.

acopic (ə-kŏp′ĭk) adj. relieving
tiredness.

acouasm (ə-kōō′ə-zəm) n. a ringing sound in the head.

acousticophobia (ə-kōōs″tĭ-kō-
fō′bĭ-ə) n. fear of noise.

acraein (ă-krē′ĭn) n. a substance
secreted by certain butterflies
making them unpalatable to their
enemies.

acritochromacy (ăk″rĭ-tə-krō′mə-
sē) n. color blindness; *achroma-
topsy*.

acroamatic (ăk″rō-ə-măt′ĭk) adj.
esoteric, abstruse, profound.
acroatic, pertaining to profound
learning.

acrocephalic (ăk″rō-sə-făl′ĭk) adj.
pertaining to pointed heads. –n.
someone with a pointed head.

acrology (ə-krŏl′ə-jē) n. the science
of representing names using initials, pictures, etc.

acronical (ə-krŏn′ĭ-kəl) adj.
happening at sunset or twilight.
also *acronycal, -ichal, -ychal*.

acronyx (ăk′rō-nĭks) n. an ingrow-
ing nail.

ACTH. see *adrenocorticotropic hormone.*

acushla (ə-kōōsh′lə) n. darling. see
cushlamochree (Irish).

acutiator (ə-kū′shĭ-ā″tər) n. in
medieval times, a sharpener of
weapons.

acyanoblepsia (ə-sī″ə-nō-blĕp′sĭ-ə)
n. inability to distinguish blue;
blue-blindness.

acyesis (ā-sī-ē′sĭs) n. female sterility. –syn. *atocia.*

acyrology (ə-sĭr-ŏl′ə-jē) n. poor
diction.

Adamitism (ăd′əm-īt″ĭz-əm) n.
going naked for God; imitating
Adam for religious reasons.

adda (ăd′ə) n. the common Egyptian skink, one-time curer of lep-
rosy, so they say.

adephagous (ə-dĕf′ə-gəs) adj. gluttonous.

adeps (ăd′ĕps) n. the purified fat of
the hog's abdomen.

adespoton (ə-dĕs′pə-tən) n. an

anonymous poem or saying.

adevism (ăd'ə-vĭz"əm) n. the denial of legendary gods.

adiaphoretic (ăd"ĭ-ă-fə-rĕt'ĭk) n. a drug to inhibit sweating. -adj. pertaining to sweat prevention.

adiaphoristic (ăd"ĭ-ă-fə-rĭs'tĭk) adj. theologically indifferent.

adiaphorous (ăd-ĭ-ăf'ôr-əs) adj. neutral; neither right nor wrong; neither deleterious nor salubrious.

adipose (ăd'ĭ-pōz) adj. fatty.-n. fat.

adit (ăd'ĭt) n. a mine entrance; generally, a drainage or ventilation tunnel.

adjectitious (ăj-ĕk-tĭ'shəs) adj. added, thrown in (obs.).

adlittoral (ăd-lĭt'ə-rəl) adj. pertaining to the shallow water near the shore.

admanuensis (ăd-măn"ū-ĕn'sĭs) n. one who takes an oath by touching the Bible (obs.).

adminicle (ăd-mĭn'ĭ-kəl) n. something that helps or supports; corroboratory evidence; explanatory proof.

adnomination (ăd-nŏm"ĭ-nā'shən) n. punning. also ag-, an-.

adonize (ăd'ə-nīz) v.t. to beautify [men].

adosculation (ăd-ŏs"kū-lā'shən) n. fertilization by external contact only.

adoxography (ăd-ŏks-ŏg'rə-fē) n. good writing on a trivial subject.

adrenocorticotropic, -trophic (ă-drĕn"ō-kôr"tĭ-kō-trŏp'ĭk, -trŏf'ĭk) hormone n. (ACTH) the hog's pituitary hormone, effective against rheumatoid and allergic disorders.

adrogation (ăd-rō-gā'shən) n. adoption of a boy under fourteen years or of a girl under twelve.

adscititious (ăd-sĭ-tĭsh'əs) adj. sup-

plementary, extra, additional.

adulterine (ă-dŭl'tər-īn) n. an illegitimate child.

adumbrate (ă-dŭm'brāt) v.t. to outline in a hazy sort of way; to over- or foreshadow.

aduncity (ă-dŭn'sĭ-tē) n. crookedness, hookedness.

advena (ăd-vĕn'ə) n. one who has not become a citizen of his adopted country.

advenient (ăd-vēn'ĭ-ənt) adj. due to outside causes.

adversaria (ăd-vŭr-sĕr'ĭ-ə) n. a miscellaneous collection of notes or remarks; commentaries on a text or document.

advesperate (ăd-vĕs'pər-āt) v.i. to draw toward evening (obs.).

adytum (ăd'ĭ-təm) n. an inner sanctum.

aegrotat (ē-grō'tăt) n. 1. a student's written medical excuse. 2. the degree given to a student prevented by illness from taking final exams.

aelurophile (ē-lŏŏr'ə-fīl) n. a cat-lover; aelurophobe (fōb) n. a cat-hater.

aeneous (ă-ēn'ĭ-əs) adj. brassy; like brass in color and luster.

aeolistic (ē-ə-lĭs'tĭk) adj. long-winded.

aeonian (ē-ō'nĭ-ən) adj. everlasting.

aeromancy (ĕr'ə-măn"sē) n. fortunetelling by air or wind; weather forecasting.

aerugo (ē-rōō'gō) n. the rust of any metal, especially of brass or copper; verdigris.

aes (ēz) n. bronze or copper; bronze or copper money (Roman antiquity).

aesculapian (ĕs-kū-lā'pĭ-ən) adj. medical (from Aesculapius, god of healing).

affabrous (àf'ə-brəs) *adj.* work-manlike.

affabulation (à-fàb"ū-lā'shən) *n.* the moral of a fable (obs.).

afflatus (à-flā'təs) *n.* an artistic inspiration.

affy (à-fē') *v.t.* 1. to confide or trust (+ *to* or *in*) 2. to betroth, join closely. 3. to make affidavit.

afterages (àf'tər-āj"əz) *n.* a child born long after its siblings (slang).

afterwit (àf'tər-wĭt) *n.* the locking of the barn door after the cows have gone (slang).

agamic (ā-gàm'ĭk) *adj.* asexual; parthenogenic.

agapemone (àg-ə-pĕm'ən-ē) *n.* British commune of 1846 sanctioning free love (cap.); any such group.

agapetae (àg-ə-pē'tē) *n.* early churchwomen who lived (strictly platonically) with avowedly celibate men.

agar-agar (ā'gòr-ā"gòr) *n.* a gelatinous substance extracted from certain seaweeds and used for culture media, laxatives, and oriental soups.

agastopia (à-gàs-tō'pĭ-ə) *n.* admiration of a particular part of someone's body.

agathism (àg'ə-thĭ"zəm) *n.* the concept that all is for the better.

agathokakological (àg"ə-thə-kàk"ō-lòj'ĭ-kəl) *adj.* composed of both good and evil.

agenhina (à-jĕn'ĭ-nə) *n.* a guest at an inn, who, after having stayed for three nights, was considered one of the family (Saxon law).

agennesic (àj-ən-ēs'ĭk) *adj.* sterile; impotent. −*syn.* acarous, apogenous, anandrious.

agenocratia (à-jĕn"ō-krà'tĭ-ə) *n.* opposition to birth control.

agerasia (àj-ə-rā'sĭ-ə) *n.* youthful appearance in an older person.

ageusia (à-gū'sĭ-ə) *n.* loss of or damage to the sense of taste.

aggeration (àj-ər-ā'shən) *n.* amassing, heaping up; an accumulation.

agiotage (àj'ĭ-ō-tāj") *n.* stock speculation.

agistment (à-jĭst'mənt) *n.* 1. taking care of someone's cattle; the fee paid. 2. a land tax.

agley (àg-lī') *adj.* awry (Scottish).

agminate (àg'mĭn-āt) *adj.* bunched together.

agnogenic (àg-nō-jĕn'ĭk) *adj.* of unknown cause.

agnoiology (àg-nō-yòl'ə-jē) *n.* the study of ignorance.

agnomen (àg-nō'mən) *n.* an additional name describing some exploit; a nickname.

agnosy (àg'nō-sē) *n.* ignorance; especially ignorance shared by the whole human race.

agomphious (à-gòm'fĭ-əs) *adj.* toothless.

agonistic (à-gən-ĭs'tĭk) *adj.* combative; strained for the sake of effect. also *agonistical*.

agoraphobia (àg"ər-ə-fō'bĭ-ə) *n.* fear of public places and open spaces.

agouara (ò-gōō-ò'rò) *n.* 1. any of various wild dogs of South America. 2. the crab-eating raccoon.

agrestian (à-grès'tĭ-ən) *adj.* growing wild.

agriologist (àg-rĭ-òl'ə-jĭst) *n.* an authority on primitive peoples.

agrizoiatry (àg"rĭ-zō-ī'ət-rē) *n.* branch of medicine specializing in wild animals.

agroof (à-grōōf') *adj.* flat on one's face (Scottish).

agrostographer (à-gròs-tòg'rə-fûr) *n.* someone who writes about grasses; *agrostologist*.

agrypnia (à-grĭp'nĭ-ə) *n.* sleeplessness.

agunah (ŏ-gōō-nŏ') *n.* a woman whose husband has deserted her and who may not marry without divorce or proof of his death.

agyiophobia (ăj"ĭ-ō-fō'bĭ-ə) *n.* fear of crossing busy streets.

ahimsa (ä-hĭm'sə) *n.* Gandhi's doctrine of passive resistance.

ai (ŏ'ē) *n.* the three-toed South American sloth.

aichmophobia (īk-mō-fō'bĭ-ə) *n.* fear of needles and other pointed objects.

Ainu (ī'nōō) *n.* a primitive light-skinned race of Japan; their language. *–adj.* pertaining to the race or language.

aischrolatreia (īs"krō-lə-trī'ə) *n.* worship of filth, dirt, smut; obscenity cult. *aischrology* (īs-krŏl'ə-jē) *n.* "dirty" language.

aissaoua (ī-sŏ'ōō-ŏ) *n.* a sect of Moroccan dervishes.

ait (āt) *n.* a small island in a river or lake.

ajaja (ŏ-yŏ'yŏ) *n.* the roseate spoonbill. also *aiaiai* (ī-ī'ī).

albescent (ăl-bĕs'ənt) *adj.* becoming white; whitish.

Alcoranist (ăl-kō-răn'ĭst) *n.* a strict follower of the Koran.

aleatory (ăl'ĭ-ə-tôr"ē) *adj.* pertaining to or relying on chance.

alectryomachy (ă-lĕk"trĭ-ŏm'ə-kē) *n.* cockfighting.

alembic (ă-lĕm'bĭk) *n.* 1. a glass or metal apparatus formerly used for distillation. 2. something that purifies or refines.

alethiology (ă-lē"thĭ-ŏl'ə-jē) *n.* the study of truth.

aleuromancy (ăl-yōŏr'ə-măn"sē) *n.* fortunetelling with flour or meal.

alexia (ă-lĕk'sĭ-ə) *n.* inability to read.

alexipharmic (ă-lĕk"sĭ-fŏr'mĭk) *adj.* antidotal. *–n.* an antidote; *alexiteric*.

alforja (ăl-fôr'hŏ) *n.* a leather bag; saddlebag (Southwestern U.S.)

algedonica (ăl-jə-dŏn'ĭks) *n.* the science of pleasure and pain. *algedonic, adj.* pertaining to pain, especially when associated with pleasure. *algetic,* causing pain.

algific (ăl-jĭf'ĭk) *adj.* that which produces cold.

algolagnia (ăl-gō-lăg'nĭ-ə) *n.* sexual satisfaction resulting from giving or receiving pain; sadism or masochism; *algophilia.* also *algolagny.*

algophobia (ăl-gō-fō'bĭ-ə) *n.* fear of pain.

algorism (ăl'gər-ĭz"əm) *n.* 1. Arabic numbers. 2. the decimal system. 3. computation.

algorithm (ăl'gō-rĭth"əm) *n.* a rule of procedure for solving recurrent mathematical problems.

alible (ăl'ĭ-bəl) *adj.* nutritive, nourishing (obs.).

aljamiado (ŏl-hŏm-yŏ'dō) *n.* a work written in Spanish with Arabic characters.

alkahest (ăl'kə-hĕst) *n.* the universal solvent vainly sought by alchemists.

allantiasis (ăl-ən-tē'ə-sĭs) *n.* food poisoning resulting from inadequate or improper preserving methods. *–syn. botulism.*

alliaceous (ăl-ĭ-ā'shəs) *adj.* smelling or tasting like onions or garlic.

allicient (ă-lĭsh'ənt) *n.* attracting, alluring. *–n.* that which attracts.

allision (ă-lĭzh'ən) *n.* the ramming of one object by another.

allochroous (ă-lŏk'rō-əs) *adj.* multicolored; changing color.

màn; māde; lĕt; bē; sĭp; wīne; hŏt; cōld; sôre; dŭll; fūgue; bûrp; gŏŏd; fōōd; out; gĕt; thin; this; year; azure; ō'mən"; viN; fūr; Bach

allochthonous (à-lŏk'thən-əs) *adj.*
foreign. *-ant. autochthonous.*

allocochick (ăl'ō-kə-chĭk″) *n.·* Indian shell money formerly used in
northern California.

allograph (ăl'ō-grăf) *n.* a signature
made for someone else.

allonymous (ă-lŏn'ĭ-məs) *adj.*
ghosted; ghostwritten.

alloo (à-lōō′) *v.t.* to set on; to incite
(obs.).

allophylian (ăl-ō-fĭl'ĭ-ən) *adj.* referring to Asiatic and European
languages other than Indo-Euro-
pean or Semitic. also *allophylic.*

allotheism (ăl-ō-thē'ĭz″əm) *n.* worship of strange gods.

allotriophagy (ăl″ō-trē-ŏf'ə-jē) *n.*
the craving for weird food.

almagest (ăl'mə-jĕst) *n.* Ptolemy's
tome on astronomy; any such
treatise.

almoner (ăl'mən-ûr) *n.* a person in
charge of distributing money re-
ceived through charity.

alogism (ăl'ō-jĭz″əm) *n.* unreason-
ableness; absurdity.

alopecia (ăl-ō-pē'shĭ-ə) *n.* baldness. *-syn. acomia, atrichia, calvities, phalacrosis.*

alopecoid (ă-lō-pē'koid) *adj.* foxy.

alouatte (ăl-ōō-ăt′) *n.* the South
American howling monkey.

alphabetterments (ăl-fə-bĕt'ər-
mĕnts) *n.* government measures
and agencies to promote economic recovery and social security (slang).

alphitomancy (ăl-fĭt'ō-măn″sē) *n.*
fortunetelling with barley meal.

alphonsin (ăl-fŏn'zĭn) *n.* a three-
armed forceps for extracting
bullets from wounds (invented by
Alphonso Ferri, c. 1552).

altiloquence (ăl-tĭl'ə-kwĕns) *n.*
pompous speech.

altitudinarian (ăl″tĭ-tōō-dĭ-nêr'ĭ-

ən) *adj.* aspiring to great heights.

altricial (ăl-trĭsh'əl) *adj.* having the
young hatched in such an imma-
ture condition that extra care is
required for some time.

altrigenderism (ăl-trī-jĕn'də-
rĭz″əm) *n.* the developmental
period when one becomes at-
tracted to someone of the opposite sex.

altruipathia (ăl″trōō-ĭ-păth'ĭ-ə) *n.*
pathologic altruism.

alveolate (ăl-vē'ō-lət) *adj.* with
many small cavities; like a honeycomb.

ama (ä'mə) *n.* 1. a wine receptacle,
especially one for the Eucharist in
early Christendom. 2. the en-
largement of the semicircular
canal in the inner ear.

amadelphous (ăm-ə-dĕl'fəs) *adj.*
gregarious.

amanuensis (ă-măn″ū-ĕn'sĭs) *n.*
one who takes dictation; a secre-
tary.

amaranthine (ăm-ə-răn'thĭn) *adj.*
1. pertaining to the amaranth, an
imaginary flower that never dies
or fades. 2. everlasting, unfad-
ing. 3. like the color, amaranth,
reddish purple.

amarity (à-măr'ĭ-tē) *n.* biterness.

amasesis (ăm-ə-sē'sĭs) *n.* inability
to chew.

amate (am-āt′) *v.t.* to terrify.

amathophobia (ăm″ə-thō-fō'bĭ-ə)
n. fear of dust.

amatorculist (ăm-ə-tôr'kū-lĭst) *n.*
an insignificant or hypocritical
lover (obs.).

amaxophobia (ă-măks″-ō-fō'bĭ-ə)
n. fear of riding in a car.

ambagious (ăm-bāj'əs) *adj.* talking or doing things in an indirect
manner; devious.

ambitus (ăm'bĭ-təs) *n.s.&pl.* 1. cir-
cumference, edge, border. 2. a

canvassing for votes in ancient Rome.

amblotic (ăm-blŏt'ĭk) *adj.* causing abortion. *n.* a drug that does this. also *ambolic.*

ambry (ăm'brē) *n.* 1. a cupboard. 2. a niche in a church for sacred odds and ends.

ambsace (ām'zās) *n.* double aces, the lowest throw at dice; bad luck; the least; most worthless.

ambulophobia (ăm"bū-lō-fō'bĭ-ə) *n.* fear of walking.

amelus (ăm'ə-lŭs) *n.* a limbless fetus.

amener (ā-mèn'ər) *n.* a yes-man (British slang).

amerceable (ă-mûr'sĭ-bəl) *adj.* lawfully punishable, particularly by fine.

amnicolist (ăm-nĭk'ə-lĭst) *n.* someone living near a river.

amort (ă-môrt') *adj.* as if dead; lifeless, spiritless.

amotion (ă-mō'shən) *n.* the ousting of an official; removal.

amphibological (ăm"fĭ-bō-lŏj'ĭ-kəl) *adj.* ambiguous.

amphierotism (ăm-fĭ-èr'ō-tĭz"əm) *n.* capacity of erotic reaction toward either sex.

amphigean (ăm-fĭ-jē'ən) *adj.* found or occurring throughout the world.

amphigory (ăm'fĭ-gôr"ē) *n.* nonsensical writing.

amphiscians (ăm-fĭsh'ənz) *n.pl.* tropical people.

amphitryon (ăm-fĭt'rĭ-ən) *n.* a dinner-giver or host (from the legendary Theban king).

amphoric (ăm-fôr'ĭk) *adj.* having a hollow sound similar to that produced by blowing across the mouth of a bottle.

amplectant (ăm-plĕk'tənt) *adj.* entwining; clasping.

ampollosity (ăm-pō-lŏs'ĭ-tē) *n.* bombast; pompous style.

amulierosis (ă-mū"lĭ-ər-ō'sĭs) *n.* result of sexual privation, as seen in U.S. prisons.

amurcous (ă-mûr'kəs) *adj.* stinking; filled with dregs.

amusia (ă-mū'zĭ-ə) *n.* the inability to play or sing.

amyctic (ă-mĭk'tĭk) *adj.* irritating; abrasive.

amygdalate (ă-mĭg'də-lāt) *adj.* made of almonds.

amylaceous (ăm-ĭ-lā'shəs) *adj.* pertaining to starch.

amyous (ā'mĭ-əs) *adj.* without strength.

ana (ā'nə) *n.* 1. the collection of memorable sayings, writings, or other information, of an interesting person. (ăn'ə) *adv.* of each *an,* a quantity used in prescripttions.

anabamous (ăn-ā'bə-məs) *adj.* able to climb.

anabasis (ăn-ā'bə-sĭs) *n.* a military expedition (from the expedition led by Cyrus the Younger, 401 B.C.).

anabiotic (ăn"ə-bī-ŏ'tĭk) *adj.* apparently dead, but capable of being revived.

anacalypsis (ăn"ə-kăl-ĭp'sĭs) *n.* an unveiling; a revelation.

anacampserote (ăn-ə-kămp'sèr-ōt) *n.* something which can bring back a lost love.

anacamptic (ăn-ə-kămp'tĭk) *adj.* reflecting or reflected.

anacardic (ăn-ə-kôr'dĭk) *adj.* pertaining to the cashew nut.

anachorism (ăn-ăk'ər-ĭz"əm) *n.* foreign to a certain locality; geographically impossible.

anaclitic (ăn-ə-klĭ'tĭk) *adj.* overly dependent on another.

anacreontic (ăn-ăk"-rĭ-ŏn'tĭk) *adj.* erotic; convivial (from *Anacreon,* a Greek poet who knew how to live).

anacrisis (ăn-ə-krī'sĭs) *n.* 1. preliminary hearing. 2. interrogation accompanied by torture (law).

anacrusis (ăn-ə-krōō'sĭs) *n.* an upbeat (music).

anadem (ăn'ə-dĕm) *n.* a flowery headband.

anadipsic (ăn-ə-dĭp'sĭk) *adj.* pertaining to excessive thirst.

anagapesis (ăn"ə-găp-ē'sĭs) *n.* lack of interest in former loved ones.

anaglyptography (ăn"ə-glĭp-tŏg'rə-fē) *n.* the art of making a drawing or etching look like relief work.

anagnorisis (ăn-ăg-nôr'ĭ-sĭs) *n.* the dénouement or unraveling of a dramatic plot.

anagogical (ăn-ə-gŏ'jĭ-kəl) *adj.* mysterious, ephemeral, spiritual.

analect (ăn'ə-lĕkt) *n.* a literary fragment; short saying.

analeptic (ăn-ə-lĕp'tĭk) *adj.* restorative, comforting. -*n.* a restorative.

analysand (ăn-ăl'ĭ-zănd) *n.* a person being psychoanalyzed.

anamnestic (ăn-ăm-nĕs'tĭk) *adj.* reminiscent; aiding the memory.

anamorphosis (ăn-ə-môr'fə-sĭs) *n.* 1. a distorted image which loses its distortion when viewed through a special device, like an *anamorphoscope.* 2. the making of such images. 3. an evolutionary change in form.

anandrious (ăn-ăn'drĭ-əs) *adj.* sterile. -*syn. acarpous, agennesic, apogenous.*

ananym (ăn'ə-nĭm) *n.* a name written backward.

anaphalantiasis (ăn"ə-făl-ən-tī'ə-sĭs) *n* the falling out of the eyebrows.

anaphrodisiac (ăn-ăf"rŏ-dē'zĭ-ăk) *adj.* tending to reduce sexual desire. -*n.* anything which does this.

anapodictic (ăn"ə-pō-dĭk'tĭk) *adj.* undemonstrable.

anastatic (ăn-əs-tăt'ĭk) *adj.* raised, embossed; having raised characters.

anatine (ăn'ə-tīn) *adj.* ducklike.

anatopism (ăn-ăt'ə-pĭz"əm) *n.* misplacement; faulty or inharmonious arrangement.

anatreptic (ăn-ə-trĕp'tĭk) *adj.* defeating, refuting.

anautarchia (ăn-ô-tòr'kĭ-ə) *n.* perpetual unhappiness.

anaxiphilia (ăn-ăks"ĭ-fĭl'ĭ-ə) *n.* act of falling in love with a schtoonk by someone who ought to know better.

ancipital (ăn-sĭp'ĭ-təl) *adj.* having two edges.

anconal (ăng'kə-nəl) *adj.* pertaining to the elbow; also *anconeal.*

androcracy (ăn-drŏk'rə-sē) *n.* male supremacy or domination.

androlepsia (ăn-drō-lĕp'sĭ-ə) *n.* international governmental kidnapping for political gain.

anemography (ăn-ə-mŏg'rə-fē) *n.* description of the winds; recording a wind's force and direction.

anepigraphous (ăn-ē-pĭg'rə-fəs) *adj.* without an inscription.

aneroid (ăn'ə-roid) *adj.* without liquid, as in an *aneroid barometer.*

anfractuous (ăn-frăk'chōō-əs) *adj.* full of windings and turnings.

angang-angang (ăn'găng-ăn"găng) *n.* a type of Javanese gong.

angary (ăng'gə-rē) *n.* the right of a warring nation to use or destroy a neutral's property, subject to full indemnification (international law).

angekok (àng'gə-kòk) *n.* añ Eskimo medicine man.

anguineous (àng-gwĭn'ē-əs) *adj.*
snakelike.

angustate (àng-gŭs'tāt) *adj.*
narrowed; narrowing.

angustirostrate (àng-gŭs"tĭ-
ròs'trāt) *adj.* having a narrow
beak or nose.

anhedonia (àn-hĭ-dō'nĭ-ə) *n.* the inability to be happy.

anhelation (àn-hə-lā'shən) *n.* 1.
panting, breathless. 2. a breathless or eager wanting.

anhidrotic (àn-hĭ-drò'tĭk) *n.* an
antiperspirant. -*adj.* tending to inhibit sweating.

aniconic (àn-ī-kòn'ĭk) *adj.* 1.
figurative rather than literal. 2.
opposed to the use of idols.

anicular (àn-ĭk'ū-lər) *adj.* old-
womanish, weak; feeble-minded.
-*syn. anile.*

anidian (àn-ĭd'ĭ-ən) *adj.* shapeless.

anililagnia (àn-ī"lĭ-làg'nĭ-ə) *n.* sexual desire for older women.

animadversion (àn"ĭ-màd-vûr'żən)
n. censure; hostile criticism.

animalcule (àn-ĭ-màl'kūl) *n.* a
microscopic animal.

animastic (àn-ĭ-màs'tĭk) *adj.*
spiritual.

anisognathous (àn"ĭ-sòg'nə-thəs)
adj. having the upper and lower
teeth unlike.

anisosthenic (àn-ĭs"ŏs-thèn'ĭk) *adj.*
of unequal force or strength.

anlage (òn'lò"gə) *n.* 1. the first
traces of an organ seen in the
embryo; rudiment. 2. bent, inclination.

annotinous (àn-òt'ĭn-əs) *adj.* a year
old.

anoclassociation (à-nō"sĭ-ə-sō"sĭ-
ā'shən) *n.* the prevention of shock
in surgery.

anoetic (àn-ō-èt'ĭk) *adj.* unthink-
able.

anomia (àn-ō'mĭ-ə) *n.* the inability
to remember names.

anomy (àn'ō-mē) *n.* lawlessness in
society or in an individual in
which all rules of conduct are
thrown to the winds.

anonymuncule (àn-òn"ĭ-mùng'kūl)
n. an insignificant anonymous
writer.

anopisthographic (àn"ō-pĭs-thō-
gràf'ĭk) *adj.* having writing or
printing on one side only.

anorchous (àn-ôr'kəs) *adj.* without testicles.

anosognosia (àn- òs"ŏg-nō'żĭ-ə) *n.*
the lack of interest or belief in the
existence of one's disease; *anoso-
diaphoria.*

ansate (àn'sāt) *adj.* having a handle.

Anschauung (òn'shou"ŏŏng) *n.* intuition; sense awareness or per-
ception.

anserine (àn'sər-ēn) *adj.* pertaining to a goose; stupid.

antaean (àn-tē'ən) *adj.* pertaining
to the legendary Antaeus, an
invincible wrestler as long as he
was touching ground.

antaphroditic (ànt"àf-rō-dĭt'ĭk) *n.*
a remedy for venereal disease
(obs.).

anteambulo (àn-tē-àm'bə-lō) *n.* an
usher.

antecibal (àn-tē-sī'bəl) *adj.* happening before meals; *anteprandial.*

antelucan (àn-tē-lōō'kən) *adj.*
before dawn.

antepaschal (àn-tē-pàs'kəl) *adj.*
before Passover or Easter.

antephialtic (àn-tèf"ĭ-àl'tĭk) *adj.*
preventing nightmare. -*n.* a nightmare preventive. also *antiephial-
tic.*

anteprandial (ăn-tē-prăn'dĭ-əl) *adj.* before dinner; *antecibal.*

anthomania (ăn-thō-mā'nĭ-ə) *n.* flower mania.

anthracomancy (ăn"thrə-kō-măn"sē) *n.* fortunetelling with burning coal.

anthropometry (ăn-thrō-pŏm'ət-rē) *n.* measuring the human body and its functions. *anthropometrist.* one who does this. *anthropometrical. adj.*

anthropophobia (ăn"thrō-pō-fō'bĭ-ə) *n.* fear of meeting people; fear of society.

anthropopithecus (ăn"thrō-pō-pĭth'ə-kəs) *n.* hypothetical animal thought of as the "missing link."

anthroposcopy (ăn-thrō-pŏs'kə-pē) *n.* character-reading from facial features.

antibiosis (ăn"tē-bī-ō'sĭs) *n.* relationship between two organisms, beneficial to one but harmful to the other.

antibromic (ăn-tĭ-brō'mĭk) *n.&adj.* deodorant.

antidisecestablishmentarian (ăn"tĭ-dĭ-sĕk"əs-tăb"lĭsh-menter'ĭ-ən) *n.* one against dissection (slang).

antigram (ăn'tĭ-grăm) *n.* an anagram whose meaning is opposite to the original word or phrase.

antigropelos (ăn-tĭ-grŏp'ə-ləs) *n.s.&pl.* waterproof leggings.

antilogous (ăn-tĭl'ə-gəs) *adj.* contrary; inconsistent.

antinganting (ŏn'tĭng-ŏn-tĭng") *n.* an amulet or charm.

antinomian (ăn"tĭ-nō'mĭ-ən) *n.* a Christian who believes that faith alone will see her through. *-adi.* pertaining to such a doctrine.

antinomy (ăn-tĭn'ə-mē) *n.* a contradiction between two seemingly reasonable principles; a paradox.

antiphlogistic (ăn"tĭ-flō-jĭs'tĭk) *adj.* reducing inflammation or fever. also *n.*

antiphrasis (ăn-tĭf'rə-sĭs) *n.* a word used to mean its opposite.

antipruritic (ăn"tĭ-prə-rĭt'ĭk) *adj.* that which relieves itching.

antipudic (ăn-tĭ-pū'dĭk) *adj.* covering one's genitals.

antiscians (ăn-tĭsh'ənz) *n.* people living on the same meridian, but on different sides of the equator, thus casting shadows at noon in opposite directions.

antistasis (ăn-tĭs'tə-sĭs) *n.* the defense of an action that prevented something worse from happening.

antisyzygy (ăn-tĭ-sĭz'ĭ-jē) *n.* a union of opposites.

antithalian (ăn-tĭ-thăl'ĭ-ən) *adj.* against enjoyment.

antonomasia (ăn"tŏn-ō-mā'zĭ-ə) *n.* use of an epithet for a proper name.

anuloma (ăn-ōō-lō'mə) *adv.* according to custom, said of a man marrying a woman of inferior class. compare *pratiloma* (Hindu law).

anuptaphobia (ăn-ŭp"tə-fō'bĭ-ə) *n.* fear of staying single.

aosmic (ā-ŏz'mĭk) *adj.* odorless.

apagogic (ăp-ə-gŏ'jĭk) *adj.* pertaining to a proof by *reductio ad absurdum;* an indirect demonstration of proof.

apanthropy (ă-păn-thrə-pē) *n.* dislike of being with people; love of solitude.

apatetic (ăp-ə-tĕt'ĭk) *adj.* camouflaged.

aperient (ă-pĭr'ĭ-ənt) *n.&adj.* laxative.

aphelion (ă-fēl'ĭ-ən) *n.* the point farthest from the sun in a planet's orbit; opposite to *perihelion.* also

---

măn; māde; lĕt; bē; sĭp; wīne; hŏt; cōld; sôre; dŭll; fūgue; bŭrp; gŏŏd; fōōd; out; gĕt; thin; this; year; aźure; ō'mən"; viN; fŭr; Bach

figurative.

aphesis (ăf'ə-sĭs) n. the gradual dis-appearance of an unstressed in-itial syllable or vowel. *aphetic, adj.*

aphilophrenia (ă-fĭl"ō-frē'nĭ-ə) n. a feeling that one is unloved or unwanted.

aphnology (ăf-nŏl'ə-jē) n. the science of wealth.

aphthong (ăf'thŏng) n. unpro-nounced letter or letters.

Apician (ə-pĭsh'ən) adj. epicurean (from *Apicianus*, a Roman gour-mand).

apinoid (ăp'ĭn-oid) adj. clean, dirt-free.

apishamore (ə-pĭsh'ə-môr) n. a saddle blanket, usually of buf-falo skin; a bed (Algonquian).

apistia (ə-pĭs'tĭ-ə) n. faithlessness in marriage.

apocarteresis (ă"pō-kŏr"tə-rē'sĭs) n. suicide by starvation.

apocatastasis (ă"pō-kə-tăs'tə-sĭs) n. reestablishment or restora-tion.

apocope (ă-pŏk'ə-pē) n. omission of the last letter or syllable of a word.

apodiabolosis (ă"pō-dī"ə-bō-lō'sĭs) n. diabolical treatment.

apodictic (ă-pō-dĭk'tĭk) adj. clearly and undeniably true.

apodysophilia (ă"pō-dĭ-sō-fĭl'ĭ-ə) n. feverish desire to undress.

apogenous (ă-pŏj'jə-nəs) adj. sterile, impotent. -syn. *acarpous, agennesic, anandrious.*

apographal (ă-pŏg'rə-fəl) adj. per-taining to *apograph*, a copy or transcript.

apolaustic (ă-pō-lôs'tĭk) adj. fond of pleasure; self-indulgent.

apologue (ă'pō-lôg) n. a fable with a moral.

aponic (ă-pŏn'ĭk) adj. pertaining to painlessness.

apoop (ăpo͞op') adv. toward the back; astern.

apopemptic (ă"pō-pĕmp'tĭk) adj. pertaining to farewell.

apopemptoclinic (ă"pō-pĕm-tō-klĭn'ĭk) adj. inclined toward divorce.

apophasis (ă-pŏf'ə-sĭs) n. mention-ing something by saying it won't be mentioned: "We won't men-tion his filthy habits."

aporetic (ă-pō-rĕt'ĭk) n.&adj. skep-tic (obs.).

apositic (ă-pō-sĭt'ĭk) adj. without appetite. -syn. *anorectous.*

aposterioristic (ā-pŏs-tĭr"ĭ-ō-rĭs'tĭk) adj. 1. inductive, the op-posite of *aprioristic*. 2. pertain-ing to empirical knowledge.

apostrophize (ă-pŏs'trə-fīz) v.t.&i. to address someone or some-thing present or not, usually ex-clamatorily and as a digression.

apotropaic (ă-pŏt"rō-pā'ĭk) adj. pertaining to turning aside or averting.

appanage (ăp'ən-āj) n. 1. a king's or prince's money or property as-signed to his younger sons. 2. a tip or gratuity. 3. a territorial de-pendency.

appersonation (ă-pûr"sən-ā'shən) n. a form of insanity in which the patient thinks she is a famous person.

appetent (ăp'ə-tənt) adj. eagerly desirous.

applanate (ăp'lən-ət) adj. flattened out.

appropinquate (ăp-rō-pĭn'kwāt) v.i. to approach.

apricate (ăp'rĭ-kāt) v.t.&i. to ex-pose to sunlight.

aprioristic (ā-prī-ō-rĭs'tĭk) adj. 1. deductive, the opposite of *apos-terioristic*. 2. innate, presumptive.

aprosexia (ăp-rō-sĕks'ĭ-ə) *n.* inability to concentrate.

apterium (ăp-tîr'ē-əm) *n.* a featherless spot on a bird; a bird's bald spot.

aptronym (ăp'trə-nĭm) *n.* a name that sounds like its owner's occupation (coined by Franklin P. Adams).

aptyalism (ăp-tī'ə-lĭz″əm) *n.* loss of saliva.

aqueosalinocalcalinocetaceoaluminosocuprevitriolic *n.* a sesquipedalian acid.

arachidic (ăr-ə-kĭd'ĭk) *adj.* caused by or pertaining to peanuts.

arachnoid (ă-răk'noid) *adj.* cobwebby.

araphorostic (ăr″ə-fər-ŏs'tĭk) *adj.* seamless. also *arrhaphostic*.

archaeolatry (ör-kĭ-ŏl'ə-trē) *n.* worship of anything archaic.

archididascalos (ör″kĭd-ĭ-dăs'kə-ləs) *n.* a school principal.

archilowe (ör'hĭ-lou) *n.* a drinker's return treat. also *archilagh*, *archilogh* (Scottish).

archimage (ör'kĭ-māj) *n.* 1. the high priest of the Persian fire worshipers. 2. a great magician or wizard.

architectonics (ör″kĭ-tĕk-tŏn'ĭks) *n.* the science of architecture; good design in general.

archology (ör-kŏl'ə-jē) *n.* the science of origins; the science (?) of government.

archon (ör'kŏn) *n.* a ruler or high official; originally, an Athenian magistrate.

arctoid (örk'toid) *adj.* like a bear.

arenose (ăr'ĭ-nōs) *adj.* sandy; *arenoid*.

areology (ĕr-ē-ŏl'ə-jē) *n.* the study of Mars.

aretaics (ăr-ə-tā'ĭks) *n.* the study of virtue.

argh (örh, örg) *adj.* timid; cowardly.

argillaceous (ör-jĭl-ā'shəs) *adj.* clayey; containing clay.

argus (ör'gəs) *n.* 1. eternally vigilant (from *Argus*, of Greek mythology, a humanoid monster with 100 eyes, some of which were always awake). 2. a type of butterfly with many circular eyespots on its wings.

arletation (ör″ĕ-ə-tā'shən) *n.* butting like a ram; the using of a battering ram; striking.

ariolation (ör″ĭ-ō-lā'shən) *n.* fortunetelling.

aristarchian (ăr-ĭs-tör'kĭ-ən) *adj.* extremely critical (from *Aristarch*, who didn't care for Homer's poetry).

aristarchy (ăr'ĭs-tör″kē) *n.* government by the most qualified people.

aristology (ăr-ĭs-tŏl'ə-jē) *n.* the art of dining.

aristophrenia (ăr-ĭs″tō-frē'nĭ-ə) *n.* condition of having a superior intellect.

arithmancy (ă-rĭth'mən-sē) *n.* fortunetelling by numbers.

arithmocracy (ă-rĭth-mŏk'rə-sē) *n.* rule of the numerical majority.

arpagee (ör-pə-jē') *n.* a raped woman.

arpentator (ör-pĕn-tā'tər) *n.* a land surveyor.

arras (ăr'əs) *n.* a richly woven tapestry (from *Arras*, France, famed for tapestries).

arrect (ă-rĕkt') *adj.* alert, intent.

arriviste (ör-ē-vēst') *n.* an overly ambitious person; an opportunist (French).

arrogate (ăr'ə-gāt) *v.t.* to appropriate or claim unjustly; to attribute unreasonably.

---

măn; māde; lĕt; bē; sĭp; wīne; hŏt; cōld; sôre; dŭll; fūgue; bûrp; gŏŏd; fōŏd; out; gĕt; thin; this; year; azure; ō'mən″; viN; fūr; Bach

artuate (är′chōō-āt) *v.t.* to tear limb from limb (obs.).

asana (ŏ′sən-ŏ) *n.* a contorted posture for meditation, part of Yoga training.

asanka (ŏ-sŏng′kə) *n.* one, followed by forty-five zeros = one quattuordecillion (Buddhist).

ascham (ăs′kəm) *n.* a box for keeping bows and arrows dry.

ascian (ăsh′ĭ-ən) *n.* one without a shadow; applied to the inhabitants of the torrid zone, where the sun is vertical at noon for a few days every year.

ascob (ăs′kŏb) *n.* a cocker spaniel of Any Solid Color Other than Black.

ashram (ŏsh′rəm) *n.* a religious retreat (India).

asomatous (ă-sō′mə-təs) *adj.* bodiless, incorporeal.

aspergillum (ăs-pûr-jĭl′əm) *n.* a short-handled brush, or perforated globe holding a sponge, used for sprinkling holy water.

aspheterism (ăs-fĕt′ər-ĭz″əm) *n.* denial of private property. •

asportation (ăs-pôr-tā′shən) *n.* theft.

assanka (ŏ-sŏng′kə) *n.* one followed by sixty-three zeros = one vigintillion (Ceylonese).

assart (ă-sŏrt′) *v.t.* to make forest land arable by clearing it of trees and bushes. *-n.* land cleared this way.

asseverate (ă-sĕv′ər-āt) *v.t.* to state positively, emphatically.

assonant (ăs′ən-ənt) *adj.* pertaining to a similarity of sound or a fudged rhyme.

assuetude (ăs′wē-tōōd) *n.* custom or habit.

asteism (ăs′tē-ĭz″əm) *n.* an ingeniously polite insult.

astereognosis (ăs-tĕr′ē-ŏg-nō′sĭs)

n. loss of ability to recognize the shapes of objects by touch.

asthenia (ăs-thēn′ĭ-ə) *n.* loss of strength.

astorgia (ăs-tôr′jĭ-ə) *n.* lack of interest in one's children.

astragalomancy (ăs-trăg′ə-lō-măn″sē) *n.* fortunetelling using dice.

astrogation (ăs-trō-gā′shən) *n.* space navigation.

asyndeton (ă-sĭn′də-tŏn) *n.* the omission of conjunctions.

ataraxia (ăt-ər-ăks′ĭ-ə) *n.* imperturbability; utter calmness.

ataxia (ă-tăks′ĭ-ə) *n.* loss of muscular coordination.

ateknia (ă-tĕk′nĭ-ə) *n.* childlessness.

athanasia (ăth-ən-āż′ĭ-ə) *n.* immortality.

athenaeum (ăth-ən-ē′əm) *n.* an intellectual club; a building or room so used; a library or reading room.

athetise (ăth′ə-tīz) *v.t.* to spurn, reject.

atluk (ăt′lŭk) *n.* a seal's breathing hole in the ice.

atmatertera (ăt-mŏ-tĕr′tə-rŏ) *n.* a great-grandfather's grandmother's sister.

atocia (ă-tō′shĭ-ə) *n.* female sterility. *-syn. acyesis.*

atony (ăt′ən-ē) *n.* 1. lack of muscular tone; abnormal relaxation. 2. lack of stress in a syllable.

atpatruus (ăt-pŏt′rōō-əs) *n.* a great-grandfather's grandfather's brother.

atrabilarian (ăt″rə-bĭ-lĕr′ĭ-ən) *n.* a hypochondriac.

atramental (ăt-rə-mĕn′təl) *adj.* jet black.

atrichia (ă-trĭ′kĭ-ə) *n.* baldness. *-syn. acomia, alopecia.*

attrahent (ăt′rə-hĕnt) *adj.* attracting; that which attracts.

atychiphobia (ă-tī″kǐ-fō′bǐ-ə) *n.* fear of failure. see *kakorrhaphiophobia.*

aubade (ō-bǎd′) *n.* morning music (as opposed to *serenade,* *nocturne,* or evening music).

aubaine (ō-bān′) *n.* the disposition of a dead foreigner's belongings (French law).

auctorial (ôk-tôr′ǐ-əl) *adj.* of or like an author.

Augean (ô-jē′ən) *adj.* utterly filthy (refers to the legendary king, *Augeas,* whose stable held 3,000 oxen for thirty redolent years).

aularian (ô-lĕr′ǐ-ən) *adj.* pertaining to a hall.

aulete (ôl′ēt) *n.* a flutist.

auricomous (ôr-ĭk′ə-məs) *adj.* golden-haired; blond.

auricular (ôr-ĭk′ū-lər) *adj.* 1. pertaining to the ear or sense of hearing. 2. spoken in the ear; private.

auriphrygiate (ôr-ĭ-frǐj′ət) *adj.* fringed or otherwise ornamented with gold embroidery.

aurocephalous (ô-rō-sĕf′əl-əs) *adj.* blond.

aurochs (ôr′ŏks) *n.* the extinct wild ox, ancestor of modern cattle.

auroral (ôr-ôr′əl) *adj.* pertaining to dawn.

auscultate (ôs′kəl-tāt) *v.t.&i.* to examine by listening; to examine with a stethoscope.

austral (ôs′trəl) *adj.* 1. southern. 2. Australian.

autarchia (ô-tär′kǐ-ə) *n.* perpetual happiness.

autarky (ô′tär-kē) *n.* economic self-sufficiency of a country. also *autarchy.*

autocephalous (ô-tō-sĕf′ə-ləs) *adj.* ecclesiastically self-governing.

autochthonous (ô-tŏk′thə-nəs) *adj.* native, indigenous. -ant. *alloch-*

thonous.

autodidact (ô′tō-dǐ-dăkt″) *n.* one self-taught. *autodidactic, adj.*

autognosis (ôt-ŏg-nō′sǐs) *n.* self-awareness, especially of one's emotional make-up.

autologophagist (ô″tō-lō-gò′fə-jǐst) *n.* one who eats her words.

automysophobia (ô″tō-mī-sō-fō′bǐ-ə) *n.* fear of being dirty.

autonomasia (ôt″ən-ō-mā′żə) *n.* the accepted use of a common name for a specific one.

autophagia (ôt-ō-fā′jǐ-ə) *n.* biting oneself; nourishment from body tissues.

autophobia (ô-tō-fō′bǐ-ə) *n.* fear of oneself, or of being alone.

autoptic (ô-tŏp′tǐk) *adj.* pertaining to evidence based on observation.

autoschediastic (ô″tō-skē-dǐ-ăs′tǐk) *adj.* impromptu; on the spur of the moment.

autotelic (ô-tō-tĕl′ǐk) *adj.* for its own sake (art for art's sake). see *heterotelic.*

autotomy (ô-tŏ′tə-mē) *n.* self-mutilation.

aval (ā′vəl) *adj.* pertaining to grandparents.

avatar (ă-və-tôr′) *n.* incarnation (Sanskrit).

avenage (ă′və-nəj) *n.* oats paid by a tenant to a landlord in lieu of rent (old law).

avering (ă-vûr′ĭng) *n.* a boy's begging in the nude to arouse sympathy.

averruncator (ă-vər-ŭng′kā″tər) *n.* a pole for pruning trees.

avinosis (ă-vǐ-nō′sǐs) *n.* airsickness.

avunculocal (ă-vŭng″kū-lō′kəl) *adj.* belonging to or centered around a maternal uncle. compare *matrilocal, patrilocal, nelo-*

cal.

awm (ôm) *n.* forty gallons of wine in old England.

awu (ä-wōō′, ô-wōō′, ʼō-wōō′, ā-wōō′, ô′wōō, ä′wōō, ā′wōō) *n.* acronym for Atomic Weight Unit = one sixteenth of the atomic weight of oxygen (1 awu=1.660 × 10^{-24}g.).

axilla (ăks-ĭl′ə) *n.* the armpit.

axiology (ăks-ĭ-ŏl′ə-jē) *n.* a branch of philosophy dealing with values (moral, esthetic, etc.).

axiopisty (ăks′ĭ-ō-pĭs″tē) *n.* the quality which makes something believable.

axolotl (ăks′ə-lŏt″əl) *n.* the sala-mander of Mexico and the western U.S.

axunge (ăks′ŭnj) *n.* 1. pig fat or goose grease. 2. lard prepared for medicinal use.

ayne (ān) *adj.* eldest.

azoic (ă-zō′ĭk) *adj.* lifeless: specific-ally: pertaining to the geologic period before life appeared on earth.

azygophrenia (ă-zī″gō-frē′nĭ-ə) *n.* the psychoneurosis of everyday unmarried life.

azygous (ăz′ĭ-gəs) *adj.* odd, un-paired.

azymic (ă-zĭm′ĭk) *adj.* pertaining to unleavened bread; *azymous.*

B

baba (bŏ′bŏ) *n.* a kind of fruit cake (French).

babery (bā′be-rē) *n.* 1. finery to please a baby (obs.). 2. grotesque ornamentation or absurdity (obs.).

babyolatry (bā-bē-ŏl′ə-trē) *n.* baby worship.

bacillary (bă′sĭ-lĕr″ē) *adj.* 1. rod-shaped. 2. bacterial: pertaining to bacilli.

backberend (băk′bĕr″ənd) *adj.* a thief caught with the goods.

bactrian (băk′trĭ-ən) *n.* (cap.) an ancient Iranian people. *-adj.* (also cap.) pertaining to *Bactria*, a satrapy of ancient Persia. *bactrian camel*: the two-humped variety.

baculine (băk′ū-līn) *adj.* pertaining to a rod, or *baculus* (see below); punishing with a rod.

baculus (băk′ū-ləs) *n.* a staff or power symbol.

baetylus (bēt′ĭ-ləs) *n.* a stone serving as a sacred symbol.

baggit (băg′ĭt) *n.* a salmon that has recently spawned (Scottish).

baggywrinkle (băg′ē-rĭnk″el) *n.* frayed-out rope used on ship rigging to prevent chafing.

bain-marie (băN″mə-rē′) *n.* a large double boiler (French).

baisemain (băz′măN) *n.* hand-kissing (French *baise* = kiss + *main* = hand).

baksheesh (băk′shēsh) *n.* a tip; gratuity (in Egypt and points east).

balaclava (băl-ə-klă′və) *n.* a full beard (British slang).

balatron (băl′ə-trŏn) *n.* a joker; a clown.

balayeuse (băl-ā-yūz′) *n.* a strip of cloth on the inside hem of a long dress (French *balayeur* = a sweeper).

balbriggan (băl-brĭg′ən) *n.* a fine cotton used mainly for underwear like that made in *Balbriggan*, Ireland.

balbutient (băl-bū′shənt) *adj.* stuttering.

baldachin (bôl′də-kĭn) *n.* 1. a rich brocade. 2. a canopy carried in religious processions, or placed over a throne. 3. a canopy-like structure made of stone to adorn a church altar.

baldric (bôl′drĭk) *n.* a belt worn

---

măn; māde; lĕt; bē; sĭp; wīne; hŏt; cōld; sôre; dŭll; fūgue; bûrp; gōōd; fōōd; out; gĕt; thin; this; year; aẑure; ŏ′mən″; viN; fūr; Bach

diagonally from the shoulder to, or below, the waist, for military or decorative reasons. 2. a wide belt.

ballhooter (bôl'hoot"ər) *n.* a lumberjack who rolls logs down a hill.

ballistophobia (bă-lĭs"tō-fō'bĭ-ə) *n.* fear of missiles; fear of being shot.

ballock (bǎl'ək) *n.* a testicle; ball.

balnearii (bǎl"nē-ō-rē'ē) *n. pl.* those who stole clothes in the public baths (Roman law).

balneology (bǎl-nē-ŏl'ə-jē) *n.* the science of therapeutic bathing.

balsamical (bǎl-sǎm'ĭ-kəl) *adj.* unctuous, mitigating, soothing, balmy.

bam (bǎm) *v.t. &i.* to trick; play a joke on.

banausic (bǎn-ô'sĭk) *adj.* pertaining to a mechanic or mechanic's workshop.

bandog (bǎn'dôg) *n.* a tethered watchdog; a bloodhound.

bandoline (bǎn'dō-lĭn) *n.* a smelly hair goo made from boiled quince pips.

bangboard (bǎng'bôrd) *n.* 1. an extra board attached to a wagon to keep the corn from rebounding after overenthusiastic tossing. 2. a plywood tennis practice board with a line painted at net height.

banlieue (bôN'lyü) *n.* a suburb (French).

bantling (bǎnt'lĭng) *n.* a brat.

barabara (bǒ-rə-bǒ'rə) *n.* an underground hut (Aleutian Islands Russian dialect).

baragouin (bǎr'ə-gwĭn) *n.* gibberish.

barathrum (bǎr'ə-thrəm) *n.* 1. a pit (into which ancient Greek criminals were thrown). 2. figuratively: a glutton or extortionist.

barbaralalia (bǒr"bə-rə-lā'lĭ-ə) *n.* a speech impairment manifested when speaking a foreign language.

barbellate (bǒr'bə-lāt) *adj.* hairy; covered with bristles.

bardolatry (bǒr-dŏl'ə-trē) *n.* Shakespeare worship.

barm (bǒrm) *n.* yeast formed on brewing liquors. *-v.i.* to ferment.

barmecide (bǒr'mə-sīd) *n.* a false benefactor. *-adj.* deceptive, false.

barnumize (bǒr'nəm-īz) *v.i.* to advertise with outrageous or lavish claims (after P.T. *Barnum*).

baroxyton (bǎ-rŏks'ĭ-tŏn) *n.* a large brass musical instrument.

barranca (bǒ-rŏng'kǒ) *n.* a steep ravine. also *barranco*.

barratrous (bǎr'ə-trəs) *adj.* pertaining to the habitual causing of fights.

barrio (bǒr'ĭ-ō) *n.* 1. a suburb. 2. a Spanish-speaking neighborhood in a U.S. city (Spanish).

barylalia (bǎr-ĭ-lā'lĭ-ə) *n.* indistinct speech, due to imperfect articulation.

barythymia (bǎr-ĭ-thĭm'ĭ-ə) *n.* nervousness, depression.

bashi-bazouks (bǒsh"ē-bǒ-zōōks) *n.* Ottoman volunteer soldiers of the nineteenth century noted for their cruelty, lack of discipline, and lawlessness.

basial (bā'zĭ-əl) *adj.* pertaining to kissing.

basophobia (bā-sō-fō'bĭ-ə) *n.* inability to stand because of a fear of falling.

bat-fowler (bǎt'foul"ər) *n.* one who captures birds at night by driving them toward a light and netting them there.

bathetic (bǎ-thě'tĭk) *adj.* falsely sentimental.

bathybic (bă-thĭ'bĭk) *adj.* pertaining to deep sea.

bathycolpian (bă-thĭ-kŏl'pĭ-ən) *adj.* deep-bosomed.

batophobia (băt-ō-fō'bĭ-ə) *n.* fear of heights or of being close to high buildings.

batrachoid (băt'rə-koid) *adj.* froglike.

battological (băt-ə-lŏ'jĭ-kəl) *adj.* pertaining to unnecessarily repetitive writing or speaking.

battue (băt'ū) *n.* 1. a hunt where the game is driven into the arms of the hunters. 2. the game slaughtered. 3. any kind of mass slaughter of the unresisting.

batule (bă-tūl') *n.* a springboard; *batule-board*.

bauchle (bô'kəl) *v.t.* 1. an old shoe, or one with worn heels. 2. anything worn-out or worthless.

baxa (băks'ə) *n.* a kind of sandal; a comedian's shoes.

bdellotomy (dĕl-ŏt'ə-mē) *n.* 1. the act of cutting a sucking leech to increase its suction. 2. use of the *bdellometer*, a mechanical leech substitute.

bdelygmia (dĕl-ĭg'mĭ-ə) *n.* nausea.

beatster (bēt'stûr) *n.* a fishnet repairer.

beautilitarianism (bū-tĭl"ĭ-tĕr'ĭ-ən-ĭz"əm) *n.* practical art; the conception of beauty, with utility (slang).

bechic (bē'kĭk) *adj.* tending to relieve coughs. *-n.* a cough remedy.

bedizen (bĭ-dī'zən) *v.t.* to dress flashily; to overdecorate.

bedlamite (bĕd'lem-īt) *n.* a madman.

bedswerver (bĕd'swûr"vər) *n.* an unfaithful spouse (obs.).

beeswing (bēz'wĭng) *n.* a film formed in old wine; the wine itself.

beguine (bĭ-gēn') *n.* 1. a religious order of do-gooding women founded in the twelfth century by Lambert le *Begue*, the Stammerer 2. (Cap.) a Martinique dance.

belcher (bĕl'chər) *n.* the neckerchief of Jim *Belcher*, a British boxer; any small blue scarf with white dots.

beldam (bĕl'dəm) *n.* an ugly old hag; old woman (French *belle dame* = beautiful woman).

belletristic (bĕl-ə-trĭs'tĭk) *adj.* pertaining to *belles-lettres*, or fine literature.

belling (bĕl'ĭng) *n.* 1. mating sound of deer; hounds' cry in a fox hunt. 2. a noisy serenade to a bridal couple.

bellipotent (bĕl-ĭp'ə-tənt) *adj.* powerful in war.

bellonion (bĕl-ōn'ĭ-ən) *n.* a mechanically operated musical instrument of twenty-four trumpets and two drums.

bellwether (bĕl'wĕth"ər) *n.* a leader of a sheeplike and foolish crowd.

belomancy (bĕl'ō-măn"sē) *n.* fortunetelling with arrows.

belonephobia (bĕl"ən-ē-fō'bĭ-ə) *n.* fear of pins and needles.

belton (bĕl'tən) *n.* 1. a two-toned color combination, used in describing dogs' coats. 2. a dog with such a coat.

belvedere (bĕl'və-dĭr) *n.* 1. a building overlooking a fine view. 2. a cigar, shorter and thinner than a corona. 3. the summer cypress.

benedick (bĕn'ə-dĭk) *n.* a recent bridegroom previously a confirmed bachelor; a married man also *benedict*.

benison (bĕn'ĭ-zən) *n.* a blessing.

benthopelagic (bĕn"thō-pĕl-ăj'ĭk) *adj.* inhabiting the ocean deep.

---

măn; māde; lĕt; bē; sĭp; wīne; hŏt; cōld; sôre; dŭll; fūgue; bûrp; gŏŏd; fōŏd; out; gĕt; thin; this; year; ažure; ō'mən"; viN; fūr; Bach

beray (bē-rā') *v.t.* to make foul; to soil.

besom (bē'zəm) *n.* a broom; any cleaning utensil.

betweenity (bē-twēn'ĭ-tē) *n.* indecision (slang).

bever (bĕv'ər) *v.i.* to tremble. -*n.* 1. a drink. 2. a between-meal snack.

bezoardic (bē-zôr'dĭk) *adj.* used as an antidote; a remedy.

bhang (băng) *n.* an intoxicant made from Indian hemp; hashish, majoon; cannabis indica.

bibacious (bī-bā'shəs) *adj.* addicted to alcohol. -*syn. bibulous.*

bibble (bĭb'əl) *v.t.&i.* 1. to drink often or much. 2. to drink or eat noisily.

bibelot (bēb-lō') *n.* a small art object (French).

bibleback (bī'bəl-băk) *n.* a preacher; a sanctimonious person (slang).

biblioclasm (bĭb'lĭ-ō-klăz"əm) *n.* Bible destruction; destruction of books.

bibliomancy (bĭb'lĭ-ō-măn"sē) *n.* fortunetelling by random Bible-passage picking.

bibliopegy (bĭb-lĭ-ŏp'ə-jē) *n.* book-binding.

bibliopolist (bĭb-lĭ-ŏp'ə-lĭst) *n.* a rare-book dealer.

bibliotaph (bĭb'lĭ-ō-tăf") *n.* one who hoards or hides books.

bibulous (bĭb'ū-ləs) *adj.* addicted to alcohol. -*syn. bibacious.*

bicorne (bī'kôrn) *n.* a two-horned animal; a monster that has grown fat from eating patient husbands (Old French). see *chichevache.*

bicrural (bī-krōōr'əl) *adj.* having two legs.

biduous (bĭd'ū-əs) *adj.* lasting two days.

bight (bīt) *n.* 1. a small bay. 2. a rope loop. 3. a bend, fork, or hollow in the body. 4. a coastal curve.

bilberry (bĭl'bĕr"ē) *n.* the whortle-berry.

bilboes (bĭl'bōz) *n.pl.* leg irons; foot shackles.

bildungsroman (bĭl'dŭngz-rō-mŏn") *n.* a novel dealing with the protagonist's early development or education. see *entwicklungsroman.*

billabong (bĭl'ə-bông) *n.* a pool formed by a backwater channel (Australian).

billingsgate (bĭl'ĭngz-gāt) *n.* coarse or abusive talk.

bindle (bĭn'dəl) *n.* 1. a bedroll. 2. an envelope containing morphine or cocaine. 3. any small package or bundle (slang). *bindlestiff,* n. a hobo (slang).

biolysis (bī-ŏl'ĭ-sĭs) *n.* the destruction of living matter. 2. sewage decomposition by tiny organisms.

bionomics (bī-ō-nŏm'ĭks) *n.pl.* a branch of biology dealing with life's adaptation to its environment.

biophilism (bī-ŏf'ĭ-lĭz"əm) *n.* belief that animals have rights which human beings should respect.

bioscopy (bī-ŏs'kə-pē) *n.* medical examination to discover the presence of life.

biota (bī-ō'tə) *n.* an area's flora and fauna.

biparous (bĭp'ər-əs) *adj.* bearing twins.

bipennis (bī-pĕn'ĭs) *n.* a double-edged battle-ax.

biretta (bĭ-rĕt'ə) *n.* the hat of a Catholic priest (black), bishop (purple) or cardinal (red). also *baretta, beretta, birretta.*

birl (bûrl) *v.t.* 1. to revolve a log in the water while standing on it. 2.

to spin [a coin].

bismer (bĭz'mûr) *n.* 1. shame, disgrace, scorn. 2. a disgraceful person. 3. a steelyard. 4. the fifteen-spined stickleback.

bissextile (bĭ-sĕks'tĭl) *adj.* pertaining to February twenty-ninth or leap year. -*n.* leap year.

bittern (bit'ərn) *n.* the booming heron.

biunial (bī-ū'nĭ-əl) *adj.* combining two in one.

blabagogy (blăb'ə-gō"jē) *n.* criminal environment.

blague (blăg) *n.* joking; trickery (French).

blancmange (blóN-mȯNŻ') *n.* a dessert made from Irish moss, isinglass, cornstarch, arrowroot, and boiled with milk.

blandiloquence (blănd-ĭl'ō-kwəns) *n.* mildly flattering talk.

blattnerphone (blăt'nər-fōn) *n.* tape recorder (invented by Ludwig *Blattner*).

blaubok (blou'bŏk) *n.* 1. the large South African antelope, now extinct. 2. a smaller, still surviving version.

blebby (blĕb'ē) *adj.* full of blebs (small swellings, blisters).

blepharospasm (blĕf'ər-ō-spă"zəm) *n.* persistent winking.

bletonism (blĕt'ən-ĭz"əm) *n.* the alleged ability to perceive an underground water supply.

blinkard (blĭng'kərd) *n.* one with bad eyes; a stupid or obtuse person; someone who ignores or avoids something.

blissom (blĭs'əm) *adj.* in heat. -*v.t.* to copulate with a ewe.

bloodguiltiness (blŭd-gĭlt'ĭ-nĕs) *n.* the guilt of murder or bloodshed.

blumba (blŏŏm'bə) *n.* a certifying metal tag attached to kosher meat.

boanthropy (bō-ăn'thrə-pē) *n.* a type of insanity in which a man thinks he's an ox.

boation (bō-ā'shən) *n.* a loud noise.

bocking (bŏk'ĭng) *n.* the red herring.

bodaciously (bō-dā'shəs-lē) *adv.* wholly, completely (slang).

bodega (bō-dā'gə) *n.* a small grocery or liquor store (Spanish).

bodewash (bŏd'wŏsh) *n.* cow dung. see *bushwah.*

bolide (bō'līd) *n.* a shooting star; an exploding meteor.

bolshephobia (bŏl-shə-fō"bĭ-ə) *n.* fear of Bolshevism (slang).

bolus (bō'ləs) *n.* a horse pill.

bombilate (bŏm'bĭ-lāt) *v.i.* to hum, buzz, boom, or drone.

bombous (bŏm'bəs) *adj.* convex, rounded.

bombycine (bŏm'bĭ-sīn) *adj.* pertaining to silk (obs.).

bonamano (bō-nə-mȯ'nō) *n.* a tip; gratuity (Italian).

bonhomie (bŭn-ə-mē') *n.* cheerfulness (French *bon* = good + *homme* = man).

bonification (bŏn"ĭ-fĭ-kā'shən) *n.* 1. improvement, betterment. 2. payment of a bonus. 3. a partial rebate of customs duty on the exportation of bonded goods.

bonnyclabber (bŏn'ē-klă"bər) *n.* coagulated sour milk; *clabber.*

boobocracy (bōōb-ŏk'rə-sē) *n.* government by boobs; plebianism ad absurdum (slang).

booboisie (bōōb-wȯ-zē') *n.* the mass, rabble (coined by H.L. Mencken).

boobook (bōō'bōōk) *n.* the Australian morepork.

boobopolis (bōōb-ŏp'ə-lĭs) *n.* an imaginary hick town (slang).

boomer (bōōm'ər) *n.* the giant

kangaroo of Australia; a booster (slang).

boopic (bō-ŏp′ik) *adj.* ox-eyed.

bootician (bōō-tĭ′shən) *n.* "a high-toned big-city bootlegger" (a 1925 Mencken coinage).

borachio (bôr-ŏ′chō) *n.* a drunkard (from *Borachio*, one of Don Juan's drunken followers in Shakespeare's *Much Ado About Nothing*).

borborygm (bôr′bə-rĭm) *n.* the noise made by gas in the bowels; a fart.

boreal (bôr′ē-əl) *adj.* pertaining to the north wind; northern.

bosky (bŏs′kē) *adj.* wooded; covered with or shaded by underbrush, bushes, or trees.

boss (bôs) *n.* a protuberant ornament as a buckle, knob. *-v.t.* to adorn with such an ornament.

boswellize (bŏz′wəl-īz) *v.i.* to eulogize in a biography (slang).

bothy (bŏ′thē) *n.* a small hut for farm hands.

botryoidal (bŏt-rī-oi′dəl) *adj.* formed like a grape cluster. see *aciniform*.

bouchée (bōō-shā′) *n.* a pastry shell (French *bouche* = mouth).

boudin (bōō′dăn) *n.* sausage made by stuffing ground buffalo meat into a piece of the large intestine.

bourn (bôrn) *n.* 1. boundary. 2. objective or goal. 3. domain. 4. a small river. also *bourne, burn* (in Britain, often appearing as a suffix in names of towns on rivers).

boustrophedon (bōōs-trō-fē′dən) *n.* an ancient style of writing in which the direction of the lines alternated.

bovarism (bō′və-rĭz″əm) *n.* man's romantic conception of himself (from Flaubert's *Madame Bovary*).

bovrilise (bŏv′rĭl-īz) *v.t.* to condense an ad to essentials; to epitomize.

bowyer (bō′yər) *n.* a bow-maker or dealer.

bozart (bō′zŏrt) *n.* fine arts (slang from *Beaux-Arts*).

bozzeto (bŏt-sĕt′ō) *n.* a small, rough clay model for a larger sculpture (Italian).

brabble (bră′bəl) *n.* quarrelsome chatter. *-v.i.* to quarrel over nothing.

brachiation (brā-kĭ-ā′shən) *n.* locomotion.

brachygraphy (brā-kĭg′rə-fē) *n.* stenography; writing in shorthand.

brachylogy (brā-kĭl′ō-jē) *n.* brevity; condensation omitting all non-essentials.

bradyarthria (brăd-ĭ-ôr′thrĭ-ə) *n.* slow talking.

branular (brăn′ū-lər) *adj.* pertaining to the brain; cerebral.

brashy (brăsh′ē) *adj.* 1. pertaining to *brash*, an acid taste in the mouth. 2. broken, crumbly. 3. pertaining to a cloudburst.

brassard (brăs′ŏrd) *n.* an arm band with a badge, worn as a mark of rank or eminence.

bratticing (brăt′ĭ-sĭng) *n.* a board fence around something dangerous.

breastsummer (brĕst′sŭm″ər) *n.* a beam or girder set over an opening, as a doorway, for supporting the superstructure. also *brest-*.

bree (brē) *n.* 1. an eyelid, eyelash, or eyebrow. 2. liquor or broth (Scottish).

breedbate (brēd′bāt) *n.* someone looking for an argument.

breme (brēm) *adj.* 1. distinct, apparent, fierce, severe, and cruel.

breve (brĕv) *n.* 1. a mark (˘) over a

vowel indicating a short sound, as màn; lĕt; sĭp; hŏt; dŭll. 2. the same mark over a short or unstressed syllable. 3. an official letter. 4. a musical note = two whole notes. 5. a legal writ or brief. 6. the Sumatra antthrush.

brevirostrate (brĕv-ĭ-rŏs'trāt) adj. having a short nose.

brickkiln (brĭk'kĭln) n. a kiln in which bricks are baked.

brimborion (brĭm-bôr'ĭ-ən) n. something useless or nonsensical.

brills (brĭlz) n. 1. the hair on a horse's eyelids. 2. spectacles.

brindled (brĭn'dəld) adj. flecked or streaked with a darker color.

brobdingnagian (brŏb-dĭng-nàg'ĭ-ən) adj. gigantic, enormous (from *Brobdingnag*, land of the giants, in *Gulliver's Travels*).

broché (brō-shā') adj. 1. brocaded; lavishly woven. 2. sewn like a pamphlet or brochure (French).

brockage (brŏk'əj) n. 1. an imperfectly minted coin. 2. faulty or damaged goods.

brocked (brŏkt) adj. mottled with black and white.

brockie (brŏk'ē) n. 1. a cow with a black and white face. 2. a person with a dirty face.

brockle (brŏk'əl) adj. 1. breakable; variable (as weather). 2. of cattle: apt to break a fence. -n. rubbish; • fragments.

broma (brō'mə) n. 1. food that is chewed. 2. a cocoa-bean preparation without the oil.

bromatology (brō-mə-tŏl'ə-jē) n. the science of nutrition.

bromidrosiphobia (brō"mĭ-drō-sĭ-fō'bĭ-ə) n. fear of body smells.

bromopnea (brŏm"ŏp-nē'ə) n. bad breath.

brontophobia (brŏn-tō-fō'bĭ-ə) n. fear of thunderstorms.

brool (brōōl) n. a low roar; a deep murmur or humming.

brott (brŏt) n. broken pieces; fragments; leavings.

brotus (brō'tùs) n. any extra measure without charge, such as a baker's dozen.

bruit (brōōt) v.t. to tell publicly (French *bruit* = noise).

brumal (brōō'məl) adj. pertaining to winter.

brummagem (brŭm'ə-jəm) adj. phony; cheap. -n. something cheap or gaudy, especially phony jewelry (slang from *Birmingham*, England, where cheap gift items, primarily jewelry, were made).

brumous (brōō'məs) adj. misty, foggy.

brunneous (brùn'ē-əs) adj. dark brown.

bruxomania (brùks-ō-mā'nĭ-ə) n. the habit of unconsciously grinding the teeth, especially in sleep, or under stress.

bubbybush (bŏŏb'ē-bŏŏsh) n. the Carolina allspice.

bubukie (bū'bə-kəl) n. a red pimple.

buccinal (bùk'sĭn-əl) adj. like a trumpet in sound or shape.

buccula (bùk'ū-lə) n. the double chin.

Bucephalus (bū-sĕf'ə-ləs) n. Alexander the allegedly Great's horse.

buckeen (bùk-ēn') n. a young man of the lesser gentry aping the manners of the greater; an idle, shabby young dandy (Irish).

buckish (bùk'ĭsh) adj. foppish, lively, lewd, or stinking.

buhlwork (bōōl'wûrk) n. elaborate inlaid work of wood, metal, ivory, etc. also *buhl, boule, boulle,* and *boulework*.

bukra (bùk'rə) n. a white man (Gullah dialect from Georgia and

South Carolina).

buldering (bŭl′dər-ĭng) *adj.* hot and muggy.

bulimic (bū-lĭm′ĭk) *adj.* constantly hungary.

bulla (bŏŏl′ə) *n.* 1. a case for one's amulet, attached to a cord and worn around the neck. 2. an ornament used as a pendant. 3. a seal attached to papal bulls with the faces of Peter and Paul on one side and the current pope's name on the other. 4. a bony prominence under the ear of many mammals. 5. a juicy bleb or large blister. 6. a vesicle in the lung. 7. (cap.) a genus of marine gastropods.

bullary (bŏŏl′ər-ē) *n.* 1. a collection of papal bulls. 2. a place where salt is boiled.

bumfodder (bŭm′fŏd″ər) *n.* toilet paper; an opprobrious name for a collection of documents; *bumf.*

bungfu (bŏŏng′fŏŏ) *adj.* drunk.

buran (bŏŏ-rŏn′) *n.* a violent snowstorm on the Steppes of central Asia.

burble (bûr′bəl) *v.i.* to mix up sounds beyond repair (from Carroll's *Jabberwocky*).

burdalane (bûrd′əl-ān) *adj.* all alone and friendless. *-n.* the last surviving child. also *birdalane, burdalone.*

burghbote (bûrg′bŏt) *n.* a contribution for building or repairing castles.

burke (bûrk) *v.t.* to smother people in order to sell their bodies for dissection (from *William Burke,* the first known practitioner, who ended up on the dissecting table

himself after being tried and executed).

burletta (bûr-lĕt′ə) *n.* a comic opera.

burrasca (bŏŏ-rŏs′kŏ) *n.* a musical passage imitating a storm.

busby (bŭz′bē) *n.* 1. a kind of bushy wig. 2. a British army cap trimmed with fur.

bushelman (bŏŏsh′əl-mən) *n.* a tailor specializing in alterations.

bushranger (bŏŏsh′rān″jər) *n.* one who lives, or (more likely) hides among bushes (Australia).

bushwah (bŏŏsh′wŏ) *n.* something poor, mean, contemptible (the French *bois de vache* = cow's wood or dried dung produced *bodewash,* which became *bushwah,* a slang euphemism for *bullshit).*

bushwhacker (bŏŏsh′wă″kər) *n.* one who whacks bushes; a sickle or other instrument for whacking bushes; a guerrilla fighter or backwoodsman.

busk (bŭsk) *n.* 1. a corset stay. 2. the corset. *-v.t.* to prepare, equip, dress. *-n.* a Creek Indian harvest feast.

busker (bŭs′kər) *n.* a street musician.

butyric (bū-tĭr′ĭk) *adj.* pertaining to butter.

byrnie (bûr′nē) *n.* chain-mail body armor of the early Scandinavians.

byrthynsak (bûr′thĭn-sàk) *n.* the theft of a calf, sheep, or as much as the thief can carry (old English law).

byssus (bĭs′əs) *n.* an elegant mummy-wrapping fabric.

C

caballetta (kŏ-bŏ-lĕt′ŏ) *n.* 1. a melody imitating a horse's gallop. 2. the last, fast strains of an aria (Italian).

caballine (kăb′ə-līn) *adj.* horselike.

cabotage (kăb′ō-tŏj) *n.* coastal navigation.

cabotin (kă-bō-tăN′) *n.* a charlatan.

cabriole (kăb′rĭ-ōl) *n.* a curved furniture leg that ends as a paw clutching a ball (Queen Anne and chippendale).

cacafuego (kŏ-kō-fwä′gō) *n.* a spitfire (slang, literally, shit-fire).

cacation (kă-kā′shən) *n.* excretion.

cacemphaton (kă-kĕm′fə-tən) *n.* a harsh-sounding word or phrase.

cacestogenous (kăk-əs-tŏj′ən-əs) *adj.* caused by unfavorable home environment.

cachet (kă-shā′) *n.* 1. a mark establishing authenticity or quality. 2. a capsule for medicine.

cachexia (kă-kĕks′ĭ-ə) *n.* poor physical or mental health.

cachinnation (kă-kĭ-nā′shən) *n.* boisterous laughter.

cacidrosis (kă-kĭ-drō′sĭs) *n.* smelly sweat.

cacique (kŏ-sēk′) *n.* 1. a slightly pompous person. 2. a political boss.

cacodoxical (kă-kō-dŏks′ĭ-kəl) *adj.* heretical.

cacoepy (kă-kō′ĭ-pē) *n.* incorrect pronunciation.

cacoethes (kă-kō-ē′thĕz) *n.* a mania or bad habit.

cacogen (kă′kō-jən) *n.* an antisocial person.

cacography (kă-kŏg′rə-fē) *n.* bad writing or spelling.

cacology (kă-kŏl′ə-jē) *n.* poor pronunciation or diction.

caconym (kă′kō-nĭm) *n.* 1. a generic name rejected for linguistic reasons. 2. a bad name.

cacophemism (kă-kŏf′ə-mĭz″əm) *n.* an unfairly harsh or derogatory word or description. *-ant. euphemism.*

cacophonophilist (kă-kŏf″ən-ŏf′əl-ĭst) *n.* lover of harsh sounds.

cacophrenic (kă-kō-frĕn′ĭk) *adj.* pertaining to an inferior intellect.

cacotechny (kăk′ō-tĕk″nē) *n.* a corrupt state of art.

cacuminate (kă-kū′mĭn-āt) *v.t.* to

make sharp or pointed.

cade (kād) *adj.* abandoned by the mother; bottle-fed; pampered; spoiled. -*v.t.* to spoil or pamper. -*n.* 1. a *cade* animal or child (one who is spoiled or pampered). 2. the European juniper. 3. a barrel of 500 herrings or 1,000 sprats.

caduceus (kȧ-dōō'sĭ-əs) *n.* Mercury's staff as a symbol of the medical profession.

caducity (kȧ-dōō'sĭ-tē) *n.* 1. dropping or falling off, especially at an early age. 2. perishable; temporary. 3. lapse of a will's legacy through the later birth of an heir.

cagamosis (kȧg-ȧ-mō'sĭs) *n.* unhappy marriage.

cagmag (kȧg-'mȧg) *n.* inferior food. -*adj.* inferior (British slang).

caique (kȯ-ēk') *n.* 1. a long narrow rowboat. 2. a small sailboat (Middle East).

cairn (kẽrn) *n.* a heap of stones used either as a memorial or as a landmark for surveyors.

caitiff (kāt'ĭf) *n.* a mean or cowardly person. -*adj.* mean or cowardly.

calceate (kȧl'sē-āt) *v.t.* to shoe.

calcitrate (kȧl'sĭ-trāt) *v.t.* to kick.

calcographer (kȧl-kŏg'rȧ-fȧr) *n.* one who draws with crayons.

caldarium (kȧl-dẽr'ĭ-əm) *n.* a room for hot baths in the old Roman bathhouse or *thermae.*

calecannon (kāl-kȧn'ən) *n.* a stew made mostly from potatoes and greens (Irish).

calefactory (kȧl-ȧ-fȧk'tȧ-rē) *n.* 1. a heated room in a monastery. 2. a warming pan.

calembour (kȧl'əm-bōōr) *n.* a pun (French).

calendographer (kȧl-ən-dŏg'rȧ-fȧr) *n.* a calendar maker.

calenture (kȧl'ən-chȧr) *n.* 1. a tropical fever; sunstroke. 2. passion, ardor, glow. -*v.t.* to make feverish.

calf-slobber (kȧf'slŏb"bȧr) *n.* meringue on a pie (slang).

caliginous (kȧl-ĭj'in-əs) *adj.* obscure, dark, or veiled.

calix (kā'lĭks) *n.* a cup or goblet.

callidity (kȧl-ĭd'ĭ-tē) *n.* craftiness.

callipygian (kȧl-ĭ-pĭj'ĭ-ən) *adj.* having shapely buttocks.

callistela (kȧl-ĭs-tī'ə) *n.pl.* beauty prizes (Greek).

callithumpian (kȧl-ĭ-thŭmp'ĭ-ən) *n.* a noisy demonstration.

callomania (kȧl-ō-mā'nĭ-ə) *n.* the delusion that one is beautiful.

calumet (kȧl'ū-mět) *n.* an Indian peace pipe.

calvities (kȧl-vĭsh'ĭ-ēz) *n.* baldness. -*syn. acomia, alopecia, atrichia, phalacrosis.*

camarilla (kȧm-ȧ-rĭl'ə) *n.* 1. a small private meeting room. 2. a leader's confidential advisers. 3. a clique or cabal.

cambistry (kȧm'bĭs-trē) *n.* the science of exchange in international finance.

camelopard (kȧ-mĕl'ȧ-pȯrd) *n.* giraffe.

cameralistics (kȧm"ȧr-ȧl-ĭs'tĭks) *n.* the science of public finance.

cameriere (kȧm-ȧr-yẽr'ə) *n.* a waiter or valet (Italian).

camorra (kȯ-môr'ȯ) *n.* 1. a notoriously powerful Italian crime syndicate of the early nineteenth century. 2. any such society.

campanologist (kȧmp-ȧ-nŏl'ȧ-jĭst) *n.* a bell expert.

campestral (kȧm-pĕs'trȧl) *adj.* pertaining to or thriving on level ground.

canaille (kȧ-nīy') *n.* the mob, rabble, riffraff.

canescent (kȧn-ĕs'ənt) *adj.* becoming white.

cangue (kàng) *n.* a square wooden collar with openings for the head and hands, once used for punishment of minor crimes.

canicular (kàn-ìk'ū-lər) *adj.* pertaining to the "dog days" of July and August.

canities (kàn-ìsh'ĭ-ēz) *n.* having gray or white hair.

cannabidulia (kàn-àb''ĭ-dōōl'ĭ-ə) *n.* addiction to hashish.

cannelured (kàn'əl-ûrd) *adj.* grooved.

cannulate (kàn'ū-lāt) *v.t.* to make hollow -*adj.* hollow, with room for thread or wire inside, such as in a *cannulated* (surgical) needle.

canonicals (kàn-òn'ĭ-kəlz) *n.pl.* clerical battle array.

canoodle (kàn-ōō'dəl)*v.i.*to caress.

canophilist (kàn-òf'ĭ-lìst) *n.* a doglover.

canorous (kàn-ôr'əs) *adj.* melodious.

cantabank (kàn'tə-bànk) *n.* 1. second-rate ballad singer (slang). 2. a singer on a platform (Italian *cantabanco*).

cantharides (kàn-thòr'ĭ-dēz) *n.pl.* Spanish fly.

cantonment (kàn'tən-mənt) *n.* a military training camp.

caoine (kēn) *n.* traditional Irish death song. also *keen.*

caoutchouc (kōō'chōōk) *n.* natural, pure, or Indian rubber.

capax (kā'pàks) *adj.* legally competent.

capeline (kàp'ə-lĭn) *n.* 1. a small steel skullcap worn by foot soldiers in the Middle Ages. 2. a hoodshaped bandage for the head, shoulder, or stump of an amputated limb.

capernoited (kàp'ər-noi''təd) *adj.* tipsy, lightly pifflecated, slightly

nimptopsical.

capillose (kàp'ĭ-lōs) *adj.* hairy.

capistrate (kàp'ĭs-trāt) *adj.* hooded.

capnomancy (kàp'nō-màn''sē) *n.* fortunetelling with smoke.

caponize (kàp'ən-īz) *v.t.* to castrate [a chicken].

capric (kàp'rĭk) *adj.* goatlike; coming from a goat.

caprification (kàp''rĭ-fĭ-kā'shən) *n.* pollination of the domestic fig by hanging flowering branches of the wild fig, or *caprifig*, in the fig tree, making it easier for the fig wasp to carry and distribute the pollen; artificial fertilization (slang).

capriole (kàp'rĭ-ōl) *n.* a leap. -*v.t.* to leap.

capripede (kàp'rĭ-pēd) *n.* a satyr.

caprylic (kàp-rĭl'ĭk) *adj.* like an animal's strong smell.

captation (kàp-tā'shən) *n.* 1. the act of controlling another's mind. 2. trying to cadge acceptance by flattery. 3. formerly, the first stage of a hypnotic trance.

capuchin (kàp'ōō-shĭn) *n.* 1. a hooded cape like that worn by Capuchin monks. 2. a pigeon whose head looks like a monk's cowl. 3. a South American monkey with the same problem.

carbonado (kər-bō-nā'dō) *n.* 1. grilled meat or fish. 2. a large, dark, opaque diamond used for drills.

carboy (kòr'boi) *n.* a large green bottle encased in wicker.

carcanet (kòr'kə-nèt) *n.* an ornamental collar or necklace.

carceral (kòr'sə-rəl) *adj.* pertaining to a prison.

carcinomorphic (kòr''sĭn-ō-môr'fĭk) *adj.* crablike.

cardinalize (kòr'dĭn-ə-līz) *v.t.* to

redden by boiling.

cardophagus (kòr-dòf'ə-gəs) *n.* a donkey or other thistleivorous being.

carfax (kòr'făks) *n.* an intersection of four or more roads.

carioca (kàr-ĭ-ō'kə) *n.* a South American dance or its music.

caritative (kă-rĭt'ə-tĭv) *adj.* charitable.

carminative (kòr'mĭ-nā"tĭv) *adj.* pertaining to farting. *-n.* a medicine to induce farting.

carmot (kòr'mŏt) *n.* in alchemy, the alleged material of the philosopher's stone.

carnificial (kòr-nĭ-fĭsh'əl) *adj.* pertaining to a public executioner or butcher (in either case, to a *carnifex*).

carphology (kòr-fŏl'ə-jē) *n.* picking motions at the bedding, as happens in certain prolonged diseases.

carpogenous (kòr-pŏj'ə-nəs) *adj.* fruit-producing.

carrell (kàr'əl) *n.* a small reading area in the stacks of a library.

carucage (kàr'ōō-kāj) *n.* the act of plowing.

caryatid (kàr-ĭ-ăt'ĭd) *n.* a draped female sculpture serving as a pillar.

cascaron (kàs-kə-rŏn') *n.* an eggshell filled with confetti and emptied on certain festive occasions (Spanish *cascarón* = eggshell).

caseic (kă-sē'ĭk) *adj.* cheeselike.

cassation (kă-sā'shən) *n.* 1. an annulment (applied legally and politically). 2. open-air music (eighteenth century).

castellated (kàs'təl-ā"təd) *adj.* built like a castle; [an area] having many castles.

castrametation (kàs"trə-mē-tā'shən) *n.* the laying out or planning of a camp.

castrophrenia (kàs-trō-frē'nĭ-ə) *n.* the belief that one's thoughts are being stolen by enemies.

catabaptist (kăt-ə-băp'tĭst) *n.* a foe of baptism.

catabatic (kăt-ə-băt'ĭk) *adj.* an abating; a military retreat; pertaining to the downward motion of air, also *katabatic*.

catachresis (kăt-ə-krē'sĭs) *n.* incorrect use of a word or phrase, especially from any etymological misunderstanding.

catachtonian (kăt-ăk-thō'nĭ-ən) *adj.* underground.

catafalque (kăt'ə-fàlk) *n.* a coffin support used in elaborate funerals.

catagelophobia (kăt"ə-jĕl-ō-fō'bĭ-ə) *n.* fear of being ridiculed.

catalo (kăt'ə-lō) *n.* what you get when you cross a buffalo with a cow (U.S.).

catamenia (kăt-ə-mē'nĭ-ə) *n.* menstruation.

catamite (kăt'ə-mīt) *n.* a boy used in homosexual relations.

catamount (kăt'ə-mount) *n.* the North American cougar or lynx (from cat-o-mountain).

catapedamania (kăt"ə-pĕd-ə-mā'nĭ-ə) *n.* mania to jump from high places.

cataphasia (kăt-ə-fā'zĭ-ə) *n.* verbal repetition.

catarolysis (kăt-ər-ŏl'ĭ-sĭs) *n.* letting off steam by cursing.

catastasis (kăt-ăs'tə-sĭs) *n.* the section of ancient Greek drama just before the climax.

catasterism (kăt-ăs'tər-ĭz"əm) *n.* the use of mythological creatures for names of constellations; the constellations themselves.

catawamptious (kăt-ə-wòmp'shəs) *adj.* 1. fierce, destructive. 2. diagonal or crooked.

---

catchpoll (kàch'pōl) *n.* a police-man who arrests debtors (obs.).

catechetical (kàt-ə-kĕt'ĭ-kəl) *adj.* consisting of questions and answers.

catechumen (kàt-ə-kū'mən) *n.* one getting instructions in funda-mentals, especially Christian.

cathexis (kàth-ĕks'ĭs) *n.* mental or emotional concentration on an idea or object (Freud).

cathisophobia (kàth"ĭ-sō-fō'bĭ-ə) *n.* fear of sitting.

catholicon (kà-thŏl'ĭ-kən) *n.* a cure-all; panacea.

catlap (kàt'làp) *n.* a weak drink, fit only for cats to lap.

catmalison (kàt'màl"ĭ-sən) *n.* a cupboard in the ceiling near the chimney.

catoptromancy (kàt-ŏp'trə-màn"sē) *n.* fortunetelling with mirrors.

cauponize (kôp'ən-īz) *v.t.* to mix and adulterate for profit.

causerie (kōz-rē') *n.* 1. informal or light conversation; a chat. 2. a short, chatty article or para-graph (French).

causeuse (kô-zūz') *n.* a sofa for two people (French *causer* = to chat).

cecity (sē'sĭ-tē) *n.* blindness.

cecutiency (sē-kū'shən-sē) *n.* par-tial blindness; tendency toward blindness.

ceilidh (kā'lē) *n.* 1. a visit. 2. a private conversation. 3. an evening's musical entertainment (Anglo-Irish and Scottish).

celation (sĕl-ā'shən) *n.* hiding, es-pecially of pregnancy or child-birth.

cenacle (sĕn'ə-kəl) *n.* 1. a dining room or *cenaculum;* (cap.) the room where the "last supper" was allegedly eaten. 2. a female

religious retreat house. 3. a liter-ary group headed by Victor Hugo.

cencerro (sĕn-sĕr'ō) *n.* the leader in a pack-mule train (southwestern U.S.).

cenobite (sĕn'ō-bīt) *n.* a monk living with other monks.

cenophobia (sĕn-ō-fō'bĭ-ə) *n.* fear of empty spaces.

cenotaph (sĕn'ō-tàf) *n.* a monu-ment or empty tomb honoring a dead person whose body lies else-where.

centesimation (sĕn-tĕs"ĭ-mā'shən) *n.* an old Roman punishment of executing one hundredth of a group, usually of soldiers.

centonism (sĕn'tən-ĭz"əm) *n.* col-lating of old or borrowed mater-ial into a new form (music, art, literature).

cepaceous (sĕp-ā'shəs) *adj.* of or like an onion.

cephalonamancy (sĕf-əl-ŏn'ə-màn"sē) *n.* fortunetelling by boil-ing an ass head.

ceraunograph (sĕr-ŏn'ə-gràf) *n.* an instrument for chronologically recording thunder and lightning.

ceraunoscopy (sĕr"ən-ŏs'kə-pē) *n.* fortunetelling with lightning.

cerberus (sûr'bûr-əs) *n.* a rough watchful guard (in Greek myth-ology, *Cerberus* guarded the en-trance to Hades).

cercopithecan (sûr-kō-pĭth'ə-kən) *adj.* pertaining to monkeys.

cerements (sĭr'mənts) *n.* burial clothes.

cereous (sĭr'ē-əs) *adj.* waxen.

cernous (sûr'nū-əs) *adj.* hanging down, like a flower.

ceromancy (sĭr'ō-màn"sē) *n.* for-tunetelling with melted wax dropped in water.

cervicide (sûr'vĭ-sīd) *n.* deer-killing.

cervisial (sûr-vĭs'ĭ-əl) *adj.* pertaining to beer.

cespitose (sĕs'pĭ-tōs) *adj.* pertaining to turf; growing in clumps; matted.

cetologist (sē-tŏl'ə-jĭst) *n.* a student of whales.

chaetiferous (kē-tĭf'ər-əs) *adj.* having bristles, also *chaetrophorous.*

chafferer (chăf'ər-ûr) *n.* a buyer, bargainer.

chaldean (kăl-dē'ən) *adj.* pertaining to astrology or mysticism. *-n.* an astrologer or mystic.

chalybeous (kə-lĭb'ē-əs) *adj.* looking like tempered steel; steel-blue.

chamade (shò-mŏd') *n.* the drum beat or trumpet blast which announces a surrender.

champaign (shăm-pān') *n.* flat or open country. *-adj.* pertaining to flat or open country.

champerty (shăm'pər-tē) *n.* an illegal deal between litigants and an outsider who shares the court costs for a cut of the proceeds.

chandala (chăn-dŏl'ò) *n.pl.* an outcast, untouchable (India).

chankings (chănk'ĭngz) *n.pl.* spat-out food, such as rind or pits; *champings* (dialect).

chantage (shòn-tŏž') *n.* blackmail (French).

chanterelle (shòn-tə-rĕl') *n.* 1. an edible mushroom that smells like a plum. 2. the highest-pitched string of a musical instrument, also *chantarelle.*

chaology (kā-ŏl'ə-jē) *n.* the study of chaos.

charette (shò-rĕt') *n.* 1. the eleventh-hour efforts of architecture students to solve their design-problem assignments. 2. applied more generally to other

work with specific due dates. 3. a cart or chariot.

Chargoggagoggmanchauggagoggchaubunagungamaugg (chŭm'lē?) *n.* Indian name for a Massachusetts lake. ("You fish on your side, I fish on my side, nobody fish in the middle.")

charientism (kăr'ĭ-ən-tĭz"əm) *n.* a gracefully veiled insult.

charivari (shà-rĭv'ər-ē) *n.* a noisy demonstration, especially one for newlyweds.

chartaceous (kòr-tā'shəs) *adj.* paperlike.

charuk (shò-rōōk') *n.* an old Turkish sandal with turned-up tips.

chasmophilous (kăz-mŏf'ĭ-ləs) *adj.* fond of nooks, crannies, crevices, and chasms.

chatelaine (shăt'ə-lān) *n.* 1. a female castle-keeper. 2. an ornamental chain suspended between two pins, worn by women.

chatoyment (shă-toi'mənt) *n.* play of colors in a mineral, also *adj.*

chawdron (shôd'rən) *n.* entrails (archaic).

cheechako (chē-chò'kō) *n.* a newcomer, tenderfoot (from the Chinook jargon of Alaska and northwestern U.S.).

cheeseparings (chēz'pèr"ĭngz) *n.pl.* cheese peels, saved only by the very poor or the tightwad; worthless scraps. *-adj. s.* miserly economizing; scrimping.

cheimaphilic (kī"mə-fĭl'ĭk) *adj.* fond of winter, or of cold.

chela (kē'lə) *n.* 1. a disciple. 2. a crustacean claw (India).

chelonian (kē-lō'nĭ-ən) *adj.* pertaining to tortoises or turtles. *-n.* a tortoise or turtle.

chemiloon (shĕm-ĭ-lōōn') *n.* a pant-slip (*chemise* + pant*aloon*).

chemurgy (kĕm'ûr-jē) *n.* chemical

---

măn; mãde; lĕt; bē; sĭp; wīne; hŏt; cōld; sôre; dŭll; fūgue; bûrp; gŏŏd; fōōd; out; gĕt; thin; thĭs; year; ažure; ō'mən"; viN; fũr; Bach

soil cultivation for produce not associated with food or clothing (i.e., soy beans as used in plastics manufacturing).

chermany (chûr'mə-nē) *n.* a type of baseball (southern U.S.).

cherophobia (kĭr"ō-fō'bĭ-ə) *n.* fear of gaiety.

cherubimical (chĕr-ə-bĭm'ĭ-kəl) *adj.* drunk (in a list compiled by Benjamin Franklin. see *nimptopsical*).

chevaline (shĕv'ə-lĭn) *adj.* horse-like. *-n.* horseflesh.

chevelure (shĕv-əl-yōōr') *n.* 1. the head of a comet. 2. a head of hair (French).

chevy (chĕv'ē) *n.* a hunting cry; the hunt. *-v.t. &i.* 1. to hunt. 2. to tease or torment.

chewink (chĭ-wĭnk') *n.* the red-eyed towhee.

chiasmus (kĭ-àz'məs) *n.* the inversion of a phrase that produces a complementary one (never eat to live; but live to eat).

chichevache (shēsh'vŏsh) *n.* a medieval monster, said to have fed on patient wives, and was therefore very lean. see *bicorne*.

chiliad (kĭl'ĭ-əd) *n.* one thousand [years].

chiloschisis (kĭ-lòs'kĭ-sĭs) *n.* hare-lip.

chimopelagic (kĭ"mō-pə-làj'ĭk) *adj.* pertaining to certain deep-sea organisms that surface only in winter.

chinch (chĭnch) *n.* bedbug.

chionablepsia (kĭ"ŏn-ə-blĕp'sĭ-ə) *n.* snow blindness.

chirognomy (kĭ-rŏg'nə-mē) *n.* palmistry.

chirogymnast (kĭ-rō-jĭm'nàst) *n.* a finger-exercise machine for pianists.

chirology (kĭ-rŏl'ə-jē) *n.* talking with one's hands; the study of the hand.

chirospasm (kĭ'rō-spàz"əm) *n.* writer's cramp.

chirotonsor (kĭ'rō-tòn"sər) *n.* barber (a 1924 coinage voted on and accepted by 3,000 chirotonsorial representatives).

chirotony (kĭ-ròt'ə-nē) *n.* 1. an election by a show of hands. 2. the laying on of hands by a priest for ordination and sundry blessings.

chittering-bite (chĭt'ər-ĭng-bīt") *n.* a piece of bread put in the mouth to prevent the teeth from chattering.

chitterlings (chĭt'ər-lĭngz) *n.pl.* 1. the edible smaller intestines of cattle and pork. 2. *(s.)* a frill or ruffle on a shirt front. also *childing, chitter, chitteril, chitling,* and *chitlin'.*

chockablock (chŏk'ə-blŏk) *adj.* crowded, squeezed together.

cholangiocholecystocholedoch-ectomy (see *Chargoggagogg-manchauggagoggchaubunagun-gamaugg* for pronunciation) *n.* cutting out of the hepatic duct, common bile duct, and gall bladder.

chopin (chŏp'ĭn) *n.* 1. a ceramic cup. 2. a liquid measure varying from a half pint to a quart (Scottish).

choralcelo (kôr"əl-sèl'ō) *n.* an electric piano.

chorea (kôr-ē'ə) *n.* St. Vitus's dance.

choregus (kôr-ē'gəs) *n.* the "angel" or backer of a play in ancient Greece.

choreomania (kôr"ē-ō-mā'nĭ-ə) *n.* dancing mania, sometimes occurring in epidemics.

chorography (kôr-òg'rə-fē) *n.* regional delineation of maps.

---

mǎn; mǎde; lět; bē; sǐp; wīne; hǒt; cōld; sôre; dǔll; fūgue; bûrp; gōōd; fōōd; out; gět; thin; this; year; azure; ō'mən"; viN; fûr; Bach

chowry (chou're) *n.* an East Indian fly swatter made from a yak's tail.

chrematophobia (krēm"ə-tō-fō'bl-ə) *n.* fear of money.

chreotechnics (krē-ō-těk'nĭks) *n.* the necessary trades, especially farming, manufacturing, and selling.

chrestomathy (krès-tŏm'ə-thē) *n.* a collection of choice literary pieces.

chrisom (krĭs'əm) *n.* 1. a child that dies within a month. 2. a white cloth thrown over a child when baptized.

chronogram (krŏn'ō-grăm) *n.* an inscription containing the correlative date in Roman numerals (*M*an of s*C*ience and hu*M*anity, Bertrand Russe*L*L's e*X*ample g*I*ves life e*X*tra meaning = MCMLXIX or 1969, the year of Bertrand Russell's death).

chrysology (krĭ-sŏl'ə-jē) *n.* the study of value and production of precious metals (a branch of political economy).

chrysophilist (krĭ-sŏf'ə-lĭst) *n.* a gold-lover.

chthonian (thō'nĭ-ən) *adj.* pertaining to underworld gods.

chthonophagia (thŏn-ō-fā'jĭ-ə) *n.* eating dirt; *geophagy*.

chummage (chŭm'əj) *n.* 1. roommates. 2. expense of money due from each roommate. 3. money demanded by old prisoners of new ones (British slang).

churriguerism (chōō-rē'gər-ĭz"əm) *n.* grossly ornamental architecture (from *Churríguera*, a gross eighteenth-century Spanish architect).

cibarious (sĭ-bĕr'ĭ-əs) *adj.* pertaining to food; edible.

cibophobia (sĭ-bō-fō'bĭ-ə) *n.* fear

of food.

cicada (sĭ-kā'də) *n.* the seventeen-year locust.

cicisbeo (sĭ-sĭs'bē-ō) *n.* the known lover of a married woman.

ciconine (sĭk'ō-nīn) *adj.* storklike.

cidevant (sē-də-vŏN') *adj.* has-been (pertaining to an ex-officer or other notable).

cienega (sē-ĕn'ə-gə) *n.* a marsh or swamp (Spanish and U.S.).

cilicious (sĭl-ĭsh'əs) *adj.* made of haircloth (obs.).

cimex (sī'mĕks) *n.* bedbug. *pl. cimices.* see *chinch*.

cimmerian (sĭ-mĭr'ĭ-ən) *adj.* dark, gloomy (Homerian people whose land is perpetually misty and dark).

cincinate (sĭn-sĭn'ət) *adj.* curled in ringlets.

cinerescent (sĭn-ər-ĕs'ənt) *adj.* ashen, grayish; *cinereous*.

cingular (sĭng'gū-lər) *adj.* ring-shaped.

circumforaneous (sûr"kùm-fər-ān'ĭ-əs) *adj.* wandering from market to market, or place to place.

cisatlantic (sĭs-ăt-lăn'tĭk) *adj.* on this (the speaker's or writer's) side of the Atlantic.

cist (sĭst) *n.* 1. a primitive stone tomb. 2. a box of sacred oddments.

cisvestitism (sĭs-vĕs'tĭ-tĭz"əm) *n.* wearing weird or inappropriate clothes.

cittosis (sĭ-tō'sĭs) *n.* an abnormal desire for strange foods.

cixiid (sĭks'ē-ĭd) *n.* an insect related to the lantern fly.

clabber (klăb'ər) *n.* 1. curdled milk; *bonnyclabber*. 2. mud, mire. *-v.t.&i.* to curdle.

clairaudience (klĕr-ô'dĭ-əns) *n.* the alleged ability to hear sounds too

distant for the normal ear:
claimed by psychics and other
such frauds.

clamjamfry (klăm-jăm'frē) *n.* the
mob or rabble (Scottish).

clang-tint (klăng'tĭnt) *n.* timbre.

clappermaclaw (klăp'ər-mə-klô")
v.i. to claw or scratch; to scold.
also *clapperclaw.*

claqueur (klà-kûr') *n.* a member of
a *claque.*

clarigate (klăr'ĭ-gāt) *v.i.* to declare
war formally (obs.).

claudicant (klô'dĭ-kənt) *adj.* lim-
ping; lame.

claver (klā'vər) *n.* gossip.

clavicytherium (klăv"ĭ-sĭ-thĕr'ĭ-
əm) *n.* a harpsichordlike musical
instrument.

claviger (klăv'ĭ-jər) *n.* a caretaker,
or the man with the keys.

clavis (klā'vĭs) *n.* a clue in de-
ciphering, or translating foreign
writings; a glossary or key (Latin
clavis = key).

cledonism (klĕ'dən-ĭz"əm) *n.* use of
euphemisms for protection
against the black magic perpe-
trated by plain words.

clematite (klĕm'ə-tīt) *n.* the European birthwort.

cleocentric (klē-ō-sĕn'trĭk) *adj.*
pertaining to the belief that fame
is everything.

clepsydra (klĕp'sĭ-drə) '*n.* a water
clock.

clerihew (klĕr'ĭ-hū) *n.* an amusing
quatrain about contemporary
notables (from *Edmund Clerihew
Bentley,* 1875-1956, its origin-
ator).

cleromancy (klĕr'ō-măn"sē) *n.* fortunetelling with dice.

climacophobia (klī"mə-kō-fō'bĭ-ə)
n. fear of falling downstairs.

clinchpoop (klĭnch'pōōp) *n.* a lout,
jerk, clod, boor, slob, boob, fat-

head, sap.

clinomania (klī-nō-mā-nĭ-ə) *n.* excessive desire to stay in bed.

clinquant (klĭng'kənt) *adj.* glitter-
ing, showy, or specious.

clish-ma-claver (klĭsh'mə-klā"vər)
n. foolish gossip (Scottish).

clishpen (klĭsh'pən) *v.t.* to break
something by dropping it (slang).

cloaca (klō-ā'kə) *n.* a sewer or
toilet; excretion passage in animals.

clodpolish (klŏd'pŏl"ĭsh) *adj.* awkward (slang).

clonic (klŏ'nĭk) *adj.* spastic.

clough (klŭf) *n.* gully.

clyster (klĭs'tər) *n.* an injection into
the anus; an enema.

cnemial (nē'mĭ-əl) *adj.* pertaining
to the shinbone or tibia.

cnicin (nī'sĭn) *n.* "the crystalline
bitter principle of the blessed
thistle (Cnicus benedictus)."

coacervate (kō-ăs'ər-vāt) *v.t.* to
accumulate, amass, heap up.

coaction (kō-ăk'shən) *n.* compulsion.

coadjuvancy (kō-ăj'ōō-văn"sē) *n.*
cooperation.

coadunate (kō-ăj'ən-āt) *adj.*
joined, united.

coaptation (kō-ăp-tā'shən) *n.* the
mutual adaptation *(co-*adapta-
tion) of broken parts to each
other, as the edges of a wound,
etc.

coarct (kō-ŏrkt') *v.t.* to restrain, re-
strict (obs.).

cockabaloo (kŏk"ŏ-bə-lōō') *n.* a
bullying boss (slang).

cockalorum (kŏk-ə-lôr'əm) *n.* 1. a
small rooster. 2. a little man with
delusions of grandeur.

cockarouse (kŏk'ə-rouz) *n.* an im-
portant person (obs.).

coctile (kŏk'tĭl) *adj.* baked.

coffle (kŏf'əl) *n.* a caravan of slaves

---

măn; māde; lĕt; bē; sĭp; wīne; hŏt; cōld; sôre; dŭll; fūgue; bûrp;
gŏŏd; fōōd; out; gĕt; thin; this; year; ažure; ō'mən"; viN; fūr; Bach

or cattle chained together. -*v.t.* to fasten together in a *coffle*.

cogger (kŏ'gər) *n.* a phony flatterer.

cogitabund (kŏ'jĭ-tə-bŭnd″) *adj.* meditative.

coign (koin) *n.* corner or angle. *coign of vantage.* vantage point.

colletic (kŏl-ĕt'ĭk) *adj.* pertaining to glue; made of glue. -*n.* a glue.

collier (kŏl'yər) *n.* 1. a coal miner. 2. a coal ship. 3. the dolphin fly. 4. Wilson's plover. *colliery, n.* a coal mine.

collieshangie (kŏl-ĭ-shǎng'ē) *n.* a noisy or confused fight.

colligation (kŏl-ĭ-gā'shən) *n.* a binding together.

collimate (kŏl'ĭ-māt) *v.t.* to make parallel.

collocate (kŏl'ō-kāt) *v.t.* to arrange; to place side by side.

collop (kŏl'əp) *n.* a small slice or piece.

colluctation (kŏl-ək-tā'shən) *n.* conflict.

colluvial (kŏl-ōō'vĭ-əl) *adj.* pertaining to a mass of filth. *colluvies, n.* a collection, or mass of nasties.

collybist (kŏl'ĭ-bĭst) *n.* a usurer or miser.

collywobbles (kŏl'ĭ-wŏb″əlz) *n.* pain or looseness in the bowels.

coloquintida (kŏl-ō-kwĭn'tĭ-də) *n.* the bitter apple; related to the watermelon, its juice is used as a cathartic. *colocynth* (kŏl'ō-sĭnth) *n.*

colporter (kŏl'pôr″tər) *n.* a traveling Bible salesman or distributor. also *colporteur.*

colubrine (kŏl'ū-brīn) *adj.* snaky, sneaky, cunning.

columbine (kŏl'əm-bīn) *adj.* dovelike; like a dove's neck.

comate (kō'māt) *adj.* hairy.

combololo (kŏm-bō-lō'yō) *n.* a Mohammedan rosary of ninety-nine beads.

comedo (kŏm'ĭ-dō) *n.* a blackhead.

comeling (kŭm'lĭng) *n.* an immigrant or temporary resident.

comity (kŏm'ĭ-tē) *n.* courtesy, politeness.

commasculation (kō-màs″kū-lā'shən) *n.* homosexuality between men.

commatic (kō-mǎt'ĭk) *adj.* having short phrases or sentences; brief.

commensal (kō-mĕn'səl) *n.* living and eating together.

commentitious (kŏm-ĕn-tĭ'shəs) *adj.* imaginary.

commination (kŏm-ĭn-ā'shən) *n.* denunciation; threatening or cursing.

comminution (kŏm-ĭn-ū'shən) *n.* a wearing away.

commisure (kŏm'ĭ-shûr) *n.* a seam or joint.

commonition (kŏm-ə-nĭ'shən) *n.* warning (obs.).

commorant (kŏm'ər-ənt) *n.* a resident. -*adj.* residing.

commorient (kŏm-ôr'ĭ-ənt) *adj.* dying together.

comose (kō'mōs) *adj.* hairy, tufted.

companage (kŏm-pŏ-nŏž') *n.* food eaten with bread.

compeer (kŏm-pĭr') *n.* an equal.

compesce (kŏm-pĕs') *v.t.* to restrain.

complect (kŏm-plĕkt') *v.t.* to connect together; to intertwine.

comploration (kŏm-plôr-ā'shən) *n.* wailing and weeping together.

compotation (kŏm-pō-tā' shən) *n.* drinking together, *compotator,* fellow drinker.

comprachico (kŏm-prə-chē'kō) *n.* one who buys or sells children after first deforming them (Spanish).

comprecation (kŏm-prə-kā'shən) *n.* a prayer meeting.

comprivigni (kôm-prē-vēn'yē) *n.* children of present couple's former marriages in relation to each other.

compurgation (kŏm-pər-gā'shən) *n.* vindication; that which vindicates.

compursion (kŏm-pûr'żən) *n.* wrinkling one's face.

conation (kō-nā'shən) *n.* mental effort.

concamerate (kŏn-kăm'ər-āt) *v.t.* to arch over; to vault.

concatenation (kŏn-kăt″ə-nā'shən) *n.* connection in a series; a connected series.

concatervate (kŏn-kăt'ər-vāt) *adj.* heaped up.

conchologist (kŏng-kŏl'ə-jĭst) *n.* a shell collector or specialist.

concliabule (kŏn-sĭl'ĭ-ə-būl″) *n.* a secret meeting of plot-hatchers.

concinnity (kŏn-sĭn'ĭ-tē) *n.* skillful blending; harmony.

concionative (kŏn'shə-nā″tĭv) *adj.* pertaining to public speaking or preaching.

concitation (kŏn-sī-tā'shən) *n.* the act of exciting or stirring up.

concubitant (kŏn-kū'bĭ-tənt) *adj.* marriageable.

concupiscence (kŏn-kū'pĭ-səns) *n.* strong appetite; excessive sexual desire.

condign (kŏn-dīn') *adj.* deserved or suitable [punishment].

condottiere (kŏn-dô-tyèr'è) *n.* head of a mercenary army.

conduce (kŏn-dōōs') *v.t. &i.* to contribute; tend to.

confitent (kŏn'fĭ-tənt) *n.* one who confesses.

conflate (kŏn-flāt') *adj.* blown or brought together, blended, consolidated. *-v.t.* to blow or bring

together; to collect.

congeries (kŏn-jĭr'ēz) *n.* heap, pile.

congiary (kŏn'jĭ-ĕr″ē) *n.* a gift of food or money to Roman soldiers and others.

conglaciate (kŏn-glăs'ĭ-āt) *v.t. &i.* to freeze.

conglobe (kŏn-glōb') *v.t. &i.* to form into a ball. *conglobation, n.* the process of *conglobing* or the product itself.

congreet (kŏn-grēt') *v.i.* to greet mutually (Shakespeare).

coniaker (kŏ'nĭ-ăk″ər) *n.* a coin counterfeiter.

connate (kŏn'āt) *adj.* 1. coexisting since birth. 2. cognate (having the same origin).

conquassate (kŏn-kwăs'ət) *v.t.* to shake violently (obs.).

consarcination (kŏn-sŏr″sĭnā'shən) *n.* the act of patching.

consectaneous (kŏn-sĕk-tā'nĭ-əs) *adj.* logical consequence; corollary.

conspectable (kŏn-spĕk'tə-bəl) *adj.* easily seen (obs.).

conspissation (kŏn-spĭ-sā'shən) *n.* thickness; the act of thickening.

conspue (kŏn-spū') *v.t.* to spurn contemptuously.

conspurcate (kŏn'spər-kāt) *v.t.* to pollute, defile.

constuprate (kŏn'stū-prāt) *v.t.* to violate, to debauch.

consuetude (kŏn'swĭ-tūd) *n.* custom, tradition.

contabescent (kŏn-tə-bĕs'ənt) *adj.* wasting away, atrophied.

contabulate (kŏn-tăb'ū-lāt) *v.t.* to floor with boards (obs.).

contect (kŏn-tĕkt') *v.t.* to cover.

contemn (kən-tĕm') *v.t.* to be contemptuous; to disdain, scorn.

contesseration (kŏn-tĕs″ər-ā'shən) *n.* the act of making friends.

conticent (kŏn'tĭ-sənt) *adj.* quiet,

hushed.

contortuplicate (kŏn″tôr-tōōp′lĭ-kət) *adj.* twisted back upon itself.

contraremonstrant (kŏn″trə-rē-mŏn′strənt) *n.* a remonstrator against remonstrance.

contrectation (kŏn-trĕk-tā′shən) *n.* handling; the love play preceding sexual intercourse; act of caressing someone, especially furtively or against her will.

contriturate (kŏn-trĭt′yər-āt) *v.t.* to pulverize; to triturate.

contubernial (kŏn-tōō-bûr′nĭ-əl) *adj.* living together familiarly.

conventicle (kŏn-vĕn′tĭ-kəl) *n.* 1. a secret religious meeting or assembly. 2. the place where this is held.

convertite (kŏn′vər-tīt) *n.* a reformed prostitute.

cooster (kōōs′tər) *n.* a worn-out libertine (slang).

coparcener (kō-pŏr′sən-ûr). *n.* a joint heir.

coprolalia (kŏp-rō-lā′lĭ-ə) *n.* the use of words relating to dirt or excrement. see *eschrolalia.*

coprology (kŏp-rŏl′ə-jē) *n.* the study of pornography.

coprophemia (kŏp-rō-fē′mĭ-ə) *n.* obscene language.

coprophilia (kŏp-rō-fĭl′ĭ-ə) *n.* a feces fancier.

copula (kŏp′ū-lə) *n.* 1. something that joins together. 2. a connecting tissue or bone (Medicine). 3. a verb form connecting subject with predicate. 4. the connecting link between a proposition's subject and predicate (logic). 5. sexual intercourse.

coradicate (kō-răd′ĭ-kāt) *adj.* derived from the same root (linguistics).

cordate (kôr′dāt) *adj.* heart-shaped.

cordillera (kôr-dē-yĕr′ə) *n.* a mountain range (Spanish).

cordwainer (kôrd′wān″ər) *n.* a shoemaker.

coriaceous (kôr-ĭ-ā′shəs) *adj.* pertaining to something resembling leather; tough.

cormorant (kôr′mər-ănt) *n.* a bird that preys on fish; a gluttonous or avaricious person.

corncrake (kôrn′krāk) *n.* a long-legged bird with a grating call.

cornobbled (kôr′nŏb″əld) *adj.* hit with a fist.

cornopean (kôr-nō′pĭ-ən) *n.* the valve trumpet.

cornuted (kôr-nū′təd) *adj.* cuckolded (Latin *cornutus* = horned).

corody (kŏr′ə-dē) *n.* a food, drink, or clothing subsidy.

coronach (kŏr′ō-năk) *n.* a dirge played on bagpipes (Scotch and Irish).

corregidor (kō-rĕg′ə-dôr) *n.* the chief magistrate of a town formerly in Spanish territory.

corrigent (kŏr′ĭ-jənt) *n.* something used to mitigate the effect of something else; corrective.

corroboree (kō-rŏ′bə-rē) *n.* a noisy Australian victory celebration; an uproar. *-v.i.* to indulge in such goings-on.

corvee (kôr-vā′) *n.* slave labor.

corvine (kôr′vĭn) *adj.* of the crow family.

corybantism (kôr-ĭ-bănt′tĭz″əm) *n.* a frenzied, sleepless delirium accompanied by wild and frightening hallucinations, also *corybantiasm.*

corydon (kôr′ĭ-dŏn) *n.* a shepherd or young country lout.

coryphaeus (kôr-ĭ-fē′əs) *n.* leader of the ancient Greek dramatic chorus; chorus leader.

---

coryphee (kôr-ĭ-fā') *n.* prima ballerina.

coryza (kôr-ī'-zə) *n.* a head cold.

coscinomancy (kŏs'ĭ-nō-măn″sē) *n.* fortunetelling with a sieve suspended on shears (Voodoo).

cosher (kŏsh'ər) *v.t.&i.* to live off someone; to have a friendly chat.

cosmotellurian (kŏz″-mō-tĕl-ōōr'ĭ-ən) *adj.* relating to or affecting the earth and sky.

cosseted (kŏs'ə-təd) *adj.* cuddled, coddled, pampered, or petted.

costal (kŏs'təl) *adj.* pertaining to the ribs or rib area.

costard (kŏs'tərd) *n.* 1. a large English apple. 2. the head (British slang).

costermongering (kŏs'tər-mŭng″gər-ĭng) *n.* 1. apple-selling. 2. tampering with a great composer's orchestral or choral works (from Sir Michael *Costa's* tamperings with Handel. British slang).

costive (kŏs'tĭv) *adj.* constipated.

costumbrista (kōs-tōōm-brēs'tə) *adj.* illustrating local customs in art and literature.

cothurnus (kō-thûr'nəs) *n.* 1. a boot worn by actors in ancient Greek and Roman tragedies. 2. the somewhat stilted spirit of classical tragic drama. *cothurnal, adj.*

cotquean (kŏt'kwēn) *n.* 1. a man who does "women's work." 2. a vulgar, shrewish woman.

couchée (kōō-shā) *n.* bedtime; a bedtime visit.

countercaster (koun'tər-kàs″tər) *n.* a contemptuous word for a bookkeeper or accountant; a person dealing in numbers.

couscous (kōōs'kōōs) *n.* a West African dish of baobab leaves.

couvade (kōō-vŏd') *n.* symbolic portrayal of childbirth by the husband while his wife is actually in labor.

couveuse (kōō-vûz') *n.* an incubator for premature infants (French).

covinous (kŭv'ĭn-əs) *adj.* deceitful, conspiring.

cowan (kou'ən) *n.* a non-Mason who claims membership in order to penetrate Masonry's dark secrets.

coypu (koi'pōō) *n.* South American aquatic rodent, source of nutria.

crambo (krăm'bō) *n.* a rhyme (derogatory).

crantara (krăn-tô'rə) *n.* a piece of half-burned wood dipped in blood and carried from clan to clan, once used as a rallying signal in Scotland; the fiery cross.

crapaudine (krà-pō-dēn') *adj.* swinging on top and bottom pivots like a door. *-n.* 1. the socket for a swinging-door pivot. 2. a horse's ulcer.

crapulous (krăp'ū-ləs) *adj.* overeating or drinking; coarse.

crassilingual (krăs-ĭ-lĭng'gwəl) *adj.* thick-tongued.

crawk (krôk) *n.* an animal imitator (radio slang).

creancer (krē'ən-sûr) *n.* guardian.

crebrity (krē'brĭ-tē) *n.* frequency.

crenulate (krĕn'ū-lāt) *adj.* notched; scalloped, also *crenulated.*

creodont (krē'ō-dŏnt) *n.* a primitive, carnivorous, small-brained mammal.

creophagous (krē-ŏf'ə-gəs) *adj.* carnivorous.

crepehanger (krāp'hàng″ər) *n.* a gloomy person; a pessimist (slang).

crepitate (krĕp'ĭ-tāt) *v.i.* to make repeated crackling noises; to crackle or rattle.

crepitus (krĕp'ĭ-təs) n. fart.

cretated (krē'tā"təd) adj. rubbed with chalk.

cribiform (krĭb'rĭ-fôrm) adj. sieve-like.

crinal (krī'nəl) adj. hairy; crinatory.

crine (krīn) v.i. to shrink, shrivel up.

crinigerous (krī-nĭj'ər-əs) adj. overgrown with hair (obs.).

crispate (krĭs'pāt) adj. curled.

crithomancy (krĭth'ō-măn"sē) n. fortunetelling with cake dough, scattering it over sacrificial victims.

criticaster (krĭ'tĭ-kăs"tər) n. an incompetent, inferior critic.

croakumshire (krō'kəm-shər) n. a croaking sound peculiar to the Northumberland dialect resulting from a supposed inability to sound the letter R (British).

croft (krôft) n. a small field or farm (British).

cromlech (krŏm'lĕk) n. a prehistoric tomb or monolithic monument.

cromnyomancy (krŏm'nĭ-ō-măn"sē) n. fortunetelling with onions.

cronk (krŏnk) n. a horse made sick so that it will lose the race (slang).

croodle (krōō'dəl) v.t. & i. to cling to; nestle together.

cropsick (krŏp'sĭk) adj. sick from overeating or drinking.

croquignole (krō'kĭn-yōl) n. the curling of one's hair with a curling iron.

crotaline (krŏt'ə-lĭn) adj. pertaining to rattlesnakes.

crounotherapy (krōōn-ə-thĕr'ə-pē) n. therapy using mineral waters.

cruor (krōō'ôr) n. clotted blood; gore.

crurophilous (krûr-ŏf'ĭl-əs) adj.

liking legs.

crustose (krŭs'təs) adj. thick-skinned.

crwth (krōōth) n. a six-stringed Welsh ancestor of the violin.

cryogeny (krī-ŏj'ə-nē) n. refrigeration.

ctetology (tē-tŏl'ə-jē) n. the study of acquired characteristics.

cubatory (kū'bə-tôr"ē) adj. reclining, resting. -n. a dormitory.

cuck (kŭk) v.t. & i. to excrete. -n. excrement.

cuckquean (kŭk'wē-ən) n. a female cuckold. -v.t. to make a cuck-quean of.

cuculine (kū'kū-lĭn) adj. pertaining to the cuckoo.

cuddy (kŭd'ē) n. 1. a gift or bribe to the landlord. 2. a small cabin under the poop deck; any small room. 3. a blockhead. 4. the young coalfish. 5. a rustic swain. 6. four Arabian nusfiahs (= one gallon).

cuerpo (kwĕr'pō) n. the body. in cuerpo, without a shirt of jacket; undressed, unprotected.

cuggermugger (kŭg'ər-mŭg"ər) n. whispered gossiping.

cuirass (kwĭr-ăs') n. armor for the chest and back; protective bony covering [on animals].

culch (kŭlch) n. odds and ends of meat (slang).

culiciform (kū-lĭs'ĭ-fôrm) adj. goat-like. see capric.

cunctative (kŭngk'tə-tĭv) adj. tardy, dilatory; cunctatious.

cunctipotent (kŭngk-tĭp'ə-tənt) adj. omnipotent.

cuniculous (kū-nĭk'ū-ləs) adj. full of holes, windings, or rabbits.

cunnilingus (kŭn-ĭ-lĭng'gəs) n. the licking of female genitals.

cunningman (kŭn'ĭng-mən) n. someone who alleges recovery of stolen goods; a phony fortune-teller.

curiological (kyoor"ĭ-ō-lŏj'ĭ-kəl) *adj.* pertaining to a form of hiero-glyphics which represents things by graphic illustrations rather than by abstract symbols.

curpin (kûr'pĭn) *n.* a fowl's rump; anyone's rump. also *curpon.*

curple (kûr'pəl) *n.* the buttocks.

curtein (kûr-tān') *n.* the blunted sword used in English corona-tions, supposed to symbolize the sword of mercy.

curtilage (kûr'tĭ-lāj) *n.* a yard belonging to and adjoining a house.

cushlamochree (koosh"lə-mə-krē') *n.* darling (Irish = "vein of my heart"). also *cushlamachree.* see *acushla.*

cwm (koom) *n.* a steep hollow in a mountain (Welsh).

cyaneous (sī-ān'ĭ-əs) *adj.* sky-blue.

cyclostomate (sī-klŏs'tō-māt) *adj.* having a round mouth.

cyesthes (sī-ēs'thēz) *n.pl.* clothes worn by pregnant women to mini-mize the maximum.

cygnet (sĭg'nət) *n.* a young swan.

cymotrichous (sī-mŏt'rĭ-kəs) *adj.* having wavy hair.

cynanthropy (sī-năn'thrə-pē) *n.* a type of insanity in which a per-son thinks she's a dog.

cynegetics (sī-nə-jĕt'ĭks) *n.* hun-ting with dogs.

cynolatry (sī-nŏl'ə-trē) *n.* dog worship.

cynghanedd (kĭn-hŏ'nĕth) *n.* a strict rhyme and alliteration sys-tem used in Welsh poetry.

cynophobia (sī-nō-fō'bĭ-ə) *n.* 1. fear of dogs. 2. *lyssophobia,* or a fear of rabies accompanied by its usual symptoms; *hydropho-bophobia.*

cynosure (sī-nə-shoor) *n.* some-thing that guides; a person or thing in the limelight; the con-stellation Ursa Minor, or the North Star therein.

cyprian (sĭp'rĭ-ən) *adj.* lecherous, licentious, and lewd. -*n.* a prosti-tute.

cypripareunia (sĭp"rĭ-pər-ū'nĭ-ə) *n.* sexual intercourse with a prosti-tute.

cywydd (kĭ'wĭth) *n.* a Welsh couplet of seven-syllable lines with varying *cynghanedd.*

czigany (tsĭ'gŏ-nē") *n.* a gypsy (Hungarian).

D

dabchick (dăb′chĭk) *n.* the little grebe, a small diving bird.

dacnomania (dăk-nō-mā′nĭ-ə) *n.* a mania for killing.

dacrygelosis (dăk″rĭ-jə-lō′sĭs) *n.* condition of alternating crying and laughing.

dactylion (dăk-tĭl′ĭ-ən) *n.* 1. a finger-exerciser for pianists invented in 1835 by Henri Herz. 2. webbed fingers or toes.

dactylology (dăk-tĭl-ŏl′ə-jē) *n.* the study or act of communicating by finger-language, or sign language.

dactyloscopy (dăk-tĭl-ŏs′kə-pē) *n.* identification by or classification of fingerprints.

dadaism (dŏ′dŏ-ĭz″əm) *n.* an art movement characterized by symbolism, formlessness, and satire, it became the forerunner of surrealism (the meaningless word, *dada*, was coined by poet Tristan Tsara, who founded the movement in Paris in 1916).

daggle (dăg′əl) *v.t.&i.* to soil by dragging in the mud, also *draggle*.

damassin (dăm′ə-sĭn) *n.* a brocade with gold or silver threads.

dandiprat (dăn′dĭ-prăt) *n.* 1. a little fellow: used both critically and complimentarily. 2. a silver coin issued by Henry VII, also *dandeprat*.

danism (dăn′ĭz″əm) *n.* usury. - syn. *defeneration, feneration*.

dap (dăp) *v.i.* 1. to fish by placing bait on the water. 2. to skip [a stone] on water.

daphnean (dăf′nē-ən) *adj.* pertaining to *Daphne;* shy, bashful.

dapifer (dăp′ĭ-fər) *n.* someone who brings meat to the dinner table; the steward of a royal household.

darraign (dă-rān′) *v.t.&i.* to settle an argument (law).

darrain (dă-rān′) *v.t.&i.* to prepare for battle; to deploy troops (obs.).

dasypygal (dăz-ĭ-pī′gəl) *adj.* having hairy buttocks.

dasyure (dăs′ĭ-yər) *n.* the Tasmanian devil, the pouched mouse, or the banded anteater (Australian).

dauw (dô) *n.* the South African zebra resembling the *quagga*.

dealbation (dē-ăl-bā′shən) *n.* hair bleaching.

---

dearbought (dĭr'bôt) *adj.* bought at a high price.

deblaterate (dē-blăt'ər-āt) *v.i.* to babble.

deboswellize (dē-bŏz'wəl-īz) *v.i.* to deprecate in a biography. —

debuiliate (dē-bŭl'ĭ-āt) *v.i.* to boil over.

decadic (dē-kăd'ĭk) *adj.* pertaining to the decimal system.

decalcomania (dē-kăl″kō-mā'nĭ-ə) *n.* decal; using decals.

decameron (dē-kăm'ər-ən) *n.* 1. a collection of 100 stories written by Boccaccio in the fourteenth century. 2. any book divided into ten parts; a decade.

decerptible (dē-sûrp'tĭ-bəl) *adj.* removable, as clothing.

decoction (dē-kŏk'shən) *n.* an extraction of the essence by boiling.

decollate (dē-kŏl'at) *v.t.* to behead.

decorticate (dē-kôr'tĭ-kāt) *v.t.* to remove the outer covering.

decrement (dĕk'rĭ-mənt) *n.* 1. a loss or waste. 2. amount lost by waste.

decrepitation (dē-krĕp″ĭ-tā'shən) *n.* the crackling noise which salt or minerals make over fire.

decubital (dē-kū'bĭ-təl) *adj.* pertaining to or resulting from lying down.

decuman (dĕk'ū-mən) *adj.* every tenth, thought of as the largest in a series; huge, enormous, especially waves.

decussate (dē-kŭs'āt) *v.t.&i.* to make an X; intersect. -*adj.* intersected.

dedal (dē'dəl) *adj.* ingenious, highly skilled, intricate and varied. also *daedal* (from *Daedalus,* a mythical Greek artist and inventor who built a labyrinth in Crete, was later imprisoned in it, then escaped with his son, Icarus, by means of homemade wings).

dedans (dû-dôN') *n.* that part of the tennis court used by spectators (French *dedans* = inside).

dedentition (dē-dĕn-tī'shən) *n.* loss of teeth.

dedition (dē-dĭ'shən) *n.* surrender.

deedeed (dē'dēd) *adj.* d----d, a euphemism for damned (1845).

defaicate (dē-făl'kāt) *v.i.* to embezzle.

defeneration (dē-fĕn″ər-ā'shən) *n.* usury. -syn. *danism, feneration.*

defenestration (dē-fĕn″əs-trā'shən) *n.* throwing out of a window.

deflagrable (dē-flăg'rə-bəl) *adj.* pertaining to a sudden bursting into flame, sudden vaporization, or fast burning.

defluous (dĕf'lōō-əs) *adj.* that which falls off or flows down.

defoedation (dĕf-ō-dā'shən) *n.* pollution; making filthy.

defossion (dē-fŏ'żən) *n.* live burial.

degarnishment (dē-gŏr'nĭsh-mənt) *n.* the stripping of furniture.

deglutitious (dē-glōō-tī'shəs) *adj.* pertaining to swallowing.

dehiscence (dē-hĭs'əns) *n.* the bursting open of an organ, capsule, or pod in order to discharge its contents.

dehorner (dē-hôr'nər) *n.* a rubbing-alcohol addict (law).

dehortatory (dē-hôr'tə-tôr″ē) *adj.* dissuading.

deictically (dīk'tĭk-lē) *adv.* pointedly, specifically, definitely.

deiparous (dē-ĭp'ər-əs) *adj.* giving birth to a god.

deipnosophist (dīp-nŏs'ə-fĭst) *n.* a skillful dinner conversationalist (from *Deipnosophistai* of Athens who sparked the dinner conversation of smart men).

dejecture (dē-jĕk'chər) *n.* excrement; *dejecta, n.pl.*

---

măn; māde; lĕt; bē; sĭp; wīne; hŏt; cōld; sôre; dŭll; fūgue; bûrp; gŏŏd; fōōd; out; gĕt; thin; this; year; ażure; ō'mən″; viN; fūr; Bach

delator (dē-lāt'ər) n. an informer or accuser.

delenda (dē-lĕn'də) n.pl. things to be deleted.

deligation (dĕl-ĭ-gā'shən) n. bandaging.

delignate (dē-lĭg'nāt) v.t. to remove trees; to strip wood from.

deliquesce (dĕl-ĭ-kwĕs') v.i. to dissolve by absorbing moisture from the air.

delirament (dē-lĭr'ə-mənt) n. raving; a foolish story.

delitescent (dĕl-ĭ-tĕs'ənt) adj. hidden; inactive.

delphic (dĕl'fĭk) adj. ambiguous.

deltiologist (dĕl-tĭ-ŏl'ə-jĭst) n. someone who collects postcards. *deltiology, n.*

dementi (dā-mŏN-tē') n. an official denial.

demersal (dē-mûr'səl) adj. pertaining to sinking to the bottom, as certain fish eggs.

demesne (dē-mān') n. an area [of activity].

demiquaver (dĕm'ĭ-kwā'vər) n. the sixteenth note according to musical Britons. see *quaver*, for other values.

demisemiquaver (dĕm'ĭ-sĕm"ĭ-kwā"vər) n. the thirty-second note. see above.

demit (dē-mĭt') v.i. to resign.

demiurge (dĕm'ĭ-ûrj) n. 1. a secondary god who (a) created evil; (b) created the material world. 2. an old Grecian magistrate.

demology (dē-mŏl'ə-jē) n. the study of social conditions.

demophobe (dĕm'ō-fōb) n. a people-hater.

demulcent (dē-mŭl'sənt) adj. softening, soothing. -n. something that soothes.

denary (dĕn'ə-rē) adj. pertaining to the number ten.

dendrochronology (dĕn"drō-krŏn-ŏl'ə-jē) n. the science of computing time by counting tree rings.

dendrophilous (dĕn-drŏf'ĭ-ləs) adj. loving trees, loving them so much as to live in them.

dentiloquist (dĕn-tĭl'ə-kwĭst) n. someone who speaks with closed teeth.

deodand (dē'ō-dănd) n. the object causing someone's death which was forfeited to the crown ("to be applied to pious uses"; English law).

deontology (dē"ŏn-tŏl'ə-jē) n. the theory of morality or ethics.

deoppilate (dē-ŏp'ĭ-lāt) v.t.&i. to remove obstruction.

deorsumversion (dē-ôr"səm-vûr'ẑən) n. a turning downward; *deorsumduction, deorsumvergence.*

deosculate (dē-ŏs'kū-lāt) v.i. to kiss affectionately (obs.).

depascent (dē-păs'ənt) adj. feeding; eating.

depeculation (dē-pĕk"ū-lā'shən) n. an embezzling of public funds.

deperition (dĕp-ər-ĭ'shən) n. destructive process.

dephlegmate (dē-flĕg'māt) v.t. to distill.

dephlogisticate (dē-flō-jĭs'tĭ-kāt) v.t. to make fireproof.

deplumation (dē-plōō-mā'shən) n. 1. molting. 2. shedding of the eyelashes.

depone (dē-pōn') v.t.&i. 1. to testify under oath. 2. to depose. 3. to bet.

depredicate (dē-prĕd'ĭ-kāt) v.t. to publish, proclaim, announce.

depuration (dĕp-yər-ā'shən) n. purification.

deraign (dē-rān') v.t. to settle a dispute by combat between the litigants (old law).

derodidymus (dĕr"ō-dĭd'ĭ-məs) *n.* a two-headed monster. see *disomus.*

desecate (dĕs'ə-kāt) *v.i.* to cut off.

desiderata (dē-sĭd'ər-ŏ'tə) *n.pl.* things wanted and needed (Latin).

desidious (dē-sĭd'ĭ-əs) *adj.* slothful. also *desidiose.*

desipient (dē-sĭp'ĭ-ənt) *adj.* foolish, silly.

desparple (dĕs-pŏr'pəl) *v.t.&i.* to scatter.

desponsories (dē-spŏn'sər-ēz) *n.s.&pl.* a formal written announcement of an engagement (obs.).

despumate (dĕs'pū-māt) *v.t.&i.* to skim; to take the scum off.

desquamate (dĕs'kwə-māt) *v.i.* to peel off.

desudation (dē-sōō-dā'shən) *n.* extreme sweating.

desuetude (dĕs'wĭ-tūd) *n.* disuse.

detenebrate (dē-tĕn'ə-brāt) *v.t.* to lighten.

detinue (dĕt'ĭ-nū) *n.* 1. illegal detention of personal property. 2. measures taken for recovery of such property.

detrition (dē-trĭ'shən) *n.* erosion by friction.

detumescence (dē-tōō-mĕs'əns) *n.* subsidence of swelling.

deuteragonist (dōō-tər-ăg'ən-ĭst) *n.* a supporting actor (Greek).

deuterogamist (dōō-tər-ŏg'əm-ĭst) *n.* a widow or widower who remarries.

deuteroscopy (dōō-tər-ŏs'kə-pē) *n.* hidden meaning or second sight.

devenustate (dē-vĕn-ūs'tāt) *v.i.* to deprive of beauty.

devolve (dē-vŏlv') *v.i.* to pass on; to transfer.

devorative (dē-vôr'ə-tĭv) *adj.* capable of being swallowed whole.

dewdropper (dū'drŏp"ər) *n.* one who sleeps by day and plays by night (slang).

dextral (dĕks'trəl) *adj.* right, right-handed, on the right.

dextrosinistral (dĕks-trō-sĭn'ĭs-trəl) *adj.* naturally left-handed but trained to use the right hand in writing.

dghaisa (dī'sə) *n.* a small Maltese boat that looks like a gondola.

dhabb (dăb) *n.* the dried flesh of the skink, used as medicine.

dharna (dŏr'nə) *n.* in India, a way of collecting debts by sitting on the debtor's doorstep until the money is paid or the collector has starved to death.

dhole (dōl) *n.* the wild dog of Asia (Cuon alpinus).

dhyana (dyŏ'nə) *n.* profound or ecstatic religious meditation (Hinduism, Buddhism).

diaconate (dī-ăk'ən-āt) *n.* 1. a deacon's office or term. 2. a board of deacons. 3. a bunch of deacons.

diacope (dī-ăk'ə-pē) *n.* 1. the separation of a word by the interpolation of another or others, as in *absogoddamlutely.* 2. a deep cut or wound.

dianoetic (dī"ə-nō-ĕt'ĭk) *adj.* relating to logical reasoning.

diaphoretic (dī"ə-fôr-ĕt'ĭk) *adj.* producing or increasing sweat; a medicine that does this.

diaskeuasis (dī-əs-kū'ə-sĭs) *n.* editorial revision.

Diaspora (dī-ăs'pôr-ə) *n.* literally, "dispersion," applied collectively 1. to the dispersion of the Jews after the Babylonian captivity. 2. to any religious group isolated from its church.

diathesis (dī-ăth'ə-sĭs) *n.* an in-

dibble (dĭb'əl) *n.* a small hand tool used to make holes in the ground. -*v.t.* to plant with a *dibble.* -*v.i.* 1. to *dib,* or dip bait into the water in angling; to dip, generally. 2. to dabble or trifle. 3. to drink like a duck, lifting up the head after each sip.

dicacity (dī-kàs'ĭ-tē) *n.* oral playfulness; talkativeness.

dichastasis (dī-kàs'tə-sĭs) *n.* spontaneous subdivision.

dickcissel (dĭk-sĭs'əl) *n.* a sparrow-like bird, Spiza americana, of central North America.

dicty (dĭk'tē) *adj.* dictatorial; high-class (slang).

didgerydoo (dĭj"ər-ĭ-dŏō') *n.* an Australian aboriginal musical instrument.

didine (dī'dĭn) *adj.* dodolike.

diegesis (dī-ə-jē'sĭs) *n.* a recitation; a narration.

dieresis (dī-èr'ə-sĭs) *n.* 1. the separation of a diphthong into two syllables. 2. an *umlaut,* or mark placed over the second vowel to indicate such pronunciation.

diffugient (dī-fū'jĭ-ənt) *adj.* scattering.

digamous (dĭg'ə-məs) .*adj.* married a second time.

digenesis (dī-jèn'ə-sĭs) *n.* alternately sexual and asexual reproduction.

digenous (dĭj'ən-əs) *adj.* bisexual.

dight (dīt) *v.t.* to equip or adorn, usually used as past participle.

digitigrade (dĭj'ĭ-tĭ-grād") *adj.* walking on the toes, opposite of *plantigrade,* walking on the soles.

digitorium (dĭj-ĭ-tôr'ĭ-əm) *n.* a silent machine for piano practicing.

digladiate (dī-glàd'ĭ-āt) *v.t.* to fence, or otherwise fight (Latin *digladiari* = to fight).

digoneutic (dī-gō-nū'tĭk) *adj.* reproducing twice a year.

digraph (dī'gràf) *n.* one sound represented by two letters.

dike-louper (dīk'lŏ"pər,-lŏō"pər) *n.* one who jumps fences; a transgressor (slang).

dikephobia (dĭk-ə-fō'bĭ-ə) *n.* fear of justice.

dilaniate (dī-lā'nĭ-āt) *v.t.* to rip, tear in shreds.

dildo (dĭl'dō) *n.* 1. an artificial penis. 2. an effeminate man (both slang). 3. a West Indian cactus with pink flowers.

dilogical (dī-lòj'ĭ-kəl) *adj.* ambiguous; having a double meaning.

dimication (dĭm-ĭ-kā'shən) *n.* a fight or contest.

dimidiate (dĭm-ĭd'ĭ-āt) *v.t.* to halve or reduce to half. -*adj.* divided into two equal parts.

dingle (dĭng'gəl) *n.* 1. a small secluded valley. 2. a storeroom or storm door. 3. a ringing. -*v.t.&i.* 1. to ring. 2. to tremble.

dingo (dĭng'gō) *n.* a wild Australian dog with pointed ears and a bushy tail.

dinic (dĭn'ĭk) *adj.* pertaining to dizziness.

dinkey (dĭnk'ē) *n.* 1. a small locomotive. 2. a small streetcar. 3. a penis, especially a small one (slang).

dinmont (dĭn'mənt) *n.* a *wether* (castrated ram) between one and two years old or between his first and second shearing.

dinomania (dĭn-ō-mā'nĭ-ə) *n.* a mania for dancing. see *chorea.*

dioecious (dī-ē'shəs) *adj.* unisexual; having separate sexes (in plants).

dioestrum (dī-ĕs'trəm) *n.* the time a female animal is *not* in heat.

dioristically (dī-ō-rĭs'tĭk-lē) *adv.* in a distinguishing manner.

diorthosis (dī-ôr-thō'sĭs) *n.* 1. straightening out, putting in order. 2. reshaping deformed limbs.

di petto (dē pĕt'ō) *adj.* from the chest: said of the natural singing voice, opposite of *falsetto*.

diplasiasmus (dī-plăs"ĭ-ăz'məs) *n.* the incorrect doubling of a singgle [sic] letter.

dippoldism (dĭp'əl-dĭz"əm) *n.* beating or whipping school children (from Herr *Dippold*, one of the best).

dipsetic (dĭp-sĕt'ĭk) *adj.* a thirst provoker.

diptych (dĭp'tĭk) *n.* 1. a picture painted on two hinged surfaces. 2. anything folded in two.

dirdum (dûr'dəm) *n.* a loud rebuke (Scottish dialect).

diremption (dī-rĕmp'shən) *n.* a violent or final separation.

direption (dī-rĕp'shən) *n.* looting; plundering.

diriment (dĭr'ĭ-mənt) *adj.* making void, nullifying (law).

disboscation (dĭs-bŏs-kā'shən) *n.* deforesting; clearing forest land.

discalceate (dĭs-kăl'sē-āt) *v.t.&i.* to take the shoes off.

discerptible (dĭs-ûrp'tĭ-bəl) *adj.* divisible, breakable.

discinct (dĭs-ĭnkt') *adj.* beltless; dressed loosely.

discobolus (dĭs-kŏb'ə-ləs) *n.* a discus-thrower.

discubation (dĭs-kū-bā'shən) *n.* reclining at meals; *accubation*, *cubation*.

disembogue (dĭs-əm-bōg') *v.t.&i.* to disgorge, emerge, discharge [usually a river into the sea].

disespoused (dĭz-ĕs-pouzd') *adj.* left, broken off, divorced.

diseuse (dē-zûz') *n.* an actress specializing in monologues or recitations (French).

disgregate (dĭs'grē-gāt) *v.t.&i.* to separate; to disperse.

dislimn (dĭs-lĭm') *v.t.* to blot out the outlines of.

disomus (dī-sō'məs) *n.* a two-bodied [one-headed] monster. see *derodidymus*.

dispope (dĭs-pōp') *v.t.* to remove from popehood.

disquisition (dĭs-kwĭ-zĭ'shən) *n.* a formal discourse or treatise.

dissentaneous (dĭs-ən-tān'ē-əs) *adj.* disagreeable; negative.

dissilient (dĭs-ĭl'ĭ-ənt) *adj.* bursting apart.

distich (dĭs'tĭk) *n.* a poetic couplet.

distrain (dĭs-trān') *v.t.&i.* to grab property as security.

ditation (dī-tā'shən) *n.* the act of making rich (obs.).

dithyrambic (dĭth-ē-răm'bĭk) *adj.* 1. pertaining to *dithyramb*, a wildly passionate Greek choric hymn in honor of Dionysus. 2. passionately lyrical; rhapsodic.

ditokous (dĭt'ə-kəs) *adj.* producing twins.

dittography (dĭt-ŏg'rə-fē) *n.* the accidental repetition of letters in writing.

dittology (dĭt-ŏl'ə-jē) *n.* a dual interpretation.

diurnal (dī-ûr'nəl) *adj.* daily; pertaining to daytime; living one day; active in daytime.

diuturnal (dī-ū-tûr'nəl) *adj.* pertaining to long duration.

divagate (dī'və-gāt) *v.i.* to wander, digress.

divarication (dī-văr"ĭ-kā'shən) *n.* 1. a branching out or apart. 2. a difference of opinion.

diversivolent (dī-vər-sĭv'ō-lənt) *adj.* looking for trouble or an argument.

divulsion (dĭ-vŭl'shən) *n.* a tearing apart.

dixit (dĭks'ĭt) *n.* an unconfirmed, sometimes dogmatic statement.

dizygotic (dī-zī-gŏt'ĭk) *adj.* derived from two separate and separately fertilized eggs; fraternal twins.

docent (dō'sənt) *n.* a visiting teacher or lecturer.

doch-an-doris (dŏk"ən-dŏr'ĭs) *n.* a parting drink; a nightcap.

docity (dŏs'ĭ-tē) *n.* ability to comprehend or be taught quickly.

doddard (dŏd'ərd) *n.* a tree whose branches have decayed; a stump. also used figuratively.

dokhma (dŏk'mə) *n.* a circular stone wall up to thirty feet high on which the Parsis exposed their dead to the vultures.

dolabriform (dō-lăb'rĭ-fôrm) *adj.* shaped like an ax or hatchet head.

dolent (dō'lənt) *adj.* sad.

dolichoprosopic (dŏl"ĭ-kō-prō-sŏp'ĭk) *adj.* having a disproportionately long face.

dolorifuge (dō-lôr'ĭ-fūj) *n.* something that relieves sadness.

dolus (dō'ləs) *n.* fraud; malicious deceit (law).

domatologist (dō"mə-tŏl'ə-jĭst) *n.* a professional housekeeper.

domatophobia (dō"mə-tō-fō'bĭ-ə) *n.* fear of being house-bound.

domiculture (dŏm'ĭ-kŭl"chər) *n.* home economics.

dominical (dō-mĭn'ĭ-kəl) *adj.* pertaining to Sunday or Jesus.

dompteuse (dôN-tûz') *n.* a female animal-trainer.

donnered (dŏn'ərd) *adj.* stupefied; stunned.

dooab (dōō'ăb) *n.* a piece of land between two rivers. also *doab,*

duab (East India).

doodlebug (dōō'dəl-bŭg) *n.* the larva of the ant lion.

doodlesack (dōō'dəl-săk) *n.* bagpipe.

dopolavoro (dō"pō-lò-vôr'ō) *n.* a workers' recreation program sponsored by the Italian fascists.

Doppelgänger (dôp'əl-gĕng"ər) *n.* the ghost or double of a living person; *doubleganger.*

doramania (dôr-ə-mā'nĭ-ə) *n.* mania to possess furs.

Dorcas (dôr'kəs) *n.* a Biblical woman who made clothes for poor people (Acts IX: 36-41).

dorty (dôr'tē) *adj.* bad-tempered.

doseh (dō'sə) *n.* a Mohammedan custom of riding over the prostrate bodies of dervishes.

doss (dŏs) *n.* a bed in a flophouse; *doss house,* flophouse (British slang).

dosser (dòs'ər) *n.* 1. a basket carried on someone's back, or by two horses. 2. a tapestry for the back of a throne. 3. one who frequents *doss houses.*

dotard (dō'tərd) *n.* one in his dotage.

dotation (dō-tā'shən) *n.* an endowing or endowment.

dotterel (dŏt'ər-əl) *n.* 1. a dupe, a fool. 2. a decaying tree. 3. the European or Asian plover.

dottle (dŏt'əl) *n.* 1. a plug or stopper. 2. the tobacco left in a pipe.

douceur (dōō-sûr') *n.* 1. a sweet or charming manner. 2. a gift; a tip, bribe, or reward.

doughfaced (dō'făst) *adj.* having a false face or mask.

dowcet (dou'sət) *n.* a deer's testicle. also *doucet.*

downgyred (doun'gī"ərd) *adj.* descending in circular wrinkles, as stockings (obs.).

doxastic (dŏks-ăs'tĭk) *adj.* pertaining to opinion.

doxy (dŏks'ē) *n.* 1. a creed or doctrine, especially a religious one. 2. a prostitute.

doyen (doi'ən) *n.* senior; dean.

draconian (drȧ-kŏ'nĭ-ən) *adj.* inhumanly severe; cruel (from *Draco*, a harsh Athenian statesman of the seventh century B.C.).

draconic (drȧ-kŏn'ĭk) *adj.* of or like a dragon.

dragade (drȧ-gād') *n.* the breaking up [of glass] by pouring it, when molten, into water.

dragoman (drăg'ō-mən) *n.* a guide or interpreter (Arabic, Turkish, and Persian).

dragonnade (drăg-ən-ād') *n.* a military persecution (from the time of Louis XIV, who used the dragoons to persecute Protestants).

drapetomania (drăp"ə-tō-mā'nĭ-ə) *n.* intense desire to run away from home.

dromomania (drō-mō-mā'nĭ-ə) *n.* compulsive traveling.

droze (drōz) *v.i.* to melt irregularly and drip, as a candle. also *drose*.

drumble (drŭm'bəl) *v.i.* to act sluggishly (obs.).

drung (drŭng) *n.* a narrow road or path to a pasture.

druxy (drŭks'ē) *adj.* semi-rotten; having decayed spots: said of trees. also *druxey*.

dryasdust (drī'ăz-dŭst) *n.* a dull, pedantic speaker or writer (after *Dr. Jonas Dryasdust*, a fictitious character to whom Scott dedicated some of his novels).

drynurse (drī'nûrs) *n.* a woman who raises a child without breastfeeding.

duddyfunk (dŭd'ē-fŭnk) *n.* a pie made of beef, lamb, or venison, and salt pork and ground cloves (New England).

dug (dŭg) *n.* animal nipple or teat.

dugong (dōō'gŏng) *n.* the sea cow, a whalelike herbivorous mammal.

dugway (dŭg'wā) *n.* a dug road.

dulciloquy (dŭl-sĭl'ə-kwē) *n.* softness in speaking (obs.).

dulcorate (dŭl'kôr-āt) *v.t.* to sweeten.

dulocracy (dū-lŏk'rə-sē) *n.* a government dominated by privileged slaves or servants.

dulosis (dū-lō'sĭs) *n.* enslavement as practiced by some ants who bag enemy young and raise them.

dulysis (dū'lĭ-sĭs) *n.* breaking of an addiction.

duma (dōō'mə) *n.* Russian parliament started by Nicholas II in 1905, now defunct.

dumose (dōō'mōs) *adj.* bushy.

dunnage (dŭn'əj) *n.* 1. packing used around a ship's cargo. 2. personal baggage.

duomachy (dōō-ŏm'ə-kē) *n.* a fight between two people.

dupion (dū'pĭ-ən) *n.* 1. a cocoon spun by two silkworms working together. 2. the silk thus spun.

durance (dōōr'əns) *n.* long confinement.

durity (dûr'ĭ-tē) *n.* hardness.

dustoory (dŭs-tōōr'ē) *n.* a bribe given to servants by those wishing the patronage of their masters (India).

dvandva (dvŏn'dvŏ) *n.* a compound word, neither element of which is subordinated to the other, as *bitter-sweet* (Anglo-Saxon).

dwaible (dwā'bəl) *adj.* unstable. also *dwaibly* (Scottish).

dwergmal (dwûrg'məl) *n.* an echo;

literally, dwarf-language, the echoing rocks being the supposed homes of the dwarfs (Norse saga).

dyadic (dī-ăd'ĭk) *adj.* pertaining to a pair.

dysania (dĭs-ā'nĭ-ə) *n.* having a hard time waking up in the morning.

dysbulia (dĭs-blĭ-ə) *n.* loss of will power.

dysgenics (dĭs-jĕn'ĭks) *n.pl.* the science dealing with hereditary deterioration; *cacogenics.*

dyslogistic (dĭs"lə-jĭs'tĭk) *adj.* unfavorable; antagonistic; opposite of *eulogistic.*

dysnomy (dĭs'nə-mē) *n.* bad legislation; passing bad laws.

dyspathy (dĭs'pə-thē) *n.* without sympathy; unsympathetic.

dysphemism (dĭs'fəm-ĭz"əm) *n.* the opposite of *euphemism.*

dysphoria (dĭs-fôr'ĭ-ə) *n.* a generalized feeling of physical and mental discomfort; opposite of *euphoria.*

dysthymic (dĭs-thĭm'ĭk) *adj.* chronically sad or depressed.

dystychiphobia (dĭs-tĭk"ĭ-fō'bĭ-ə) *n.* fear of accidents.

dziggetai (dzĭg'ə-tī) *n.* the wild ass of central Asia.

dzo (zō, dzō) *n.* a hybrid between the yak and the domestic cow.

eagre (ē′gər) *n.* a sudden tidal flood; a tidal wave.

ean (ē′ən) *v.t.&i.* to give birth; *yean.*

eanling (ēn′lĭng) *n.* a young lamb or kid.

ebberman (ĕb′ər-mən) *n.* one who fishes below bridges.

ebenezer (ĕb-ən-ē′zər) *n.* 1. a memorial stone, especially one commemorating alleged divine assistance. 2. an opprobrious term for a house of worship.

eboulement (ā-bool-mòN) *n.* 1. a landslide. 2. the collapse of a fortification wall.

ebriection (ē-brĭ-ĕk′shən) *n.* mental breakdown from too much boozing.

ebrious (ē′brĭ-əs) *adj.* tending to overimbibe; slightly drunk.

eburnean (ē-bûr′nē-ən) *adj.* pertaining to or made of ivory.

ecaudate (ē-kô′dāt) *adj.* without a tail.

ecballium (ĕk-băl′ĭ-əm) *n.* the squirting cucumber.

eccaleobion (ĕk-ăl″ē-ō-bī′ən) *n.* an incubator.

ecchymosis (ĕk-ĭ-mō′sĭs) *n.* a black-and-blue spot.

ecclesiolatry (ĕk-lēz″ĭ-ŏl′ə-trē) *n.* an all-consuming devotion to the church.

ecdemic (ĕk-dĕm′ĭk) *adj.* of foreign origin.

ecdemomania (ĕk″dē-mō-mā′nĭ-ə) *n.* compulsive wandering.

ecdysiast (ĕk-dē′zĭ-ăst) *n.* a stripper (a Menckenism derived from *ecdysis,* the zoological term for shedding skin, or any other outer covering).

echinate (ĕk′ĭn-āt) *adj.* prickly, bristled. also *echinated.*

echolalia (ĕk-ō-lā′lĭ-ə) *n.* repeating another's words.

echopraxia (ĕk-ō-prăks′ĭ-ə) *n.* a habit of mimicking people; *echomimia. echopractic,* adj.

eclaircissement (ĕk-lĕr″sĕs-mòN′) *n.* clarification.

eclogue (ĕk′lôg) *n.* a short poem or shepherd's dialogue. (Virgil's *Eclogue*) also *eclog.*

ecmnesia (ĕk-nē′zə) *n.* loss of recent memory, with retention of earlier memories.

ecomania (ĕk-ō-mā′nĭ-ə) *n.* attitude of humility toward super-

ecophobia (ĕk-ō-fō′bĭ-ə) *n.* fear of home.

ectad (ĕk′tăd) *adv.* toward the exterior, opposite of *entad*. *ectal*, *adj.* external.

ectene (ĕk′tēn) *n.* a prayer where the minister leads and the people respond.

ectype (ĕk′tīp) *n.* a copy or reproduction of an *archetype* or a *prototype*.

ecu (ĕk-ōō′) *n.* 1. a medieval shield. 2. a French coin of the seventeenth and eighteenth centuries.

edacious (ē-dā′shəs) *adj.* eats a lot; voracious.

edea (ē-dē′ə) *n.* the external genitals.

edentate (ē-dĕn′tāt) *adj.* 1. toothless. 2. pertaining to an order of mammals *(edenta)* whose members may be toothless.

edipol (ĕd′ĭ-pōl) *n.* a mild oath.

edulcorate (ē-dŭl′kə-rāt) *v.t.* to sweeten or purify.

eesome (ē′səm) *adj.* pleasing to the eye.

effable (ĕf′ə-bəl) *adj.* something that can be expressed.

efflation (ĕf-lā′shən) *n.* an emanation; a puff; the act of blowing or puffing.

effleurage (ĕf-lûr-ŏž′) *n.* a gentle rubbing with the palm of the hand.

effodient (ĕf-ō′dĭ-ənt) *adj.* burrowing.

effulgent (ĕf-ŭl′jənt) *adj.* shining brightly.

egersis (ē-gûr′sĭs) *n.* abnormal wakefulness.

egest (ē-jĕst′) *v.t.* to excrete.

egger (ĕg′ər) *n.* 1. an egg collector. 2. an inciter. 3. a moth.

eglomerate (ē-glŏm′ər-āt) *v.t.* to unwind (obs.).

egotheism (ē′gō-thē″ĭz-əm) *n.* self-deification.

egredouce (ĕg′rə-dōōs) *n.* a tangy sauce; literally a sweet-and-sour sauce. 2. a fourteenth-century rabbit curry.

eider (ī′dər) *n.* a duck with black and white feathers.

eidetic (ī-dĕt′ik) *adj.* pertaining to the ability of visualizing something previously seen.

eidolon (ī-dōl′ən) *n.* a ghost, an apparition. also *eidola*.

eigne (ān) *adj.* first-born, eldest, heir apparent.

eisegesis (ī-sə-jē′sĭs) *n.* the interpretation of a text by sneaking in one's own ideas as the author's.

eisteddfod (ā-stĕth′vŏd) *n.* an annual assembly of Welsh poets and musicians.

ejoo (ē′jōō) *n.* the Malay gomuti.

ejuration (ĕj-ûr-ā′shən) *n.* renunciation, repudiation, abjuration.

elapidation (ē-lăp″ĭ-dā′shən) *n.* a clearing away of stones.

eldritch (ĕld′rĭch) *adj.* weird, eerie, ghastly.

electragist (ē-lĕk′trə-jĭst) *n.* a seller and installer of electrical apparatus who is a member of the Association of Electragists International.

electrolethe (ē-lĕk′trə-lēth) *n.* a suggested name for the electric chair.

eleemosynary (ĕl-ē-mŏs′ĭ-nĕr″ē) *adj.* 1. pertaining to charity. 2. living on charity.

eleutheromania (ē-lōō″thər-ō-mā′nĭ-ə) *n.* a mania for freedom.

elflock (ĕlf′lŏk) *n.* tangled hair (as if by elves).

ellipsis (ē-lĭp′sĭs) *n.* 1. deletion of words from a sentence: [I am] having [a] wonderful time [but I] wish [that] you were here [to

share it with me] 2. brackets
[...] indicating deletion: *eclipsis*.

eloign (ē-loin′) *v.t.* 1. to carry away
[property]. 2. beyond legal limits.

elucubrate (ē-lōō′kū-brāt) *v.t.* to
work studiously.

elumbated (ē-lùm′bāt″əd) *adj.*
weak in the loins.

elute (ē-lōōt′) *v.t.* to wash out.

eluxate (ē-lùks′āt) *v.t.* to disjoint.

elydoric (èl-ĭ-dôr′ĭk) *adj.* painting
with a combination of oil and
water color.

emarcid (ē-mòr′sĭd) *adj.* wilted.

emarginate (ē-mòr′jĭn-āt) *v.t.* to
take away the margin of.

embonpoint (ðN-bôN-pwôN′) *n.*
stoutness, corpulence (French).

embouchure (òm-bōō-shōōr′) *n.* 1.
the mouth of (a) a river; (b) a
river valley; (c) a musical instrument (mouthpiece). 2. the position of the mouth in playing a
wind instrument.

embracery (èm-brā′sər-ē) *n.* the
attempt to influence a court by
bribery or other means.

embrocation (èm-brō-kā′shən) *n.*
1. lubricating or rubbing the body
with liniment, oil, etc. 2. the
liquid used for this.

embulalia (èm-bū-lā′lĭ-ə) *n.* insertion of nonsense into speech, as in
schizophrenia. also *embololalia*.

embusque (òm-bōōs-kā′) *n.* a
shirker, a slacker (French = in
ambush or hiding).

emeute (ē-mūt′) *n.* an insurrec-
tion; a popular uprising.

emgalla (èm-gòl′ə) *n.* the South
African wart hog.

emmenology (èm-ən-òl′ə-jē) *n.* the
study of menstruation.

emmet (èm′ət) *n.* an ant. also *emet,
amet, amt.*

empasm (èm-pàz′əm) *n.* deodorant
powder.

emphysematous (èm-fĭ-sèm′ə-təs)
adj. 1. bloated, swollen. 2. pertaining to *emphysema*.

empleomania (èm-plē″ō-mā′nĭ-ə)
n. a mania for holding public
office.

empressement (òm-près′mðN) *n.*
extreme politeness.

emption (èmp′shən) *n.* the act of
buying.

empyrean (èm-pĭr-ē′ən) *n. & adj.*
the highest heaven; firmament.

emuscation (èm-əs-kā′shən) *n.* a
freeing from moss.

enatation (ē-nä-tā′shən) *n.* a swimming out; escape by swimming
(obs.).

enate (ē-nāt′) *adj.* 1. growing out. 2.
related through the mother.
enatic, adj.

enceinte (òN-sànt′) *n.* 1. pregnant.
2. the main enclosure of a for-
tress. 3. a fortified town.
enceinteship, n. pregnancy.

enchiridion (èn-kĭr-ĭd′ĭ-ən) *n.* a
manual or handbook.

enchorial (èn-kôr′ĭ-əl) *adj.* 1.
native, endemic. 2. pertaining to
certain Egyptian hieroglyphics.

encraty (èn′krə-tē) *n.* abstinence,
self-restraint.

endeictic (èn-dīk′tĭk) *adj.*
demonstrative (applied to certain
Platonic dialogues).

endiablee (òN-dyä-blā′) *v.t.* to put
the devil into.

endogamous (èn-dòg′ə-məs) *adj.*
pertaining to marriage within
one's group; pertaining to in-
breeding, opposite of *exogamous*
(which see).

endue (èn-dū′) *v.t.* 1. imbue. 2. to
digest (said of birds). also *indue*.

energumen (èn″ər-gū′mən) *n.* 1. a
person supposedly possessed by
an evil spirit. 2. a fanatic.

enew (èn-ū′) *v.t.* to plunge into

---

măn; māde; lĕt; bē; sĭp; wīne; hŏt; cōld; sôre; dùll; fūgue; bûrp;
gŏŏd; fōōd; out; gĕt; thin; this; year; aźure; ō′mən″; viN; für; Bach

water (French *en eau* = in water).

engastration (ĕn-găs-trā'shən) *n.* the stuffing of one bird inside another.

engastrimyth (ĕn-găs'trĭ-mĭth) *n.* a ventriloquist (obs.).

engouement (ŏN-gōō-mŏN') *n.* infatuation (French).

enigmatology (ē-nǐg"mə-tŏl'ə-jē) *n.* the science of solving enigmas.

enissophobia (ĕn-ĭs"ō-fō'bĭ-ə) *n.* fear of being reproached. see *enosiophobia*.

ennead (ĕn'ē-əd) *n.* 1. the number nine. 2. any group of nine objects.

enneatic (ĕn-ē-ăt'ĭk) *adj.* occurring once every nine times, days, years, etc; every ninth.

ennomic (ĕn-ŏm'ĭk) *adj.* within the law; lawful.

enoptromancy (ĕn-ŏp'trə-măn"sē) *n.* fortunetelling with a mirror.

enosiophobia (ĕn-ō"sĭ-ō-fō'bĭ-ə) *n.* fear of having committed an unpardonable sin. see *enissophobia*.

enquete (ŏN-kĕt') *n.* inquiry; investigation (French).

ensiform (ĕn'sĭ-fôrm) *adj.* swordshaped.

ensky (ĕn-skī') *v.t.* to make immortal.

ensorcell (ĕn-sôr'səl) *v.t.* to bewitch. also *ensorcel*.

ensynopticity (ĕn-sĭn"ŏp-tĭs'ĭ-tē) *n.* the ability of taking a general view of something.

entad (ĕn'tăd) *adv.* inward; toward the center; opposite of *ectad*.

entheal (ĕn'thē-əl) *adj.* divinely inspired (obs.).

entheomania (ĕn"thē-ō-mā'nĭ-ə) *n.* an abnormal state in which one thinks one is inspired.

entortilation (ĕn-tôr"tĭl-ā'shən) *n.* a turning into a circle.

entremets (ŏN-trə-mā') *n.* 1. a side dish. 2. any entertainment be-

tween courses at a banquet. 3. an interlude.

entrepot (ŏN-trə-pō') *n.* a warehouse or other distributing outlet for merchandise (French).

entresol (ŏN-trə-sŭl') *n.* mezzanine (French).

entwicklungsroman (ĕnt-vĭk"lōōngks-rō-mŏn') *n.* a novel dealing with the protagonist's character development from childhood to maturity. see *bildungsroman*.

enucleate (ē-nōō'klē-āt) *v.t.* to extract the kernel or truth or nucleus from.

enuresis (ĕn-ū-rē'sĭs) *n.* bedwetting.

envermeil (ĕn-vûr'mĭl) *v.t.* to make red.

envoutement (ŏN-vōōt-mŏN') *n.* the use of someone's picture in order to put a hex on her (Old French).

eoan (ē-ō'ən) *adj.* pertaining to the dawn or the east.

eolian (ē-ō'lĭ-ən) *adj.* pertaining to or caused by the wind. also *aeolian*.

eonism (ē'ən-ĭz"əm) *n.* acting and dressing like a woman; transvestitism.

eoproligery (ē"ō-prō-lĭj'ər-ē) *n.* ability to reproduce early.

eosophobia (ē-ō"sō-fō'bĭ-ə) *n.* depression caused by fear of dawn.

epactal (ē-păk'təl) *adj.* additional.

epaulion (ē-pôl'ĭ-ən) *n.* the day after the wedding (Greek).

epenthesis (ĕp-ĕn'thə-sĭs) *n.* insertion of a letter or syllable into a word for pronunciation ease (the b in mum*b*le).

epergne (ĕp-ĕrn') *n.* a centerpiece of bowls arranged in tiers or branches containing edible goodies or flowers for the table.

epexegetic (ĕp-ĕks″ə-jĕt′ĭk) *adj.* pertaining to further explanation.

ephemeromorph (ĕf-ĕm′ər-ō-môrf″) *n.* low forms of life that defy animal or vegetable classification.

epicaricacy (ĕp″ĭ-kər-ĭk′ə-sē) *n.* taking pleasure in others' misfortune.

epicedian (ĕp-ĭ-sē′dĭ-ən) *adj.* sad, mournful.

epicene (ĕp′ĭ-sēn) *adj.* pertaining to both sexes.

epicrisis (ē-pĭk′rĭ-sĭs) *n.* detailed criticism, especially of the Old Testament. (ĕp′ĭ-krī″sĭs) *n.* the secondary crisis of a disease (medicine).

epideictic (ĕp-ĭ-dīk′tĭk) *adj.* impressive; for display purposes; exhibitable.

epidermophytosis (ĕp-ĭ-dûr″mō-fĭ-tō′sĭs) *n.* athlete's foot.

epigamic (ĕp-ĭ-găm′ĭk) *adj.* tending to attract the opposite sex during mating season.

epigean (ĕp-ĭ-jē′ən) *adj.* living close to the ground, as some insects.

epigonous (ē-pĭg′ə-nəs) *adj.* of a later generation; pertaining to an imitative school of art or science.

epilate (ĕp′ĭ-lāt) *v.t.* to remove hair.

epilegomenon (ĕp″ĭl-ə-gŏm′ə-nŏn) *n.* an added remark.

epimyth (ĕp′ĭ-mĭth) *n.* the moral of a story.

epinicion (ĕp-ĭ-nĭsh′ən) *n.* a song of victory; anthem.

epiphoric (ĕp-ĭ-fôr′ĭk) *adj.* pertaining to a torrent of tears.

episcopicide (ē-pĭs′kō-pĭ-sīd″) *n.* the killing of a bishop.

epistaxis (ĕp-ĭs-tăks′ĭs) *n.* nosebleed.

epistemology (ē-pĭs″təm-ŏl′ə-jē) *n.* the study of knowledge.

epistemonic (ē-pĭs″tə-mŏn′ĭk) *adj.* pertaining to knowledge as a kind of experience; intellectual.

epistemophilia (ē-pĭs″tĕm-ō-fĭl′ĭ-ə) *n.* abnormal preoccupation with knowledge.

epithalamium (ĕp″ĭ-thə-lā′mĭ-əm) *n.* a song or poem honoring the bride, groom, or both; a nuptial song.

epithymetic (ĕp″ĭ-thī-mĕt′ĭk) *adj.* pertaining to appetite, sexual and otherwise.

epitonic (ĕp-ĭ-tŏn′ĭk) *adj.* overstrained.

epizeuxis (ĕp-ĭ-zōōk′sĭs) *n.* emphatic verbal repetition.

epizootic (ĕp″ĭ-zō-ŏt′ĭk) *adj.&n.* an animal epidemic, or pertaining to one.

eponym (ĕp′ən-ĭm) *n.* 1. someone after whom a country or institution is named. 2. someone whose name has become closely associated with some period, movement, or theory.

epopee (ĕp-ō-pē′) *n.* an epic poem or its subject. *epos,* a primitive epic poem or series of epic events handed down by word of mouth, *epopoeist* (ĕp-ō-pē′ĭst) *n.* an epic poet.

epopt (ĕp′ŏt) *n.* an initiate in the Eleusinian mysteries (secret religious rites of ancient Greece).

epulotic (ĕp-ū-lŏt′ĭk) *adj.* having healing power. -*n.* a medicine that heals.

epuration (ĕp-ū-rā′shən) *n.* the act of purifying.

epure (ē-pyōōr′) *n.* building plans traced on a wall or floor, on a one-to-one ratio (1:1 scale).

equilibrist (ē-kwĭl′ĭ-brĭst) *n.* a tightrope walker.

equitant (ĕk′wĭ-tənt) *adj.* 1. sitting or riding on a horse. 2. overlapping, as leaves.

equivoque (ĕk'wĭ-vōk) *n.* an ambiguous expression; a pun.

equivorous (ē-kwĭv'ər-əs) *adj.* eating horsemeat.

eremic (ē-rĕm'ĭk) *adj.* pertaining to deserts or sandy areas.

eremite (ĕr'ə-mīt) *n.* a hermit, especially a religious one.

eremophobia (ĕr'ə-mō-fō'bĭ-ə) *n.* fear of loneliness.

ereption (ē-rĕp'shən) *n.* the act of snatching away.

erethism (ĕr'ə-thĭz"əm) *n.* excessive irritability or excitability.

erf (ûrf) *n.* a half-acre in South Africa.

ergasiophobia (ûr-găs"ĭ-ō-fō'bĭ-ə) *n.* 1. fear of or aversion to work. 2. a surgeon's fear of operating in spite of demonstrable need.

ergatocracy (ûr-gə-tŏk'rə-sē) *n.* government by the workers.

ergophile (ûr'gō-fīl) *n.* someone who loves work.

eric (ĕr'ĭk) *n.* a blood fine: payment to the family of the victim by the murderer (old Irish law).

erigible (ĕr'ĭ-jĭ-bəl") *adj.* capable of being erected.

erinaceous (ĕr-ĭn-ā'shəs) *adj.* pertaining to the hedgehog.

eristic (ĕr-ĭs'tĭk) *adj.* pertaining to argument or controversy; argumentative. *-n.* disputation; a disputant.

erlking (ûrl'kĭng) *n.* a bad elf who hates children (German folklore, naturally).

erose (ē-rōs') *adj.* uneven, as the edge of a chewed leaf.

erostrate (ē-rŏs'trāt) *adj.* without a beak.

eroteme (ĕr'ō-tēm) *n.* the question mark (?).

erotographomania (ĕr-ŏt"ō-grăf-ō-mā'nĭ-ə) *n.* mania for writing love letters.

erotophobia (ē-rŏ"tō-fō'bĭə) *n.* fear of sexual love.

errabund (ĕr'ə-bŭnd) *adj.* wandering; erratic.

errhine (ĕr'īn) *adj.* 1. sneeze provoking. 2. snuffable substance.

ers (ûrs) *n.* the bitter vetch. see *vetch.*

eructation (ē-rŭk-tā'shən) *n.* 1. belching or something produced by belching. 2. any violent expulsion.

erugate (ĕr'ōō-gāt) *adj.* freed from wrinkles, smoothed; smooth.

erumpent (ē-rŭm'pənt) *adj.* bursting forth.

erythrophobia (ē-rĭth"rō-fō'bĭ-ə) *n.* fear of red lights or of blushing.

eschatology (ĕs-kə-tŏl'ə-jē) *n.* the study or doctrine of final things, such as death, resurrection, immortality.

eschrolalia (ĕs-krō-lā'lĭ-ə) *n.* dirty (fecal) language. see *coprolalia* (Greek *aischros* = shameful).

esclandre (ĕs-klän'dər) *n.* notoriety; disturbance; a disgraceful occurrence or scene.

esclavage (ĕs-klō-vòž') *n.* a necklace that resembled eighteenth-century slave chains (French *esclavage* = slavery).

escudero (ĕs-kōō-dèr'ō) *n.* a shield-bearer or noble's factotum.

esculent (ĕs'kū-lənt) *adj.* edible.

espalier (ĕs-păl-yā') *n.* a trellis for training trees or bushes to grow flat; the tree itself. *-v.t.* to train trees or bushes to grow flat.

espringal (ĕs-prĭng'gəl) *n.* a medieval stone-throwing machine.

esquamate (ē-skwā'māt) *adj.* having no scales.

esquisse (ĕs-kēs') *n.* preliminary

sketch or model.

essling (ĕs'lĭng) *n.* a young salmon (British dialect).

essoin (ĕs-oin') *n.* the giving of an excuse for not apppearing in court; the excuse given. -*v.t.* to excuse for a no-show in court. *essoiner, n.* someone who essoins; a lawyer who essoins for his client.

esssse (ĕsh'ə) *n.* obsolete form of ashes.

estafette (ĕs-tŏ-fĕt') *n.* a courier on horseback.

estale (ĕs-tāl') *v.t.* to hang with drapery.

estaminet (ĕs-tŏ"mĭn-ā) *n.* a coffee-house (French).

estiferous (ĕs-tĭf'ər-əs) *adj.* producing heat. also *aes-*.

estival (ĕs'tĭ-vəl) *adj.* relating to summer. also *aes-*.

estovers (ĕs-tō'vərz) *n.pl.* necessities allowed by law, such as alimony, child support, etc.

estrade (ĕs-trād') *n.* a platform or raised section of a room.

estrapade (ĕs-trə-pād') *n.* a horse's attempt to dump his rider.

estuous (ĕs'tū-əs) *adj.* excited, passionate.

esurient (ē-sûr'ĭ-ənt) *adj.* hungry, greedy, voracious. -*n.* someone who is all of the above.

etaac (ā-tŏts') *n.* the South African blaubok.

etaoin shrdlu (ĕt'oin shûrd'lōō) *n.* two sequences of letters on a linotype machine: if the machine jams, the entire slug may drop right into the family newspaper.

etesian (ē-tē'żən) *adj.* annual; every summer; usually applied to Mediterranean winds.

ethmoid (ĕth'moid) *adj.* 1. sievelike. 2. pertaining to the ethmoid bones that form part of the wall of the nasal cavity.

ethnarch (ĕth'nörk) *n.* a governor.

ethnocentrism (ĕth-nō-sĕn'trĭ"zəm) *n.* the attitude that one's race or tribe is superior.

ethnophaulism (ĕth-nō-fôl'ĭz"əm) *n.* any racial pejorative.

etiolate (ē'tĭ-ō-āt") *v.t.&i.* to bleach by lack of sunlight.

ettle (ĕt'əl) *v.t.* to plan, try, aim, design, prepare, suppose.

etui (ĕt'wē) *n.* a case for small articles, as needles. also *etwee*.

et uxor (ĕt ŭks'ôr) *n.* "and wife," usually abbreviated to *et ux* (law).

etymon (ĕt'ĭ-mŏn) *n.* an original root or meaning.

euania (ū-ā'-nĭ-ə) *n.* ease of waking up in the morning.

eucrasy (ū'krə-sē) *n.* a normal state of good health. ant. *dyscrasy*.

eudaemonia (ū-də-mŏn'ĭə) *n.* true happiness, which, according to Aristotle, results from a life of reason. also *eudemonia*.

eugeria (ū-jĕr'ĭ-ə) *n.* normal and happy old age.

euhemerism (ū-hĕm'ər-ĭz"əm) *n.* the theory that all myths are based on reality (from *Euhemerus*, a so-called philosopher of 300 B.C. Sicily).

eumoirous (ū-moi'rəs) *adj.* someone who is lucky or happy as a result of being good.

eumorphous (ū-môr'fəs) *adj.* well-formed.

euneirophrenia (ū-nī"rō-frē'nĭ-ə) *n.* peace of mind after a pleasant dream.

eunuchate (ū'nōō-kāt) *v.t.* to make a eunuch; emasculate.

euodic (ū-òd'ĭk) *adj.* aromatic.

euphelicia (ū-fə-lĭs'ĭ-ə) *n.* healthiness resulting from having all one's wishes granted.

euphuism (ū'fōō-ĭz"əm) *n.* affected, high-flown speech or writing.

euripize (ū'rĭ-pīz) *v.i.* to fluctuate.

euthermic (ū-thûr'mĭk) *adj.* inducing warmth.

euthymia (ū-thĭm'ĭ-ə) *n.* mental tranquillity.

euxine (ūks'ĭn) *adj.* relating to the Black Sea (Pontus *Euxinus*).

evagation (ē-vă-gā'shən) *n.* mental wandering; digression.

evaginate (ē-văj'ĭn-āt) *v.t.&i.* to turn inside out; evert.

evancalous (ē-văn'kə-ləs) *adj.* pleasant to embrace (Greek).

evasé (ā-vŏ-zā') *adj.* enlarging gradually, like a funnel.

eventerate (ē-věn'tər-āt) *v.t.* to rip open; to open by ripping the belly.

eviration (ĕv-ĭr-ā'shən) *n.* emasculation, castration.

evulgate (ē-vŭl'gāt) *v.t.* to publish, divulge.

ewery (ū'ər-ē) *n.* a room for ewers (pitchers), basins, and towels.

Ewig-Weibliche (ā"vĭk-vīp'lĭ-kə) *n.* according to Goethe, "eternal-feminine characteristics."

exallotriote (ĕks-əl-ō'trĭ-ōt) *adj.* foreign.

exanimous (ĕks-ăn'ĭ-məs) *adj.* lifeless.

exarch (ĕks'ŏrk) *n.* 1. a Byzantine big shot. 2. a Bulgarian ecclesiastical big shot. 3. an ecclesiastical batman.

exaugurate (ĕgz-ôg'yŏŏr-āt) *v.t.* to secularize; to desecrate.

excalceate (ĕks-kăl'sē-āt) *v.t.* to make barefooted.

excerebrose (ĕks-ĕr'ĭ-brōs) *adj.* having no brains.

exclave (ĕks'klāv) *n.* a territory politically allied but geographically separated from another territory.

excogitation (ĕks-kŏj"ĭ-tā'shən) *n.* an invention; being invented.

exeat (ĕks'ē-ət) *n.* a permit for temporary leave [from college or monastery].

exegesis (ĕks-ə-jē'sĭs) *n.* critical literary analysis, especially of the Bible.

exennium (ĕks-ēn'ĭ-əm) *n.* a New Year's gift.

exenterate (ĕks-ĕn'tər-āt) *v.t.* 1. to literally or figuratively disembowel. 2. to remove (surgically) an organ.

exequies (ĕks'ə-kwēz) *n.pl.* 1. funeral rites; obsequies. 2. a funeral procession.

exfodiate (ĕks-fō'dĭ-āt) *v.t.* to dig out.

exheredate (ĕks-hĕr'ə-dāt) *v.t.* to disinherit.

exiguous (ĕks-ĭg'ū-əs) *adj.* scanty, little, small, meager.

exilic (ĕks-ĭl'ĭk) *adj.* of exile, especially the exile of the Jews in Babylon.

eximious (ĕgz-ĭm'ĭ-əs) *adj.* most distinguished; excellent.

exinanition (ĕks-ĭn"ən-ĭ'shən) *n.* an emptying. 2. loss; destitution.

exoculate (ĕks-ŏk'ū-lāt) *v.t.* to put out the eyes of.

exoduster (ĕks'ō-dŭs"tər) *n.* one who leaves in a hurry (slang).

exogamy (ĕks-ŏg'ə-mē) *n.* marriage outside the tribe or class, outbreeding.

exophagy (ĕks-ŏf'ə-jē) *n.* cannibalism outside the tribe.

exoptable (ĕks-ŏp'tə-bəl) *adj.* extremely desirable.

exordium (ĕgz-ôr'dĭ-əm) *n.* the beginning or introductory part of anything, especially of a discourse or treatise.

exornation (ĕks-ôr-nā'shən) *n.* ornament, decoration, embellishment.

exosculate (ĕks-ŏs'kū-lāt) *v.t.* to kiss, especially to kiss heartily (obs.).

exoteric (ĕks-ō-tĕr'ĭk) *adj.* 1. adapted for the layman, such as a theory. 2. understood by the layman. 3. ordinary or simple. -ant. *esoteric.*

expergefaction (ĕks-pûr"jə-făk'shən) *n.* an awakening.

experientialism (ĕks-pĭr"ē-ĕn'shəl-ĭz"əm) *n.* the philosophic theory that experience is the origin and test of all knowledge.

expiscate (ĕks-pĭs'kāt) *v.t.* to examine or discover skillfully.

explaterate (ĕks-plăt'ər-āt) *v.i.* to talk a lot (slang).

explicitrize (ĕks-plĭs'ĭt-rīz) *v.t.* to censure (slang).

exponible (ĕks-pō'nĭ-bəl) *adj.* needing further explanation.

expromission (ĕks-prō-mĭsh'ən) *n.* being responsible for another's debt.

exsibilate (ĕks-ĭb'ĭ-lāt) *v.t.* to reject with a hissing sound.

exsiccate (ĕks'ĭ-kāt) *v.t.&i.* to dry up or out.

exspuition (ĕks-pū-ĭsh'ən) *n.* a spitting.

exsuccous (ĕks-ŭk'əs) *adj.* dry, sapless.

exsufflate (ĕks-ŭf'lāt) *v.t.* to blow out or away.

extersion (ĕks-tûr'żən) *n.* the act of wiping or rubbing out.

extradictionary (ĕks-trə-dĭk'shən-ĕr"ē) *adj.* consisting not in words, but in deeds (obs.).

extraforaneous (ĕks"trə-fôr-ān'ī-əs) *adj.* outdoor.

exundation (ĕks-ŭn-dā'shən) *n.* an overflowing.

exungulate (ĕgz-ŭng'gū-lāt) *v.t.* to trim, cut, or cut off the nails or hoofs.

exuviate (ĕgz-ū'vĭ-āt) *v.t.&i.* to shed; to molt.

eyeservice (ī'sûr"vĭs) *n.* 1. work done only when the boss is watching. 2. admiring looks (slang).

eyot (ī'ət) *n.* an islet. *eyoty* (ī'ə-tē) *adj.*

---

mǎn; māde; lĕt; bē; sĭp; wīne; hŏt; cōld; sôre; dŭll; fūgue; bûrp; gŏŏd; fōŏd; out; gĕt; thin; this; year; ażure; ō'mən"; viN; fūr; Bach

F

fabliau (fàb'lǐ-ō) *n.* a ribald, medieval French poem.

fabrile (fàb'rǐl) *adj.* pertaining to a skilled artisan or mechanic.

facetiae (fà-sē'shǐ-ē) *n.* witty, ribald books or stories.

facient (fā'shənt) *n.* a doer or agent; in mathematics, the multiplier.

facinorous (fā-sǐn'ə-rəs) *adj.* infamous.

facundity (fà-kŭn'dǐ-tē) *n.* eloquence.

faffle (fàf'əl) *v.i.* 1. to stutter or mumble. 2. to luff (flap, as the sail of a boat heading into the wind).

fagin (fā'gǐn) *n.* a teacher of crime; an old criminal (from Dickens' *Oliver Twist*).

fagotto (fà-gô'tō) *n.* bassoon; a bassoonlike organ stop (Italian).

faineant (fā'nē-ənt) *adj.* lazy, indolent. *-n.* a loafer, idler (Old French *fait* = does + *nient* = nothing).

falcate (fàl'kāt) *adj.* curved like a sickle; crescent-shaped; *falciform.*

faltboat (fàlt'bōt) *n.* collapsible or folding boat somewhat like a kayak (German *faltboot* = folding boat).

famble (fàm'bəl) *v.i.* to stutter.

famicide (fā'mǐ-sīd) *n.* a slanderer; a destroyer of one's reputation.

familistere (fàm″ǐl-ǐs-tèr') *n.* a house for communal living.

famulus (fàm'ū-ləs) *n.* the servant of a medieval scholar or magician.

fanfaronade (fàn″fər-ō-nād') *n.* bravado; braggadocio.

fantassin (fàn'tə-sǐn) *n.* an infantry soldier.

fantoccini (fàn-tô-chē'nē) *n.* puppets moved either mechanically, or manually, by strings; puppet shows.

farandole (fàr'ən-dōl) *n.* a Provencal dance or its music.

farceur (fòr-sûr') *n.* a writer of or actor in farces; a joker (French).

fard (fòrd) *v.t.* 1. to put on make-up. 2. to minimize a fault. *-n.* 1. make-up. 2. a date tree common to eastern Arabia and western California.

farfel (fòr'fəl) *n.* noodles (Yiddish).

farkleberry (fòr'kəl-bèr″ē) *n.* a multiseeded blackberry bush.

farraginous (fă-răj'ĭ-nəs) *adj*. mixed; heterogeneous.

farrago (fă-rā'gō) *n*. hodgepodge, mishmash, jumble.

farrier (făr'ĭ-ər) *n*. 1. an unqualified horse doctor. 2. a blacksmith. 3. a cavalry officer in charge of horses.

farsang (fôr'săng) *n*. the Persian mile (equal to four U.S. miles).

fartleberries (fôr'təl-běr"ēz) *n.pl*. excrement clinging to the hairs around the anus; also *dilberries*.

fasciation (făsh-ĭ-ā'shən) *n*. bandaging; becoming bound up.

fascicle (făs'ĭ-kəl) *n*. 1. a small bundle. 2. a serial installment of a book.

fasgrolia (făs-grō'lĭ-ə) *n*. *FASt-GROwing Language of Initialisms and Acronyms*.

fashious (făsh'əs) *adj*. troublesome.

fastigate (făs'tĭ-gāt) *v.t*. to make pointed.

fastigium (făs-tĭj'ĭ-əm) *n*. 1. the top of a building. 2. the apex of the roof of the fourth cerebral ventricle.

fastuous (făs'chōō-əs) *adj*. arrogant, stuck-up, or showy.

fatidic (fă-tĭd'ĭk) *adj*. prophetic.

fatiferous (făt-ĭf'ər-əs) *adj*. destructive; deadly.

fatiscent (făt-ĭs'ənt) *adj*. cracked; having cracks.

fatling (făt'lĭng) *n*. a young animal fattened for slaughter.

faubourg (fō'bŏŏrg) *n*. suburb (French).

fautress (fôt'rəs) *n*. patroness.

favaginous (făv-ăj'ĭ-nəs) *adj*. like a honeycomb.

favillous (făv-ĭl'əs) *adj*. resembling ashes.

favonian (făv-ō'nĭ-ən) *adj*. like the west wind; mild.

feak (fēk) *n*. a lock of hair; a dangling curl. -*v.t*. to twitch. -*v.i*. to fidget. *v.t.&i*. to wipe [the hawk's beak] after feeding (falconry).

feazings (fē'zĭngz) *n*. an unraveled rope end.

febrifuge (fĕb'rĭ-fūj) *adj*. describing a fever-reducing agent or medicine; the medicine.

februation (fĕb-rōō-ā'shən) *n*. exorcism; religious purification.

feckless (fĕk'ləs) *adj*. weak, worthless, and incompetent.

fedifragous (fĕd-ĭf'rə-gəs) *adj*. treacherous, deceitful.

feedy (fē'dē) *adj*. gorged; overfed.

fefnicute (fĕf'nĭ-kūt) *n*. hypocrite; sneak.

felicific (fē-lĭ-sĭf'ĭk) *adj*. producing happiness.

fellatio (fĕl-ā'shĭ-ō) *n*. sucking the penis.

fellmonger (fĕl'mŭng"gər) *n*. a dealer in sheepskins.

fellness (fĕl'nəs) *n*. destructive cruelty.

feneration (fĕn-ər-ā'shən) *n*. usury. also *foeneration*. -*syn*. *danism*, *defeneration*.

fenestral (fē-nĕs'trəl) *n*. a window with panes of cloth or paper instead of glass; windowlike.

fenks (fĕngks) *n.pl*. leftover whale blubber used as manure.

feoffee (fĕf'ē) *n*. someone to whom land is given as payment.

feracious (fŭr-ā'shəs) *adj*. productive; fruitful.

ferd (fûrd) *n*. 1. an army troop. 2. a large number. 3. fear.

feretory (fĕr'ĭ-tôr"ē) *n*. a portable shrine for saints' relics.

feriation (fĭr-ĭ-ā'shən) *n*. taking a holiday; not working.

ferly (fûr'lē) *adj*. a sudden, surprising, or unusual sight. also *ferlie*.

fernticled (fûrn'tĭk"əld) *adj.*
freckled, or covered with *fern-
ticles* (or *ferntickles* or *ferni-
ticles*).

ferruminate (fèr-ōō'mĭ-nāt) *v.t.* to
unite; solder [metals].

fescennine (fès-ən-īn') *adj.* vulgar,
dirty (from the Etrurian city
Fescennia, famous for its dirty
poetry).

fescue (fès'kū) *n.* a straw or twig
used as a pointer in school; grass,
genus *Festuca*.

festination (fès-tĭn-ā'shən) *n.* walking faster and faster involuntarily.

fetation (fē-tā'shən) *n.* pregnancy.
also *foetation*.

feticide (fē'tĭ-sīd) *n.* killing a fetus;
aborting.

feuilletonistic (fû"yə-tŭn-ĭs'tĭk)
adj. pertaining to a *feuilleton*, or
newspaper section devoted to
literary trivia.

fewterer (fū'tûr-ər) *n.* a dog-keeper;
generally, someone in charge,
used with a defining prefix.

fico (fē'kō) *n.* 1. giving the finger. 2.
a worthless trifle.

fictile (fĭk'tĭl) *adj.* 1. capable of
being molded; tractable. 2. made
of clay. 3. pertaining to pottery.

fiddleback (fĭd'əl-bàk) *n.* a ripple
in sycamore or maple, used for
fiddle backs.

fideism (fī'dē-ĭz"əm) *n.* depending
upon faith rather than reason.

fidgin-fain (fĭj'ĭn-fān) *adj.* restless
with delight; eager, excited. also
fidgin fain and *fidging-fain*.

fidicinal (fĭd-ĭs'ĭ-nəl) *adj.* pertaining to stringed instruments.

fidimplicitary (fĭd-ĭm-plĭs'ĭ-tèr"ē)
adj. fully trusting someone.

FIDO (fī'dō) *n.* Fog, Intensive Dis-
persal Of (military).

figgum (fĭg'əm) *n.* juggling; the fire-

spitting trick.

figulate (fĭg'ū-lāt) *adj.* made of
clay.

fike (fīk) *n.* 1. an itch; anything
causing one to fidget. 2. anxiety.
-*v.i.* to fidget. -*v.t.* to annoy.

filaceous (fĭl-ā'shəs) *adj.* consisting of threads; *filamentous*.

filiate (fĭl'ĭ-āt) *v.t.* to determine
paternity officially.

filibeg (fĭl'ĭ-bèg) *n.* the Scottish kilt,
also *philibeg*.

filiopietistic (fĭl"ĭ-ō-pī"ə-tĭs'tĭk)
adj. pertaining to ancestor worship.

filipendulous (fĭl-ĭ-pèn'dū-ləs) *adj.*
suspended by a thread.

fimblefamble (fĭm'bəl-fàm"bəl) *n.*
excuse, particularly a phony one;
a lying answer.

fimbriate (fĭm'brĭ-āt) *adj.* fringed.
also *fimbriated*.

fimetarious (fĭm-ə-tèr'ĭ-əs) *adj.*
growing or living in excrement.

finewed (fĭn'ūd) *adj.* moldy.

finific (fĭn-ĭf'ĭk) *n.* a limiting quality.

fipple (fĭp'əl) *n.* 1. the lower lip. 2. a
stopper.

firkin (fûr'kĭn) *n.* 1. a small wooden
barrel for butter and cheese. 2. a
British measure equalling about
nine gallons.

firnification (fûrn"ĭf-ĭ-kā'shən) *n.*
the process of snow being
changed to *neve* or *firn* (granular
snow, especially that on the upper
end of a glacier).

fissilingual (fĭs-ĭ-lĭng'gwəl) *adj.*
having a forked tongue.

fitch (fĭch) *n.* a long-handled brush
for painting those hard-to-get-to
places.

fitz (fĭts) *n.* a twelfth-century
patronymic for royal bastards
(French *fils* = son).

fizgig (fĭz'gĭg) *n.* 1. a flirtatious

woman. 2. a firework which hisses when exploded. 3. a *whirligig*, or noisy toy. 4. a barbed harpoon.

fjeld (fyèld) *n.* a high barren plateau in Scandinavia.

flabellation (flàb-ə-lā'shən) *n.* fanning, or otherwise cooling [someone].

flacket (flàk'ət) *v.i.* to rustle like a taffeta dress. *-n.* a barrel-shaped bottle or flask.

flagitate (flàj'ì-tāt) *v.t.* to plead.

flagitious (flà-jìsh'əs) *adj.* heinously, shamefully wicked or criminal.

flam (flàm) *v.t.&i.* to deceive, cheat. *-n.* 1. a lie. 2. a quick two-note drumbeat. 3. the flared portion of a ship's bow.

flammulated (flàm'ū-lā"təd) *adj.* ruddy, reddish.

flaneur (flò-nûr') *n.* a loafer or idler (French).

flapdragon (flàp'dràg"ən) *n.* a game of catching candy from burning brandy.

flatulopetic (flàch"əl-ō-pèt'ìk) *adj.* 1. pertaining to gas production in the bowels. 2. pretentious, pompous, inflated.

flaught (flôt) *n.* 1. a spark. 2. a snowflake. 3. a handful. 4. a flight or flutter. 5. a roll of wool. *-adv.* lying with outstretched arms; eagerly.

flavescent (flà-vès'ənt) *adj.* yellowish.

fleam (flēm) *n.* 1. a kind of lancet. 2. a stream or ditch.

fleer (flîr) *v.i.* to laugh lecherously or derisively. *-n.* 1. such a look. 2. a jeer. 3. someone who does all this.

flender (flèn'dər) *v.i.* to go fast (southern U.S.).

flense (flèns) *v.t.* to strip the cover-

ing off.

fletcher (flèch'ər) *n.* someone who makes arrows.

Fletcherism (flèch'ər-ìz"əm) *n.* ridiculously thorough chewing, advocated by Horace *Fletcher* (1849-1919), a U.S. health nut.

flews (flōōz) *n.* the hanging upper lip of dogs who look like bloodhounds.

flexanimous (flèks-àn'ì-məs) *adj.* mentally flexible.

fliffis (flìf'əs) *n.* a twisting double somersault performed on the trampoline. also *fliffus*.

flitwite (flìt'wīt) *n.* a fine for fighting.

floccify (flòk'sì-fī) *v.t.* to consider worthless.

floccillation (flòk-sìl-ā'shən) *n.* picking motions at the bedding, as happens in certain prolonged diseases; *carphology*.

floccinaucinihilipilification (flòk'sì-nō-sì-nē"hē-lē-pē"lì-fì-kā'shən) *n.* the categorizing of something as worthless trivia. Eton's Grammar considers this humorous (Latin *flocci* = trivia + *nauci* = consider worthless + *nihili* = nothing + *pili* = particle).

flocculent (flòk'ū-lənt) *adj.* like, consisting of, or covered with, soft woolly tufts.

florilegium (flôr-ìl-èj'ì-əm) *n.* an anthology.

flugel (flōō'gəl) *n.* a grand piano or harpsichord (German).

flumen (flōō'mən) *n.* the right to direct excess rain water from one's roof to the neighbor's yard.

flummadiddle (flùm'ə-dìd"əl) *n.* a New England holiday mess consisting of stale bread, pork fat, molasses, cinnamon, allspice, and cloves.

màn; māde; lèt; bē; sìp; wīne; hòt; cōld; sôre; dùll; fūgue; bûrp; gōōd; fōōd; out; gèt; thin; thìs; year; ažure; ō'mən"; viN; fûr; Bach

flyblow (flī'blō) *n.* blowfly larvae. -*v.t.* to fill with maggots or *flyblows;* to contaminate.

fnast (fnàst) *v.i.* to pant. -*n.* breath.

fnese (fnēz) *v.i.* to breathe heavily; snore.

focillate (fòs'îl-āt) *v.t.* to comfort.

fodient (fō'dì-ənt) *adj.* pertaining to digging.

fogram (fō'grəm) *adj.* old-fashioned; passé.

foinery (foin'ər-ē) *n.* making thrusts with a fencing foil; fencing, swordplay.

folie à deux (fùl"ē-ò-dû') *n.* a shared psychosis or delusion, especially one passed from one to another.

folkmoot (fōk'mōōt) *n.* a general assembly of people, such as a town or district meeting.

footle (fōō'təl) *v.i.* to waste time, talk nonsense. -*n.* foolishness.

foozle (fōō'zəl) *v.i.* to bungle or fumble. -*v.i.* to be clumsy, fumble, especially in golf.

foraminous (fôr-àm'ĭn-əs) *adj.* full of holes.

foraneous (fôr-ā'nē-əs) *adj.* pertaining to a law court or a market.

forcemeat (fôrs'mēt) *n.* chopped-up and seasoned meat or fish served alone or as stuffing.

forel (fôr'əl) *n.* a book jacket.

forfend (fôr-fènd') *v.t.* to defend, protect.

forfex (fôr'fèks) *n.* scissors.

forfoughten (fôr-fôt'ən) *adj.* worn out or exhausted from fighting.

forisfamiliate (fôr"ĭs-fə-mĭl'ĭ-āt) *v.t.* to disinherit; to shed parental authority.

forjeskit (fôr-jès'kĭt) *adj.* exhausted from work (Scottish).

forlie (fôr-lē') *v.t.* 1. to smother by lying upon. 2. to lie with.

formicary (fôr'mĭ-kèr"ē) *n.* an ant-hill (Latin *formica* = ant).

formication (fôr-mĭ-kā'shən) *n.* the feeling that bugs are crawling on you.

formist (fôr'mĭst) *n.* a creator of geometric word puzzles.

forslack (fôr-slàk') *v.t.* to hinder or delay by laziness.

forslug (fôr-slùg') *v.t.* to lose or destroy by sluggishness.

foss (fòs) *n.* a ditch or canal; an artificial stream.

fossarian (fòs-èr'ĭ-ən) *n.* a clergyman moonlighting as a grave-digger.

fossick (fòs'ĭk) *v.i.* 1. to undermine someone else's digging. 2. to search for waste gold in abandoned claims. 3. to search for anything for possible profit.

fosterlean (fòs'tər-lēn) *n.* money allowance for foster child support.

foudroyant (fōō-drwà-yòN') *adj.* 1. striking, as lightning. 2. sudden; dazzling. 3. sudden or severe onset of disease.

fourragere (fōō-rò-żèr') *n.* a shoulder ornament or award, usually made of cord.

foveate (fō'vē-ət) *adj.* pitted; pock-marked.

frab (fràb) *v.t.&i.* to scold, nag.

fraise (fràz) *n.* 1. a neck ruff. 2. a defense of pointed stakes. 3. a fluted reamer for enlarging holes. 4. a tool for cutting wheel teeth. 5. a disturbance. 6. empty talk. 7. a strawberry; strawberry-colored. -*v.t.* 1. to ream out and enlarge. 2. to defend with a *fraise.* -*v.t.&i.* to flatter, praise.

frampold (fràm'pōld) *adj.* peevish, touchy, quarrelsome.

frangible (fràn'jĭ-bəl) *adj.* breakable, fragile.

---

mǎn; māde; lèt; bē; sìp; wīne; hòt; cōld; sôre; dùll; fūgue; bûrp; gōōd; fōōd; out; gèt; thin; this; year; aʒure; ō'mən"; viN; fùr; Bach

franion (frăn'yən) *n.* the perennial hedonist, reveler.

frankalmoigne (frănk'əl-moin) *n.* land grant to a religious organization paid with prayer.

frateries (frăt'ər-ēz) *n.pl.* dining halls in monasteries.

freemartin (frē'mòr"tĭn) *n.* a sterile cow, born as a twin of a bull.

fremd (frěmd) *adj.* alien, strange, unfriendly.

fremescent (frē-měs'ənt) *adj.* an incipient murmur; becoming noisy.

frescade (frès-kād') *n.* a cool or shady place.

freshet (frěsh'ət) *n.* 1. a sudden rise in a river. 2. a stream.

fretum (frē'təm) *n.* a narrow waterway or canal.

friable (frī'ə-bəl) *adj.* easily destroyed; fragile.

fribusculum (frī-bùs'kŭ-ləm) *n.* a legal separation.

fricatrice (frĭk'ə-trĭs) *n.* a whore.

frigorific (frĭg-ə-rĭf'ĭk) *adj.* producing cold.

frim (frĭm) *adj.* flourishing, thriving.

friseur (frē-zûr') *n.* a hairdresser (French).

frist (frĭst) *n.* delay; respite.

fritinancy (frĭt'ĭn-ăn"sē) *n.* insect noises; twittering, buzzing.

froise (froiz) *n.* a large, thick pancake, sometimes with bacon.

frondescence (frŏn-děs'əns) *n.* sprouting leaves; foliage.

frotteur (frô-tûr') *n.* someone who gets her kicks by rubbing against people in crowds.

froward (frō'wərd) *adj.* perverse, obstinate.

frugivorous (frōō-jĭv'ər-əs) *adj.* fruit-eating.

frumentacious (frōō-mən-tā'shəs) *adj.* pertaining to wheat or other grain.

frush (frùsh) *v.t.* 1. to break. 2. to carve. 3. to polish. 4. to arrange. -*v.i.* to rush. -*n.* clash of weapons. 3. din. -*adj.* 1. fragile. 2 flabby.

frustraneous (frùs-trān'ē-əs) *adj.* vain, useless.

fubar (fōō'bòr) *adj.* Fucked-Up Beyond All Recognition (slang). see *snafu* for more of the same.

fubb (fùb) *adj.* Fucked-Up Beyond Belief (slang). see *snafu* for more of the same.

fubsy (fùb'zē) *adj.* short and stout.

fucatory (fŭk'ə-tôr"ē) *adj.* counterfeit; deceitful.

fucivorous (fū-sĭv'ər-əs) *adj.* eating seaweed and related foods of the deep.

fucold (fū'koid) *adj.* resembling seaweed.

fud (fùd) *n.* 1. rump. 2. an animal's tail. 3. wool leavings (after spinning).

fugacious (fū-gā'shəs) *adj.* flying, fleeing; of short duration.

fugleman (fū'gəl-mən) *n.* a political leader; formerly, a model soldier.

fukfuk (fùk'fùk) *n.* an animal's innards.

fulcible (fùl'sĭ-bəl) *adj.* capable of being supported.

fulgent (fùl'jənt) *adj.* shining brightly.

fulgurous (fùl'gū-rəs) *adj.* producing lightninglike flashes.

fuliginous (fū-lĭj'ĭn-əs) *adj.* 1. sooty. 2. pertaining to a sooty color.

fulvous (fùl'vəs) *adj.* tawny; dull brownish-reddish yellow.

fulyie (fōōl'yē) *n.* 1. a leaf; gold leaf. 2. street sweepings; manure.

fumacious (fū-mā'shəs) *adj.* 1. smoky. 2. addicted to smoking.

fumarole (fū'mə-rōl) *n.* a fuming hole in or near a volcano.

fumet (fū'mət) *n.* 1. a flavoring agent for sauces. 2. deer shit.

fumtu (fùm'tōō) *adj.* Fucked-Up More Than Usual; (slang) see *snafu* for more of the same.

funambulist (fū-nàm'bū-lĭst) *n.* a tightrope walker.

funest (fū-nĕst') *adj.* harbinger of evil or death; dire.

fungible (fùn'jĭ-bəl) *adj.* interchangeable: applied mostly to goods.

funkify (fùnk'ĭ-fī) *v.t.* to retreat fearfully.

furacious (fyōōr-ā'shəs) *adj.* thievish.

furfuraceous (fûr-fər-ā'shəs) *adj.* covered with dandruff.

furibund (fûr'ĭ-bùnd) *adj.* furious, enraged.

furr-ahin (fûr'ə-hĭn) *n.* the right rear horse in plowing (Scottish).

fuscous (fùs'kəs) *adj.* pertaining to a brownish-grayish color.

fusiform (fū'zĭ-fôrm) *adj.* spindle-shaped; tapering at each end.

fusil (fū'zĭl) *adj.* fusing, melting.

fussock (fùs'ək) *n.* 1. a big, fat woman. 2. a fluffy mass of cotton.

fustigate (fùs'tĭ-gāt) *v.t.* to beat; to criticize severely.

fustilugs (fùs'tĭ-lùgz) *n.* a fat, unwieldy person.

futhorc (fōō'thôrk) *n.* the runic alphabet—so called from the first six letters: FUTHORC.

fyke (fīk) *n.* a long, bag-shaped fishnet held open by hoops.

fylfot (fīl'fŏt) *n.* the swastika.

fyrd (fûrd) *n.* 1. the military in old England. 2. the obligation to serve in the ranks.

fyrdung (fīr'dùng) *n.* an army prepared for battle; a military expedition.

G

gaberlunzie (găb-ûr-lŭn′zē) *n.* a
wandering or licensed beggar.

gair (gèr) *adj.* sharp, eager, greedy.
-*n.* a corner section of unplowed
land.

gajo (gô′jō) *n.* a nongypsy.

galactophagist (găl-ăk″tō-fā′jĭst)
n. a milk drinker.

galang-galang (gà-lòng″gà-lòng′)
n. the Australian locust.

galantine (găl-ən-tēn′) *n.* a cold
dish of pressed meat covered with
aspic.

galbe (gălb) *n.* the general contour
or outline of a rounded object.

galeanthropy (găl-ē-ăn′thrə-pē) *n.*
the delusion that one has become
a cat.

galeated (gā′lē-ā″təd) *adj.* helmet-
shaped; wearing a Roman
helmet.

galempung (găl-ĕm′pŭng) *n.* a
Javanese zither. also *galempong,
tjalempoeng. calempun.*

galericulate (găl-ər-ĭk′ū-lāt) *adj.*
covered with a hat.

galimatias (găl-ĭ-mā′shĭ-əs) *n.*
gibberish; confused, meaningless
jargon.

gallongee (găl-yən-jē′) *n.* a Turkish sailor.

galliardise (găl′yûr-dēz) *n.* great
merriment.

galligaskins (găl-ĭ-găs′kĭnz) *n.*
loose, baggy pants (British slang).

gallimaufry (găl-ĭ-môf′rē) *n.* 1. a
hash made of sweetbreads,
brains, and other such goodies. 2.
any preposterous mixture.

gallinaceous (găl-ĭ-nā′shəs) *adj.*
like a chicken or pheasant.

gallinipper (găl′ĭ-nĭp″ər) *n.* 1. a
large mosquito or crane fly. 2.
any biting or stinging insect.

gallionic (găl-ĭ-òn′ĭk) *adj.* indifferent; careless; irresponsible.

gallipot (găl′ĭ-pòt) *n.* 1. a small
medicine jar. 2. a druggist
(colloquial).

galp (gòlp) *v.i.* to yawn; to gape.
-*v.t.* to belch. -*n.* gaping.

galways (găl′wāz) *n.* a kind of
beard worn to represent a stage
Irishman. also *gallaway.*

galyak (găl′yàk) *n.* 1. a hybrid between *Galloway* (black, hornless,
Scottish) cattle and a yak. 2.
lamb or goat fur (Russian).

gamashes (găm-àsh′ēz) *n.pl.*
leggings worn for protection

---

mān; māde; lĕt; bē; sĭp; wīne; hŏt; cōld; sôre; dŭll; fūgue; bûrp;
gŏŏd; fōōd; out; gĕt; thin; this; year; aźure; ō′mən″; viN; fûr; Bach

(especially by horsemen).

gambist (găm'bĭst) *n.* a viola da gamba player.

gambrinous (găm-brī'nəs) *adj.* full of beer.

gamdeboo (găm'dĭ-bōō) *n.* a hardwood tree of South Africa.

gamic (găm'ĭk) *adj.* 1. sexual. 2. developing after fertilization.

gammacism (găm'ə-sĭz″əm) *n.* 1. difficulty in pronouncing guttural consonants, as g and k; guttural stammering. 2. childish talk.

gammadion (găm-ā'dĭ-ŏn) *n.* a cross resembling the swastika made of four capital gammas.

gammer (găm'ər) *n.* an old wife; an old woman. -*v.i.* to idle.

gammon (găm'ən) *n.* 1. a foot, leg, or thigh. 2. smoked ham or bacon. 3. backgammon. 4. *gammoning, n.* the iron band by which a ship's bowsprit is tied to the stem. -*v.t.* 1. to smoke or dry [bacon, etc.] 2. to beat in backgammon by getting a *gamon.* 3. to tie [a ship's bowsprit].

gamophobia (găm-ō-fō'bĭ-ə) *n.* fear of marriage.

gamp (gămp) *n.* 1. a large umbrella. 2. a midwife (from *Mrs. Gamp,* a character in Dickens' *Martin Chuzzlewit,* who was a midwife with a large umbrella).

ganch (gănch) *v.t.* 1. to execute by impaling on stakes or hooks. 2. to wound with a tusk. -*v.i.* 1. to gnash the teeth; to snarl. 2. to stammer; stutter. -*n.* 1. apparatus used in *ganching;* execution by *ganching;* 2. a wound made by a boar's tusk.

ganger (găng'ûr) *n.* 1. a pedestrian. 2. a stranger. 3. a well-running horse. 4. a gang foreman. 5. a short length of chain

cable. -*v.i.* to *gangrene* (to produce or be affected with gangrene).

ganja (gŏn'jŏ) *n.* marijuana or hashish in India and Jamaica.

gapeseed (găp'sēd) *n.* 1. anything that causes stares. 2. someone who stares. *to buy,* or *sow gapeseed,* to stare idly.

gapingstock (găp'ĭng-stŏk) *n.* an object of open-mouthed curiosity.

gapo (gà-pō') *n.* a forest near a river, which is partly inundated every rainy season.

garboil (gŏr'boil) *n.* confusion. -*v.t.* to confuse, to garble.

gardyloo (gŏr-dē-lōō') *n.* a warning cry given before tossing slops and garbage from the windows of old Edinburgh.

garlion (gŏrl'yən) *n.* a cross between garlic and onion.

gasconade (găs-kən-ād') *n.* boasting; bravado. -*v.i.* to brag, *gasconader, n.*

gastriloquist (găs-trĭl'ō-kwĭst) *n.* a ventriloquist.

gastromancy (găs'trō-măn″sē) *n.* fortunetelling by ventriloquism or crystal-gazing.

gaud(s) (gŏd[z]) *n.(pl.)* 1. a trick or practical joke; a fraud. 2. jewelry or other ornaments. 3. (mostly *pl.*) a showy display or ceremony. 4. a bead marking a division in a rosary. -*v.i.* to make merry. -*v.t.* to decorate with *gauds.*

gavage (gà-vàž') *n.* 1. feeding through a stomach tube. 2. force-feeding poultry.

gavelock (găv'əl-ŏk) *n.* 1. a spear or dart. 2. an iron lever.

gawsie (gô'sē) *adj.* large and jolly; lusty. also *gawsy, gawcie.*

gazooney (gà-zōōn'ē) *n.* a passive

male homosexual. see *gunzel*.

gazophylacium (găz″ō-fĭl-ā′shĭ-əm) *n.* a treasury (slang).

geck (gĕk) *n.* 1. an object of scorn; a dupe. 2. an expression or gesture of scorn or contempt. *-v.t.&i.* to deride, cheat; tò toss the head in derision.

gegenschein (gā′gən-shīn) *n.* a faint, glowing spot in the sky, exactly opposite the sun, best seen in September and October. also called *counterglow*.

Gehenna (gĕ-hĕn′ə) *n.* 1. a valley near Jerusalem, scene of Israeli sacrifice, later used as a garbage dump. 2. hell in the New Testament. 3. a prison or torture chamber.

gelastic (jĕl-ăs′tĭk) *adj.* pertaining to or used in laughing.

gelogenic (jĕl-ō-jĕn′ĭk) *adj.* laughter-provoking.

geloscopy (jĕl-ŏs′kə-pē) *n.* determining someone's character or future by the way she laughs.

gemebund (jĕm′ə-bŭnd) *adj.* a constant moaning.

gemeled (jĕm′əld) *adj.* coupled, paired.

gemelliparous (jĕm-əl-ĭp′ər-əs) *adj.* pertaining to a *gemellipara*, a woman who has given birth to twins.

gemsbok (gĕmz′bŏk) *n.* a large, good-looking South African oryx.

genarch (jĕn′örk) *n.* head of the family. also *genarcha*.

genethliac (jĕn-ĕth′lĭ-ăk) *adj.* pertaining to birthdays.

genethliacon (jĕn″ĕth-lī′ə-kŏn) *n.* a birthday poem.

genicon (jĕn′ĭ-kən) *n.* a sexual partner imagined by one who is dissatisfied with her actual partner.

geniculate (jĕn-ĭk′ū-lāt) *adj.* 1.

bent at an angle, as a bent knee. *-v.t.* to form joints in.

genocratia (jĕn-ō-krăt′ĭ-ə) *n.* birth control.

gentilitial (jĕn-tĭl-ĭsh′əl) *adj.* 1. pertaining to a people: national. 2. pertaining to a family. 3. of gentle birth, well-born.

geocentricism (jē-ō-sèn′trĭ-sĭz″əm) *n.* belief that the earth is the center of the universe.

geodesic (jē-ō-dē′zĭk) *adj.* the shortest distance between two points on a spherical surface: arc of a great circle.

geogenous (jē-ŏj′ən-əs) *adj.* growing on or in the ground.

georgic (jôr′jĭk) *n.* a bucolic poem. *-adj.* pertaining to agriculture and country life.

gephyrophobia (jĕf″ĭ-rō-fō′bĭ-ə) *n.* fear of crossing bridges.

gerascophobia (jĕr-ăs″kō-fō′bĭ-ə) *n.* fear of growing old.

gerent (jĭr′ənt) *adj.* bearing, carrying. *-n.* one who rules or manages.

gerful (jûr′fəl) *adj.* changeable. also *gereful, gerie, gerish*.

geromorphism (jĕr-ō-môr′fĭz″əm) *n.* condition of appearing older than one is.

gerontocomium (jĕr-ŏn″tō-kō′mĭ-əm) *n.* an institution for care of the aged.

gerontocracy (jĕr-ən-tŏk′rə-sē) *n.* government by old people.

gestic (jĕs′tĭk) *adj.* relating to body movement: consisting of gestures, especially in dancing.

gharnao (gàr-nô′ō) *n.* a raft made of inverted ceramic pots (Ganges Valley).

ghawazee (gà-wô′zē) *n.pl.* Egyptian female dancers who do not marry outside the tribe. also *ghawazi*.

---

mǎn; māde; lĕt; bē; sĭp; wīne; hŏt; cōld; sôre; dŭll; fūgue; bûrp; gōōd; fōōd; out; gĕt; thin; thìs; year; azure; ō′mən″; viN; fūr; Bach

ghee (gē) *n.* that part of buffalo butter, which, after being melted and cooled, is poured off.

Ghibelline (gĭb'ə-lĭn, -lĭn) *n.* a political faction of medieval Italy supporting the ruling German emperors. opposite of the *Guelphs.*

ghoom (gōōm) *v.i.* to hunt in the dark (Anglo-Indian).

ghurry (gŭr'ē) *n.* 1. a Hindu period of twenty-four minutes; an Anglo-Indian hour. 2. a *clepsydra.* or water clock. 3. any timepiece.

giaour (jour) *n.* an infidel, i.e., a Christian.

giardinetto (jŏr-dē-nĕt'ō) *n.* precious stones arranged into a spray of flowers for a ring or brooch.

gibbed (gĭbd) *adj.* castrated, said usually of cats.

gibus (jī'bəs) *n.* an opera hat, so named from the original maker in Paris.

giddhom (gĭd'thəm) *n.* a frantic galloping movement made by cows when plagued with flies.

giffgaff (gĭf'gàf) *n.&v.i.* mutual accommodation; give-and-take; informal conversation.

gilliver (jĭl'ĭ-vər) *n.* the common wallflower of Europe.

gillygaloo (gĭl-ē-gə-lōō') *n.* a mythical bird that lays square eggs (slang).

gilravage (gĭl-ràv'əj) *v.i.* to celebrate noisily; to go on a rampage. also *n.*

gime (gīm) *n.* a hole washed in an embankment by water pouring through a leak.

gimmaces (gĭm'ə-sĕz) *n.pl.* chains used in hanging criminals.

gingival (jĭn'jĭ-vəl) *adj.* 1. pertaining to the gums. 2. pronounced

with the tip of the tongue near the upper gums. -*n.* a *gingival* sound.

girandole (jĭr'ən-dōl) *n.* 1. a radiating, showy composition, as a cluster of skyrockets fired together. 2. an ornamental, branched candleholder. 3. a mirror in an ornamental, circular frame (U.S.). 4. an earring with small stones clustered around a larger one (French *girare* = to revolve).

girasol (jĭr'ə-sòl) *n.* 1. the Jerusalem artichoke. 2. a fire opal.

girn (gûrn) *v.i.* to snarl, whine. -*v.t.* to bare the teeth in rage; to utter with a *girn* or snarl (Scottish, English dialect).

givy (gĭv'ē) *adj.* relaxed (U.S.).

glabrous (glā'brəs) *adj.* smooth; without hairs or projections; *glabrate. glabrescent* means slightly glabrous.

glaciology (glā-shĭ-òl'ə-jē) *n.* the study of glaciers and their effects on animal and plant life.

glaikit (glā'kĭt) *adj.* foolish, thoughtless, giddy. also *glaiket.*

glair (glèr) *n.* 1. raw egg white used in sizing or glazing. 2. a size or glaze made of egg white. -*v.t.* to smear with *glair.* also *glaire.*

glandaceous (glàn-dā'shəs) *adj.* acorn-colored.

glaucous (glô'kəs) *adj.* green with a grayish-blue cast.

glebous (glē'bəs) *adj.* full of clods; like a clod, earthy; *gleby.*

gledge (glĕj) *n.&v.i.* squint.

gleed (glēd) *n.* 1. a live coal. 2. a flame or ray. 3. *pl.* cinders. -*adj.* 1. squint-eyed; blind in one eye. 2. crooked, awry, astray.

gleek (glēk) *n.* 1. a trick or deception. 2. an enticing glance. 3. a card game for three people; three cards of the same rank in one hand; a trio.

gleet (glēt) *n.* 1. slime, ooze, greasy filth. 2. phlegm like that found in a hawk's stomach. 3. mucous discharge from the urethra. 4. a chronic inflammation of the nasal cavities -*v.i.* to ooze, as *gleet;* to flow slowly; *gleety, adj.*

gliff (glĭf) *n.* 1. a fleeting glance; a faint sound. 2. a brief moment. 3. a sudden shock. -*v.t.* to frighten.

glin (glĭn) *n.* haze or vapor on the horizon at sea, signaling an approaching storm.

glink (glĭnk) *v.i.* to look at slyly, sideways.

glock (glŏk) *v.t.* 1. to swallow in huge gulps. 2. to make a gulping sound.

gloppen (glŏp'ən) *v.t.&i.* to surprise, or be surprised; to worry or be worried.

gloss (glŏs) *n.* 1. a definition in a glossary or dictionary. 2. a glossary. 3. a misleading definition. 4. a word requiring explanation. 5. a type of poetry. 6. a commentary on Roman law of the twelfth and thirteenth centuries. *glossarist,* a *gloss*-writer or commentator; *glossographer.*

glossolalia (glòs-ō-lā'lĭ-ə) *n.* nonsensical talk; gibberish.

glossology (glòs-òl'ō-jē) *n.* 1. the study of language or linguistics. 2. the writing of glossaries; *glossonomy.* 3. the study of the tongue and its diseases.

glottogonic (glòt-ō-gòn'ĭk) *adj.* of or pertaining to the origin of language, *glottogonist.*

glutition (gloo-tĭsh'ən) *n.* swallowing; *deglutition.*

glycolimia (glī-kō-lĭm'ĭ-ə) *n.* a craving for sweets.

glyph (glĭf) *n.* 1. a channel or groove, usually vertical. 2. a carved figure or character in relief.

glyptic (glĭp'tĭk) *n.* the art of engraving on gems. also *adj.*

gnathic (nàth'ĭk) *adj.* pertaining to the jaw.

gnathonic (nà-thòn'ĭk) *adj.* flattering, deceitful; *gnathonical.*

gnoff (nòf) *n.* churl, lout, boor.

gnomonics (nō-mòn'ĭks) *n.* the science of dial construction, especially sundials.

goadsman (gōd'mən) *n.* a man who uses a *goad,* or pointed stick, to urge his plow horses onward.

gobbet (gòb'ət) *n.* 1. a piece [of flesh]. 2. a lump [of metal, clotted blood, mud, or fat]; a mass. -*v.t.* 1. to swallow in *gobbets.* 2. to divide into pieces.

gobemouche (gòb-mōōsh') *n.* a gullible person. -*adj.* gullible; literally, one who swallows flies.

god-box (gòd'bòks) *n.* organ (slang).

godemiche (gōd'mēsh) *n.* a dildo.

godhopping (gòd'hòp'ĭng) *v.i.* pretending an interest in religion in order to receive aid from missionaries (slang).

goditorium (gòd-ĭ-tôr'ĭ-əm) *n.* a church (slang).

godling (gòd'lĭng) *n.* a puny or small-time god.

godwit (gòd'wĭt) *n.* a long-billed wading bird of the snipe family.

goety (gō'ə-tē) *n.* black magic.

gomeral (gòm'ûr-əl) *n.* a fool.

gomphiasis (gòm-fī'ə-sĭs) *n.* toothache; looseness of the teeth.

gonemous (gō'nə-məs) *adj.* bearing many children.

gonfalonier (gòn"fə-lòn-ĭr) *n.* one who carries the *gonfalon,* or flag.

gongoozler (gòn-gōōz'lər) *n.* someone who stares for hours at anything out of the ordinary.

googol (gŏŏ'gəl) *n.* ten to the hundredth power (coined by Dr. Edward Kasner's nine-year old nephew. From *Mathematics and the Imagination* by Kasner and James Newman.

googolplex (gŏŏ'gəl-plĕks) *n.* one, followed by a *googol* zeros (same etymology as above).

goonch (gŏŏnch) *n.* Indian licorice seeds.

gooney (gŏŏn'ē) *n.* 1. a booby, dunce. 2. the black-footed albatross. also *goony; gony.*

gorgonize (gôr'gən-īz) *v.t.* to petrify; to stare at, with a *Gorgon* look.

gossoon (gŏ-sŏŏn') *n.* 1. a young man. 2. a waiter (French *garçon* = a waiter or a young man).

gracile (grăs'ĭl) *adj.* graceful and slender.

gradine (gră-dēn') *n.* a toothed chisel used by sculptors.

Graf (grŏf) *n.* a German, Austrian, and Swedish title of nobility (equal to an English *earl* or French *comte*).

graip (grāp) *n.* a pitchfork or dungfork.

graith (grāth) *n.* 1. readiness. 2. furniture, dress, apparatus or accouterments for work, sport, etc.; gear. 3. material. 4. soapy water. -*v.t.* 1. to prepare. 2. to furnish, adorn. 3. to make or build. -*adj.* prepared.

gralloch (grăl'ôĥ) *n.* the viscera of a dead deer. -*v.t.* to disembowel.

gramercy (grăm-ûr'sē) *interj.* 1. many thanks. 2. an exclamation meaning *mercy on us!* 3. a thank-you; an acknowledgment (French *grand-merci* = many thanks).

graminivorous (grăm-ĭn-ĭv'ər-əs) *adj.* grass-eating.

grammalogue (grăm'ə-lôg) *n.* a word represented by a *logogram,* or symbol. also *grammalog.*

grammaticaster (grăm-ăt'ĭ-kàs"tər) *n.* a petty grammarian; a pretentious grammatical pedant.

grammatolatry (grăm"ə-tŏl'ə-trē) *n.* worship of letters or words.

grandgousier (grŏn-gŏŏz-yā') *n.* a glutton; someone with an enormous gullet who will swallow anything (father of Rabelais's *Gargantua*).

grangerism (grăn'jər-ĭz"əm) *n.* cutting out pictures and designs from the books of others in order to illustrate your own (so called from the Reverend James Granger, whose *Biographical History of England* (1769) was so richly illustrated).

grapholagnia (grăf-ō-lăg'nĭ-ə) *n.* a more than passing interest in obscene pictures.

graphospasm (grăf'ō-spăz"əm) *n.* writer's cramp.

grassation (grăs-ā'shən) *n.* act of attacking violently; a lying in wait to attack.

gravamen (gră-vā'mən) *n.* a grievance; a formal complaint.

gravedo (gră-vē'dō) *n.* a head cold.

graveolent (grăv'ē-ō-lĕnt") *adj.* stinking.

gravid (gră'vĭd) *adj.* pregnant.

grayslick (grā'slĭk) *adj.* a state of the sea when the wind has died down and the still water takes on a "glassy" look.

grebe (grēb) *n.* a four-toed podicipoid diving bird without tail feathers. *little grebe,* the European *dabchick.*

greegree (grē'grē) *n.* 1. an African charm or fetish. 2. a buzzard. 3. the sassy-tree.

greffier (grĕf'ĭ-ûr) *n.* a registrar or

recorder.

gregal (grē'gəl) *adj.* pertaining to, or like a flock; gregarious.

gregale (grā-gŏl'ä) *n.* a dry, cold, northeast wind that occasionally blows over Malta.

gremial (grē'mĭ-əl) *n.* 1. a close friend. 2. a member of a society or university. 3. an apron used by a bishop at Mass or during ordination ceremonies. -*adj.* 1. being a member of a society. 2. pertaining to the aforementioned episcopal garment.

gressible (grès'ĭ-bəl) *adj.* able to walk.

gressorial (grès-ôr'ĭ-əl) *adj.* adapted for walking, as the feet of certain birds and insects; pertaining to the *Gressoria*, a division of insects; *gressorious.*

grice (grīs) *n.* a young pig.

griffonage (grē-fô-nŏz') *n.* careless handwriting; illegible scribble.

grifter (grĭf'tər) *n.* a concessionaire at a circus, carnival, or amusement park, especially one who operates a prize wheel or other game of chance; a thief (U.S. slang).

grig (grĭg) *n.* 1. a tiny person or creature; a dwarf. 2. a cricket or grasshopper. 3. a small domestic fowl. 4. a little eel. 5. a lively person, usually with *merry.* 6. a farthing. 7. heather. -*v.i.* to fish for *grigs.* -*v.t.* to tantalize; irritate.

grilse (grĭls) *n.* young salmon after their first return from the sea.

grimalkin (grĭm-ŏl'kĭn) *n.* a female cat; an old woman.

grimgribber (grĭm'grĭb"ər) *n.* technical jargon, especially legal.

grinagog (grĭn'ə-gŏg) *n.* a perpetual grinner (slang).

grisaille (grē-zī') *n.* 1. a style of painting in gray tones imitating bas-relief. 2. a painting thus executed. 3. a French dress material with cotton warp and woolen filling.

griskin (grĭs'kĭn) *n.* 1. the spine of a hog. 2. the lean part of a pork loin. 3. a small piece of meat for roasting.

grith (grĭth) *n.* 1. refuge or asylum. 2. mercy. 3. short for *church-grith,* the asylum of a church.

grivoiserie (grēv-wŏz-rē') *n.* lewd and lascivious behavior; a lewd act.

groak (grōk) *v.i.* to watch people silently while they're eating, hoping they will ask you to join them.

grobianism (grō'bĭ-ən-ĭz"əm) *n.* rudeness; boorishness.

groschen (grō'shən) *n.* 1. the tenpfennig piece of Germany. 2. in Austria, a bronze coin = 1/100 of a schilling.

grosz (grŏsh) *n.* 1/100 of a zloty (Polish).

grummels (grŏŏm'əlz) *n.pl.* sediment; dregs.

Grundyism (grŭnd'ē-ĭz"əm) *n.* conventionalism as personified by Mrs. Grundy (in Morton's *Speed the Plough*).

gruntling (grŭnt'lĭng) *n.* a young pig.

Guelph (gwĕlf) *n.* a political faction in medieval Italy which opposed the ruling German emperors; opposite of the *Ghibellines.*

guerdon (gûr'dən) *n.* a reward. -*v.t.* to give *guerdon* to; to reward.

gufa (gŏŏ'fə) *n.* a round boat made of wickerwork, used in old Mesopotamia. also *goofa, goofah.*

gugusse (gŭ-gŏŏs') *n.* a young, effeminate man who trysts with priests.

guignol (gēn-yùl') *n.* 1. cap. the main character in French puppet shows. 2. a puppet show or one of the puppets; a marionette theater. 3. the *Grand Guignol* (a small theater in Paris, specializing in horror plays).

guitguit (gwĭt'gwĭt) *n.* the American honey creeper (so called from its song).

gulosity (gū-lòs'ĭ-tē) *n.* enormous appetite; greediness.

gunnel (gùn'əl) *n.* a small, slimy, elongate marine blenny found on both sides of the Atlantic.

gunzel (gùn'zəl) *n.* 1. a passive, orally oriented, male homosexual. see *gazooney*. 2. a brat. 3. an informer (slang).

gurry (gùr'ē) *n.* 1. diarrhea. 2. whale garbage resulting from efforts to extract its oil. 3. a small car, sleigh, or wheelbarrow. 4. a fort.

gutta-percha (gùt'ə-pûr"chə) *n.* a substance like rubber which comes from the latex of certain Malaysian trees: used for electrical insulation and temporary tooth fillings.

guttatim (gù-tā'tĭm) *adv.* drop by drop: used in prescriptions (Latin *gutta* = drop).

gyascutus (gī-əs-kū'təs, jī-) *n.* a huge, imaginary, four-legged beast with legs on one side longer than on the other, enabling it to walk easily on steep hillsides (U.S.).

gyle (gīl) *n.* 1. wort about to ferment. 2. a vat in which beer is fermented.

gymnophobia (jĭm-nō-fō'bĭ-ə) *n.* fear of nudity.

gymnosophist (jĭm-nòs'ə-fĭst) *n.* 1. an ancient sect of Hindu ascetics found in India by Alexander T.A.G.* 2. a nudist.

gynandry (gī-nàn'drē, jĭ-) *n.* 1. hermaphroditism. 2. a woman who looks like a man.

gynarchy (gī'nòr-kē", jĭn') *n.* 1. government by women. 2. an insect society where only the female parent takes part in establishing the colony.

gyneolatry (gī"nē-òl'ə-trē, jĭn") *n.* worship of women.

gynotikolobomassophile (gī-nòt"ĭ-kō-lō"bō-màs'ō-fīl) *n.* one who likes to nibble on a woman's earlobe (Greek *gyne* = woman + *otikos* = of the ear + *lobos* = lobe + *masso* = chew + *philos* = loving).

gyre (jīr) *n.* 1. a circular motion, revolution. 2. a circular or spiral form, a ring or vortex. 3. an evil spirit. -*v.t.&i.* to turn around, to gyrate.

gyromancy (jī'rō-màn"sē) *n.* fortunetelling by walking in a circle until dizzy; the fortune is determined by where the person falls.

gyrovagues (jī'rō-vāgz) *n.pl.* monks accustomed to wander from monastery to monastery.

gyve (jīv) *n.* a shackle, usually in *pl.* -*v.t.* to shackle, to chain.

*The Allegedly Great

H

habilitate (hà-bǐl'ǐ-tāt) *v.t.* to supply with money, clothes, or equipment. *-v.i.* to qualify oneself, as for teaching.

habnab (hàb'nǎb) *adj.* at random; hit or miss.

haboob (hà-boōb') *n.* a violent desert sandstorm of North Africa and India.

habromania (hàb-rō-mā'nǐ-ə) *n.* extreme euphoria.

hachure (hà-shûr') *n.* a short line used for shading in drawing and engraving.

hadeharia (hā-dē-hà'rǐ-ə) *n.* constant use of the word *hell*.

hadj (hàj) *n.* the pilgrimage to Mecca; any pilgrimage.

haecceity (hĕk-sē'ǐ-tē) *n.* that which makes something different from anything else; individuality. see *quiddity*.

haffle (hàf'əl) *v.i.* to stutter, hesitate.

haft (hàft) *n.* 1. the handle of a sword. 2. a holder for spun fibres. 3. a place for settling down; a pasture, a home. *-v.i.* to be shifty. *-v.t.&i.* to familiarize; to settle down.

hagborn (hàg'bôrn) *adj.* born of a hag or witch.

hagiarchy (hàg'ǐ-ŏr"kē) *n.* government by religious types.

hagiolatry (hàg-ǐ-ŏl'ə-trē) *n.* worship of saints. *hagiolatrous, adj.*

haha (hŏ'hŏ) *n.* a sunken wall, invisible from a distance.

hakenkreuz (hŏ'kən-kroits) *n.* swastika: *hakenkreuzler,* a fanatic nationalist.

hakim (hŏ'kēm) *n.* a Moslem judge or ruler.

halberd (hàl'bûrd) *n.* 1. a long-handled weapon used in the fifteenth and sixteenth centuries. 2. a frame into which soldiers were placed to be whipped.

halfpace (hàf'pās) *n.* 1. a platform with stairs, used for thrones or altars. 2. a staircase landing or broad step between two half-flights going in different directions.

halidom (hàl'ǐ-dùm) *n.* holiness; a storehouse for holy relics.

halieutics (hàl-ǐ-ū'tǐks) *n.* fishing.

haliography (hàl-ǐ-ŏg'rə-fē) *n.* description of the sea. *halio-*

---

màn; māde; lèt; bē; sǐp; wīne; hŏt; cōld; sôre; dùll; fūgue; bûrp; goōd; foōd; out; gèt; thin; ᴛhis; year; aᴢure; ŏ'mən"; viN; für; Bach

grapher, *n.*

halitus (hăl′ĭ-təs) *n.* exhalation, breath. *halituous*, *adj.*, *halituosity*, *n.*

hallelujatic (hăl″ē-lōō-yŏt′ĭk) *adj.* pertaining to or containing *hallelujahs*.

hallux (hăl′ŭks) *n.* the big toe; a bird's rear toe. *hallucal*, *adj.*

halobios (hăl-ō-bī′əs) *n.* sea flora and fauna.

haloid (hăl′oid) *adj.* saltlike.

halomancy (hăl′ō-măn″sē) *n.* fortunetelling with salt.

halotic (hăl-ŏ′tĭk) *adj.* easy to catch.

halsen (hôl′sən) *v.t.* to predict.

hamartiology (hăm-ôr′tĭ-ŏl′ə-jē) *n.* the study of sin.

hamartithia (hăm-ôr-tĭth′ĭ-ə) *n.* mistake-prone.

hamartophobia (hăm-ôr″tō-fō′bĭ-ə) *n.* fear of sin or sinning.

hamble (hăm′bəl) *v.t.* to cut off the balls of dogs' feet to make them useless for hunting. *-v.i.* to limp.

hamesucken (hām′sŭk″ən) *n.* the assaulting of a person in her own house.

hamiform (hā′mĭ-fôrm) *adj.* nook-shaped.

hamirostrate (hā-mĭ-rŏs′trāt) *adj.* having a hooked beak.

hanaper (hăn′ə-pər) *n.* a box for documents.

handsel (hăn′səl) *n.* 1. good luck, or a good-luck token. 2. a gift made as a good-luck token, as the first receipts of a new store or a groom's present to his bride. *-v.t.* 1. to celebrate the beginning of something. 2. to use or do for the first time; to try experimentally.

haole (hou′lā) *n.* a white person or foreigner in Hawaii.

haplography (hăp-lŏg′rə-fē) *n.* in writing, the inadvertent omission of one or more adjacent and similar letters, syllables, words, or lines.

haplology (hăp-lŏl′ə-jē) *n.* in pronunciation, the omission of one or more syllables; syllabic syncope.

haptodysphoria (hăp″tō-dĭs-fôr′ĭ-ə) *n.* unpleasant sensation felt by some people when touching peaches, cotton, or similar surfaces.

harageous (hăr-ā′jəs) *adj.* rough and bold.

haramaitism (hăr-ə-mā′-ĭ-tĭz″əm) *n.* Hindu child marriages.

hardscrabble (hŏrd′skră″bəl) *adj.* the eking out of a living. *-n. hardscrabble* land.

harengiform (hăr-ĕn′jĭ-fôrm) *adj.* herring-shaped.

hariolate (hăr′ĭ-ō-lāt″) *v.i.* to practice fortunetelling or ventriloquism; to predict.

harpactophagous (hŏr-păk-tŏf′ə-gəs) *adj.* predatory: used especially of insects.

harpaxophobia (hŏr-păks″ō-fō′bĭ-ə) *n.* fear of robbers or of being robbed.

harpocratic (hŏr-pō-kră′tĭk) *adj.* relating to silence.

hartal (hŏr-tŏl′) *n.* a strike to protest a governmental action [in India].

haruspex (hăr′ŭs-pĕks) *n.* a fortuneteller who used animal innards and lightning for her predictions. *pl. -spice.*

hasenpfeffer (hŏ′zən-fĕf″ər) *n.* 1. highly seasoned rabbit stew. 2. a card game like euchre.

havelock (hăv′lŏk) *n.* a cloth sunshade hung from the back of a military cap.

havier (hăv′yər) *n.* a castrated deer.

haybote (hā′bōt) *n.* wood or thorns

allowed a tenant for repair of her hedges or fences; the right to take such material; *hedgebote*.

haznadar (hăz-nə-dòr') *n.* a treasurer (Turkish).

heautontimorumenos (hē-ô"tòn-tĭm-ō-rōō'mən-ŏs) *n.* masochist (title of a play by Menander).

hebdomadal (hĕb-dòm'ə-dəl) *adj.* weekly.

hebephrenia (hē-bə-frē'nĭ-ə) *n.* a type of schizophrenia occurring usually at puberty and characterized by extreme silliness.

hebesphalmology (hē-bēs"făl-mŏl'ə-jē) *n.* study of juvenile delinquency.

hebetic (hē-bĕt'ĭk) *adj.* happening at puberty.

hebetude (hĕb'ə-tūd) *n.* dullness, stupidity. *hebetudinous, adj.*

hecatomb (hĕk'ə-tōōm) *n.* religious sacrifice of 100 oxen; any mass slaughter.

hecatompedon (hĕk-ə-tòm'pə-dòn) *n.* 1. the *cella* of the Parthenon or of Athena's Temple. 2. any building 100 feet long or wide.

hectare (hĕk'tĕr) *n.* 100 acres.

hector (hĕk'tər) *v.t.* to verbally threaten or intimidate. *-v.i.* to bully.

hederaceous (hĕd-ər-ā'shəs) *adj.* pertaining to ivy. *hederaceously, adv.*

hederate (hĕd'ər-āt) *v.t.* to decorate with ivy.

hednon (hĕd'nən) *n.* a wedding present.

hedonics (hē-dòn'ĭks) *n.* the study of pleasant and unpleasant sensations. the relationship of duty to pleasure.

hegemony (hē-jĕm'ən-ē) *n.* dominance or control, as 'he mind over the body, or one nation over another.

hegira (hē-jī'rə) *n.* Mohammed's flight from Mecca (A.D. 622 = first year of the Moslem era); any flight.

hegumen (hē-gū'mən) *n.* the head of a small monastery.

heliolater (hē-lĭ-òl'ə-tər) *n.* a sun worshiper. *heliolatrous, adj.*

hellhag (hĕl'hăg) *n.* an evil old woman; a hellcat.

hellkite (hĕl'kīt) *n.* a fierce bird of prey; an extremely cruel person.

helminthophobia (hĕl-mĭn"thō-fō'bĭ-ə) *n.* fear of being, or becoming, infested with worms.

helobious (hē-lō'bĭ-əs) *adj.* living in marshy places.

helotry (hĕl'ŏt-rē) *n.* helots, or slaves, collectively; slavery.

helve (hĕlv) *n.* 1. the handle of a tool or weapon. *-v.t.* to supply with a *helve*.

hematopoiesis (hĕm"ə-tō-poi-ē'sĭs) *n.* the formation of blood.

hemeralopia (hĕm"ər-ə-lō'pĭ-ə) *n.* day blindness; able to see only in the dark. opposite of *nyctalopia*.

hemeraphonia (hĕm"ər-ā-fō'nĭ-ə) *n.* able to speak only at night.

hemipenis (hĕm-ĭ-pē'nĭs) *n.* one of the paired sex organs of many reptiles.

hempen (hĕmp'ən) *adj.* pertaining to hemp or a hangman's noose.

henbane (hĕn'bān) *n.* a poisonous herb similar to belladonna, whose extract is used medically.

hendecasyllable (hĕn"dĕk-ə-sĭl'ə-bəl) *n.* a metrical line of eleven syllables.

henhussy (hĕn'hŭz"ē) *n.* a sexist term for a man who does housework.

henism (hĕn'ĭz"əm) *n.* the theory that existence is a single principle; *monism*.

henotic (hĕn-ŏ'tĭk) *adj.* harmonizing.

hent (hĕnt) *v.t.* 1. to seize, carry away. 2. to experience. 3. to reach. *-n.* a grab; that which is grabbed.

hepaticocholangiocholecysten-terostomy (hē-păt″ĭ-kō-lăn″jē-ō-kō″lə-sĭs″tən-tĕr-ŏs'tə-mē) *n.* surgically created link between the gall bladder and hepatic duct, and between the intestine and gall bladder. also *hepaticochole-cystostcholecystenterostomy.*

heredipety (hĕr-ə-dĭp'ĭ-tē) *n.* legacy hunting; trying to cadge an inheritance.

hereism (hĭr'ē-ĭz″əm) *n.* faithfulness in marriage.

heresiarch (hĕr'ĭ-sĭ-ärk″) *n.* the leader of a heretical sect.

heresiography (hĕr″ĭ-sĭ-ŏg'rə-fē) *n.* a treatise on heresy. *heresiographer, n.*

hermeneutics (hûr-mə-nū'tĭks) *n.* 1. Bible interpretation. 2. the study of interpretation. *hermenutic, adj.* interpretative.

herzog (hĕrts'ōh) *n.* a high-ranking German or Austrian noble (before 1919).

hesperian (hĕs-pĭr'ĭ-ən) *adj.* 1. western, occidental. 2. pertaining to *Hesperia,* a name given by the Greeks to Italy and by the Romans to Spain. 3. pertaining to the *Hesperides:* (a) nymphs who guarded the golden apples Gaea gave to Hera; (b) the western garden producing the apples. 4. pertaining to the *Hesperiidae,* or skipper butterflies.

hesternal (hĕs-tûr'nəl) *adj.* pertaining to yesterday.

hesternopothia (hĕs-tûr″nō-pŏth'ĭ-ə) *n.* a pathologic yearning for the good old days.

hesychastic (hĕs-ĭ-kăs'tĭk) *adj.* 1. soothing, calming, as some ancient Greek music. 2. pertaining to the *Hesychasts,* fourteenth-century Eastern mystics who contemplated their navels, seeing therein the Divine Light.

hetaerism (hē-tĭr'ĭz″əm) *n.* extra-marital sex; communal marriage.

heterize (hĕt'ər-īz) *v.t.* to transform. *heterization, n.*

heterochthonous (hĕt-ər-ŏk'thə-nəs) *adj.* foreign, opposite of *autochthonous.*

heteroclite (hĕt'ər-ō-klīt″) *adj.* irregular, unorthodox, abnormal. *-n.* 1. irregular, as verbs, declensions, etc. 2. any thing or person deviating from the common rule.

heteronym (hĕt'ər-ō-nĭm″) *n.* a word spelled like another, but differing in meaning and sound.

heterophemy (hĕt'ər-ō-fē″mē) *n.* Freudian slipsism.

heterotelic (hĕt″ər-ō-tĕl'ĭk) *adj.* existing for an outside or extraneous purpose.

heuristic (hū-rĭs'tĭk) *adj.* 1. helping to learn; encouraging further investigation. 2. pertaining to a certain teaching method which encourages students to learn for themselves.

hiant (hī'ənt) *adj.* gaping. *hiate* (hī'āt) *v.i.* to gape; to cause a hiatus.

hibernaculum (hī-bər-năk'ū-lŭm) *n.* 1. the dormant part of a plant. 2. protective covering during winter. 3. winter quarters; *hibernacle.* 4. the epiphragm of a snail.

hibernicism (hī-bûr'nĭ-sĭz″əm) *n.* the quality of being Irish; an Irish trait or custom.

hidrotic (hĭd-rŏt'ĭk) *adj.* causing sweating. *n.* a medicine that induces sweating; a diaphoretic or a sudorific.

hield (hēld) *v.i.* 1. to incline, to be favorable. 2. to decline or droop. 3. to yield. 4. to turn away. -*v.t.* 1. to tip over. 2. to pour, to shed. -*n.* an incline, slope. also *heald.*

hiemal (hī′ē-məl) *adj.* pertaining to winter.

hierodule (hī′ər-ō-dūl″) *n.* a temple slave. *hierodulic, adj.*

hierofastidia (hī″ər-ō-fås-tĭd′ĭ-ə) *n.* dislike of "holy" things.

hieromachy (hī-ər-ŏm′ə-kē) *n.* a fight between men or women of the cloth.

hieromancy (hī′ər-ō-măn″sē) *n.* fortunetelling by observing and interpreting various sacrifices.

hilding (hĭl′dĭng) *adj.* mean; cowardly. -*n.* 1. a mean or cowardly person. 2. (cap.) the foster father of Fridthjof and Ingeborg.

hilo (hē′lō) *v.t.* to grow dizzy or seasick. -*n.* 1. dizziness, seasickness. 2. a small seam of ore.

hindermate (hĭn′dər-māt) *n.* a mate who is a hindrance. opposite of *helpmate.*

hinnible (hĭn′ĭ-bəl) *adj.* able to whinny.

hippiater (hĭp′ĭ-ā″tər) *n.* a horse doctor.

hippocampine (hĭp-ō-kăm′pĭn) *adj.* pertaining to sea horses.

hippocrepiform (hĭp-ō-krĕp′ĭ-fôrm) *adj.* horseshoe-shaped.

hippodamist (hĭp-ŏd′ə-mĭst) *n.* 1. a city planner (from *Hippodamus,* a fifth-century Greek architect, who planned the first city). 2. a horse tamer.

hippomaniac (hĭp-ō-mā′nĭ-ăk) *n.* a horse lover; someone who really *loves* horses.

hippometer (hĭp-ŏm′ĭ-tər) *n.* an

upright with a movable arm to measure the height of a horse.

hippopotomonstrosesquipedalian (hĭp″ō-pŏt-ə-mŏn″strō-sĕs″kwĭ-pə-dā″lĭ-ən) *adj.* pertaining to a very, very long word. see *sesquipedalian.*

hipshot (hĭp′shŏt) *adj.* having one hip lower than the other, due to a dislocation.

hipsy (hĭp′sē) *n.* a drink consisting of wine, water, and brandy.

hirci (hĭr′sē) *n.* armpit hair.

hircine (hûr′sĭn) *adj.* goatlike, especially in smell; lewd.

hircismus (hĭr-sĭz′məs) *n.* stinky armpits.

hirr (hĭr) *v.t.* to order a dog forward [to attack, round up sheep, etc.].

hirrient (hĭr′ĭ-ənt) *adj.* strongly trilled, as the letter *r.* -*n.* a strongly or harshly trilled sound.

hirsutorufous (hĭr-sōō′tər-ōō″fəs) *adj.* red-haired.

historionomer (hĭs-tôr″ĭ-ŏn′ə-mər) *n.* an expert on historical laws, principles, and phenomena.

histrion (hĭs′trĭ-ŏn) *n.* an actor.

hlonipa (hlō-nĭp′ô) *n.* constant change of vocabulary to avoid confusion among words that sound alike, especially the names of Zulu relatives and headmen.

hobberdehoy (hŏb′ər-dē-hoi″) *n.* a youth entering manhood.

hodiernal (hō-dĭ-ûr′nəl) *adj.* pertaining to today.

hodman (hŏd′mən) *n.* 1. a hod carrier. 2. a hack; assistant.

hodophobia (hō-dō-fō′bĭ-ə) *n.* fear of road travel.

hoggaster (hŏg′ås″tər) *n.* a three-year-old boar. 2. a young sheep; a hog or hogget.

hoggerel (hŏg′ər-əl) *n.* 1. vulgar songs or poetry. 2. a *hogget.* see below.

hogget (hŏg'ət) *n*. 1. a two-year-old boar. 2. a year-old sheep or colt.

Hogmanay (hŏg'mə-nā″) *n*. New Year's Eve in Scotland, when children cadge treats from neighbors.

hogo (hō'gō) *n*. a strong smell or flavor; a highly flavored dish (dialect).

hogshead (hŏgz'hĕd) *n*. 1. a large barrel containing over sixty-three gallons. 2. a measure of sixty-three gallons. 3. any large liquid measure.

hoitzitzillin (hoit-zĭt-zĭl'ən) *n*. a showy American bird.

hoker (hō'kər) *n*. scorn; derision. -*v.t. &i.* to scorn, mock.

holagogue (hŏl'ə-gŏg) *n*. a medication which removes all trace of a disease.

holarctic (hōl-ärk'tĭk) *adj*. pertaining to the arctic regions collectively.

holluschick (hŏl'ŭs-chĭk) *n*. a young male fur seal; a bachelor.

holm (hōm) *n*. 1. the *holm* oak. 2. holly. 3. the sea. 4. a small island in a river or lake (common in English place names).

holmgang (hōm'găng) *n*. a duel fought on an island.

holocryptic (hŏl-ō-krĭp'tĭk) *adj*. incapable of being deciphered without a key.

hologram (hŏl'ō-grăm) *n*. a three-dimensional image produced by two laser beams.

holograph (hŏl'ō-grăf) *n*. a personally written and signed document. also *adj*.

holophrasis (hŏl-ō-frā'sĭs) *n*. a whole phrase or idea expressed in one word. also *holophrase*. *holophrastic, adj*.

homoerotism (hō-mō-ĕr'ə-tĭz″əm)

n. homosexuality. *homoerotic, adj*.

homograph (hō'mō-grăf) *n*. a word agreeing in spelling and pronunciation with another word, but not in meaning.

homonym (hŏm'ō-nĭm) *n*. a word pronounced like another word, but spelled differently.

homophobia (hō-mō-fō'bĭ-ə) *n*. fear of sameness, of monotony.

homunculus (hō-mŭng'kū-ləs) *n*. 1. a perfectly proportioned dwarf. 2. the little man who wasn't there (psychiatry). 3. the human fetus.

hondo (hŏn'dō) *n*. a broad, deep gully or dry gulch.

honorificabilitudinitatibus (ŏn-ər-ĭf″ĭ-kà-bĭl-ĭ-tū″dĭn-ĭt-àt'ĭ-bəs) *n*. with honorablenesses (a nonsense word derived from medieval literature). this is the longest word in Shakespeare, specifically in *Love's Labour's Lost*, Act V, scene 1, but ĭt isn't Shakespeare's coinage.

hopo (hō'pō) *n*. a V-shaped hedge with a pit at the angle to trap game.

hopple (hŏp'əl) *v.t.* 1. to tie an animal's feet. 2. to hobble, entangle. -*n*. a fetter used for grazing animals, or for controlling a horse's gait (usually *pl.*).

horaphthia (hôr-ăf'thĭ-ə) *n*. a neurotic preoccupation with one's youth.

hordeaceous (hôr-dē-ā'shəs) *adj*. pertaining to barley.

horography (hôr-ŏg'rə-fē) *n*. making clocks, watches, sundials, etc.; *horologiography*.

horrent (hôr'ənt) *adj*. 1. upright; bristling. 2. expressing horror.

horripilation (hôr-ĭp-ĭ-lā'shən) *n*. 1. goose pimples. 2. a bristling of the hair.

horrisonant (hôr-ĭs'ən-ənt) *adj.* terrible-sounding.

hortative (hôr'tə-tĭv) *adj.* advisory; exhortative. *-n.* an exhortation; advice.

hortensial (hôr-tĕn'shĭ-əl) *adj.* grown in a garden; *hortensian.*

hortulan (hôr'tū-lən) *adj.* pertaining to a garden.

hospice (hŏs'pĭs) *n.* 1. an inn for travelers often run by a religious order. 2. a hostel for students, poor people, the sick, or the elderly.

hosticide (hŏs'tĭ-sīd) *n.* one who kills her enemy.

hotspur (hŏt'spûr) *n.* a hotheaded, impetuous man (from *Hotspur* in Shakespeare's *Henry V*).

houri (hoo'rē) *n.* a perpetually young and beautiful virgin of the Mohammedan paradise.

housage (hou'zəj) *n.* storage; storage fee.

housel (hou'zəl) *n.* the giving or receiving of the Eucharist. *-v.t.* to give the Eucharist.

Hreidmar (hrād'môr) *n.* (of *Volsunga Saga* fame) he demanded, and got, wergild from the gods for killing his son, Otter, but was then dispatched by his other son, Fafnir.

Hrimthursar (hrĭm'thûr"sòr) *n.* the frost-giant who lived under the roots of Ygdrasil (Norse mythology).

hubristic (hū-brĭs'tĭk) *adj.* insolent; contemptuous.

hui (hwā) *n.* 1. a secret society (China). 2. a partnership (Hawaii). 3. a purposeful gathering of people, like the old town meeting (New Zealand).

humdudgeon (hŭm-dŭj'ən) *n.* an imaginary illness or pain; a loud complaint about nothing. also

humdurgeon.

humectant (hū-mĕk'tənt) *adj.* retaining moisture. *-n.* a moistening agent.

humhum (hŭm'hŭm) *n.* a rough Indian cotton cloth (like those used in *hammams,* or Turkish baths).

humicubation (hū-mĭk"ū-bā'shən) *n.* lying on the ground in penitence.

humstrum (hŭm'strŭm) *n.* a second-rate or defective musical instrument.

humuhumunukunukuapuaa (hoo"moo-hoo-moo-noo"koo-noo-koo-ò-poo'ò-ò) *n.* a small tropical Hawaiian fish.

hunkerousness (hŭnk'ə-ùs-nĕs") *n.* opposition to progress; old-fogyism.

hurley-hacket (hûr'lē-hăk"ət) *n.* 1. sledding down a hill. 2. a wobbly horse-drawn carriage.

hurst (hûrst) *n.* a grove or sandbank, used often in place names.

hushion (hŭsh'ən) *n.* 1. a stocking without a foot. 2. a useless creature.

hussif (hŭs'ĭf) *n.* a housewife; a hussy.

hustlerati (hŭs-lər-òt'ē) *n.* a mercenary racist writer (slang).

huttoning (hŭt'ən-ĭng) *n.* manipulation of a dislocated or stiff joint (after Richard and Robert *Hutton,* two English bonesetters).

hwyl (hū'əl) *n.* an emotional outburst of eloquence (Welsh).

hyaline (hī'ə-lĭn) *n.* 1. the sea or atmosphere when smooth, clear, or transparent. 2. the main constituent of the walls of hydatid cysts.

hydrodynamic (hī"drō-dī-năm'ĭk) *adj.* pertaining to water power.

hydrography (hī-drŏg'rə-fē) *n.* 1.

the study of seas, lakes, and rivers. 2. surveying the bottom of a harbor.

hydromancy (hī'drō-măn"sē) n. fortunetelling by observing the tide.

hydromel (hī'drō-mĕl) n. 1. mead. 2. a laxative of honey and water.

hydrophanous (hī-drŏf'ən-əs) adj. made transparent by wetting.

hydrophobophobia (hī"drō-fō-bō-fō'bĭ-ə) n. fear of hydrophobia.

hydroponics (hī-drō-pŏn'ĭks) n. chemically grown plants.

hyetal (hī'ĭ-təl) adj. pertaining to rain; rainy.

hygeiolatry (hī-jē-ŏl'ə-trē) n. health fanaticism.

hygiology (hī-jĭ-ŏl'ə-jē) n. the science of hygiene.

hygrophobia (hī-grō-fō'bĭ-ə) n. fear of liquids.

hylic (hī'lĭk) adj. pertaining to matter; material. *hylism*, n. materialism, especially of the Ionian philosophers.

hylogenesis (hī-lō-jĕn'ə-sĭs) n. the genesis of matter; *hylogeny*.

hymnography (hĭm-nŏg'rə-fē) n. composing and writing hymns.

hypaethral (hĭp-ēth'rəl) adj. open to the sky; not roofed over (architecture).

hypengyophobia (hī-pĕn"jĭ-ō-fō'bĭ-ə) n. fear of responsibility.

hyper (hī'pər) v.i. to be active or busy.

hyperborean (hī-pər-bôr'ē-ən) adj. 1. northern; very cold. 2. pertaining to the *Hyperboreans*, Apollo cultists of the Far North. 3. any arctic peoples, especially the tribes of northeastern Asia and Alaska.

hyperdulia (hī-pər-dū'lĭ-ə) n. mariolatry.

hyperhedonia (hī"pər-hē-dō'nĭ-ə)
n. abnormal pleasure from doing ho-hum things.

hypermimia (hī-pər-mĭm'ĭ-ə) n. excessive gesticulating while talking.

hypermnesia (hī-pûrm-nē'zĭ-ə) n. unusually sharp memory.

hyperthermalgesia (hī"pər-thûr-məl-jē'zĭ-ə) n. abnormally increased sensitivity to heat.

hypertridimensional (hī"pər-trī-dĭm-ĕn'shən-əl) adj. having more than three dimensions.

hypnomogia (hĭp-nō-mō'jĭ-ə) n. insomnia.

hypnopompic (hĭp-nō-pŏm'pĭk) adj. pertaining to hallucinations occurring immediately after waking (or somnolent state) and persisting until the wide-awake state.

hypobulia (hī-pō-bū'lĭ-ə) n. difficulty in making decisions.

hypogeal (hī-pō-jē'əl) adj. 1. underground construction. 2. pertaining to living or occurring underground; subterranean.

hypogeiody (hī-pō-jī'ə-dē) n. underground surveying, as of mines.

hypomnematic (hĭp"ŏm-nə-măt'ĭk) adj. consisting of notes or memoranda.

hypophobia (hī-pō-fō'bĭ-ə) n. lack of fear; *pantaphobia*.

hyporchema (hĭp-ôr-kē'mə) n. a happy song and dance in honor of Apollo or Dionysus.

hypostasis (hī-pŏs'tə-sĭs) n. 1. foundation, groundwork; essence. 2. sediment. 3. the suppressing action of one gene over another (genetics). 4. resulting from downward pressure (pathology).

hystricine (hĭs'trĭ-sīn) adj. pertaining to porcupines.

I

iatramelia (ī-ăt″rə-mē′lĭ-ə) *n.* medical negligence.

iatrapistia (ī-ăt″rə-pĭs′tĭ-ə) *n.* lack of faith in doctors or medicine.

iatrogenic (ī-ăt″rō-jĕn′ĭk) *adj.* illness or disease caused by doctors; resulting from prescribed treatment.

iatrology (ī″ə-trŏl′ə-jē) *n.* the science of healing, or a treatise on it. *iatreusiology* (ī″ə-trōō-sē-ŏl′ə-jē) *n.* therapeutics.

iatromisia (ī-ăt″rō-mē′zĭ-ə) *n.* dislike of doctors.

icarian (ī-kĕr′ĭ-ən) *adj.* pertaining to Icarus; hazardous.

ichneutic (ĭk-nū′tĭk) *adj.* pertaining to tracking or trailing.

ichnogram (ĭk′nō-grăm) *n.* a footprint.

ichor (ī′kôr) *n.* 1. the fluid coursing through the veins of Greek gods. 2. a watery discharge from a wound, or from the temples of a musk elephant. 3. a mineral-rich magma.

ichthyomancy (ĭk′thē-ō-măn″sē) *n.* fortunetelling with fish offal.

icker (ĭk′ər) *n.* an ear of corn (Scottish).

iconolagny (ī-kòn′ō-làg″nē) *n.* sexual stimulation from pictures or statues.

icosahedron (ī″kō-sə-hē′drən) *n.* a twenty-sided solid.

icosian (ī-kō′sĭ-ən) *adj.* of or relating to twenty.

ictic (ĭk′tĭk) *adj.* 1. caused by a blow; abrupt. 2. pertaining to metrical stress.

iddat (ĭ-dòt′) *n.* a period of three to four months in which a Moslem widow or divorcée may not remarry.

ideation (ī-dē-ā′shən) *n.* the process of forming ideas.

ideogenous (ĭd-ē-ŏj′ə-nəs) *adj.* mental in origin.

ideogram (ĭd′ē-ō-grăm) *n.* a pictorial symbol representing an idea rather than a word.

idiograph (ĭd′ē-ō-grăf″) *n.* a trademark.

idiolalia (ĭd″ĭ-ō-lā′lĭ-ə) *n.* mental state characterized by use of invented language.

ideoplastia (ĭd″ē-ō-plàs′tĭ-ə) *n.* hypnotically suggestive.

ideopraxist (ĭd″ē-ō-pràks″ĭst) *n.* one who puts ideas into practice.

---

màn; māde; lĕt; bē; sĭp; wīne; hòt; cōld; sôre; dŭll; fūgue; bûrp; gōōd; fōōd; out; gĕt; thin; this; year; aźure; ō′mən″; viN; fūr; Bach

Idioticon (ĭd-ē-ŏt'ĭ-kŏn) *n.* a dialect dictionary.

Idoneous (ī-dō'nē-əs) *adj.* apt; suitable.

iele (ē'ā-ē"ā) *n.* the Hawaiian screw pine.

ignavia (ĭg-nā'vĭ-ə) *n.* idleness, laziness.

igneous (ĭg'nē-əs) *adj.* 1. pertaining to fire. 2. produced by underground heat.

ignescent (ĭg-nĕs'ənt) *adj.* producing sparks; scintillating. *-n.* an *ignescent* substance.

ignipotent (ĭg-nĭp'ō-tənt) *adj.* having power over fire.

ignivomous (ĭg-nĭv'ō-məs) *adj.* vomiting fire.

ignoscency (ĭg-nŏs'ən-sē) *n.* forgiveness; a forgiving nature.

ihram (ē-rŏm') *n.* 1. the sacred robes of Moslem pilgrims. 2. the pilgrim's holy state while wearing these robes.

iiwi (ē-ē'wē) *n.* a Hawaiian bird whose brilliant red feathers were used for regal capes.

illachrymable (ĭl-ăk'rĭ-mə-bəl) *adj.* unable to cry.

illaqueate (ĭl-ăk'wē-āt) *v.t.* to catch or trap.

illation (ĭl-ā'shən) *n.* inferring; inference or conclusion.

illicitator (ĭl-ĭs'ĭ-tā"tər) *n.* an auctioneer's shill.

illinition (ĭl-ĭ-nĭsh'ən) *n.* 1. rubbing with liniment. 2. treatment of metals with corrosives; the crust produced by so doing.

illision (ĭl-ĭzh'ən) *n.* striking against something.

illth (ĭlth) *n.* being poor or miserable, the opposite of wealth.

illuminati (ĭl-ōōm"ĭn-ŏ'tē) *n.pl.* 1. the newly baptized. 2. members of a secret rationalist anticlerical sect founded by Adam

Weishaupt, professor of canon law at Ingolstadt. 3. people who claim exceptional spiritual or intellectual insight: sometimes used satirically.

illutation (ĭl-ū-tā'shən) *n.* a mud bath.

imagism (ĭm'ə-jĭz"əm) *n.* early twentieth-century free-verse style stressing clarity and simplicity, and favoring everyday speech and rhythm.

imago (ĭm-ā'gō) *n.* 1. a wax portrait like those carried in Roman funeral processions. 2. a mature insect. 3. unconsciously retained childhood fantasies involving parents.

imam (ĭm-ŏm') *n.* 1. Mohammedan priest who leads the service. 2. a caliph or other prince. 3. any theological or legal authority.

imaret (ĭm-ŏr'ĕt)*-n.* a Turkish inn or hostel.

imbibition (ĭm-bĭ-bĭ'shən) *n.* absorption, saturation, steeping.

imbonity (ĭm-bŏn'ĭ-tē) *n.* lack of good qualities.

imbosk (ĭm-bŏsk') *v.t.&i.* to hide, conceal.

imbrication (ĭm-brĭ-kā'shən) *n.* 1. an overlapping, like shingles or fish scales. 2. a design resembling this. *imbricated, adj.*

immarcescible (ĭm"ŏr-sĕs'ĭ-bəl) *adj.* indestructible.

immerd (ĭm-ûrd') *v.t.* to cover with excrement.

immiscible (ĭm-ĭs'ĭ-bəl) *n.* things that cannot be mixed (oil and water, for example).

immorigerous (ĭm"ŏr-ĭj'ər-əs) *adj.* rude, boorish.

immund (ĭm-ŭnd') *adj.* filthy, dirty; filthy dirty.

impanation (ĭm-pā-nā'shən) *n.* cannibalistic doctrine of baking

Christ into the Eucharistic cookie.

imparl (ĭm-pörl′) *v.i.* to confer with opposing counsel prior to out-of-court settlement (law).

impavid (ĭm-pă′vĭd) *adj.* fearless.

impeccant (ĭm-pĕk′ənt) *adj.* sinless.

imperdible (ĭm-pûr′dĭ-bəl) *adj.* incapable of being lost.

impetrate (ĭm′pə-trāt) *v.t.* to get by pleading; to entreat.

impi (ĭm′pē) *n.pl.* Kaffir warriors of South Africa.

impignorate (ĭm-pĭg′nə-rāt) *adj.* to put up as security; pawn, mortgage.

impinguate (ĭm-pĭng′gwāt) *v.t.* to fatten.

implex (ĭm′plĕks) *adj.* involved, intricate, complex.

impofo (ĭm-pŏ′fō) *n.* the eland.

imprest (ĭm-prĕst′) *v.t.* to lend money. *-adj.* lent. *-n.* 1. a loan. 2. salary advance to the military.

imprimatur (ĭm-prĭ-mā′tər) *n.* 1. a license to publish. 2. approval by censors. 3. general approval.

improbity (ĭm-prŏ′bĭ-tē) *n.* immorality; crookedness.

improcreant (ĭm-prŏ′krē-ənt) *adj.* impotent.

improlificate (ĭm-prŏ-lĭf′ĭ-kāt) *v.t.* to impregnate.

improvvisatore (ĭm″prō-vēz-ō-tôr′ä) *n.* one who recites her own improvised poetry.

impuberal (ĭm-pū′bər-əl) *adj.* not having reached puberty.

impudicity (ĭm-pū-dĭs′ĭ-tē) *n.* immodesty.

imsonic (ĭm-sŏn′ĭk) *adj.* onomatopoeic.

imu (ē′mōō) *n.* a baking pit dug in the Hawaiian sand.

inaniloquent (ĭn-ăn-ĭl′ō-kwənt) *adj.* loquacious, windy, garrulous. also *inaniloquous.*

inaurate (ĭn-ôr′āt) *adj.* gilded. *-v.t.* to gild.

inby (ĭn′bī) *adv.* inwardly, within. *-adj.* nearby, beside. *-prep.* beside. *-n.* an inner room (all Scottish).

incalescent (ĭn-kăl-ĕs′ənt) *adj.* becoming warmer.

incameration (ĭn-kăm″ər-ā′shən) *n.* addition to papal property.

incarn (ĭn-kärn′) *v.t.&i.* to heal over, as skin.

incarnadine (ĭn-kär′nə-dīn) *adj.* pertaining to blood red or crimson. *-n.* an *incarnadine* color. *-v.t.* to dye *incarnadine.*

incatenate (ĭn-kăt′ən-āt) *v.t.* to restrain with chains; to fetter.

inchling (ĭnch′lĭng) *n.* a small living thing that will grow larger.

inchoate (ĭn′kō-āt) *v.t.&i.* to begin, start, initiate.

incicurable (ĭn-sĭk′ū-rə-bəl) *adj.* untamable.

inconcinnity (ĭn-kŏn-sĭn′ĭ-tē) *n.* unsuitableness; ineptitude.

incondite (ĭn-kŏn′dĭt) *adj.* crude, unfinished.

incrassate (ĭn-krăs′āt) *adj.* thickened. *-v.t.&i.* to thicken. see *inspissate.*

increpation (ĭn-krə-pā′shən) *n.* criticism, censure.

incruental (ĭn-krōō-ĕn′təl) *adj.* bloodless.

incubus (ĭn′kū-bŭs) *n.* 1. an imaginary devil who rapes sleeping women. 2. something that oppresses or worries one, as a nightmare. 3. a nightmare.

inculpate (ĭn′kŭl-pāt) *v.t.&i.* to blame, accuse, incriminate.

incunabula (ĭn-kū-năb′ū-lə) *n.pl.* 1. extant books printed before 1500 A.D. 2. early stages of anything.

incuse (ĭn-kūz′) *adj.* stamped. *-n.* relief design on the head produced by stamping a coin on the tail. -*v.t.* to stamp [a coin].

indaba (ĭn-dò'bò) *n.* a native South African conference.

indehiscent (ĭn-dē-hĭs'ənt) *adj.* staying closed at maturity.

indign (ĭn-dīn') *adj.* unbecoming; undignified; disgraceful.

indite (ĭn-dīt') *v.t.* to write literarily; to describe or inscribe.

indocible (ĭn-dòs'ĭ-bəl) *adj.* unteachable.

inductile (ĭn-dŭk'tĭl) *adj.* unyielding, inflexible.

indurate (ĭn'dū-rāt) *v.t.* 1. to harden. 2. to inure; make stubborn. -*v.i.* to harden.

ineluctable (ĭn-ē-lŭk'tə-bəl) *adj.* inevitable; irresistible.

inenarrable (ĭn-ē-nàr'ə-bəl) *adj.* indescribable.

inermous (ĭn-ûr'məs) *adj.* without thorns or prickles, as some leaves.

inexpugnable (ĭn-ĕks-pŭg'nə-bəl) *adj.* incapable of being overthrown.

inexsuperable (ĭn-ĕks-ū'pûr-ə-bəl) *adj.* insurmountable, impassable.

infandous (ĭn-făn'dəs) *adj.* too horrible to mention; unspeakably awful.

infangthief (ĭn'făng-thēf) *n.* the right of a feudal lord to punish thieves.

infare (ĭn'fĕr) *n.* 1. a housewarming given by a recently married couple. 2. an entrance.

infaust (ĭn-fôst') *adj.* unlucky. *infausting, n.* making unlucky.

infibulation (ĭn-fĭb"ū-lā'shən) *n.* sewing up the vulva or sewing down the foreskin to prevent sexual intercourse.

inficete (ĭn-fĭ-sēt') *adj.* dull, unfunny, deadly serious, humorless.

infracaninophile (ĭn"frə-kə-nĭn'ŏ-fĭl) *n.* champion of the underdog (Christopher Morley in preface to the *Complete Sherlock Holmes*, 1930).

infralapsarianism (ĭn"frə-làp-sèr'ĭ-ən-ĭz"əm) *n.* Calvinist doctrine of crime and punishment after the Fall.

infrapose (ĭn-frə-pōz') *v.t.* to place beneath.

infucation (ĭn-fū-kā'shən) *n.* putting on make-up.

infumate (ĭn'fū-māt) *v.t.* to smoke, as sturgeon.

infundibular (ĭn-fŭn-dĭb'ū-lər) *adj.* shaped like a funnel.

ing (ĭng) *n.* a low-lying pasture.

ingannation (ĭn-gän-ā'shən) *n.* deception; fraud.

ingerence (ĭn'jər-əns) *n.* interference.

ingestar (ĭn-gès'tòr) *n.* a large seventeenth-century decanter.

ingle (ĭng'gəl) *n.* 1. a fire or fireplace. 2. an angle. 3. a homosexual boy-in-residence. -*v.t.* to fondle; cajole.

ingluvious (ĭn-glōō'vĭ-əs) *adj.* gluttonous.

ingravidate (ĭn-gràv'ĭ-dāt) *v.t.* to impregnate.

ingustable (ĭn-gŭs'tə-bəl) *adj.* tasteless.

inlagary (ĭn-làg'ə-rē) *n.* legal restitution of criminals.

inlapidate (ĭn-làp'ĭ-dāt) *v.t.* to petrify.

innascible (ĭn-às'ĭ-bəl) *adj.* without a beginning.

innubilous (ĭn-ū'bĭl-əs) *adj.* cloudless; clear.

in petto (ĭn pĕt'ŏ) *adj.* in the breast; figuratively: not yet made public.

inquinate (ĭn'kwĭ-nāt) *v.t.* to corrupt.

insalubrious (ĭn-sə-lōō'brĭ-əs) *adj.*

unhealthy, deleterious.

insanable (ĭn-sàn′ə-bəl) *adj.* incurable.

insapory (ĭn-sàp′ə-rē) *adj.* tasteless.

insclent (ĭn′shənt) *adj.* having insight.

insecable (ĭn-sĕk′ə-bəl) *adj.* that cannot be cut with a knife; indivisible.

insigne (ĭn-sīn′) *adj.* 1. distinguished. 2. singular of *insignia*.

insolate (ĭn′sō-lāt) *v.t.* to expose to sunlight.

inspissate (ĭn-spĭs′āt) *v.t.&i.* to thicken; *incrassate*.

instauration (ĭn-stôr-ā′shən) *n.* 1. restoration, renovation. 2. inaugurating something.

insuetude (ĭn′swē-tūd) *n.* state of disuse.

insulse (ĭn-sŭls′) *adj.* tasteless, flat, insipid.

insusurration (ĭn-sōō′sər-ā′shən) *n.* whispering in the ear; insinuation.

intactible (ĭn-tăk′tĭ-bəl) *adj.* imperceptible to the touch.

intaglio (ĭn-tăl′yō) *n.* opposite of bás-relief or cameo; a hollowed-out design used for producing relief work.

integument (ĭn-tĕg′ū-mənt) *n.* an outer covering.

intemerate (ĭn-tĕm′ər-āt) *adj.* 100 percent pure.

intempestive (ĭn-tĕm-pĕs′tĭv) *adj.* untimely; inopportune.

intenerate (ĭn-tĕn′ər-āt) *v.t.* to soften, sensitize.

interamnian (ĭn-tər-ăm′nĭ-ən) *adj.* between rivers.

interaulic (ĭn-tər-ôl′ĭk) *adj.* existing only between two royal households.

intercalate (ĭn-tûr′kə-lāt) *v.t.* 1. add a day, week, etc., to the calendar. 2. to interpolate.

intercolumniation (ĭn″tər-kō-lŭm″nĭ-ā′shən) *n.* 1. space between two columns. 2. system of measuring space between columns.

interdigitate (ĭn-tər-dĭj′ĭ-tāt) *v.t.&i.* to interlace the fingers.

interfenestration (ĭn″tər-fĕn-əs-trā′shən) *n.* 1. space between two windows. 2. placing windows.

intergern (ĭn-tər-gûrn′) *v.i.* to snarl back.

interlacustrine (ĭn″tər-lă-kŭs′trĭn) *adj.* between lakes.

interlucation (ĭn″tər-lōō-kā′shən) *n.* thinning out trees in a forest to let in some light.

intermundane (ĭn″tər-mŭn-dān′) *adj.* existing between stars or planets.

internecion (ĭn-tər-nē′shən) *n.* mutual destruction.

internuncio (ĭn-tər-nŭn′shĭ-ō) *n.* 1. a low-ranking papal nuncio. 2. a messenger.

interpellation (ĭn″tər-pə-lā′-shən) *n.* demanding explanation of a government official's act or policy.

intersidereal (ĭn″tər-sĭ-dĭr′ĭ-əl) *adj.* interstellar.

intersilient (ĭn-tər-sĭl′ĭ-ənt) *adj.* suddenly emerging in the midst of something.

intertessellation (ĭn″tər-tĕs-əl-ā′shən) *n.* an intricate design, as mosaic.

introjection (ĭn-trō-jĕk′shən) *n.* 1. throwing oneself into one's work. 2. the theory that perceived objects are merely copies.

intromission (ĭn-trō-mĭ′shən) *n.* 1. inserting the penis into the vagina. 2. general insertion or admission. 3. legal or illegal meddling.

---

măn; māde; lĕt; bē; sĭp; wīne; hŏt; cōld; sôre; dŭll; fūgue; bûrp; gōōd; fōōd; out; gĕt; thin; this; year; ażure; ō′mən″; viN; für; Bach

intumulate (ĭn-tōōm'ū-lāt) v.t. to
bury.

inturgescence (ĭn-tûr-jĕs'əns) n.
swelling up.

intussusception (ĭn"tŭs-ə-
sĕp'shən) n. a taking within; invagination.

inumbrate (ĭn-ŭm'brāt) v.t. to
shade.

inusitate (ĭn-ū'zĭ-tāt) adj. obsolete.

inustion (ĭn-ŭs'chən) n. burning;
cauterization.

invaginate (ĭn-vàj'ĭn-āt) v.t. 1. to
put into a sheath (in + vagina) 2.
to fold back within itself. -v.i. to
make a pocket by turning in. -adj.
turned back upon itself; sheathed.
invagination, n. see intussusception.

invalescence (ĭn-vàl-ĕs'əns) n.
being an invalid.

invaletudinary (ĭn-vàl"ə-tōō'dĭn-
ĕr"ē) adj. unhealthy.

invultuation (ĭn-vŭl"tū-ā'shən) n.
wishing death or injury on by
melting a wax image, or sticking
it with pins.

iophobia (ī-ō-fō'bĭ-ə) n. fear of
being poisoned.

ipsedixitism (ĭp-sē-dĭks'ĭt-ĭz"əm)
n. dogmatism (Latin ipse dixit =
he himself said so).

ipseity (ĭp-sē'ĭ-tē) n. individuality.

ipsism (ĭp'sĭz"əm) n. masturbation.

iracund (ī'rə-kŭnd) adj. easily
provoked, quick-tempered,
irascible.

irpe (ûr'pē) adj. a grimace or bodily
contortion. also irp.

irrefragable (ĭr-ĕf'rə-gə-bəl) adj.
undeniable; indestructible, unyielding or stubborn.

irrefangible (ĭr-ə-frăn'jĭ-bəl) adj.
unbreakable.

irreptitious (ĭr-ĕp-tĭsh'əs) adj.
creeping stealthily.

irrorate (ĭr'ō-rāt) v.t. speckled,
dotted with color, colored with
dots.

irrugate (ĭr'ū-gāt) v.t. to wrinkle.

irrumation (ĭr-ōō-mā'shən) n.
fellatio.

isacoustic (ī-sə-kōōs'tĭk) adj. pertaining to equal intensity of
sound.

iscariotic (ĭs-kà"rī-ŏt'ĭk) adj.
traitorous (from Judas Iscariot).

ischidrosis (ĭs-kĭ-drō'sĭs) n. stopping sweat.

isochronous (ī-sŏk'rō-nəs) adj.
pertaining to equal time;
recurring regularly.

isochrous (ī-sŏk'rō-əs) adj. of uniform color.

isocracy (ī-sŏk'rə-sē) n. government where all have equal
political power.

isogenous (ī-sòj'ən-əs) adj. having
a common origin.

isonomy (ī-sòn'ə-mē) n. equal
rights; isopolity.

iter (ī'tər) n. 1. a Roman road. 2.
the Aqueduct of Sylvius.

ithyphallic (ĭth-ĭ-făl'ĭk) adj. pertaining to the phallus carried in
Bacchanalian festivals; lewd.

itinerate (ī-tĭn'ər-āt) v.i. to go on a
concert or lecture tour.

iwis (ĭ-wĭs') adj. certainly; by all
means (archaic).

izles (ī'zəlz) n.pl. specks of soot;
sparks.

izzat (ĭz'àt) n. honor, dignity,
prestige.

---

màn; māde; lĕt; bē; sĭp; wīne; hŏt; cōld; sôre; dŭll; fūgue; bûrp;
gōod; fōōd; out; gĕt; thin; thĭs; year; ażure; ō'mən"; viN; fūr; Bach

J

jaboff (jăb′ôf) *n.* an injection of any narcotic (slang).

jacal (hŏ-kŏl′) *n.* a house of woven wood and wicker, plastered on one or more sides.

jacent (jā′sənt) *adj.* recumbent.

jacinthe (jā′sĭnth) *n.* a brilliant reddish-yellow.

jackeroo (jăk-ər-ōō′) *n.* a green-horn on a sheep ranch (Australia).

jactancy (jăk′tən-sē) *n.* boasting, bragging.

jactitation (jăk-tĭ-tā′shən) *n.* 1. loud or public bragging. 2. a false claim (law). 3. excessive twitching and restlessness.

jaculative (jăk′ū-lā″tĭv) *adj.* darting, sporadic.

j'adoube (zà-dōōb′) I adjust: said when adjusting but not moving a chess piece (French).

jadu (jŏ-dōō′) *n.* magic or fortune-telling (Hindu and Persian).

jama (jŏ′mə) *n.* a long Indian cotton gown.

jambeau (jăm′bō) *n.* a piece of leg armor.

jambee (jăm-bē′) *n.* an East Indian rattan cane or the tree from which it is made.

jambone (jăm′bōn) *n.* a cards-up hand in railroad euchre.

jamdani (jŏm-dŏn′ē) *n.* a flower-patterned muslin.

jami (jŏ′mē) *n.* the main mosque (Turkey).

jampan (jăm′păn) *n.* an Indian sedan chair manned by four bearers.

janfu (jăn′fōō) *adj.* Joint Army and Navy Fuck-Up. see *snafu* for more of the same (slang).

janiceps (jăn′ĭ-sèps) *n.* a two-headed monster facing opposite directions.

jannock (jăn′ək) *n.* leavened oatmeal bread (British dialect).

japan (jà-păn′) *v.t.* 1. to varnish or lacquer. 2. to ordain [a minister].

jararacussu (jŏ-rŏ″rə-kōō′sōō) *n.* the venomous Brazilian pit viper.

jarbird (jŏr′bûrd) *n.* the nuthatch.

jarble (jŏr′bəl) *v.t.* to wet; dirty.

jargogle (jŏr′gŏ″gəl) *v.t.* to befuddle; mess up.

jarkmen (jŏrk′mèn) *n.pl.* those who forge official papers.

jar-owl (jŏr′oul) *n.* the European goatsucker.

---

jasey (jā'sē) *n.* a wig of or like Jersey yarn (British dialect).

Jataka (jŏ'tə-kə) *n.* stories about former incarnations of Buddha.

jauk (jôk) *v.i.* to trifle or toy with (Scottish).

javel (jăv'əl) *n.* a tramp or beggar.

jawab (jŏ-wŏb') *n.* a building built to match or balance another.

jazerant (jăz'ər-ənt) *n.* armor made of overlapping metal pieces, like fish scales.

jecoral (jĕk'ôr-əl) *adj.* pertaining to the liver.

jeff (jĕf) *n.* printers' dice game using pieces of type metal. *-v.i.* to gamble playing this game.

jehu (jē'hū) *v.t.&i.* to drive. *-n.* someone who loves driving; a fast driver (from *Jehu*, a fast-driving Israeli king).

jejunator (jē-jŏō-nā'tər) *n.* one who fasts.

jejune (jə-jŏōn') *adj.* insubstantial; weak, dull.

jejunojejunostomy (jē-jŏōn"ō-jē-jŏōn-ŏs'tə-mē) *n.* surgical connection between two loops of the jejunum.

jelab (jə-lŏb') *n.* a hooded jacket of North Africa.

Jemimaite (jə-mī'mə-īt) *n.* a woman who dresses as a man and opposes marriage (from *Jemima Wilkinson*, an eighteenth-century Rhode Island Quaker).

jenna (jĕn'ə) *n.* the Mohammedan paradise.

jennerize (jĕn'ər-īz) *v.t.* to vaccinate, or otherwise immunize (from *Edward Jenner*, discoverer of vaccination).

jennet (jĕn'ət) *n.* 1. a small Spanish horse. 2. a female ass.

jentacular (jĕn-tăk'ū-lər) *adj.* pertaining to breakfast.

jeofail (jĕf'āl) *n.* a lawyer's mistake and his acknowledgment of it to the court.

jeremiad (jĕr-ē-mī"əd) *n.* a woeful tirade; lament: often used sarcastically (from the Lamentations of *Jeremiah* in the Old Testament).

jerque (jûrk) *v.t.* to search for smuggled goods.

jerrican (jĕr'ĭ-kăn) *n.* a five-gallon jug.

jeziah (jĕz'yŏ) *n.* a tax levied on non-Moslems.

jheel (jēl) *n.* a rain puddle.

jhool (jŏōl) *n.* horse or elephant trappings in India.

jicara (hē'kŏ-rŏ) *n.* the calabash tree, or a bowl made from its gourd.

jigamaree (jĭg"ə-mə-rē') *n.* thingamajig: a word used for lack of a more specific one.

jihad (jē-hŏd') *n.* a Mohammedan religious war. also *jehad*.

jimberjaw (jĭm'bər-jô) *n.* a jutting chin (U.S. colloquial).

jimpricute (jĭm'prī-kūt) *adj.* well-dressed; fashionable (slang).

jingbang (jĭng'băng) *n.* crowd; she-bang.

jinnywink (jĭn'ē-wĭnk) *n.* a small derrick.

jipijapa (hē-pē-hŏ'pŏ) *n.* a palm-like plant whose leaves are used for Panama hats.

jism (jĭz'əm) *n.* 1. semen. 2. pep or vigor (slang).

jiti (jē'tē) *n.* the Rajmahal creeper.

jitneur (jĭt'nûr) *n.* a male jitney driver.

jitqazzizx (jĭt'kăz"ĭks) he does not mind; he does not feel any revulsion (Maltese).

jiva (jē'və) *n.* vital life force (Hinduism).

jivatma (jē-vŏt'mə) *n.* the individual self, spirit, or ego

(Sanskrit).

jnanendriya (jnŏ-nĕn′drē-ŏ) *n.* a sense organ (Sanskrit).

jobation (jō-bā′shən) *n.* tedious criticism.

jobbernowl (jŏb′ər-nōl) *n.* a blockhead (British colloquial).

jobmonger (jŏb′mùng″gər) *n.* one who manages corrupt jobs.

jocker (jŏk′ər) *n.* a male homosexual.

jocoque (hō-kō′kā) *n.* buttermilk (southwestern U.S.).

jocoserious (jō-kō-sĭr′ē-əs) *adj.* a combination of funny and serious.

johnboat (jŏn′bōt) *n.* a narrow flatbottomed boat usually propelled by a pole: used on inland waterways.

joinhand (join′hănd) *n.* cursive writing (obs.).

jojoba (hō-hō′bŏ) *n.* a small tree with oil-bearing seeds (southwestern U.S.).

jokul (yō′kōōl) *n.* a snow-covered mountain in Iceland.

jollop (jŏl′əp) *n.* a fowl's wattle.

jookerie (jōōk′ər-ē) *n.* trickery; swindling (Scottish).

joola (jōōl′ŏ) *n.* a Himalayan rope suspension bridge.

joom (jōōm) *n.* burning a forest, cultivating the land, and then abandoning it; the land so used.

jornada (hôr-nŏ′dŏ) *n.* 1. a full day's travel with no stops. 2. amount of land plowed in one day (southwestern U.S. and Mexico).

jorram (yōōr′əm) *n.* a Gaelic boat song.

jorum (jôr′əm) *n.* a large wine jug or bowl (colloquial).

josephinite (jō′zĕf-ĭn-īt″) *n.* a natural alloy of iron and nickel, found in stream gravel.

joss (jŏs) *n.* 1. a Chinese house god.

2. a boss. -*v.i.* to jostle.

josser (jŏs′ər) *n.* a fool, dummy, idiot (British slang).

jotation (yō-tā′shən) *n.* palatalization.

jouissance (jōō′ĭ-səns) *n.* use; enjoyment.

jouk (jōōk) *n.* 1. a trick. 2. a shelter. 3. a sudden movement. -*v.i.* to roost; sleep. -*v.t.&i.* to dodge, duck, or hide.

Ju (jōō) *n.* blue or white porcelain of the Sung dynasty (from *Ju-choco*, where it was first made). also *adj.*

jubate (jōō′bāt) *adj.* fringed with long hair, as a mane.

judex (jōō′dĕks) *n.* a legal arbitrator.

jugate (jōō′gāt) *adj.* paired; *jumelle.*

juggernaut (jŭg′ər-nôt) *n.* something huge and unrelenting that crushes everything in its path. -*v.t.* to crush under a *juggernaut.*

jugulate (jōō′gū-lāt, jŭg′) *v.t.* to cut the throat of; to strangle.

jujube (jōō′jōōb, jōō′jōō-bē) *n.* 1. edible Zizyphus fruit. 2. the Zizyphus tree. 3. jelly made from the fruit.

jumart (jōō′mŏrt) *n.* the alleged offspring of a bull and she-ass, or of a cow and he-ass.

jumelle (żōō-mĕl′) *adj.* paired; jugate.

jumentous (jōō-mĕn′təs) *adj.* 1. having a strong animal smell. 2. pertaining to the smell of horse urine.

junkettaceous (jŭnk-ə-tā′shəs) *adj.* frivolous, worthless.

jupe (żōōp) *n.* a man's shirt or jacket; a woman's blouse or skirt. also *jupon* (French *jupe* = skirt).

jural (jōōr′əl) *adj.* pertaining to law or legal obligations.

jurament (jōōr′ə-mənt) *n.* an oath.

juramentado (jōō″rŏ-mĕn-tŏ′dŏ) *n.*

a militant Moro sworn to kill someone, preferably a Christian.

jurisconsult (jûr″ĭs-kŏn-sŭlt′) *n.* a jurist; a legal expert.

jussive (jŭs′ĭv) *adj.* expressing command. -*n.* a word or mood (or tense, or case) expressing command.

justaucorps (żo͞ost-ô-kôr′) *n.s.&pl.* a seventeenth-century tight-fitting jacket (French *just* = close + *au* = to the + *corps* = body).

justice-weed (jŭs′tĭs-wēd) *n.* a white-flowered herb of the eastern U.S.

juvenescent (jo͞o-və-nĕs′ənt) *adj.* growing young.

juzgado (ho͞oz-gò′dō) *n.* hoosegow (southwestern U.S.).

jyotishi (yō′tĭ-shē) *n.* a superior fortuneteller and all-around oracle (Hindu).

K

ka (kŏ) *n.* 1. the immortal spirit or soul (ancient Egyptian religion). 2. the Scottish jackdaw.

kaaba (kŏ'ə-bŏ) *n.* Mecca's small building in the court of the Great Mosque, housing the sacred Black Stone, and toward which Moslems face when praying.

kaama (kŏ'mŏ) *n.* a large, nearly extinct African antelope, grayish-brown with yellow on its behind.

kabaya (kŏ-bŏ'yə) *n.* a loose cotton Malayan tunic.

kaberu (kŏ-bā'rōō) *n.* the Abyssinian mountain wolf.

kachina (kŏ-chē'nə) *n.* the spirit of a departed Hopi. also its impersonator either dramatic or in art works (such as the *kachina* doll). also *katcina*.

kadein (kŏ-dīn') *n.* a member of the imperial Turkish harem.

kadoodle (kŏ-dōō'dəl) *v.i.* to romp; cavort.

kafflyeh (kŏ-fē'yə) *n.* a Bedouin headdress consisting of a square kerchief bound around the head with a cord.

kaha (kŏ'hŏ) *n.* Borneo's big-nosed monkey.

kahuna (kŏ-hōō'nə) *n.* 1. a medicine man or high priest. 2. a master artisan (Hawaii).

kai (kŏ'ē) *n.* food (Maori).

kailyard (kāl'yörd) *adj.* pertaining to a style of slangy Scottish fiction.

kaivakuku (kŏ-ē″və-kōō'ōō) *n.* Papuan police hired to protect the crops.

kakapo (kă-kə-pō') *n.* a green ground-bound parrot of New Zealand.

kakemono (kŏ-kĕ-mō'nō) *n.* a painted Japanese scroll with a roller on the bottom.

kaki (kŏ'kē) *n.* 1. the Japanese persimmon. 2. the New Zealand stilt-bird.

kakidrosis (kă-kĭ-drō'sĭs) *n.* body smell.

kakistocracy (kă-kĭs-tŏk'rə-sē) *n.* government by the worst citizens.

kakkak (kă'kăk) *n.* a small bittern (Guam).

kakorrhaphiophobia (kă″kôr-ə-fē″ō-fō'bĭ-ə) *n.* fear of failure. see *atychiphobia*.

kaling (kā'lĭng) *n.* an old Halloween game in which a blindfolded person's future is predicted by the kind of cabbage she uproots (from *kale*, a type of cabbage).

kalogram (kăl'ō-grăm) *n.* a monogram using someone's name instead of initials.

kalokagathia (kăl"ō-kə-găth'ĭ-ə) *n.* a combination of the good and the beautiful in a person.

kalon (kăl'ŏn) *n.* the kind of beauty that is more than skin deep.

kalopsia (kăl-ŏp'sē-ə) *n.* condition where things appear more beautiful than they really are.

kalpa (kŭl'pə) *n.* 1,000 yugas.

kamalayka (kə-mə-lī'kə) *n.* a waterproof shirt made from seal guts.

kame (kām) *n.* a short ridge or hill (Scottish and U.S.).

kamerad (kŏ'mə-rŏd) *v.i.* to surrender (colloquial).

kamichi (kŏ'mē-shē) *n.* the horned screamer.

kanaka (kŏ-nŏk'ə) *n.* 1. a South Sea Islander. 2. a Melanesian imported to work on Australian sugar plantations; her language.

kanara (kă-nŏ'rə) *n.* a long, narrow Persian rug; a runner.

kangani (kăn-gŏ'nē) *n.* a labor boss in India, Ceylon, and Malaysia.

Kanji (kăn'jē) *n.* Chinese ideographs used in Japanese writing.

kankedort (kŏng-kə-dôrt') *n.* critical state or affair (Chaucer).

kantele (kŏn'tə-lā) *n.* an ancient five-stringed Finnish harp.

kaolin (kā'ō-lĭn) *n.* porcelain clay with fireproof color.

karao (kă-rŏ'ō) *n.* 1. a widow's marriage to her brother-in-law (Hindu law). 2. concubinage.

karimata (kŏ-rē-mŏ'tə) *n.* a two-headed Japanese arrow that whistles while it works.

karimption (kă-rĭmp'shən) *n.* a

crowd; a mass.

karma (kŭr'mə) *n.* 1. fate, destiny. 2. principle of causality. 3. future effect of any act, religious or otherwise.

karmouth (kŏr'mouth) *n.* an African fish able to live briefly in air.

kashga (kàsh'gə) *n.* an Eskimo meeting hall.

kashruth (kàsh'rŭs, -rōōth) *n.* the state of being kosher.

katchung (kàch'ŭng) *n.* the peanut or its oil.

kathenotheism (kă-thĕn'ō-thē-ĭz"əm) *n.* polytheism with a head god.

katowse (kă-tous') *n.* a ruckus, tumult, din.

katuka (kŭt'ōō-kə) *n.* Russell's viper.

katun (kŏ-tōōn') *n.* twenty Mayan years.

kava (kŏ'vŏ) *n.* an Australasian pepper used to make an intoxicating drink; the drink.

keb (kĕb) *n.* a ewe that has aborted. *-v.i.* to abort a lamb. *to keb at*, to refuse to suckle.

keck (kĕk) *v.i.* 1. to retch. 2. to express disgust. 3. to make a retching sound. *-n.* an attempt to vomit; queasiness.

keckle (kĕk'əl) *v.t.* to wrap a ship's line to prevent chafing.

kedge (kĕj) *n.* a small anchor. *-v.t.&i.* to move a boat by throwing out an anchor and hauling the boat up to it. *-adj.* lively.

kedogenous (kĕd-ŏj'ən-əs) *adj.* produced by worry.

keedug (kē'dŭg) *n.* an old sack used as a raincoat (Irish).

keek (kēk) *n.* 1. an industrial spy. 2. a peeping Tom (both slang).

keelhaul (kēl'hôl) *v.t.* 1. to punish by dragging under a ship's keel. 2. to criticize severely.

màn; māde; lĕt; bē; sĭp; wīne; hŏt; cōld; sôre; dŭll; fūgue; bûrp; gŏŏd; fōōd; out; gĕt; thin; this; year; ażure; ō'mən"; viN; für; Bach

keelivine (kē′lǐ-vīn) *n.* a lead pencil.

keest (kēst) *n.* sap, substance, marrow.

keester (kēs′tər) *n.* 1. the rectum used as a hiding place by prisoners (slang). 2. variation of *keister*, which see.

kef (kĕf) *n.* 1. drug-induced tranquility. 2. Indian hemp, the drug that can produce this state. also *kief*, *keef*.

keffel (kĕf′əl) *n.* 1. a worthless old horse. 2. a worthless or clumsy person.

keister (kēs′tər) *n.* 1. a safe or strongbox. 2. a burglar's tool kit. 3. the local jail. 4. the buttocks. 5. good luck (all slang).

keitloa (kīt′lō-ə) *n.* a black rhino whose rear horn is longer than her front one.

kellion (kĕl′ǐ-ŏn) *n.* a small monastery housing not more than three monks and three lay brothers.

kemp (kĕmp) *n.* 1. a champion soldier or athlete. 2. a harvesting contest. 3. a coarse hair. -*v.i.* to compete in a harvesting contest.

kench (kĕnch) *n.* a place where fish or skins are salted. -*v.t.* to put in a *kench*.

kenlore (kĕn′lôr) *n.* the theory of knowledge.

kennebunker (kĕn″ē-bŭnk′ər) *n.* a large suitcase (from *Kennebunk*, Maine).

kenophobia (kĕn-ō-fō′bǐ-ə) *n.* fear of empty or open spaces.

kensington (kĕn′zǐng-tən) *n.* a sewing bee.

kenspeckle (kĕn′spĕk″əl) *adj.* conspicuous; having a distinctive appearance (Scottish).

kepi (kĕp′ē) *n.* a flat-topped military cap with visor.

kerana (kĕr-ŏn′ə) *n.* a long Persian trumpet.

kerasine (kĕr′ə-sǐn) *adj.* horny; corneous.

keraunophobia (kǐr″ôn-ō-fō′bǐ-ə) *n.* fear of thunder and lightning.

keraunoscopia (kĕr-ôn″ō-skō′pǐ-ə) *n.* fortunetelling by thunder.

kerdomeletia (kûr″dō-mə-lē′shǐ-ə) *n.* excessive attention to material wealth.

kerf (kûrf) *n.* a cut or cutting; a notch.

keriarap (kûr-lăr′əp) *v.i.* to cavort; to play.

kerygma (kē-rǐg′mə) *n.* Christian preaching. *kerygmatic*, *adj.*

ketuba (kĕth-ōō-vō′) *n.* a Jewish marriage contract providing the wife with money in case of husband's death or divorce.

khamsin (kăm′sǐn) *n.* an Egyptian dust storm.

khanda (kŏng′də) *n.* a double-edged sword (Hindu).

khidmutgar (kǐd′măt-gôr) *n.* an Indian waiter.

kia ora (kē′ə ôr″ə) a Maori toast to health and happiness.

kibblerman (kǐb′lər-mən) *n.* operator of a machine that breaks up oil cake (British).

kibbling (kǐb′lǐng) *n.pl.* cut-up fish used as bait in Newfoundland.

kickshaw (kǐk′shô) *n.* 1. something fantastic; a toy. 2. a gastronomic delicacy. 3. a fantastic person. 4. *pl.* odds and ends (French *quelque chose* = something).

kife (kīf) *n.pl.* 1. prostitutes. 2. male homosexuals. -*v.t.* to swindle; to rob (slang).

kilderkin (kǐl′dər-kǐn) *n.* a half or fourth of a barrel, an Old English measure of eighteen gallons or two firkins.

kilerg (kĭl'ûrg) n. 1,000 ergs.

kilhig (kĭl'hĭg) n. a pole used to direct the fall of a tree.

killhag (kĭl'hàg) n. an Indian trap used by Maine hunters.

kincob (kĭng'kòb) n. Indian gold or silver brocade.

kindergraph (kĭn'dər-gràf) n. a photograph of a child (obs.).

kine (kīn) n.pl. cattle.

kinesophobia (kĭn″ē-sō-fō′bĭ-ə) n. fear of movement.

kingling (kĭng'lĭng) n. a small or petty king.

kinkajou (kĭnk'ə-jōō) n. a furry, tamable mammal of Central America with a prehensile tail.

kinnikinnik (kĭn″ĭ-kĭn-ĭk') n. 1. a tobacco of dried leaves and bark smoked by Indians and others in the Great Lakes region. 2. any of the plants so used.

kinology (kĭn-òl'ə-jē) n. physics of motion.

kippage (kĭp'əj) n. commotion, confusion, excitement.

kissar (kĭs'ər) n. the five-stringed Abyssinian lyre.

kitsch (kĭch) n. third-rate art or writing produced for immediate and popular appeal (German).

kitthoge (kĭth-ōg') adj.&n. 1. left-handed or awkward. 2. a left-handed or awkward person.

kittly-benders (kĭt'lē-bèn″dûrz) n. thin ice; running on thin ice (colloquial).

kiva (kē'və) n. an underground ceremonial chamber in Pueblo architecture.

kivu (kē'vōō) n. the tsetse fly.

klavierstuck (klò-vĭr'shtōōk) n. a piano composition.

kleptic (klèp'tĭk) adj. thievish.

klipspringer (klĭp'sprĭng″ər) n. a small African mammal with big ears.

knacker (nàk'ər) n. 1. a harness or saddle maker. 2. someone who buys, slaughters, and sells old horses for dog food. 3. an old worn-out horse. 4. someone who buys old ships or houses to sell the contents.

kneippism (kə-nīp′ĭz″əm) n. treating disease by walking barefoot on wet grass, originated by Dr. [of divinity] Sebastian Kneipp.

knibber (nĭb'ər) n. a male deer when the antlers first appear.

knickknackatory (nĭk-nàk'ə-tôr″ē) n. a collection or storehouse of knickknacks.

knipperdolling (nĭp'ər-dòl″ĭng) n. 1. a disciple of *Bernhard Knipperdollinck*, a German Anabaptist fanatic and polygamist. 2. a fanatic.

knissomancy (nĭs'ō-màn″sē) n. fortunetelling by incense-burning.

knout (nout) n. a lash made of twisted leather thongs and laced with wire.

kobold (kō'bōld) n. a mischievous goblin in homes or mines.

koftgari (kòft'gə-rē) n. steel inlaid with gold (India).

kohl (kōl) n. black eye make-up (antimony, soot, etc.) once used by Egyptian women.

kohlrabi (kōl'rò-bē) n. a turnip-shaped cabbage.

koimesis (koi-mē'sĭs) n. an Eastern Orthodox feast commemorating Mary's death and assumption, originally celebrated January eighteenth, now moved up to August fifteenth.

koinotropy (koi-nòt'rə-pē) n. interest in social relationships.

kokam (kō'kòm) n. the slow loris.

kokomo (kō'kə-mō) n. a cocaine addict; any drug addict (slang).

kok-saghyz (kōk-sə-gēz') n. a

rubber-producing Asian dandelion.

kokshut (kŏk'shŭt) *adj.* used up; worn out (slang).

kokum (kō'kəm) *n.* phony sympathy (British slang).

kolinsky (kō-lĭn'skē) *n.* Asiatic mink.

kombinationsfahigkeit (kŏm'bĭ-nŏts-yŏn-fō''ĭt-kīt) *n.* the way a medium picks up clues: by noting various involuntary reactions.

kompology (kŏm-pŏl'ə-jē) *n.* braggadocio.

kona (kō'nŏ) *n.* southwest wind of Hawaii.

konimeter (kō'nĭ-mē'tər) *n.* an instrument for measuring dust in the air.

koochahbee (kōō'chŏ-bē) *n.* a California Indian dish made from Lake Mono fly larvae.

kookaburra (kŏōk'ə-bŭr''ə) *n.* the laughing jackass.

koomkie (kōōm'kē) *n.* a trained female elephant used to decoy wild males.

kopophobia (kŏp-ō-fō'bĭ-ə) *n.* fear of physical or mental exhaustion.

kordax (kôr'dăks) *n.* 1. an ancient Dionysian phallic dance performed in the buff. 2. any lively Renaissance court dance. also *cordax.*

kosmokrator (kŏz-mŏk'rə-tər) *n.* the ruler of the world.

kotukutuku (kō-tōō'kōō-tōō''kōō) *n.* the New Zealand fuchsia.

krasis (krā'sĭs) *n.* dilution of the Eucharist wine.

kratogen (krăt'ō-jĕn) *n.* a dormant area next to one beset by earthquakes.

krausen (krou'zən) *v.t.* to add fermenting wort to incipient beer. *-n.* the wort.

kreatophagia (krē''ə-tō-fā'jĭ-ə) *n.* the eating of raw meat.

kreistle (krī'səl) *v.t.* to disgust (German *greiseln* = to shudder at).

kreuzer (kroit'sər) *n.* an old coin of ante-bellum Austria and Germany.

kriegspiel (krēg'shpēl) *n.* a war game (German *krieg* = war + *spiel* = game).

krobylos (krō'bĭ-lŏs) *n.* a tuft of hair on top of the head.

krummhorn (krōōm'hôrn) *n.* an obsolete reed wind instrument with a curved tube.

kuku (kōō'kōō) *n.* the New Zealand fruit pigeon.

kumiss (kōō'mĭs) *n.* a Tatar liquor made from camel's milk.

kunst (kōōnst) *n.* art; fine art.

kurveyor (kûr-vā'ər) *n.* a traveling salesman who carts his goods (South Africa).

kvetch (kvĕch) *v.i.* to complain, to whine. *-n.* someone who does this.

kwistgoed (kvīst'gŭt) *n.* a spendthrift.

kyacting (kī'ăk''tĭng) *n.* clowning at work (British slang).

kylie (kī'lē) *n.* the Australian boomerang.

kymatology (kī-mə-tŏl'ə-jē) *n.* the science of waves.

kyphorrhinos (kī-fō-rī'nŏs) *n.* a humped nose.

kyphotic (kī-fŏt'ĭk) *adj.* humpbacked.

---

laaba (lò'bə) *n.* a storage platform high enough to be beyond the reach of animals (Alaska).

laager (lò'gər) *n.* a camp protected by wagons. -*v.t.&i.* to make into such a camp (South Africa).

labefy (làb'ə-fī) *v.t.* to weaken.

labent (lā'bənt) *adj.* slipping or falling.

labile (lā'bìl) *adj.* 1. unstable, plastic; apt to change. 2. fast chemical or molecular change. 3. emotionally unstable.

laborant (làb'ər-ànt) *n.* a laboratory worker.

labret (lā'brèt) *n.* a lip ornament.

labrose (lā'brōs) *adj.* thick-lipped.

laciniate (là-sìn'ì-āt) *adj.* fringed.

laconicum (là-kòn'ì-kŭm) *n.* a sauna.

lactarium (làk-tèr'ì-əm) *n.* a dairy.

lactivorous (làk-tìv'ər-əs) *adj.* living on milk.

lacuna (là-kū'nə) *n.* a gap.

lacuscular (là-kùs'kū-lər) *adj.* pertaining to or inhabiting pools or small lakes (Latin *lacusculus* = little lake).

lacustrine (là-kùs'trìn) *adj.* pertaining to or living in lakes (Latin *lacus* = lake).

ladino (lò-dē'nō) *n.* 1. a Spanish-Hebraic patois. 2. in Spanish colonies, someone who is part Spanish and speaks a Spanish patois. 3. a vicious American horse.

ladrone (là-drōn') *n.* 1. U.S. term for a hostile Philippine soldier. 2. a mercenary. 3. any robber or thief. *ladronism. n.* robbery or intimidation by *ladrones*.

lagan (làg'ən) *n.* stuff thrown in the sea and marked by a buoy for future retrieval. also *ligan*.

lagniappe (làn-yàp') *n.* a cheap present given to good customers (Louisiana).

lagnosis (làg-nō'sìs) *n.* satyriasis.

lagotic (là-gòt'ìk) *adj.* having rabbitlike ears.

laicize (lā'ì-sīz) *v.t.* to secularize.

lairwite (lèr'wìt) *n.* a fine given a married women for adultery.

laliophobia (lā"lì-ò-fō'bì-ə) *n.* fear of speaking.

lallation (là-lā'shən) *n.* unintelligible baby talk.

lalochezia (là-lō-kē'zì-ə) *n.* talking dirty to relieve tension.

---

màn; māde; lèt; bē; sìp; wīne; hòt; cōld; sôre; dùll; fūgue; bûrp; good; fōōd; out; gèt; thin; this; year; aźure; ŏ'mən"; viN; fûr; Bach

lamassu (lŏ-màs'ōō) *n.* a Babylonian semidivine bull with a man's face.

lambative (làm'bə-tĭv) *n.* a medicine to be licked (as a cough remedy).

lambent (làm'bənt) *adj.* touching or shining softly; lightly flickering.

lambrequin (làm'brə-kĭn) *n.* 1. a scarf attached to the back of a helmet. 2. an ornamental valance. 3. a seventeenth-century ceramic design.

lamia (lā'mĭ-ə) *n.* 1. a mythological man-eater with a woman's head and a snake's body. 2. a vampire. 3. the cub shark.

lampadedromy (làm-pə-dĕd'rə-mē) *n.* an ancient Greek relay race with torches.

lampadomancy (làm-pàd'ō-màn"sē) *n.* fortunetelling with the flame of a torch.

lampas (làm'pəs) *n.* 1. an elaborately woven textile. 2. a mucous-membrane congestion in horses.

lamprophony (làm-prŏf'ən-ē) *n.* loud, ringing speech.

lancinate (làn'sĭn-āt) *v.t.* to tear, stab, lacerate.

landgrave (lànd'grāv) *n.* a German nobleman.

landlooker (lànd'lōōk"ər) *n.* a timber surveyor. *landlook*, *v.t.*

langlaufer (lòng'louf"ər) *n.* a cross-country skier.

langrets (làn'grĕts) *n.pl.* loaded dice.

languescent (làng-gwĕs'ənt) *adj.* becoming tired.

laniate (làn'ĭ-āt) *v.t.* to tear into pieces.

laniferous (làn-ĭf'ər-əs) *adj.* bearing or producing wool.

lant (lànt) *n.* stale urine used in manufacturing. *-v.t.* to wet or mix

with *lant*.

lanuginous (làn-ū'jĭn-əs) *adj.* downy.

lanx (lànks) *n.* a large metal platter (Roman).

laodicean (lā-òd"ĭ-sē'ən) *adj.* general indifference (from the inhabitants of ancient Laodicea, noted for their lack of élan).

laparohysterosalpingooophorectomy (làp"ər-ō-hĭs"tər-ō-sàl-pĭng"gō-ō"ə-fôr-ĕk'tə-mē) *n.* surgical removal of the female reproductive organs.

lapidate (làp'ĭ-dāt) *v.t.* to stone; to kill by stoning.

lapidify (làp-ĭd'ĭ-fī) *v.t.&i.* to turn into stone.

lapin (làp-èN', làp'ĭn) *n.* a euphemism for rabbit fur (French *lapin =* rabbit).

lapling (làp'lĭng) *n.* someone who enjoys resting in women's laps.

lappage (làp'əj) *n.* the amount that layers overlap.

laptea (làp'tē) *n.* a crowded tea party where guests sit in each other's laps.

larbar (lòr'bòr) *adj.* exhausted; worn-out. *-n.* an exhausted person (Scottish).

lares and penates (lā'rēz and pə-nā'tēz) *n.pl.* 1. household gods. 2. one's most treasured possessions.

larithmics (là-rĭth'mĭks) *n.* study of the quantitative aspects of population.

larmoyant (lòr-moi'yənt) *adj.* tearful.

larrigan (làr'ĭ-gən) *n.* a high moccasin used by trappers and lumbermen (U.S. and Canada).

larrikin (làr'ĭ-kĭn) *n.* a city tough; an urban slob.

larrup (làr'əp) *v.t.* to beat severely. *-n.* a severe blow (colloquial).

larvate (lòr'vāt) *adj.* hidden, ob-

màn; māde; lĕt; bē; sĭp; wīne; hòt; cōld; sôre; dùll; fūgue; bûrp; gōŏd; fōōd; out; gĕt; thin; thĭs; year; azure; o'mən"; viN; fũr; Bach

scure.

lascar (làs-kòr′) *n*. an East Indian 1. sailor on a foreign ship 2. army servant 3. poor marksman 4. tentpitcher.

lassipedes (là-sĭp′ĭd-ēz) *n.pl.* tired feet.

lasslorn (làs′lôrn) *adj*. stood up by one's girl.

latebricole (là-tĕb′rĭ-kōl) *adj*. living or hiding in holes (zoology).

latericeous (là-tər-ĭsh′əs) *adj*. brick-red. also *lateritious*.

lateropulsion (làt″ər-ō-pŭl′shən) *n*. walking sideways, as in Parkinson's disease.

latibulize (là-tĭb′ū-līz) *v.i.* to hibernate.

latifundian (là-tĭ-fŭn′dĭ-ən) *adj*. rich in real estate.

latitant (là′tĭ-tənt) *adj*. hidden; hibernating. -*n*. one in hiding.

latitudinarianism (là″tĭ-tōō-dĭn-ĕr′ĭ-ən-ĭz″əm) *n*. tolerance, especially in religious doctrines.

latrant (lā′trənt) *adj*. snarling; complaining.

latrobe (là-trōb′) *n*. a special stove which can heat the room above as well as the room it is in.

laudanum (lôd′-ə-nəm) *n*. an opium derivative.

lavaliere (làv′əl-ĭr) *n*. 1. a pendant on a chain. 2. animal coloration that looks like the above. -*adj*. pertaining to a microphone worn around the neck.

lavation (là-vā′shən) *n*. cleansing, lavage; water for washing.

Laverna (là-vûr′nə) *n*. the goddess of thieves and imposters (Roman mythology).

layboy (lā′boi) *n*. a papermaking-machine attachment that delivers sheets in piles.

laystall (lā′stôl) *n*. a garbage dump;

formerly, a cemetary.

lazaretto (làz-ə-rĕt′ō) *n*. 1. a leprosarium. 2. a building used in quarentine. 3. a storage space between ship decks.

lazarous (làz′ər-əs) *adj*. leprous.

leal (lēl) *adj*. 1. faithful, loyal, and true. 2. correct, accurate, and real. 3. legal, lawful, and just.

lecanomancy (lĕk′ə-nō-màn″sē) *n*. fortunetelling by looking at water in a basin.

lecheur (lĕsh-ûr′) *n*. a devotee of oral intercourse; a licker.

lechwe (lĕch′wē) *n*. the white-bellied antelope, almost as large as the waterbuck.

lection (lĕk′shən) *n*. reading; a lecture; a selection from the Bible read in church.

lectual (lĕk′chōō-əl) *adj*. bed-ridden.

lecythus (lĕs′ĭ-thŭs) *n*. a flagon for unguents: sometimes used as a funeral offering (archaeology).

leggiadrous (lĕj-ĭ-àd′rəs) *adj*. graceful.

legist (lĕj′ĭst) *n*. a jurist.

leguleian (lĕg-ū-lē′yən) *adj*. like a lawyer, legal; used as an epithet. -*n*. a lawyer.

leiotrichous (lī-ŏt′rĭ-kəs) *adj*. smooth-haired.

leman (lē′mən) *n*. a mistress or lover.

lenify (lĕn′ĭ-fī) *v.t.* to soften, alleviate. *lenitive, adj.*

lenitic (lē-nĭt′ĭk) *adj*. living in quiet waters.

lenocinant (lĕn-ŏs′ĭn-ənt) *adj*. lewd.

lenticular (lĕn-tĭk′ū-lər) *adj*. 1. like a lentil. 2. like a double-convex lens.

lentiginous (lĕn-tĭj′ĭ-nəs) *adj*. freckly (Latin *lentigo* = freckle).

lentor (lĕn′tôr) *n*. tenacity or sluggishness.

lenvoy (lĕn-voi′) v.t. to say good-by.

lepid (lĕp′ĭd) adj. pleasant or charming.

leporine (lĕp′ər-īn) adj. pertaining to hares.

leptorrhinian (lĕp-tə-rĭn′ĭ-ən) adj. having a long narrow nose.

leptosome (lĕp′tō-sōm) n. a thin bony body type.

letch (lĕch) n. 1. passion. 2. a muddy ditch or pond.

lethiferous (lē-thĭf′ər-əs) adj. deadly; destructive.

lethologica (lĕth-ō-lŏj′ĭ-kə) n. inability to remember the right word.

lethonomia (lĕth-ō-nō′mĭ-ə) n. tendency to forget names.

leucomelanous (loō-kō-mĕl′ə-nəs) adj. pertaining to a light complexion with dark hair and eyes.

leucous (loō′kəs) adj. white or blond; like an albino.

levant (lē-vănt′) v.i. to flee one's debtors. -n. 1. a bet made with intent to welch. 2. (cap.) countries near the eastern Mediterranean. 3. a strong eastern Mediterranean wind. 4. a leather worker who imitates goatskin grain. 5. one who *levants; a levanter.*

leveret (lĕv′ər-ĕt) n. 1. a year-old hare. 2. a mistress.

levigate (lĕv′ĭ-gāt) v.t. 1. to make smooth. 2. to make into a powder or paste. 3. to mix thoroughly. 4. to polish.

levisomnous (lĕv-ĭ-sŏm′nəs) adj. watchful.

levoduction (lē-vō-dŭk′shən) n. leftward eye movement.

lewdster (loōd′stûr) n. a lewd person.

lexiphanic (lĕks-ĭ-făn′ĭk) adj. using pretentious language.

li (lē) n. 1800 ch'ih, one millimeter, a Chinese mile, or a hundredth of a *mu.*

liana (lē-än′ə) n. any climbing plant that roots in the ground.

libant (lī′bənt) adj. sipping; slightly touching.

liberticidal (lĭ-bûr″tĭ-sī′dəl) adj. destroying or tending to destroy liberty.

liblab (lĭb′lăb) n. a nineteenth-century British trade-union supporter.

libratory (lī′brə-tôr″ē) adj. balancing.

licitation (lĭs-ĭ-tā′shən) n. selling or bidding at an auction.

ligation (lī-gā′shən) n. binding or wrapping; something that is bound (or wrapped).

ligneous (lĭg′nē-əs) adj. hard or "woody" in feeling, as a tumor.

ligyrophobia (lĭj″ĭr-ō-fō′bĭ-ə) n. fear of loud noises.

lilapsophobia (lī-lăp″sō-fō′bĭ-ə) n. fear of tornadoes.

lilly-low (lĭl′ē-lō) n. a bright flame (British dialect).

limaceous (lī-mā′shəs) adj. pertaining to slugs; *limacine.*

limbate (lĭm′bāt) adj. bordered; edged.

limberham (lĭm′bûr-hăm) n. a supple-jointed person; figuratively: a fawning or servile person.

limen (lī′mən) n. the borderline of awareness.

limicolous (lī-mĭk′ō-ləs) adj. living in mud.

limitrophe (lĭm′ĭ-trōf) adj. adjacent.

limn (lĭm) v.t. 1. to decorate with ornamental letters or borders. 2. to delineate, outline, in painting.

limnophilous (lĭm-nŏf′ĭl-əs) adj. living in fresh-water ponds.

---

măn; māde; lĕt; bē; sĭp; wīne; hŏt; cōld; sôre; dŭll; fūgue; bûrp; goōd; foōd; out; gĕt; thin; this; year; aẑure; ō′mən″; viN; für; Bach

limophoitos (lĭ-mō-foi'tōs) *n.* insanity due to lack of food.

limosis (lĭ-mō'sĭs) *n.* 1. a mania for eating chalk. 2. an insatiable craving for food.

lincture (lĭnk'chər) *n.* a thick cough syrup to be licked or sucked.

lingtow (lĭng'tō) *n.* a heavy rope used by smugglers. *lingtowman n.* (Scottish).

linguacious (lĭng-gwā'shəs) *adj.* loquacious (obs.).

linonophobia (lĭ-nŏn"ō-fō'bĭ-ə) *n.* fear of string.

linsey-woolsey (lĭn'zē-wool'zē) *adj.* neither fish nor foul (made of linen and wool) -*n.* nonsense (Shakespeare).

liparoid (lĭp'ər-oid) *adj.* fatty.

lipectomy (lĭp-ĕk'tə-mē) *n.* surgical fat removal.

lipogram (lĭp'ō-grăm) *n.* purposely eliminating certain letters in writing (Tryphiodorus's *Odyssey* lacked A's in the first book, B's in the second. . .).

lipostomy (lĭ-pŏs'tə-mē) *n.* atrophy of the mouth.

lipothymy (lĭ-pŏth'ə-mē) *n.* a fainting.

lippen (lĭp'ən) *v.t.&i.* to trust, rely on.

lipper (lĭp'ûr) *n.* 1. rippling waves; a light sea spray. 2. a thin piece of blubber used for wiping a ship's deck. 3. a tool for forming the lip on glass containers. -*v.t.* to wipe with a *lipper.* -*v.i.* to be sunk to the gunwales. -*adj.* wet.

lippitude (lĭp'ĭ-tōod) *n.* sore or bleary eyes.

lipsanographer (lĭp-sən-ŏg'rə-fûr) *n.* someone who writes about relics.

lipsanotheca (lĭp"sən-ō-thē'kə) *n.* a shrine or container for "holy" relics.

liripipium (lĭr-ĭ-pĭp'ĭ-əm) *n.* a medieval hood worn by graduates.

liripoop (lĭr'ĭ-pōōp) *n.* 1. a *liripipium.* 2. a trick. 3. a silly ass. also *liripipe.*

lirp (lûrp) *v.i.* to snap the fingers. -*n.* a snap.

lissens (lĭs'ənz) *n.pl.* in rope-making, the last strands of a rope.

lissotrichous (lĭ-sŏt'rĭ-kəs) *adj.* having straight hair.

literatim (lĭt-ər-ə'tĭm) *adv.* letter for letter, literally.

lithodomous (lĭ-thŏd'ō-məs) *adj.* burrowing in rock.

lithoglyph (lĭth'ō-glĭf) *n.* an engraving on stone, especially on a gem: an engraved stone.

lithomancy (lĭth'ō-măn"sē) *n.* fortunetelling by stones or stone charms.

lithophagus (lĭth-ŏf'ə-gəs) *adj.* eating stones or gravel; *lithodomous.*

litigious (lĭ-tĭj'əs) *adj.* 1. contentious, in a court or out of it. 2. involved in litigation or pertaining to it.

litotes (lī'tō-tēz) *n.* the use of understatement to avoid criticism or for dramatic effect.

littlin (lĭt'lĭn) *n.* a young or small child or animal.

littoral (lĭt'ō-rəl) *n.* a coastal region.

liturate (lĭ'chər-āt) *adj.* spotted.

llanero (yə-nā'rō) *n.* cowboy.

llano (yə'nō) *n.* a vast plain.

lobcock (lŏb'kŏk) *n.* 1. a dull, sluggish lout. 2. a large, relaxed penis.

loblolly (lŏb'lŏl"ē) *n.* 1. thick soup. 2. Navy medicine (slang). 3. a puddle (dialect). 4. a Bahamian pine tree.

lobola (lō'bō-lə) *n.* payment of cat-

---

màn; māde; lĕt; bē; sĭp; wīne; hŏt; cōld; sôre; dŭll; fūgue; bûrp; gŏŏd; fŏŏd; out; gĕt; thin; ţhis; year; aʒure; ō'mən"; viN; fûr; Bach

tle in exchange for a bride (South Africa).

lockrums (lĭk'rŭmz) *n.pl.* unpopular ideas.

locofoco (lō-kō-fō'kō) *n.* a self-lighting match or cigar: applied to the Equal Rights faction of the Democratic Party when the matches were used to light up their darkened meeting room.

locum tenens (lō'kəm tĕn'ənz) *n.* a substitute; temporary replacement.

lodestar (lōd'stòr) *n.* a guiding star.

loganamnosis (lŏg"ăn-əm-nō'sĭs) *n.* a mania for trying to recall forgotten words.

logastellus (lō-găs'təl-ŭs) *n.* "a person whose enthusiasm for words outstrips his knowledge of them" (John McClellan in *Word Ways*, Vol. 3 No. 3, 1970).

loggia (lō'jō) *n.* 1. a covered porch or gallery. 2. a large ornamental window (Italian).

logia (lŏg'ĭ-ə) *n.* evangelical pearls alleged to have been cast by Christ; any religious maxims.

logjam (lŏg'jăm) *n.* 1. floating logs jammed together. 2. a stalemate in negotiations.

logodaedalus (lō-gō-dĕd'ə-ləs) *n.* verbal legerdemain. also *logodaedaly.*

logogram (lŏg'ō-grăm) *n.* 1. an abbreviation or word symbol. 2. a rhyming word puzzle. 3. a *logogriph.* 4. a *phonogram.*

logogriph (lŏg'ō-grĭf) *n.* an anagrammatic puzzle.

logolept (lŏg'ō-lĕpt) *n.* a word maniac.

logology (lō-gŏl'ə-jē) *n.* 1. the science of words. 2. the pursuit of word puzzles or puzzling words; recreational linguistics (suggested by *logologist* Dmitri Borgmann).

logomachy (lō-gŏm'ə-kē) *n.* 1. war with, or about, words. 2. a word game.

logomisia (lō-gō-mĭs'ĭ-ə) *n.* disgust for certain words.

logrolling (lŏg'rōl"ĭng) *n.* 1. rolling logs to the river. 2. *birling.* 3. a *birling* contest. 4. political cooperation for a common goal. 5. mutual literary back-patting.

loimic (loi'mik) *adj.* pertaining to the plague.

lollard (lŏl'ûrd) *n.* 1. fourteenth-century Netherlands heretics. 2. Wycliffe disciples in England and Scotland. 3. a loller, or lazy clod.

lollock (lŏl'ək) *n.* a large lump.

lollybanger (lŏl'ē-bàng-ər) *n.* gingerbread with raisins.

longanimity (lông-gà-nĭm'ĭ-tē) *n.* silently suffering while planning revenge.

longear (lông'ĭr) *n.* 1. an unbranded calf. 2. an ass (colloquial).

longicaudal (lŏn-jĭ-kô'dəl) *adj.* having a long tail.

longiloquence (lŏn-jĭl'ō-kwəns) *n.* long-windedness.

longimanous (lŏn-jĭ-mā'nəs) *adj.* long-handed.

longinquity (lŏn-jĭng'kwĭ-tē) *n.* remoteness.

loob (lōōb) *n.* slimy dregs from tin ore.

looby (lōō'bē) *n.* an awkward or clumsy person; a lubber.

loof (lōōf) *n.* the palm of the hand; the inside of a cat's paw.

looping (lōōp'ĭng) *n.* the technique of voice-overs for cartoon voices, dubbing, etc.

lopadotemachoselachogale-okranioleipsanodrimhypot-rimmatosilphioparaome-litokatakechymenokichlepi-kossyphophattoperisteralek-

tryonoptekephalliokigklop-eleiolagoiosiraiobaphetrag-anopterygon
"a goulash composed of all the leftovers from the meals of the leftovers from the meals of the last two weeks." or, hash (from Aristophanes' *The Ecclesiazus-ae*).

lopper (lŏp'ər) *adj*. 1. curdled milk. 2. a blood clot. 3. slush.

loppet (lŏp'ət) *v.i.* to walk or run awkwardly.

lordosis (lôr-dō'sĭs) *n*. curvature of the spine.

loricate (lôr'ĭ-kāt) *v.t.* to cover with a protective crust or coating. *-adj*. having a *lorica*, a hard, protective shell or armor.

lorimer (lôr'ĭ-mər) *n*. a saddle-maker.

lotophagous (lō-tŏf'ə-gəs) *adj*. lotus-eating.

louche (lōōsh) *adj*. devious; oblique.

loutrophoros (lōō-trŏf'ō-rəs) *n*. a long-necked, two-handled vase used for transporting ceremonial bath water for the bride and groom (ancient Greece).

lovelock (lŭv'lŏk) *n*. a long lock of hair hanging separately; a *tendril*.

lovertine (lŭv'ər-tēn) *adj*. addicted to love-making.

lowmen (lō'mən) *n*. dice loaded to turn up low numbers.

loxotic (lŏks-ŏt'ĭk) *adj*. slanting, distorted.

luce (lōōs) *n*. 1. fleur-de-lis. 2. a pike, especially when full grown.

luciferous (lōō-sĭf'ər-əs) *adj*. illuminating, literally and figuratively.

lucifugous (lōō-sĭf'ū-gəs) *adj*. avoiding light.

lucivee (lōō'sĭ-vē) *n*. a lynx (corruption of *loup-cervier*, a Canadian lynx).

lucriferous (lōō-krĭf'ər-əs) *adj*. profitable; lucrative. *lucrifer-ousness, n*.

lucripetous (lōō-krĭp'ə-təs) *adj*. money-hungry.

luctation (lŭk-tā'shən) *n*. a struggle for success.

luctiferous (lŭk-tĭf'ər-əs) *adj*. sad and sorry.

lucubrate (lŭk'ū-brāt) *v.i.* to work by artificial light; to "burn the midnight oil." *-v.t.* to compose with effort.

luculent (lŭk'ū-lənt) *adj*. lucid, clear, transparent, shining.

ludibrious (lōō-dĭb'rĭ-əs) *adj*. ludicrous; making fun of.

ludibundness (lōō'dĭ-bŭnd"nəs) *n*. playfulness.

ludicropathetic (lōō"dĭ-krō-pă-thĕt'ĭk) *adj*. ludicrous and pathetic. also *ludicroserious*.

ludification (lōō"dĭ-fĭ-kā'shən) *n*. deriding.

lues (lōō'ēz) *n*. any widespread infectious disease. *lues venerea*, syphilis.

lulliloo (lŭl'ē-lōō) *v.t.&i.* to shout a joyous welcome.

luminiferous (lōō-mĭn-ĭf'ər-əs) *adj*. transmitting or producing light.

lungis (lŭn'jĭs) *n*. a dull clod; a lout.

lunt (lŭnt) *n*. 1. a torch. 2. pipe smoke. 3. hot air. *-v.t.&i.* to light or smoke.

lupanarian (lōō-pə-nèr'ĭ-ən) *adj*. lubricious, lascivious, and lewd. *lupanar, n*. a Roman cat house.

lurgulary (lûr'gū-lèr"ē) *n*. the act of poisoning water (Old English law).

lusk (lŭsk) *n*. a lazy person. *-v.i.* to loaf.

lusory (lōō'sər-ē) *adj*. playful.

lutarious (lōō-tèr'ĭ-əs) *adj*. pertaining to, living in, or looking like mud.

luthern (lŏŏ'thûrn) *n.* a dormer window.

lutulent (lŏŏ'tū-lənt) *adj.* muddy, turbid, thick.

lux (lŭks) *n.* the international unit of illumination, equal to 0.0929 foot-candles.

luxate (lŭks'āt) *v.t.* to displace; to put out of joint; to dislocate. also *adj.*

lycanthropy (lī-kăn'thrō-pē) *n.* insanity in which the patient thinks she's a wolf.

lygophilia (lī-gō-fĭl'ĭ-ə) *n.* love of darkness.

lygophobia (lī-gō-fō'bĭ-ə) *n.* fear of darkness.

lymacatexis (lī″mə-kàt-èks'ĭs) *n.* neurotic preoccupation with dirt.

lyncean (lĭn-sē'ən) *adj.* pertaining to a lynx; sharp-sighted.

lypophrenia (lī-pō-frē'nĭ-ə) *n.* a vague feeling of sadness, seemingly without cause.

lysis (lī'sĭs) *n.* 1. the final phase of a disease. 2. cell destruction. *lyterian, adj.*

lyssophobia (lĭs-ō-fō'bĭ-ə) *n.* fear of becoming mad.

lythcoop (lĭth'cŏŏp) *n.* an auction of household goods.

M

mab (măb) *v.t.&i.* to dress sloppily; a sloppy woman.

macarize (măk'ər-īz) *v.t.* to make happy; to praise.

macaronic (măk-ər-ŏn'ĭk) *adj.* 1. pertaining to macaroni. 2. a literary burlesque using Latin, latinized slang, and slang. 3. any literary composition of mixed languages. 4. any mix-up or jumble.

macedoine (mŏ-sä-dwŏn') *n.* 1. a dish of mixed vegetables, as a salad or garnish. 2. any mixture.

macerate (măs'ər-āt) *v.t.* 1. to oppress; torment. 2. to deny food. 3. to soften by soaking. 4. to digest. *-v.i.* to soften or wear away by soaking; to waste away.

machicolation (mə-chĭk″ō-lā'shən) *n.* 1. an opening in a parapet, or floor, for dropping missiles on attackers. 2. the act itself.

macilent (măs-Il'ənt) *adj.* lean; thin.

mackallow (mə-kăl'ō) *n.* things held in trust by parents for their foster child.

mackle (măk'əl) *n.* a blurred or double impression in printing.

-v.t.&i. to make such an impression.

macrobian (mă-krō'bĭ-ən) *adj.* long-lived.

macrography (măk-rŏg'rə-fē) *n.* 1. huge writing resulting from certain neuroses. 2. examination with the naked eye. opposite of *micrography.*

macrology (măk-rŏl'ə-jē) *n.* unnecessary repetition; redundancy.

macromastic (măk-rō-măs'tĭk) *adj.* pertaining to large breasts.

macron (mā'krŏn) *n.* the symbol for a long vowel (ā). opposite of *breve,* the symbol for a short one (ă).

macrophobia (măk-rō-fō'bĭ-ə) *n.* fear of long waits.

macrosmatic (măk-rŏz-măt'Ik) *adj.* having a supersensitive nose.

macrosomatous (măk-rō-sŏm'ə-təs) *adj.* having an abnormally large body.

macrotous (măk-rō'təs) *adj.* having big ears.

mactation (măk-tā'shən) *n.* sacrificial murder.

maculate (măk'ū-lāt) *v.t.* to stain,

---

blotch. -*adj.* stained, made impure; defiled.

maddam (màd'əm) *n.* Macromodule and Digital Differential Analyzer Machine.

madefy (màd'ə-fī) *v.t.* to wet; *madescent* (màd-ès'ənt) *adj.* becoming wet.

madstone (màd'stōn) *n.* a stone supposed to be an antidote to poisonous animal bites.

maduro (mà-dōō'rō) *adj.* strong and dark: used in describing cigars (Spanish *maduro* = mature).

Maecenas (mē-sē'nəs) *n.* a munificent patron of literature or art (Maecenas was the patron of Horace and Virgil).

maenad (mē'nàd) *n.* a bacchante.

maffick (màf'ìk) *v.i.* to celebrate noisily and boisterously. (from one such celebration after the British downed the Boers at Mafeking in 1900).

maffle (màf'əl) *v.i.* to mumble or stutter. -*v.t.* to confuse.

magged (màgd) *adj.* frayed.

magirics (mà-jī'rīks) *n.* cooking, *magirist*, *n.* a chef.

magisterialness (màj-ìs-tèr'ī-əl-nes) *n.* haughtiness; pompousness.

magma (màg'mə) *n.* 1. dregs, sediment. 2. molten rock from the earth's core.

mahajan (mò-hò'jòn) *n.* a usurer in India. also *mahajun.*

mahout (mò-hout') *n.* an elephant trainer.

maieusiophobia (mā-ū"sē-ō-fō'bī-ə) *n.* fear of childbirth.

maleutics (mā-ū'tĭks) *n.* 1. obstetrics. 2. the Socratic method.

maigre (mā'grə) *adj.* 1. pertaining to vegetarian fare for fast days. 2.

pertaining to fast days. -*n.* a large European fish.

mainour (mā'nər) *n.* stolen goods found on the thief. *with* or *in* the *mainour,* caught in the act.

maja (mò'hò) *n.* 1. a poor Spanish beauty. 2. a beautiful yellow bird.

majo (mò'hō) *n.* 1. a poor Spanish fop. 2. a tropical shrub.

majolica (mà-yòl'ì-kə) *n.* a kind of glazed and richly ornamented Italian pottery: *faience.*

makebate (māk'bāt) *n.* a troublemaker.

makimono (mò-kē-mō'nō) *n.* 1. a long picture or writing scroll rolled up and never hung. 2. anything rolled up (Japanese *maki* = roll + *mono* = thing).

malacissation (màl'ə-sì-sā'shən) *n.* the process of making something soft and pliable.

malacodermous (màl"ə-kō-dûr'məs) *adj.* soft-skinned.

malapert (màl'ə-pûrt) *adj.* impudent, outspoken, lively (Shakespeare). -*n.* a *malapert* person.

malar (màl'ör) *adj.* pertaining to the cheek.

malefic (màl-èf'ìk) *adj.* harmful, mischievous; *maleficent.*

malentendu (màl"ôN-tòN-dü') *adj.* misunderstood. -*n.* a misunderstanding.

maliferous (màl-ìf'ər-əs) *adj.* producing evil; unhealthy, as a climate.

malism (mā'lĭz"əm) *n.* the theory that the world is mostly bad.

malkin (mò'kĭn) *n.* 1. a mop for cleaning ovens. 2. a mop for cleaning cannons. 3. a cat, hare, or scarecrow.

malleate (màl'ē-āt) *v.t.* to hammer metal. -*adj.* marked as if by a hammer.

malmy (mòm'ē) *adj.* 1. clayey,

chalky soil. 2. soft like lime-stone. 3. warm and sticky, like the weather.

malneirophrenia (măl"nĭ-rō-frē'nĭ-ə) *n.* depression following a nightmare.

malnoia (măl-noi'ə) *n.* a vague feeling of mental discomfort.

malversation (măl-vûr-sā'shən) *n.* corruption in office (politics).

mamamouchi (mȯ-mȯ-mōō'chē) *n.* 1. a pompous-sounding, though bogus, Turkish title. 2. someone thus titled (Molière's *Le Bourgeois Gentilhomme*).

mamelon (măm'ə-lŏn) *n.* a low, rounded hill (from its resemblance to a woman's breast).

mameluke (măm'ə-lōōk) *n.* 1. an ex-slave converted to Islam and the military. 2. a fighting slave. 3. an aggressive supporter of the pope.

mammillated (măm'ĭ-lā"təd) *adj.* having nipples, or small protuberances like nipples.

mammock (măm'ək) *n.* a shapeless piece; a scrap. -*v.t.* to tear, break, or divide into pieces.

mammonism (măm'ən-ĭz"əm) *n.* devotion to the pursuit of wealth.

mammothrept (măm'ō-thrĕpt) *n.* 1. a child brought up by its grandmother. 2. a spoiled child.

mammoxed (măm'ŏkst) *adj.* seriously injured, mangled, mutilated (U.S. slang).

manatee (măn'ə-tē) *n.* a seal-like mammal inhabiting the Caribbean, the Amazon, the Orinoco, and waters off the West African coast.

manavelins (mə-năv'əl-ĭnz) *n.pl.* leftovers; odds and ends (slang).

manbote (măn'bōt) *n.* money paid to a lord as compensation for the killing of one of his men.

mancinism (măn'sĭn-ĭz"əm) *n.* left-handed, or -sidedness.

mancipate (măn'sĭ-pāt) *v.t.* to enslave. also *adj.*

manciple (măn'sĭ-pəl) *n.* 1. a manager, landlord, or innkeeper. 2. a slave.

mandamus (măn-dā'məs) *n.* a Superior Court order.

mandorla (mȯn'dȯr-lȯ) *n.* an almond-shaped object.

manducable (măn'dŭk-ə-bəl) *adj.* chewable or edible.

manège (măn-ĕʒ') *n.* a riding academy or horse-training school.

mang (măng) *v.t.&i.* 1. to lead or go astray. 2. to be anxious or puzzled.

mangel-wurzel (măng'gəl-wûr"zəl) *n.* a large European beet used for cattle food.

mangonize (măng'gō-nīz) *v.t.&i.* to traffic in slaves.

mania-à-potu (mā'nĭ-ə-ȯ-pō-tōō") *n.* madness resulting from too much gargle.

maniaphobia (mā"nĭ-ə-fō'bĭ-ə) *n.* fear of insanity.

maniple (măn'ĭ-pəl) *n.* 1. a handful. 2. a company of soldiers. 3. a narrow cloth band suspended on the arm by Roman Catholic Mass celebrants.

manipulandum (măn-ĭp"ū-lăn'dəm) *n.* something that is to be manipulated (psychology).

manit (măn'ĭt) *n.* man-minute, or the amount of work done by one worker in one minute.

manqué (mȯN-kā') *adj.* unrealized, as a goal; unfulfilled.

manqueller (măn'kwĕl"ər) *n.* murderer.

mansuetude (măn'swē-tōōd) *n.* tameness, gentleness, mildness.

mantic (măn'tĭk) *adj.* pertaining to

---

fortunetelling; allegedly endowed with prophetic powers. -n. fortunetelling.

mantology (măn-tŏl′ə-jē) n. fortunetelling; a fortuneteller.

manubiary (măn-ū′bĭ-ěr″ē) adj. relating to the spoils of war.

manuduction (măn-ū-dŭk′shən) n. 1. guidance, leading. 2. something that leads, a leader.

manumission (măn-ū-mĭ′shən) n. formal liberation of a slave.

manurement (măn-ūr′mənt) n. cultivation.

manustupration (măn″ū-stōō-prā′shən) n. masturbation.

manx (mănks) adj. pertaining to the Isle of Man, its inhabitants, or language. -n. the Manx cat, short-haired animal with no visible tail.

manxome (mănks′əm) adj. like a manx, the short-haired cat above (Lewis Carroll's *Jabberwocky*).

maquillage (mȯ-kē-yȯż′) n. make-up.

maquis (mȯ-kē′) n. 1. scrub bushes dotting a hillside (Latin *macula* = spot). 2. (cap.) the Second World War French underground; the resistance. 4. a member of the resistance.

marcescent (mȯr-sĕs′ənt) adj. withered, decayed, weak.

margaritaceous (mȯr″gə-rĭ-tā′shəs) adj. pearly.

margay (mȯr′gā) n. an ocelotlike cat of Central America.

marge (mȯrj) n. a river bank; any margin or boundary.

margrave (mȯr′grāv) n. English spelling of German *Markgraf*, roughly corresponding to a marquis.

maricolous (mă-rĭk′ō-ləs) adj. living in the sea.

marigenous (mă-rĭj′ən-əs) adj.

produced in or by the sea.

mariolatry (měr-ĭ-ŏl′ə-trē) n. Mary-worship.

maritodespotism (mȧr″ĭ-tō-děs′pə-tĭz″əm) n. ruthless domination by a husband.

marlish (mȯr′lĭsh) adj. easygoing. -v.t. to let [something] go.

marlock (mȯr′lŭk) v.i. to cavort, frolic. -n. a trick (dialect)

marmarize (mȯr′mə-rīz) v.t. to make into marble [from limestone].

marmoreal (mȯr-mȯr′ē-əl) adj. marblelike.

marouflage (mȯr-ōō-flȯż′) n. painting on canvas and then gluing the picture to the wall.

marplot (mȯr′plŏt) n. an officious plot-marrer.

marquetry (mȯr′kə-trē) n. inlaid work using wood, shell, stone, etc.

marrano (mə-rŏn′ō) n. a Jew or Moor Christianized in order to escape persecution.

marrowsky (mă-rou′skē) n. spoonerism (said to be named from a Polish count).

martingale (mȯr′tĭn-gāl) n. 1. a forked strap, fastened to the harness, for holding down a horse's head. 2. a stay for the jib boom (sailing). 3. a betting system of doubling the ante after every loss.

Martinmas (mȯr′tĭn-məs) n. November eleventh (feast of St. Martin).

martyrology (mȯr-tûr-ŏl′ə-jē) n. 1. a history or official catalog of martyrs and saints. 2. a branch of ecclesiastical history dealing with the lives of martyrs.

maschalephidrosis (măs″kə-lĕf-ĭ-drō′sĭs) n. massive sweating of the armpits.

mashgiach (mȯsh′gē-ȯk) n. an inspector devoted to perpetuating koshery in Jewish food stores and kitchens.

masser (màs'ûr) *n.* 1. one who attends Mass. 2. a masseur.

mastaba (màs'tə-bò) *n.* the earliest type of Egyptian tomb.

mastigophobia (màs"tǐ-gō-fō'bǐ-ə) *n.* fear of punishment.

mastigophoric (màs"tǐ-gō-fôr'ǐk) *adj.* whip-wielding.

mastodont (màs'tō-dònt) *adj.* having teeth like a mastodon's; pertaining to the mastodon.

matachin (màt'ə-chǐn) *n.* a masked sword dancer, the dance, or its music.

mataeology (màt-ē-òl'ə-jē) *n.* needless or foolish conversation. also *mateology.*

mataeotechny (màt'ē-ō-tĕk"nē) *n.* an unprofitable science or art (Greek *mataios* = vain + *techne* = art, science).

matanza (màt-àn'zə) *n.* a slaughter-house.

matelasse (mòt-lò-sā') *adj.* decorated with quilting marks. -*n.* such a fabric.

matelotage (mòt-lō-tò²') *n.* 1. boat rental. 2. West Indian communes of the eighteenth century.

mathesis (mə-thē'sǐs) *n.* learning, mental discipline, especially in mathematics.

matima (màt'ǐ-mə) *n.* a god-mother.

matrilineal (màt-rǐ-lǐn'ē-əl) *adj.* pertaining to the maternal line.

matrilocal (màt-rǐ-lō'kəl) *adj.* pertaining to marriage in which the husband lives with his wife's family.

matripotestal (màt"rǐ-pō-tès'təl) *adj.* pertaining to maternal control.

matroclinous (màt-rō-klī'nəs) *adj.* having characteristics inherited from the mother.

matronize (màt'rō-nīz) *v.t.* 1. to make a matron of; to make matronlike. 2. to chaperone.

matronymic (màt-rō-nǐm'ǐk) *adj. &n.* using the mother's name, or tracing descent matrilineally.

mattamore (màt'ə-môr) *n.* an underground storehouse.

mattock (màt'ək) *n.* a digging tool.

mattoid (màt'oid) *n.* a congenitally insane person.

maturescent (màt-ū-rès'ənt) *adj.* approaching maturity.

matutolagnia (mà-tōō"tō-làg'nǐ-ə) *n.* antemerdian sexual desire.

matutolypea (mà-tōō"tō-lǐp'ē-ə) *n.* getting up on the wrong side of the bed.

maugh (môf) *n.* a brother-in-law; a son-in-law; a friend.

maulstick (môl'stǐk) *n.* a long wooden stick used by painters for supporting the hand. also *mahlstick.*

maumetry (mô'mə-trē) *n.* idolatry.

maunderer (môn'dûr-ər) *n.* 1. someone wandering aimlessly. 2. a grumbler, mutterer; an incoherent speaker.

maundy (môn'dē) *n.* 1. a foot-cleaning ceremony occurring the Thursday (Maundy Thursday) before Good Friday. 2. dole connected with Maundy Thursday. 3. (cap.) the Last Supper. 4. a feast.

maxilla (màks-ǐl'ə) *n.* upper jaw-bone.

maypop (mā'-pòp) *n.* the passion flower, its blossom or fruit.

mazarine (màz'ər-ēn) *adj.* pertaining to Cardinal Mazarin, a successor of Richelieu. -*n.* 1. mazarine blue, a rich, medium blue. 2. a dish of chopped meat. 3. a method of cleaning chickens. 4.

a small dish when placed in a larger one. -*v.t.* to border decoratively.

mazer (mā′zûr) *n.* 1. a large drinking bowl. 2. the head. 3. a helmet. -*v.t.* to knock on the head.

mazology (mā-zŏl′ə-jē) *n.* the study of mammals; *mammalogy.*

mazomancy (mā′zō-măn″sē) *n.* fortunetelling by a nursing baby (Greek *mazos* = breast).

mazophilous (màz-ŏf′îl-əs) *adj.* pertaining to mammary mania.

mbori (əm-bôr′ē) *n.* a mild form of surra affecting camels.

meable (mē′ə-bəl) *adj.* capable of being easily penetrated.

meacock (mē′kŏk) *n.* an effeminate or cowardly man.

mease (mēz) *n.* a measure of 500 herrings. -*v.t.* to ease, calm.

meatus (mē-ā′təs) *n.* 1. a natural passage. 2. the opening of such a passage.

mechanograph (mĕk′ə-nō-grăf″) *n.* a copy of an art work, produced by mechanical means. *mechanographist, n.*

mechanomorphism (mĕk″ă-nō-môr′fĭz″əm) *n.* the doctrine that the universe is fully explicable in mechanistic terms.

mechanophobia (mĕk″ă-nō-fō′bĭ-ə) *n.* fear of machines.

meconology (mĕk-ō-nŏl′ə-jē) *n.* the study of opium and its effects.

meconophagism (mĕk-ō-nŏf′ə-jĭz″əm) *n.* opium addiction.

medicaster (mĕd′ĭ-kăs″tər) *n.* a medical quack.

mediety (mē-dī′ə-tē) *n.* 1. half. 2. middle or intermediate part or quality. 3. moderation, temperence.

meed (mēd) *n.* 1. a well-deserved reward. 2. a bribe.

megacephalous (mĕg-ə-sĕf′ə-ləs) *adj.* having a large head; *megacephalic.*

megalonisus (mĕg-ă-lŏn′ĭ-səs) *n.* a tendency to exaggerate.

megalophobia (mĕg″əl-ō-fō′bĭ-ə) *n.* fear of large things.

megalopolitan (mĕg-ə-pŏl′ĭ-tən) *adj.* pertaining to a very large city. also *megapolitan.*

megaparsec (mĕg-ə-pŏr′sĕk) *n.* a unit of measure for interstellar space, equal to 19,200,000,000,-000,000,000 miles or 3,260,000 light years.

megrim (mē′grĭm) *n.* 1. migraine headache. 2. the "blues." 3. dizziness. 4. *pl.* whim. 5. the lantern flounder.

mehari (mə-hôr′ē) *n.* a speedy camel once used by the French army in Algeria.

meinie (mā′nē) *n.* 1. a household or retinue. 2. a large number. 3. the so-called masses.

meiosis (mī-ō′sĭs) *n.* 1. an understatement in rhetoric. 2. nuclear change in cell maturation. 3. abatement of symptoms in a disease. also *miosis.*

meizoseismal (mī-zō-sīz′məl) *adj.* pertaining to the maximum destructive force of an earthquake.

mel (mĕl) *n.* honey.

melangeur (mĕl-ôN-zûr′) *n.* a machine for making chocolate syrup.

melanic (mĕl-ăn′ĭk) *adj.* dark, black; *malanian, melanotic.*

melanocomous (mĕl-ăn-ŏk′ə-məs) *adj.* dark-haired.

meldrop (mĕl′drŏp) *n.* a drop of dew, foam, or snot.

melic (mĕl′ĭk) *adj.* lyric; pertaining to song or poetry. -*n.* melic poetry.

meline (mē′lĭn) *adj.* canary yellow.

melisma (mĕl-ĭz′mə) *n.* 1. a

melody, part of an aria. 2. a
musical ornament.

melissophobia (mĕl-ĭs"ō-fō'bĭ-ə)
n. fear of bees.

mellivorous (mĕl-ĭv'ôr-əs) *adj.*
eating or living on honey.

melomaniac (mĕl-ō-mā'nĭ-ăk) *n.* a
music lover.

melophobia (mĕl-ō-fō'bĭ-ə) *n.* a
·hatred of music.

melopoeia (mĕl-ō-pē'ə) *n.* making
up melodies; the made-up
melody.

melote (mē-lō'tē) *n.* a monk's hair
coat.

menacme (mē-năk'mē) *n.* the
menstruating part of a woman's
life.

menald (mĕn'əld) *adj.* speckled,
variegated.

menarche (mē-nŏr'kē) *n.* the onset
of menstruation. see *menophania.*

mendaciloquent (mĕn-dà-sĭl'ō-
kwənt) *adj.* pertaining to lying as
a fine art.

meniscoid (mĕn-ĭs'koid) *adj.* 1.
crescent-shaped. 2. cartilage in
the knee. 3. a concave-convex
lens.

menophania (mĕn-ō-făn'ĭ-ə) *n.* 1.
the *menarche,* or onset of
menstruation. 2. false menstruation; menseslike discharge.

mensch (mĕnsh) *n.* a thoroughly
admirable and 100-percent good
person (Yiddish).

menseful (mĕns'fəl) *adj.* discreet,
considerate; neat and clean.

menticide (mĕn'tĭ-sīd) *n.* brain-
washing.

mentimutation (mĕn"tĭ-mū-
tā'shən) *n.* change of mind.

mentulate (mĕn'tū-lāt) *adj.* well-
hung (Latin *mentula* = penis).

mephitic (mə-fĭt'ĭk) *adj.* stinking.

meracious (mə-rā'shəs) *adj.* un-
adulterated, full-strength, pure.

meraculous (mûr-ăk'ū-ləs) *adj.*
demi-dirty, slightly filthy.

mercative (mûr'kə-tĭv) *adj.* pertaining to trade or commerce.

merdaille (mĕr-dīy') *n.* the mass,
rabble.

merdivorous (mûr-dĭv'ō-rəs) *adj.*
eating dung.

merenda (mĕr-ĕn'də) *n.* a between-
meals snack.

meristic (mə-rĭs'tĭk) *adj.* pertaining to or divided into segments.

meritmonger (mĕr'ĭt-mŭng"gər) *n.*
someone seeking salvation as a
reward for doing good unto his
brethren.

merkin (mûr'kĭn) *n.* 1. female
genitalia. 2. false pubic hair. 3. a
mop for swabbing cannons.

merorganization (mĕr-ôr"găn-ĭ-
zā'shən) *n.* somewhat of an
organization. *merorganized adj.*
partly organized.

Merovingian (mĕr-ō-vĭn'jĭ-ən) *adj.*
pertaining to the first Frankish
dynasty founded by Clovis I
about 500 A.D.

merse (mûrs) *n.* land near water; a
marsh. *-v.t.* to immerse.

merulator (mûr'ū-lā"tər) *n.* a wine-
bibber.

merveilleuse (mĕr-vă-yûz') *n.* an
eighteenth-century French
woman fantastically garbed; ultra
chic (French *merveilleuse* =
wonderful).

merveilleux (mĕr-vă-yû') *n.* 1. an
eighteenth-century French fop. 2.
a shiny silk fabric used for dresses
and coat linings.

merycism (mĕr'ĭ-sĭz"əm) *n.*
chewing regurgitated food;
rumination.

mesalliance (mā-zàl-yòNs') *n.*
marriage with a person of inferior social position; a *misalliance.*

mesial (mē'zĭ-əl) *adj.* middle, me-

màn; māde; lĕt; bē; sĭp; wīne; hŏt; cōld; sôre; dŭll; fūgue; bûrp;
gŏŏd; fōōd; out; gĕt; thin; this; year; ażure; ō'mən"; viN; fûr; Bach

dian. opposite of *lateral*.

mesne (mēn) *adj.* being between two extremes in time or place; intermediate, intervening.

mesomorph (mĕs'ō-môrf) *n.* a medium-sized human body.

mesothetic (mĕs-ō-thĕt'ĭk) *adj.* in the middle, intermediate.

mesquite (mĕs-kēt') *n.* 1. sugar-rich cactus of the southwestern U.S. and Mexico. 2. the screw bean.

messuage (mĕs'wĭj) *n.* a house together with its adjacent buildings and surrounding land.

metabiosis (mē″tə-bī-ō'sĭs) *n.* the preparation by one organism of the environment of another.

metage (mĕt'əj) *n.* official measurement or the charge for it.

metagnostic (mĕt-ăg-nòs'tĭk) *adj.* unknowable.

metagrobolize (mĕt-ə-gròb'ə-līz) *v.t.* to mystify.

metallege (mĕt-ăl'ə-jē) *n.* spoonerism.

metallogeny (mĕt-əl-ŏj'ən-ē) *n.* branch of geology dealing with the origin of ore deposits.

metastasis (mē-tàs'tə-sĭs) *n.* change of form or substance.

metayer (mä-tŏ-yā') *n.* a sharecropper. *metayage* sharecropping.

metempirical (mĕt-ĕm-pĭr'ĭ-kəl) *adj.* pertaining to concepts or ideas outside human experience; concerning intuitive knowledge, opposite of *empirical*.

metempsychosis (mē-tĕmp″sī-kō'sĭs) *n.* alleged transmigration of souls.

meteoromancy (mē′tē-ôr-ō-măn″sē) *n.* fortunetelling by thunder, lightning, etc.

metheglin (mē-thĕg'lĭn) *n.* mead.

methionylglutaminylarginyltyrosylglutamylserylleucylphenylalanylalanylglutaminylleucyllysylglutamylarginyllysylglutamylglycylalanylphenylalanylvalylprolylphenylalanylalanylthreonylleucylglycylaspartylprolylglycylisoleucylglutamylglutaminylserylleucyllysylisoleucylaspartylthreonylleucylisoleucylglutamylalanylglycylalanylaspartylalanylleucylglutamylleucylglycylisoleucylprolylphenylalanylserylaspartylprolylleucylalanylaspartylglycylprolylthreonylisoleucylglutaminylasparaginylalanylthreonylleucylarginylalanylphenylalanylalanylalanylglycylvalylthreonylprolylalanylglutaminylcysteinylphenylalanylglutamylmethionylleucyalanylleucylisoleucylarginylglutaminyllysylhistidylprolylthreonylisoleucylprolylisoleucylglycylleucylleucylmethionyltyrosylalanylasparaginylleucylvalylphenylalanylasparaginyllysylglycylisoleucylaspartylglutamylphenylalanyltyrosylalanylglutaminylcysteinylglutamyllysylvalylglycylvalylaspartylserylvalylleucylvalylalanylaspartylvalylprolylvalylglutaminylglutamylserylalanylprolylphenylalanylarginylglutaminylalanylalanylleucylarginylhistidylasparaginylvalylalanylprolylisoleucylphenylalanylisoleucylcysteinylprolylprolylaspartylalanylaspartylaspartylaspartylleucylleucylarginylglutaminylisoleucylalanylseryltyrosylglycylarginylglycyltyrosylthreonyltyrosylleucylleucylserylarginylalanylglycylvalylthreonylglycylalanylglutamylasparaginylarginylalanylalanylleucylprolylleucylasparaginylhistidylleucylvalylalanyllysylleucyl-

lysylglutamyltyrosylaspara-
ginylalanylalanylprolylprolylleu-
cylglutaminylglycylphenylalan-
ylglycylisoleucylserylalanylpro-
lylaspartylglutaminylvalyllysyl-
alanylalanylisoleucylaspartylal-
anylglycylalanylalanylglycyla-
lanylisoleucylserylglycylseryl-
alanylisoleucylvalyllysylisoleucyl-
isoleucylglutamylglutaminylhis-
tidylasparaginylisoleucylglu-
tamylprolylglutamyllysylmeth-
ionylleucylalanylalanylleucylly-
sylvalylphenylalanylvalylglu-
taminylprolylmethionyllysylal-
anylalanylthreonylarginylserine
the chemical name for *tryptophan synthetase A protein*, a 1,913-letter enzyme with 267 amino acids.

metis (mā-tēs′) *n.* mestizo.

metopic (mē-tŏp′ĭk) *adj.* pertaining to the forehead; frontal.

metopomancy (mĕt′ō-pō-măn″sē) *n.* fortunetelling by examining the face.

metoposcopy (mĕt-ō-pŏs′kō-pē) *n.* judging character by studying the face.

metrician (mē-trĭsh′ən) *n.* a writer or student of verse.

metrification (mĕt″rĭ-fĭ-kā′shən) *n.* versification.

metromania (mĕt-rō-mā′nĭ-ə) *n.* a mania for writing verse.

metrophobia (mĕt-rō-fō′bĭ-ə) *n.* hatred or fear of poetry.

Metternichian (mĕd-ər-nĭk′ē-ən) *adj.* pertaining to Metternich or his reactionary political ideas.

mettlesome (mĕt′əl-sŭm) *adj.* spirited, fiery.

mezonny (mə-zŏn′ē) *n.* money spent for drugs (slang).

miasmatic (mī-ăz-măt′ĭk) *adj.* noxious, contagious, blechhy.

miche (mĭch) *n.* a loaf of bread.

micracoustic (mĭk-rə-kōōs′tĭk) *adj.* made to augment faint sounds. -*n.* an instrument for doing this.

micraner (mī′krā″ər) *n.* a tiny male ant.

microcephalous (mĭk-rō-sĕf′ə-ləs) *adj.* small-headed. also *microcephalic.*

microlipet (mĭk-rō-lĭp′ət) *n.* someone bothered by trifles.

micturition (mĭk-tyûr-ĭ′shən) *n.* need for frequent urination.

midden (mĭd′ən) *n.* 1. a dunghill. 2. garbage accumulated around one's house or apartment.

mieny (mī′nē) *n.* a group of co-workers.

migniard (mĭn′yərd) *adj.* dainty, delicate; mincing.

mijnheer (mīn-hĭr′) *n.* 1. Dutch title meaning mister. 2. a Dutchman (colloquial).

milch (mĭlch) *adj.* giving milk — now applied only to domestic animals. -*v.t.* to milk. *milcher,* *n.* a milch cow.

mileway (mīl′wā) *n.* 1. the time required to walk one mile. 2. a mile long.

militaster (mĭl′ĭ-tăs″tər) *n.* an insignificant military man.

millenarianism (mĭl-ən-ĕr′ĭ-ən-ĭz″əm) *n.* belief in the coming *millennium,* or period when Christ will reign triumphant in a perfect world.

millesimal (mĭl-ĕs′ĭ-məl) *adj.* thousandth; pertaining to a thousandth. also *n.*

milpita (mĭl-pē′tə) *n.* a little cornfield.

milt (mĭlt) *n.* 1. the spleen. 2. the male reproductive glands of fishes when filled with fluid; the fluid itself. -*v.t.* to impregnate with *milt.*

---

màn; mãde; lĕt; bē; sĭp; wīne; hŏt; cōld; sôre; dŭll; fūgue; bûrp; gōōd; fōōd; out; gĕt; thin; thĭs; year; aźure; ō′mən″; viN; für; Bach

mimp (mĭmp) *n.* pursing the lips. -*v.i.* to speak affectedly.

mimsy (mĭm′zē) *adj.* prim, prudish.

minacious (mĭn-ā′shəs) *adj.* menacing; *minatory.*

minauderie (mē-nō-drē′) *n.* coquetry, usually in plural.

mingy (mĭn′jē) *adj.* mean and stingy.

miniate (mĭn′ĭ-āt) *v.t.* to paint red; to paint with red letters; to *rubricate.*

minim (mĭn′ĭm) *n.* 1. an apothecaries' measure of 0.95 grains of water, roughly equivalent to one drop. 2. a musical half note. 3. a tiny creature; pigmy.

minimifidianism (mĭn″ē-mĭ-fĭd′ĭ-ən-ĭz″əm) *n.* having almost no faith or belief.

minimus (mĭn′ĭ-məs) *n.* 1. a tiny creature. 2. the little finger or toe.

minionette (mĭn-yən-ĕt′) *adj.* small, delicate. -*n.* a type size.

miniver (mĭn′ĭ-vər) *n.* an ermine in its winter white.

minnesinger (mĭn′ē-sĭng″ər) *n.* one of a class of German lyric poets ululating from the middle of the twelfth to the same of the fourteenth century.

minuend (mĭn′ū-ĕnd) *n.* the number from which another number is to be subtracted. see *subtrahend.*

miqra (mĭk′rə) *n.* 1. the Hebrew text of the Bible. 2. a liturgical reading of the *miqra.* also *mikra.*

mirabiliary (mĭr-ə-bĭl′ĭ-èr″ē) *n.* a wonder-worker. *mirific, mirificent, adj.*

mirador (mĭr- à-dôr′) *n.* 1. a watchtower, enclosed balcony, or bay window affording a panoramic view. 2. the color reddish-orange, or *art brown.*

mird (mûrd) *v.i.* 1. to meddle. 2. to

fool around sexually. -*v.t.* to attempt.

miryachit (mēr-yò′chĕt) *n.* a neurotic condition observed in Siberia, similar to the *jumping disease* observed in New England.

mirza (mĭr′zò) *n.* a Persian title of honor used after the name of a prince and before the name of a hero, scholar, or high official.

misandry (mĭs′ăn-drē″) *n.* dislike of men.

misapodysis (mĭs′ə-pō-dĭs′ĭs) *n.* hatred of undressing in front of someone.

misarchist (mĭs′ôr-kĭst) *n.* a person who hates authority.

miscible (mĭs′ĭ-bəl) *adj.* mixable in liquid.

miscitation (mĭs-ī-tā′shən) *n.* an erroneous quotation; a misquote.

misdemeanant (mĭs-dē-mēn′ənt) *n.* someone convicted of a misdemeanor.

miserotia (mĭs-ə-ŏt′ĭ-ə) *n.* aversion to sex.

misocainia (mĭ-sō-kā′nĭ-ə) *n.* hatred of anything new or strange, such as new ideas.

misocapnist (mĭ-sō-kăp′nĭst) *n.* a hater of tobacco smoke.

misodoctakleidist (mĭ″sō-dŏk-tə-klī′dĭst) *n.* one who hates to practice the piano (Greek *misos* = hatred + *dokime* = rehearsal + *ta kleidia* = keyboard).

misogamy (mĭ-sòg′ə-mē) *n.* hatred of marriage.

misology (mĭ-sòl′ə-jē) *n.* hatred of using the intellect in argument or discussion.

misomania (mĭ-sō-mā′nĭ-ə) *n.* hatred of everything.

misoneism (mĭ-sō-nē′ĭz″əm) *n.* hatred of new things.

misopedia (mĭ-sō-pē′dĭ-ə) *n.* hatred of children, especially one's own.

misopolemiac (mĭ″sō-pō-lĕm′ĭ-ăk)
n. a war-hater.

misoscopist (mĭ-sŏs′kō-pĭst) *n.* a
hater of beauty; a recluse.

misosophy (mĭ-sŏs′ō-fē) *n.* hatred
of wisdom. *misosophist, n.*

misotheism (mĭ-sō-thē′ĭz″əm) *n.*
hatred of gods.

misotramontanism (mĭ″sō-trä-
mŏn′tən-ĭz″əm) *n.* a hatred of the
unknown.

misoxeny (mĭ-sŏks′ən-ē) *n.* a hater
of strangers. also *misoxens.*

misprision (mĭs-prĭzh′ən) *n.* 1. mis-
conduct or neglect of duty while
in office. 2. contempt, neglect,
scorn.

missionate (mĭsh′ən-āt) *v.i.* to
proselytize; act as a missionary.

mistetch (mĭs-tĕch′) *n.* a bad habit.
-*v.t.* to teach bad habits to.

mistigris (mĭs′tĭ-grĭs) *n.* a poker
game using the joker; the joker
card.

mistral (mĕs-trŏl′) *n.* a cold and dry
northerly wind of the Mediterranean provinces of France.

mithridatism (mĭth′rĭ-dā″tĭz″əm)
n. immunity to poison achieved
by taking gradually increased
doses (mythology has it that
Mithridates VI of Pontus im-
munized himself this way).

mixogamy (mĭks-ŏg′ə-mē) *n.* a sur-
plus of male fish at spawning
time.

mixty-maxty (mĭks′tē-măks″tē)
adj. mixed-up; confused. -*n.* a
mishmash.

mizmaze (mĭz′māz) *n.* a maze; confusion, bewilderment.

mizzle (mĭz′əl) *v.i.* 1. to complain
(Australian slang). 2. to dis-
appear suddenly. -*v.t.* 1. to confuse, mislead. 2. to speckle.
-*v.t.&i.* to drizzle. *n.* drizzle.

mizzy (mĭz′ē) *n.* a swamp.

mlechchha (mlĕch′chə) *n.* a non-
Hindu; a foreigner.

moa (mō′ə) *n.* a large New Zealand bird, now extinct.

moanworthy (mōn′wûr″thē) *adj.*
lamentable, pitiful.

mobby (mŏb′ē) *n.* 1. an alcoholic
drink made from sweet potatoes.
2. fruit juice for distilling brandy;
the brandy.

modena (mŏd′ē-nə) *n.* deep purple.

modoc (mō′dŏk) *n.* 1. someone
who joins the Air Force for favorable publicity. 2. a dummy used
as a target for carnival ball
tosses; also figuratively. 3. an
Indian tribe formerly of California, now relegated to Oregon
and Oklahoma.

modulus (mŏd′ū-ləs) *n.* a number
or quantity that measures a force,
function or effect.

mofette (mō-fĕt′) *n.* a volcanic fis-
sure spewing forth carbon diox-
ide, the last stages of volcanic
activity.

moggan (mŏg′ən) *n.* a long, footless stocking.

mogigraphia (mŏg-ĭ-grăf′ĭ-ə) *n.*
writers' cramp.

mogilalia (mŏg-ĭ-lāl′ĭ-ə) *n.* stuttering.

moider (moi′dər) *v.t.* 1. to worry,
confuse, distract. 2. to smother,
crowd. 3. to work (with *away*).
-*v.i.* 1. to talk incoherently or
foolishly. 2. to work (dialect).

moiety (moi′ə-tē) *n.* a half.

moil (moil) *n.* 1. a mining tool. 2.
hard work. 3. confusion, tur-
moil. 4. mud. 5. a dirty spot. 6. a
hornless ox. -*v.t.* 1. to wet; to
dirty. 2. to worry or torment. -*v.i.*
1. to dirty oneself in the mud. 2.
to work hard. 3. to worry. -*adj.*
hornless.

molendinaceous (mō-lĕn"dĭn-ā'shəs) *adj.* like a windmill.

moliminous (mō-lĭm'ĭn-əs) *adj.* massive; momentous.

moll-buzzer (mŏl'bŭz"ər) *n.* a pickpocket who picks on women (slang).

mollescent (mŏl-ĕs'ənt) *adj.* softening.

mollipilose (mŏl-ĭ-pīl'əs) *adj.* downy or fluffy.

mollitious (mŏl-ĭsh'əs) *adj.* luxuriously softening; sensuous.

molybdomancy (mō-lĭb'dō-măn"sē) *n.* fortunetelling by dropping molten lead on water.

molysmophobia (mŏl"ĭs-mō-fō'bĭ-ə) *n.* fear of dirt or contamination. see *mysophobia*.

mome (mōm) *n.* 1. a crashing bore; a buffoon. 2. a carping critic. *-adj.* soft and smooth.

momicks (mŏm'ĭks) *n.* a bad carver (slang).

mommixed (mŏm'ĭkst) *adj.* disorderly, in confusion (slang).

momzer (mŏm'zər) *n.* a really impossible person; a sponger, liar, troublemaker, and pest who is humorless and unattractive; a nothing (Yiddish).

monachal (mŏn'ə-kəl) *adj.* monastic.

monad (mō'năd) *n.* 1. an indivisible unit; the ultimate entity. 2. any one-celled organism or supreme being.

monepic (mŏn-ĕp'ĭk) *adj.* consisting of one word, or of one-word sentences.

moneyscrivener (mŭn"ē-skrĭv"ən-ûr) *n.* someone who borrows money for others.

monial (mō'nĭ-əl) *n.* a nun.

moniliform (mō-nĭl'ĭ-fôrm) *adj.* regularly segmented to look like a string of beads.

monition (mō-nĭ'shən) *n.* advice; warning.

monkshood (mŭnks'hŏŏd) *n.* a flower resembling a monk's hood.

monody (mŏn'ō-dē) *n.* 1. a lament, either in music or poetry. 2. homophony in music.

monoecious (mō-nē'shəs) *adj.* hermaphroditic.

monogenism (mō-nŏj'ən-ĭz"əm) *n.* the theory that all human races have a common ancestor.

monoglot (mŏn'ō-glŏt) *n.&adj.* [someone] fluent in only one language.

monogony (mō-nŏg'ō-nē) *n.* asexual reproduction.

monolatry (mō-nŏl'e-trē) *n.* the worship of only one of many gods.

monophobia (mŏn-ō-fō'bĭ-ə) *n.* fear of being alone.

monorchid (mŏn-ôr'kĭd) *adj.* having one testicle.

monstricide (mŏn'strĭ-sīd) *n.* the killing of a monster.

monstrum (mŏn'strəm) *n.* a box for relics; a muster of soldiers.

montane (mŏn'tān) *adj.* pertaining to or living in mountains.

mont-de-piété (mōN"də-pyĕ-tā') *n.* a public pawnshop for lending to the poor at a low rate (French = mountain of pity).

monteith (mŏn-tēth') *n.* 1. a silver punch bowl. 2. a Scottish polka dot handkerchief.

Montgolfier (mōN-gŏlf-yā') *n.* a hot-air balloon (from Joseph *Montgolfier*, who made the first one).

monticle (mŏn'tĭk"əl) *n.* a little hill.

monticule (mŏn'tĭ-kūl) *n.* a subordinate cone of a volcano.

montigenous (mŏn-tĭj'ən-əs) *adj.* produced or born on a mountain.

montjoy (mŏnt-joi') *n.* 1. (cap.) a

N

nabla (năb′lə) *n.* 1. an old Hebrew harp or Egyptian lute. 2. an operator that converts a scalar-point function to a gradient vector (mathematics).

nacelle (nà-sèl′) *n.* a small boat.

nacket (năk′ət) *n.* 1. a tennis ballboy. 2. a light lunch.

nacreous (năk′rē-əs) *adj.* pearly.

nagsman (năgz′mən) *n.* a man who rides horses in a sales ring.

Nahuatl (nȯ′wȯ″təl) *n.* the Aztec language.

nanga (năng′gə) *n.* a small Nubian harp.

nanism (năn′ĭz″əm) *n.* dwarfishness.

nankeen (năn-kēn′) *n.* 1. a durable yellow cotton cloth from China. 2. pants made from this material. 3. Nankeen yellow; Nankeen porcelain.

naology (nā-ŏl′ə-jē) *n.* the study of holy buildings.

naos (nā′ŏs) *n.* 1. a shrine or temple. 2 a star of 2.3 magnitude in the constellation *Argus Navis* or *Puppis*.

napiform (nā′pĭ-fôrm) *adj.* turnipshaped.

napoo (nà-pōō′) *adj.* nothing, finished, dead (French *il n'y a plus* = there is nothing left).

nappy (năp′ē) *adj.* 1. downy or shaggy. 2. strong, foaming, as beer or ale. -*n.* 1. ale. 2. a serving or baking bowl. 3. a diaper.

naprapathy (năp-răp′ə-thē) *n.* the manipulation of strained ligaments in the belief that they cause disease.

narcolepsy (nȯr′kō-lĕp″sē) *n.* brief sporadic lapses of deep sleep.

narcosynthesis (nȯr-kō-sĭn′thə-sĭs) *n.* sleep therapy.

narr (nȯr) *v.i.* to growl like a dog. -*n.* a legal declaration

narthex (nȯr′thĕks) *n.* 1. an old church portico. 2. an Afghanistan plant which yields asafetida.

narwhal (nȯr′wəl) *n.* a walruslike mammal with a spotted coat and long tusks, bagged for oil and ivory. also *narwal, narwhale.*

nasicornous (nā-zĭ-kôr′nəs) *adj.* horny on the nose; like a rhinoceros.

nasillate (nā′zĭl-āt) *v.i.* to speak or sing through the nose.

---

màn; māde; lèt; bē; sĭp; wīne; hŏt; cōld; sôre; dùll; fūgue; bûrp;
gŏŏd; fōōd; out; gĕt; thin; this; year; ażure; ō′mən″; viN; für; Bach

nasute (nā'sūt) *adj.* 1. having a keen sense of smell. 2. having a large nose. 3. sharp, astute.

natalitious (nă-təl-ĭ'shəs) *adj.* pertaining to someone's birthday. also *natalitial.*

natatorium (nă-tə-tôr'ĭ-əm) *n.* an indoor swimming pool.

nates (nā'tēz) *n.pl.* 1. the buttocks. 2. the umbones of a bivalve shell.

natterjack (năt'ûr-jăk) *n.* the common toad of western Europe.

natuary (năt'ū-ĕr"ē) *n.* a hospital obstetrics room.

naufragous (nôf'rə-gəs) *adj.* causing shipwrecks.

naulage (nôl'əj) *n.* payment for sea freight.

naumachy (nô'mə-kē) *n.* 1. a real or symbolic naval battle. 2. a theater in which the mock battle is enacted.

naupathia (nô-păth'ĭ-ə) *n.* seasickness.

nauscopy (nôs-kə-pē) *n.* the alleged ability to spot land or ships at sea from far away.

navicert (năv'ĭ-sûrt) *n.* a certificate exempting imports from search and seizure by the British douane.

navicular (nă-vĭk'ū-lər) *adj.* boatlike; *cymbiform, scaphoid.* -*n.* a boat-shaped bone.

nealogy (nē-ăl'ə-jē) *n.* the study of young animals.

neanic (nē-ăn'ĭk) *adj.* youthful, immature.

neanilagnia (nē-ăn"ĭ-lăg'nĭ-ə) *n.* a yen for nymphets.

neanimorphism (nē-ăn"ĭ-môr'fĭz"əm) *n.* looking younger than one's years.

neanthropic (nē-ăn-thrŏp'ĭk) *adj.* pertaining to modern man.

nearomatria (nē-ăr"ō-măt'rĭ-ə) *n.* being a young mother.

neatherd (nēt'hûrd) *n.* a cowboy.

neb (nĕb) *n.* 1. a bird's beak. 2. the tip of something. 3. a pen nib or pencil point.

nebneb (nĕb'nĕb) *n.* acacia bark used in tanning.

nebulaphobia (nĕb"ū-lə-fō'bĭ-ə) *n.* fear of fog. see *homichlophobia.*

nebulochaotic (nĕb"ū-lō-kā-ŏt'ĭk) *adj.* chaotic, confused.

necation (nē-kā'shən) *n.* killing.

necessitarianism (nĕ-sĭs"ĭ-tĕr'ĭ-ən-ĭz"əm) *n.* determinism; doctrine of inevitability resulting from hereditary or environmental causes. opposite of *free will.*

necrologist (nĕk-rŏl'ə-jĭst) *n.* an obituary writer.

necromimesis (nĕk"rō-mĭ-mē'sĭs) *n.* feigning death; the delusion of being dead.

necroponent (nĕk-rŏp'ō-nənt) *n.* someone temporarily in charge of a houshold in which a death has occurred.

necyomancy (nĕs'ĭ-ō-măn"sē) *n.* fortunetelling by summoning Lucifer.

nefandous (nē-făn'dəs) *adj.* unmentionable, unspeakable.

nefast (nē-făst') *adj.* wicked.

negus (nē'gəs) *n.* 1. the king of Ethiopia. 2. a hot wine drink.

nekton (nĕk'tŏn) *n.* swimming organisms in the ocean.

nelipot (nĕl'ĭ-pŏt) *n.* someone going barefoot.

nematode (nĕm'ə-tōd) *adj.* pertaining to the roundworm. also *nematoid.*

nemophilous (nĕm-ŏf'ĭl-əs) *adj.* loving the forest.

neocracy (nē-ŏk'rə-sē) *n.* government by tyros.

neolagnium (nē-ō-lăg'nĭ-əm) *n.* puberty.

neolocal (nē'ō-lō"kəl) *adj.* located away from the families of either spouse.

neomnesia (nē-ŏm-nē′zĭ-ə) n. good memory for recent events.

neorama (nē-ō-rò′mə) n. panorama of a building's interior.

neossology (nē-ŏs-òl′ə-jē) n. the study of young birds.

neoteinic (nē-ō-tī′nĭk) adj. pertaining to prolonged adolescence.

neoteric (nē-ō-tèr′ĭk) adj. recent, modern.

nepenthe (nĕp-ĕn′thē) n. an opiate causing forgetfulness.

nephalism (nèf′ə-lĭz″əm) n. teetotalism.

nepheligenous (nèf-ə-lĭj′ən-əs) adj. producing clouds of tobacco smoke.

nephogram (nèf′ō-gràm) n. a photograph of clouds.

nephrorrhaphy (nèf-rôr′ə-fē) n. anchoring a floating kidney to the rear abdominal wall.

nepimnemic (nĕp-ĭm-nē′mĭk) adj. childhood memory retained in the subconscious.

nepotal (nĕp′ō-təl) adj. pertaining to a nephew. also nepotic.

nepotation (nē-pō-tā′shən) n. riotous living.

nescient (nèsh′ənt) adj. uneducated, unaware, ignorant, and stupid.

nesiote (nē′sĭ-ōt) adj. living on an island.

neskhi (nès′kē) n. Arabic script used in writing religious and sometimes scientific books.

nestcock (nèst′kòk) n. a male homebody.

nestitherapy (nès-tĭ-thèr′ə-pē) n. diet therapy. also nestiatria.

netop (nē′tòp) n. friend (American colonial salutation used in greeting Indians).

neume (nūm) n. medieval musical notation, derived from the

Greeks, showing relative pitch.

neuromimesis (nū″rō-mĭm-ē′sĭs) n. psychosomatic disease.

newmarket (nū′môrk″ət) n. 1. a long, fitted coat. 2. an old card game called Pope Joan.

nexus (nèks′əs) n. 1. connection, link. 2. a connected group or series.

ngaio (ən-gò′yō) n. 1. a small New Zealand tree. 2. Ngaio Marsh, detective-story writer.

ngoko (əng-gō′kō) n. a dialect used by high-born Javanese when speaking to their social inferiors.

ngwee (əng-gwā′) n. a coin equal to 1/100 of the Zambian kwacha.

nibby-jibby (nĭb′ē-jĭb″ē) n. a narrow margin; a close call.

Nibelungenlied (nē′bə-lŏŏng-ən-lēt″) n. an anonymous twelfth-century German epic.

nicker (nĭk′ər) n. 1. an eighteenth-century London hooligan who broke windows with halfpence. 2. a sea monster. 3. a neigh or laugh. also -v.i.

nicknackatory (nĭk-nàk′ə-tôr″ē) n. a toy shop (slang).

nictation (nĭk-tā′shən) n. winking, nictate. nictitate. v.i. to wink.

niddering (nĭd′ər-ĭng) adj. cowardly.

niddle-noddle (nĭd′əl-nòd″əl) adj. having a wobbly or nodding head. -v.t.&i. to nod or wobble. also niddy-noddy, which, as a hyphenless noun, means a hand reel for yarn.

nide (nīd) n. a brood of pheasants. -v.i. to nest. also nye.

nidificate (nĭd′ĭ-fĭ-kāt″) v.i. to build a nest.

nidifugous (nĭd-ĭf′ū-gəs) adj. leaving the nest soon after birth.

nid-nod (nĭd′nòd) v.t.&i. to nod when sleepy.

nidorous (nĭd'ûr-əs) *adj.* smelling like burning or decaying animal matter.

nidulant (nĭd'ū-lənt) *adj.* nestling, embedded.

niello (nĭ-ĕl'ō) *n.* 1. a black sulfureous alloy. 2. a way of decorating metal with this material. 3. the metal so decorated. *-v.t.* to inlay with *niello*.

nieve (nēv) *n.* 1. a hand or fist. 2. a female serf.

nievie-nievie-nick-nack (nē″vē-nē-vē-nĭk'năk) *n.* a children's game using these words.

niffle (nĭf'əl) *v.t.* 1. to steal in small quantities; to pilfer. 2. to eat hurriedly. *-v.i.* to snivel or sniffle.

nigrescent (nĭ-grĕs'ənt) *adj.* blackish.

nikhedonia (nĭk-hē-dō'nĭ-ə) *n.* pleasure derived from anticipating success.

nikin (nĭk'ĭn) *n.* a very soft creature.

nilometer (nĭl-ŏm'ə-tûr) *n.* an instrument for measuring the height of water in the Nile, especially during its flood.

nimbification (nĭm″bĭ-fĭ-kā'shən) *n.* cloud formation.

nimgimmer (nĭm'gĭm″ər) *n.* a doctor who cures the clap (British slang).

nimiety (nĭm-ī'ə-tē) *n.* redundancy.

niminy-piminy (nĭm″ĭn-ē-pĭm'ĭn-ē) *adj.* affected; effeminate.

nimious (nĭm'ĭ-əs) *adj.* extravagant.

nimmer (nĭm'ər) *n.* a thief.

nimptopsical (nĭmp-tŏp'sĭ-kəl) *adj.* drunk (listed together with 227 other synonyms by Benjamin Franklin). see also *cherubimical* (slang).

nimrod (nĭm'rŏd) *n.* a tyrannical hunter (from *Nimrod*, son of Cush, Genesis X:8-10).

nimshy (nĭm'shē) *n.* a silly ass. also *nimshi.*

nipperkin (nĭp'ər-kĭn) *n.* amount of liquor roughly equivalent to a half pint.

nipperty-tipperty (nĭp″ər-tē-tĭp'ər-tē) *adj.* silly, trifling.

nippitatum (nĭp-ĭ-tā'təm) *n.* exceptionally good and strong ale.

nipter (nĭp'tər) *n.* the ceremony of foot washing on Maundy Thursday in the Eastern Orthodox church. see *maundy,* 1.

nisi (nī'sī) *conj.* unless; if not: used in legal rules, decrees, etc.

nisus (nī'səs) *n.* 1. an effort. 2. spring fever. 3. muscle contracttion while excreting.

nithing (nī'thing) *n.* a coward.

nitid (nĭt'ĭd) *adj.* bright, lustrous. also *nitidous. nitency, n.*

niveous (nĭv'ĭ-əs) *adj.* snowy; snowy white.

nixie (nĭks'ē) *n.* a letter so badly addressed that it can't be delivered (slang).

nobble (nŏb'əl) *v.t.* 1. to drug a race horse. 2. to bribe, steal, or swindle. 3. to hit on the head, stun (all British slang).

nocake (nō'kāk) *n.* Indian corn pounded into powder.

nocent (nō'sənt) *adj.* 1. harmful. 2. guilty.

noctambulation (nŏk-tăm″bū-lā'shən) *n.* somnambulism. also *noctambulism.*

noctivagation (nŏk-tĭv″ə-gā'shən) *n.* wandering around at night, once illegal.

noctuary (nŏk'tū-ĕr″ē) *n.* a diary of nighttime activities.

noddypeak (nŏd'ē-pēk) *n.* a fool; *ninnie-hammer. noddy-peaked, adj.*

nodus (nō'dəs) *n.* a knot; a knotty problem.

noematachograph (nō-ē″mə-tăk′ō-gråf) *n.* an instrument for measuring complex reaction time.

noemics (nō-ĕm′ĭks) *n.* the science of understanding.

noesis (nō-ē′sĭs) *n.* 1. ideational or conceptual knowledge. 2. cognition (psychology).

noetic (nō-ĕt′ĭk) *adj.* reasoning only in abstract or intellectual terms. *-n.* such a person or her ideas.

nolens volens (nō″lənz-vō′lənz) *adj.* willy-nilly.

noli-me-tangeretarian (nō″lĭ-mē-tăn″jə-rə-tĕr′ĭ-ən) *adj.* pertaining to a touch-me-not; rigid, unbending.

nolition (nō-lĭ′shən) *n.* unwillingness opposite of volition. also *noleity.*

nomancy (nō′măn″sē) *n.* fortune-telling by letters.

nomiatrist (nō-mī′ə-trĭst) *n.* a lawyer specializing in medical cases.

nomic (nŏm′ĭk) *adj.* 1. conventional, ordinary: applied to traditional English spelling as opposed to phonetic spelling.

nomism (nō′mĭz″əm) *n.* ethical conduct; morally legal.

nomographer (nō-mŏg′rə-fûr) *n.* a lawmaker; one who writes laws.

nonage (nŏn′əj) *n.* 1. a ninth share of a dead person's negotiable estate, formerly grabbed by the church. 2. legal minority; immaturity.

nonan (nō′nən) *adj.* happening on the ninth day.

nonnant (nŏn′ănt) *n.* at Eton, one who can't swim.

nonnock (nŏn′ŏk) *n.* a whim. *-v.i.* to waste time.

noology (nō-ŏl′ə-jē) *n.* the science of intuition.

nooscopic (nō-ŏs-kŏp′ĭk) *adj.* pertaining to mental examination.

nosathymia (nō-zə-thī′mĭ-ə) *n.* depression due to serious illness.

noseconology (nō″sē-kŏn-ŏl′əjē) *n.* the study of hospital administration.

no-see-em (nō-sē′əm) *n.* the *punkie* or black fly (colloquial).

nosism (nō′sĭz″əm) *n.* collective egotism; group conceit.

nosocomephrenia (nō″zō-kō-mə-frē′nĭ-ə) *n.* depression from prolonged hospital stay.

nosology (nō-sŏl′ə-jē) *n.* classification of diseases; diagnostic character of a disease.

nosophobia (nŏs-ō-fō′bĭ-ə) *n.* fear of becoming ill.

nostology (nŏs-tŏl′ə-jē) *n.* study of senility.

nostomania (nŏs-tō-mā′nĭ-ə) *n.* extreme homesickness.

nostrificate (nŏs′trĭ-fĭ-kāt″) *v.t.* to accept as one's own.

nothosonomia (nō″thō-sō-nō′mĭ-ə) *n.* calling someone a bastard.

nothous (nō′thəs) *adj.* illegitimate.

noumenon (nōō′mə-nŏn) *n.* an object implied by "intuition" rather than evidence. opposite of phenomenon (Kantian philosophy).

novate (nō′vāt) *v.t.* to replace by something new.

novcic (nŏf′chĭch) *n.* a coin of Montenegro, Bosnia, and Herzegovina, equal to 1/100 of a florin (Serbo-Croatian).

novercal (nō-vûr′kəl) *adj.* pertaining to a stepmother.

novercaphobia (nō-vûr″kə-fō′bĭ-ə) *n.* fear or dislike of a stepmother.

novilunar (nō-vĭ-lōō′nər) *adj.* pertaining to the new moon.

novitious (nō-vĭ′shəs) *adj.* recently invented; new.

---

noyade (nwò-yòd') *n.* a mass drowning.

nritya (ən-rĭt'yə) *n.* a Bharata Natya dance of southern India.

nubilate (nōō'bĭl-āt) *v.t.* to obscure; nubilous. *-adj.* cloudy, obscure, vague.

nucha (nōō'kə) *n.* the nape of the neck. *nuchal, adj.*

nucivorous (nōō-sĭv'ôr-əs) *adj.* nut-eating.

nucleonics (nōō-klē-òn'ĭks) *n.* physics of nucleons or atomic nucleus.

nuddle (nŭd'əl) *v.t.&i.* to nuzzle.

nudification (nōō'dĭ-fĭ-kā'shən) *n.* making naked.

nudiustertian (nōō"dĭ-əs-tĕr'shĭ-ən) *adj.* pertaining to the day before yesterday (Latin *nunc dies tertius est* = it is now the third day).

nugacity (nōō-gàs'ĭ-tē) *n.* triviality; futility.

nullah (nŭl'ə) *n.* a dry river in India which becomes a raging torrent in the rainy season.

nullibicity (nŭl-ĭ-bĭs'ĭ-tē) *n.* non-existent. also *nullicility, nullibi-quitous, adj.*

nullifidian (nŭl-ĭ-fĭd'ĭ-ən) *adj.* skeptical. *-n.* skeptic; unbeliever.

nulliparous (nŭl-ĭp'ər-əs) *adj.* pertaining to a woman who has never foaled.

numbles (nŭm'bəlz) *n.pl.* edible deer innards.

numen (nōō'mən) *n.* 1. divine power allegedly possessed by ob-

jects. 2. a god in human form.

nummamorous (nōō-màm'ôr-əs) *adj.* money-loving.

nummular (nùm'ū-lər) *adj.* 1. pertaining to money. 2. coin-shaped; *nummiform.*

nuncheon (nùn'chən) *n.* a between-meals snack.

nuncupate (nùng'kū-pāt) *v.t.* 1. to declare orally. 2. to dedicate, inscribe.

nundinal (nùn'dĭn'əl) *adj.* pertaining to a market or fair.

nutation (nū-tā'shən) *n.* involuntary nodding of the head.

nutricism (nōō'trĭ-sĭz"əm) *n.* symbiosis in which one organism is nourished or protected by the other without reciprocity.

nutshelly (nŭt'shĕl"ē) *adj.* condensed; in a nutshell.

nux (nùks) *n.* the tea served at the Leavenworth Prison mess hall.

nuzzer (nŭz'ər) *n.* a ceremonial gift.

nyanza (nyòn'zò) *n.* a large lake or river in central Africa.

nychthemeron (nĭk-thē'mər-òn) *n.* a twenty-four-hour period. *nychthemeral, adj.*

nyctalopia (nĭk-təl-ō'pĭ-ə) *n.* night blindness.

nycterent (nĭk'tər-ènt) *n.* one who hunts by night.

nympholepsy (nĭm'fō-lĕp"sē) *n.* trance incurred by erotic daydreams.

Nyx (nīks) *n.* a goddess, personification of night and daughter of Chaos.

---

màn; māde; lèt; bē; sìp; wīne; hòt; cōld; sòre; dùll; fūgue; bûrp; gōōd; fōōd; out; gèt; thin; this; year; aźure; ō'mən"; viN; fũr; Bach

oam (ōm) *n.* steam.

oast (ōst) *n.* a kiln to dry hops, malt, or tobacco.

obambulate (ŏb-ăm′bū-lāt) *v.i.* to walk about, wander. *oberration, n.*

obcordate (ŏb-kôr′dāt) *adj.* inversely heart-shaped.

obdormition (ŏb-dôr-mĭ′shən) *n.* numbness caused by pressure on a nerve; when a limb is "asleep."

obduce (ŏb-dōōs′) *v.t.* to cover with.

obeliscolychny (ŏb″əl-ĭs-kō-lĭk′nē) *n.* a lighthouse.

obelus (ŏb′əl-əs) *n.* 1. in ancient manuscripts, the mark − or ÷ which signaled the beginning of a passage suspected of being false. 2. (cap.) the constellation *Sagitta.*

obequitation (ŏb-ĕk″wĭ-tā′shən) *n.* riding around.

obex (ō′bĕks) *n.* 1. an obstacle. 2. a thin layer of cerebral gray matter.

obganiate (ŏb-găn′ĭ-āt) *v.i.* to irritate with reiteration.

oblati (ō-blŏt′ē) *n.pl.* willing slaves of the church.

oblation (ŏb-lā′shən) *n.* 1. a non-living religious sacrifice. 2. a church ante for support of the clergy or poor parishioners.

oblatrate (ŏb-lā′trāt) *v.t.* to snarl at, inveigh against.

oblectation (ŏb-lĕk-tā′shən) *n.* delight, pleasure.

obmutescent (ŏb-mū-tĕs′ənt) *adj.* becoming or remaining silent.

obnubilate (ŏb-nōō′bĭl-āt) *v.t.* to cloud, obscure. *-adj.* cloudy.

obolary (ŏb′ō-lĕr″ē) *adj.* extremely poor (having only *obols,* or coins of little value).

obreption (ŏb-rĕp′shən) *n.* creeping up on.

obrogate (ŏb′rō-gāt) *v.t.* to modify or repeal [a law] by passing a new one.

obsecrate (ŏb′sə-krāt) *v.t.* to plead, implore.

obsidional (ŏb-sĭd′ĭ-ōn″əl) *adj.* pertaining to a siege; besieged. also figurative.

obsignation (ŏb-sĭg-nā′shən) *n.* a formal ratification.

obsolagnium (ŏb-sō-lăg′nĭ-əm) *n.* waning sexual desire due to age.

obstipation (ŏb-stĭ-pā′shən) *n.* 1. act of stopping up. 2. extreme constipation.

obstringe (ŏb-strĭnj') *v.t.* to bind; to make indebted.

obstupefy (ŏb-stoōp'ə-fī) *v.t.* to stupefy.

obtenebrate (ŏb-tĕn'ə-brāt) *v.t.* to darken, as by shadow; *obumbrate.*

obtest (ŏb-tĕst') *v.t.* 1. to beg for. 2. to call as a witness. *-v.i.* to protest.

obtund (ŏb-tŭnd') *v.t.* to dull.

obturate (ŏb'tyûr-āt) *v.t.* to stop up.

obvallate (ŏb-văl'āt) *adj.* walled in.

obvention (ŏb-vĕn'shən) *n.* an occasional gift or treat.

obvolve (ŏb-vŏlv') *v.t.* to wrap up.

occamy (ŏk'ə-mē) *n.* an alloy made imitating gold or silver.

occecation (ŏk-sē-kā'shən) *n.* becoming blind; blindness.

occiduous (ŏk-sĭd'ū-əs) *adj.* western; occidental.

occision (ŏk-sĭz'ən) *n.* slaughter.

occlude (ŏk-loōd') *v.t.* 1. to shut up or out; obstruct. 2. to absorb. 3. to bring the jaws together. also *v.i.*

ocellated (ŏs'əl-āt″əd) *adj.* having or resembling eyelike spots.

ochlesis (ŏk-lē'sĭs) *n.* sickness resulting from overcrowded living conditions.

ochlocracy (ŏk-lŏk'rə-sē) *n.* mob rule.

ochlophobia (ŏk-lŏ-fō'bĭ-ə) *n.* fear of crowds.

octan (ŏk'tăn) *adj.* happening every eighth day (medicine).

octapla (ŏk'tə-plò) *n.* 1. Origen's Hebrew text and seven different Greek translations appearing side by side. 2. any text with eight such versions.

octogild (ŏk'tō-gĭld) *n.* an eight-to-one payment for injury.

octroy (ŏk-troi') *n.* 1. an import tax, where it is paid, or the agency receiving it. *-v.t.* to concede; to command, also *octroi.*

odeum (ō-dē'əm) *n.* a concert hall or theater.

odontalgia (ō-dŏn-tăl'jĭ-ə) *n.* toothache.

odonterism (ō-dŏn'tər-ĭz″əm) *n.* chattering of teeth.

odorivector (ō-dôr'ĭ-vĕk″tər) *n.* something that produces a smell.

odynophobia (ō-dĭn″ō-fō'bĭ-ə) *n.* fear of pain.

oecist (ē'sĭst) *n.* a colonizer.

oecodomic (ē-kō-dŏm'ĭk) *adj.* architectural. also *oecodomical.*

oeillade (ü-yŏd') *n.* an ogle, a flirtatious glance.

oenochoë (ē-nŏk'ō-ē) *n.* a Greek wine pitcher with a trefoil-shaped mouth.

oenology (ē-nŏl'ə-jē) *n.* the study of wines, *oenologist, n.*

oenomancy (ē'nō-măn″sē) *n.* fortunetelling with wine.

oenophilist (ē-nŏf'ĭl-ĭst) *n.* a winelover.

oenophlygia (ē-nō-flĭj'ĭ-ə) *n.* drunkenness.

oestrum (ĕs'trəm) *n.* period of sexual heat in animals, also *oestrus.*

ogdoad (ŏg'dō-ăd) *n.* 1. the number eight; a group of eight. 2. eight Gnostic Divines (or eight Divine Gnostics).

ogee (ō'jē) *n.* an S-shaped molding; any S-shaped curve.

ogive (ō'jīv) *n.* 1. a diagonal Gothic arch. 2. the curve of military projectile heads. 3. the curve of certain statistical graphs.

Ogygian (ō-jĭj'ĭ-ən) *adj.* 1. pertaining to King Ogyges, or to a terrible flood during his reign. 2. very old.

oii (ō-ē'ē) *n.* the New Zealand muttonbird (Maori).

oikofugic (oik-ō-fū'jĭk) *n.* obsessive wandering.

oikology (oi-kŏl'ə-jē) *n.* housekeeping; home economics.

oikonisus (oi-kŏn'ĭ-səs) *n.* urge to start a family.

okapi (ō-kŏ'pē) *n.* a giraffelike animal with a short neck and black and white striped forelegs.

olamic (ō-lăm'ĭk) *adj.* infinite, eternal.

oldwench (ōld'wĕnch) *n.* the triggerfish of the Atlantic and Indian Oceans; *oldwife.*

olent (ō'lənt) *adj.* fragrant.

olid (ŏl'ĭd) *adj.* fetid, stinking.

oligidria (ŏl-ĭ-jĭd'rĭ-ə) *n.* deficient sweat.

oligogenics (ŏl"ĭ-gō-jĕn'ĭks) *n.* birth control.

oligophagous (ŏl-ĭ-gŏf'ə-gəs) *adj.* eating only certain foods.

oligophrenia (ŏl"ĭ-gō-frē'nĭ-ə) *n.* feeblemindedness.

oligoria (ŏl-ĭ-gôr'ĭ-ə) *n.* disinterest in former friends or hobbies.

oligotokous (ŏl-ĭ-gŏt'ō-kəs) *adj.* laying four or fewer eggs.

olisbos (ō-lĭs'bŏs) *n.* a dildo, see *godemiche.*

olitory (ŏl'ĭ-tôr"ē) *adj.* pertaining to or grown in a kitchen garden.

olivet (ŏl'ĭ-vĕt) *n.* 1. an olive grove. 2. an imitation pearl made to deceive unsophisticated traders.

ollapodrida (ŏl"ō-pō-drē'də) *n.* hodgepodge, mishmash, motley collection.

olpe (ŏl'pē) *n.* a leather flask for liquids.

omadhaun (ŏm'ə-thôn) *n.* an idiot, fool.

ombibulous (ŏm-bĭb'ū-ləs) *adj.* someone who drinks everything (H. L. Mencken).

ombrology (ŏm-brŏl'ə-jē) *n.* the study of rain.

ombrometer (ŏm-brŏm'e-tûr) *n.* a rain gauge.

ombrophilous (ŏm-brŏf'ĭl-əs) *adj.* capable of withstanding much rain, as tropical vegetation. *ant. ombrophobous.*

ombrophobia (ŏm-brō-fō'bĭ-ə) *n.* fear of rain or of being rained upon.

ombrosalgia (ŏm-brōs-ăl'jĭ-ə) *n.* pain felt during rainy weather.

omneity (ŏm-nē'ĭ-tē) *n.* allness.

omnifarious (ŏm-nĭ-fĕr'ĭ-əs) *adj.* pertaining to all kinds; *omnigenous.*

omnilegent (ŏm-nĭl'ə-jənt) *adj.* reading everything.

omnist (ŏm'nĭst) *n.* one who believes in all religions.

omophagist (ō-mŏf'ə-jĭst) *n.* an eater of raw meat. *omophagy, n.* eating raw meat as a religious initiation rite. also *omositia, omphagie.*

omoplatoscopy (ō"mō-plă-tŏs'kə-pē) *n. scapulimancy.*

omphacine (ŏm'fə-sĭn) *adj.* pertaining to unripe fruit.

omphalomancy (ŏm'fə-lō-măn"sē) *n.* predicting the number of children a mother will bear by counting the knots in her first-born's umbilical cord.

omphalopsychite (ŏm-fə-lŏp'sĭ-kĭt) *n.* a hesychast. see *hesychastic.*

omphaloskepsis (ŏm'fə-lō-skĕp'sĭs) *n.* meditation while gazing at one's navel.

onager (ŏn'ə-jûr) *n.* 1. the wild ass of central Asia, variety of the *kiang.* 2. a kind of catapult.

onanism (ō'nə-nĭz"əm) *n.* coitus interruptus; masturbation.

oncology (ŏng-kŏl'ə-jē) *n.* the study of tumors.

---

mǎn; mǎde; lĕt; bē; sĭp; wīne; hŏt; cōld; sôre; dŭll; fūgue; bûrp; gŏŏd; fōŏd; out; gĕt; thin; this; year; aʑure; ō'mən"; viN; fûr; Bach

ondatra (ŏn-dàt'rə) *n.* the muskrat.

ondoyant (ŏN-dwô-yŏN') *adj.* wavy; pertaining to a wavy surface.

oneirataxia (ō-nī"rə-tàks'ĭ-ə) *n.* inability to differentiate between fantasy and reality.

oneirocritic (ō-nī"rō-krĭt'ĭk) *n.* an interpreter of dreams.

oneirodynia (ō-nī"rō-dī'nĭ-ə) *n.* nightmare.

onimancy (ŏn'ĭ-màn"sē) *n.* fortunetelling with the fingernails; *onychomancy.*

oniochalasia (ō"nĭ-ō-kəl-ā'zĭ-ə) *n.* buying as a means of mental relaxation.

oniomania (ō"nĭ-ō-mā'nĭ-ə) *n.* a mania for buying things.

onolatry (ō-nŏl'ə-trē) *n.* ass-worship.

onomasticon (ŏn-ō-màs'tĭ-kŏn) *n.* a dictionary, lexicon; a list of proper names. *onomastic, n.* a lexicographer. *-adj.* 1. pertaining to an *onomasticon.* 2. pertaining to the signature of a person who did not write the document she signed. opposite of *holographic.*

onomatechny (ŏn'ō-mà-tĕk"nē) *n.* fortunetelling using the letters in someone's name.

onomatomania (ŏn"ə-màt-ō-mā'nĭ-ə) *n.* preoccupation with words and names.

onomatophobia (ŏn"ō-màt-ō-fō'bĭ-ə) *n.* fear of hearing a certain word.

ontal (ŏn'təl) *adj.* see *noumenal.*

ontogeny (ŏn-tŏj'ən-ē) *n.* the life history of an individual organism.

ontology (ŏn-tŏl'ə-jē) *n.* a metaphysical system dealing with essential properties of nature and being.

onychophagy (ŏn-ĭ-kŏf'ə-jē) *n.* nail-biting.

onym (ŏn'ĭm) *n.* a technical name (biology).

oo (ō'ō) *n.* a Hawaiian bird, source of yellow feather-work since the extinction of the *mamo.*

ooaa (ō"ō-ŏ'ō) *n.* a bird of Kauai, Hawaii.

ooid (ō'oid) *adj.* egg-shaped; pertaining to eggs; *ovarious, ovicular.*

oolly (ōō'lē) *n.* a small lump of wootz steel as it leaves the melting pot (East Indian).

oology (ō-ŏl'ə-jē) *n.* the study of birds' eggs.

oom (ōm) *n.* an uncle (South Africa).

oont (ōōnt) *n.* a camel. also *unt* (Anglo-Indian, Hindi, and Urdu).

opacate (ō-pā'kāt) *v.t.* to make opaque; to darken.

operose (ŏp'ər-ōs) *adj.* requiring labor; laborious, diligent.

ophelimity (ō-fə-lĭm'ĭ-tē) *n.* 1. the ability to please sexually. 2. the ability to please generally.

ophicleide (ŏf'ĭ-klīd) *n.* musical instrument replaced by the tuba, circa 1850.

ophidiophobia (ō-fĭd"ĭ-ō-fō'bĭ-ə) *n.* fear of snakes.

ophiology (ŏf-ĭ-ŏl'ə-jē) *n.* the study of snakes. *ophic. adj.* pertaining to snakes.

ophiomancy (ŏf'ĭ-ō-màn"sē) *n.* fortunetelling with snakes.

ophrylitis (ŏf-rĭ-ī'tĭs) *n.* inflammation of the eyebrow.

ophthalmophobia (ŏf-thàl"mō-fō'bĭ-ə) *n.* fear of being stared at.

opimian (ō-pĭm'ĭ-ən) *adj.* pertaining to a 121 B.C. vintage wine when *Opimius* was consul.

opiparous (ō-pĭp'ər-əs) *adj.* sumptuous.

---

màn; māde; lĕt; bē; sĭp; wīne; hŏt; cōld; sôre; dùll; fūgue; bûrp; gŏŏd; fōōd; out; gĕt; thin; thĭs; year; aźure; ō'mən"; viN; fûr; Bach

opisthenar (ō-pĭs'thə-nòr) *n.* the back of the hand.

opisthograph (ō-pĭs'thō-grăf) *n.* a manuscript written on both sides.

opisthoporeia (ō-pĭs"thō-pôr-ē'ə) *n.* involuntary walking backward.

opodipsia (ō-pō-dĭp'sĭ-ə) *n.* a terrific yen for juices.

oppidan (ŏp'ĭ-dàn) *adj.* pertaining to a town. -*n.* 1. a town resident. 2. an English student who lives off campus.

oppignorate (ō-pĭg'nə-rāt) *v.i.* to pledge, to pawn.

oppilate (ŏp'ĭ-lāt) *v.t.* to block up, to obstruct.

oppugnant (ō-pŭg'nənt) *adj.* hostile, antagonistic.

opsablepsia (ŏp-sə-blĕp'sĭ-ə) *n.* not looking into another's eyes.

opsigamy (ŏp-sĭg'ə-mē) *n.* marriage late in life.

opsimathy (ŏp-sĭm'ə-thē) *n.* education late in life.

opsiproligery (ŏp"sĭ-prō-lĭj'ər-ē) *n.* ability to have children late in life.

opsomania (ŏp-sō-mā'-nĭ-ə) *n.* a mania for specific gourmet foods.

opsonium (ŏp-sō'nĭ-əm) *n.* an hors d'oeuvre eaten with bread.

opsophagist (ŏp-sŏf'ə-jĭst) *n.* a fastidious eater; an epicure.

opuscule (ō-pùs'kūl) *n.* an insignificant work, a little opus. also *opuscle.*

orad (ō'răd) *adv.* toward the mouth.

orage (ō-rǒz') *n.* a storm (French).

orant (ōr'ànt) *n.* a praying female figure in art.

orarian (ō-rèr'ĭ-ən) *adj.* pertaining to the seashore. -*n.* a coast-dwelling Aleut in the Bering Sea region.

orbation (ōr-bā'shən) *n.* not having parents or children; general deprivation.

orbific (ōr-bĭf'ĭk) *adj.* world-making.

orc (ôrk) *n.* 1. the *grampus* or *springer*, a dolphinlike creature. 2. the killer whale.

orchestic (ōr-kès'tĭk) *adj.* pertaining to dancing. -*n.* dancing, especially in *pl.*

orchestrion (ôr-kès'trĭ-ŏn) *n.* a large music box that sounds like an organ.

orchestromania (ōr"kəs-trō-mā'nĭ-ə) *n.* dancing mania.

orchidectomy (ōr-kĭd-ĕk'tə-mē) *n.* castration, also *orcheotomy.*

oread (ōr'ē-àd) *n.* a mountain nymph.

orectic (ōr-ĕk'tĭk) *adj.* pertaining to desire or appetite.

oreillette (ōr-ā-ĕt') *n.* a covering for the ear. also *oreillet* (French *oreille* = ear).

orexigenic (ōr-ĕks'ĭ-jĕn'ĭk) *adj.* whetting the appetite. *orexis, n.* appetite, desire, stirring.

organon (ōr'gə-nŏn) *n.* 1. a body of information to be used for further scientific or philosophic investigation. 2. an instrument for acquiring or dispensing knowledge.

orgulous (ōr'gū-ləs) *adj.* proud and haughty (humorous).

oriel (ōr'ē-əl) *n.* a large bay window.

oriency (ōr'ĭ-èn'sē) *n.* bright or strong color.

oriflamme (ōr'ĭ-flàm) *n.* 1. St. Denis's red silk banner used as a battle standard. 2. any flag vaguely reminiscent of this.

orignal (ōr-ĭg'nəl) *n.* the American moose.

orismology (ōr-ĭz-mŏl'ə-jē) *n.* definition of technical terms.

orison (ōr'ĭ-zən) *n.* a prayer.

---

ormolu (ôr'mə-loo) *n.* brass that looks like gold.

ornithocopros (ôr"nĭ-thō-kŏp'rəs) *n.* bird dung; guano.

ornithophilous (ôr-nĭ-thŏf'ĭl-əs) *adj.* bird-loving, said of plants that are pollinated by birds.

ornithorhynchus (ôr"nĭth-ər-ĭnk'əs) *n.* a creditor; a duck-billed platypus, "a beast with a bill" (Australian slang).

orology (ôr-ŏl'ə-jē) *n.* the science of mountains; *orography.*

orotund (ôr'ō-tŭnd) *adj.* 1. pertaining to vocal clarity and strength. 2. pertaining to a pompous writing or speaking style. -*n.* an *orotund* voice.

orphanotrophy (ôr"fən-ŏt'rə-fē) *n.* 1. the support of orphans. 2. an orphanage.

orrery (ôr'ə-rē) *n.* a planetarium.

ort (ôrt) *n.* a leftover tidbit. -*v.t.* to reject.

orthobiosis (ôr"thō-bī-ō'sĭs) *n.* hygenic, moral, and allegedly "normal" living.

orthodromics (ôr-thō-drō'mĭks) *n.* sailing on a straight course; great-circle sailing. also *orthodromy.*

orthoepy (ôr'thō-ē"pē) *n.* correct pronunciation; pronunciation. *phonology.*

orthogonal (ôr-thŏg'ən-əl) *adj.* right-angled; rectangular.

orthophobia (ôr-thō-fō'bĭ-ə) *n.* dislike of propriety.

orthopter (ôr-thŏp'tər) *n.* a flying machine with flapping wings; a mechanical bird.

orthotetrakaidekahedron (ôr"thō-tĕt-rə-kī"dē-kə-hē'drən) *n.* the truncated octahedron.

ortive (ôr'tĭv) *adj.* pertaining to rising; eastern.

ortolan (ôr'tō-lăn) *n.* the *bunting, wheatear, sora, rail,* or *bobolink;*

considered good birds to eat.

oryctology (ôr-ĭk-tŏl'ə-jē) *n.* the science of things dug from the earth; mineralogy or paleontology.

oryx (ôr'ĭks) *n.* the African antelope.

oryzivorous (ôr-ĭ-zĭv'ər-əs) *adj.* rice-eating.

oscitancy (ŏs'ĭ-tən-sē") *n.* yawning; drowsiness.

osculant (ŏs'kū-lənt) *adj.* embracing, clinging, kissing.

osela (ō-sā'lə) *n.* a medal of a bird ordered by the doge as a substitute for real birds usually presented to nobles on New Year's Day.

osmagogue (ŏz'mə-gŏg) *adj.* stimulating to the sense of smell.

osmonosology (ŏz"mŏn-ō-sŏl'ə-jē) *n.* study of the sense of smell.

osmophobia (ŏz-mō-fō'bĭ-ə) *n.* fear of smells.

osphresiophilia (ŏz-frē"zĭ-ō-fĭl'ĭ-ə) *n.* an inordinate love of smells.

ossature (ŏs'ə-tyûr) *n.* 1. skeleton. 2. architectural framework.

osse (ŏs) *n.* a prophecy. -*v.t.&i.* 1. to prophesy. 2. to recommend.

ossuary (ŏs'ū-ĕr'ē) *n.* a burial chamber.

ostiary (ŏs'tĭ-ĕr"ē) *n.* 1. a monastery doorman. 2. the mouth of a river.

ostler (ŏs'lûr) *n.* a stableboy.

ostreophagist (ŏs-trē-ŏf'ə-jĭst) *n.* an oyster eater.

otacoustic (ō-tə-kōōs'tĭk) *adj.* helping to hear. -*n.* a hearing device.

othergates (ŭ'thûr-gāts) *adv.* in another way.

otiant (ō'shĭ-ənt) *adj.* dormant; unemployed.

otiatrus (ŏt-ĭ-ăt'rəs) *n.* an aurist, or ear specialist.

otiose (ō'shǐ-ōs) *adj.* 1. sterile; useless. 2. *otiant.*

otolaryngologist (ō"tō-lằr-ǐn-gòl'ə-jǐst) *n.* an ear, nose, and throat specialist.

otology (ō-tòl'ə-jē) *n.* study of the ear and its diseases. *otic, adj.* pertaining to the ear; *auricular.*

otosis (ō-tō'sǐs) *n.* a hearing malfunction; not hearing correctly.

ouabain (wò-bò'ǐn) *n.* 1. the main ingredient of an arrow poison. 2. a local anesthetic and cardiac stimulant.

oubliette (ōō-blē-èt') *n.* a dungeon whose only opening is in the ceiling.

ouch (ouch) *n.* 1. a brooch or setting for a precious stone. 2. a skin sore. -*v.t.* to wear an *ouch.*

ouphe (ōōf) *n.* an elf or goblin.

outfangtheft (out'fàng-thèft) *n.* the right of a medieval English lord to prosecute one of his vassals caught off the premises.

outlier (out'lī"ər) *n.* 1. someone sleeping outdoors. 2. someone whose office is not at home. 3. an animal who strays from the fold. 4. something that has been separated from the main body.

outrance (ōō-tròNs') *n.* utmost. *à outrance* = to the bitter end.

outrecuidance (out-ər-kwē'dəns) *n.* egomania; gross conceit.

outrooper (out'rōō"pər) *n.* an auctioneer.

ouzel (ōō'zəl) *n.* the European blackbird, or other thrushes.

ovant (ō'vànt) *adj.* triumphant, as in an ovation.

overslaugh (ō'vər-slô) *n.* 1. exemption from certain military duties by being kicked upstairs. 2. a sand bar. -*v.t.* to bypass in favor of another.

ovine (ō'vīn) *adj.* sheeplike. -*n.* a sheep.

oviparous (ō-vǐp'ər-əs) *adj.* producing eggs that hatch outside the body; this kind of reproduction, opposite of *viviparous.*

ovivorous (ō-vǐv'ôr-əs) *adj.* egg-eating.

ovoviviparous (ō"vō-vǐ-vǐp'ər-əs) *adj.* producing eggs that hatch within, or immediately after expulsion from, the female.

owelty (ō'əl-tē) *n.* money paid from one property owner to another.

owler (oul'ər) *n.* someone who stares or hoots like an owl; a prowler.

owling (oul'ǐng) *n.* the act of smuggling wool or sheep, sometimes applied to smuggling in general.

oxalm (òks'àlm) *n.* a sour sauce.

oxpecker (òks'pèk"ər) *n.* a starlinglike bird that pecks cattle in search of ticks, etc.

oxter (òks'tûr) *n.* the armpit. -*v.t. &i.* to lead or support with the arm; to walk arm in arm; to put the arm around; to embrace; to elbow.

oxyacanthous (òks"ē-ə-kàn'thəs) *adj.* having sharp spines or thorns.

oxyesthesia (òks"ē-ès-thē'žǐ-ə) *n.* extreme sensitivity to touch.

oxygeusia (òks-ǐ-gū'sǐ-ə) *n.* extreme sensitivity to taste.

oxymoron (òks-ǐ-môr'ən) *n.* a statement with two seemingly contradictory words: terribly nice, etc.

oxyosphresia (òks'ǐ-òs-frē'žǐ-ə) *n.* extreme sensitivity to smell.

oxythymous (òks-ǐ-thī'məs) *adj.* quick-tempered; easily riled.

ozostomia (ō-zòs-tō'mǐ-ə) *n.* bad breath.

---

màn; māde; lèt; bē; sǐp; wīne; hòt; cōld; sôre; dùll; fūgue; bûrp; gōōd; fōōd; out; gèt; thin; this; year; ažure; ō'mən"; viN; fūr; Bach

P

paauw (pò′o͞o) *n.* the South African bustard.

pabulation (pàb-ū-lā′shən) *n.* providing food, fodder, or other nourishment; the nourishment itself.

pacation (pā-kā′shən) *n.* appeasement.

pachinko (pà-chǐng′kō) *n.* a Japanese slot machine.

pachycephalic (pàk″ē-sèf-àl′ǐk) *adj.* thick-skulled.

pachydermatous (pàk-ē-dûrm′ə-təs) *adj.* 1. thick-skinned. 2. pertaining to the elephant or rhinoceros.

paddling (pàd′lǐng) *n.* collective noun for mallards: "a *paddling* of mallards."

padmasana (pùd-mò′sən-ò) *n.* a statue's base, shaped like a lotus flower. *in padmasana,* in a cross-legged sitting position.

padnag (pàd′nàg) *n.* a horse with a pad instead of a saddle; an ambling nag. *-v.i.* to ride such a horse; to amble.

pageism (pā′jǐz″əm) *n.* masochistic fantasy of a man imagining himself as servant to a beautiful woman.

paggle (pàg′əl) *v.i.* to hang loosely; to bag.

pagophagia (pà-gō-fā′ji-ə) *n.* eating a tray of ice daily for two months to help offset iron deficiency.

pahoehoe (pò-hō′ē-hō″ē) *n.* lava that has cooled in ropy forms, unlike *aa* (Hawaiian).

paideutics (pī-dū′tǐks) *n.* pedagogy.

paillasse (pī-yòs′) *n.* 1. a straw mattress. 2. a supporting bed for masonry.

pailletee (pī-yèt′) *n.* a spangle.

paizogony (pī′zə-gòn″ē) *n.* love play. also *paraphilemia, sarmassation.*

paladin (pàl′ə-dǐn) *n.* 1. one of Charlemagne's twelve peers. 2. a knight of the round table. 3. a paragon of knighthood.

palaestra (pàl-ès′trə) *n.* 1. an exercise gym. 2. exercise, especially wrestling.

palaetiology (pàl-ē″tǐ-òl′ə-jē) *n.* explanation of past events by the laws of causation, as in geology.

palafitte (pàl′ə-fǐt) *n.* pile-built

---

màn; māde; lèt; bē; sǐp; wīne; hòt; cōld; sôre; dùll; fūgue; bûrp; gōōd; fōōd; out; gèt; thin; this; year; azure; ō′mən″; viN; fūr; Bach

structures for neolithic lake houses.

palamate (pàl'ə-māt) *adj.* web-footed.

palanquin (pàl-ən-kēn') *n.* a closed litter carried on the shoulders of four men.

palatine (pàl'ə-tīn) *adj.* 1. palatial. 2. having royal privileges. 3. pertaining to the palate. -*n.* 1. a lord with sovereign power. 2. one of the seven Roman hills. 3. a short fur stole worn first by Princess *Palatine* in 1676.

paleethnographer (pā"lē-ĕth-nŏg'rə-fûr) *n.* a specialist in prehistoric ethnography.

paleoanthropic (pā"lē-ō-ănthrŏp'ĭk) *adj.* pertaining to the earliest types of human being.

paleograph (pā'lē-ō-gràf") *n.* an ancient manuscript.

paleomnesia (pā"lē-ŏm-nē'zĭ-ə) *n.* good memory for events of the far past.

paletot (pàl'tō) *n.* a man or women's loose overcoat.

palfrenier (pàl-frə-nīr') *n.* a groom.

palfrey (pŏl'frē) *n.* a nonmilitary saddle horse; a small horse for small women.

palilalia (pàl-ĭ-lā'lĭ-ə) *n.* helplessly repeating a phrase faster and faster.

palimpsest (pàl'ĭmp-sèst) *n.* 1. writing material on which writing can be erased. 2. used writing material with erasures. 3. brass reengraved on the reverse side. -*adj.* rewritten or reengraved. -*v.t.* to write on erased writing material.

palindrome (pàl'ĭn-drōm) *n.* a word or phrase that is the same backward as forward.

palingenesis (pàl-ĭn-jèn'ə-sĭs) *n.* 1. renaissance. 2. *metempsychosis,*

or transmigration of souls. 3. formation of new rocks by refusion. 4. metamorphosis of insects.

palinode (pàl'ĭn-ōd) *n.* 1. a song or poem retracting statements in previous songs or poems. 2. retraction or recanting in general.

palinoia (pàl-ĭn-oi'ə) *n.* compulsive repetition of an act until it's perfect.

palladian (pàl-ā'dĭ-ən) *adj.* 1. pertaining to learning and wisdom. 2. pertaining to neoclassical architecture inspired by Andrea *Palladio.*

palliards (pàl'yərdz) *n.pl.* professional beggars whose parents were also beggars and who use trickery to arouse sympathy.

pallion (pàl'yən) *n.* a little piece.

palmary (pàl'mə-rē) *adj.* prizeworthy, superior; principal.

palmer (pòm'ər) *n.* 1. a pilgrim wearing palm leaves as proof of a holy visit. 2. a wood louse. 3. a stick for hitting children's hands. 4. someone who palms cards or dice. -*v.i.* to wander or stroll.

palmigrade (pòl'mĭ-grād) *adj.* plantigrade.

palpation (pàl-pā'shən) *n.* 1. medical examination of the body by touching. 2. touching or feeling.

palpebral (pàl'pə-brāl) *adj.* pertaining to the eyelids.

palpebrate (pàl'pə-brāt) *v.i.* to wink.

palter (pôl'tər) *v.i.* 1. to mumble or babble. 2. to act insincerely. 3. to bargain, haggle.

paltripolitan (pôl-trĭ-pòl'ĭ-tən) *n.* an insular city dweller *(metropolitan + paltry).*

paludal (pàl-ū'dəl) *adj.* marshy. also *paludose, paludous, palus-*

tral, palustrian, and *palustrine. paludous* means malarial, as well.

pampootee (păm-pōō'tē) *n.* an Irish moccasin.

panache (păn-ăsh') *n.* 1. flair, swagger, dash, verve, élan. 2. a bunch of feathers on a helmet; a military plume.

pandect (păn'dĕkt) *n.* 1. a complete digest of a particular branch of knowledge. 2. a fifty-book digest of Roman law. 3. any complete code of laws.

pandemic (păn-dĕm'ĭk) *adj.* 1. pertaining to all people. 2. general, universal. 3. affecting the majority, everywhere epidemic (medical). 4. sensual.

pandiculation (păn-dĭk"ū-lā'shən) *n.* stretching and yawning.

panduriform (păn-dyûr'ĭ-fôrm) *adj. obovate,* with an indentation on each side, like a violin; *pandurate.*

pandy (păn'dē) *n.* a hit on the hand. *-v.t.&i.* to hit the hand.

pangram (păn'grăm) *n.* a sentence containing every letter of the alphabet: "Q.V. Schwatzkop, Jr., bungled my fix." *pangrammatist, n.*

panivorous (păn-ĭv'ôr-əs) *adj.* living on bread.

panjandrum (păn-jăn'drəm) *n.* 1. a satiric title for a pompous official. 2. ceremonial fuss.

pannage (păn'əj) *n.* 1. feeding swine in the forest. 2. food eaten by forest swine.

pannier (păn'yər) *n.* 1. a wicker basket carried on the back. 2. a medical kit for military ambulances. 3. a whalebone hoop worn at the hips.

pannychous (păn'ĭ-kəs) *adj.* lasting all night.

panoptic (păn-ŏp'tĭk) *adj.* seeing

everything at once, or in one view; all-seeing.

panpharmacon (păn-fôr'mə-kŏn) *n.* an all-purpose medicine.

panstereorama (păn-stĕr"ē-ō-rō'mə) *n.* a relief map of a town or country.

pantagamy (păn-tăg'ə-mē) *n.* communal marriage.

pantagruelian (păn"tə-grōō-ĕl'ĭ-ən) *adj.* satiric, though ribald (Rabelais' *Pantagruel*).

pantarbe (păn-tŏrb') *n.* a mythical stone supposed to shine in the sun while attracting gold magnetically.

pantechnicon (păn-tĕk'nĭ-kən) *n.* 1. a storage warehouse. 2. a furniture van.

panthophobia (păn"thō-fō'bĭ-ə) *n.* fear of suffering and disease.

pantoffle (păn-tŏf'əl) *n.* 1. a bedroom slipper. 2. a sixteenth-century overshoe.

pantophagous (păn-tŏf'ə-gəs) *adj.* omnivorous.

pantophobia (păn"tō-fō'bĭ-ə) *n.* fear of everything; cowardice.

panurgy (păn'ûr-jē") *n.* universal skill or craft.

papaphobia (pă-pə-fō'bĭ-ə) *n.* intense fear of the pope or popery.

paparchy (pā'pŏr-kē") *n.* government by a pope. *paperchical, adj.*

papaverous (pă-păv'ər-əs) *adj.* pertaining to the poppy.

papeterie (păp'ə-trē) *n.* a box of writing materials; a kind of writing paper.

paphian (pā'fĭ-ən) *adj.* erotic; pertaining to illicit love. *-n.* 1. a prostitute. 2. an inhabitant of *Paphos,* Cyprus.

papilionaceous (pă-pĭl"ĭ-ən-ā'shəs) *adj.* like a butterfly.

papilla (păp-ĭl'ə) *n.* a nipple or nipplelike projection.

---

măn; māde; lĕt; bē; sĭp; wīne; hŏt; cōld; sôre; dŭll; fūgue; bûrp; gōōd; fōōd; out; gĕt; thin; this; year; azhure; ō'mən"; viN; für; Bach

papillote (păp'ĭl-ōt) n. 1. a paper hair curler. 2. a paper ruffle decorating a lamb-chop bone.

papiopio (pŏ-pē'ō-pē'ŏ) n. a young *ulua* (Hawaiian).

papulliferous (păp-ū-lĭf'ər-əs) adj. pimply.

parabolanus (păr'ə-bō-lā'nəs) n. a monk medic specializing in contagious diseases.

parabolize (păr-ăb'ō-līz) v.t. 1. to express in parables. 2. to make parabolic.

parachronism (păr-ăk'rō-nĭz"əm) n. an incorrect date, especially one too late.

paraclete (păr'ə-klēt) n. a legal helper; an aide.

paracoita (păr-ə-kō'ĭ-tə) n. a female sexual partner.

paracoitus (păr-ə-kō'ĭ-təs) n. a male sexual partner.

paradiastole (păr-ə-dī-ăs'tōl-ē) n. a euphemistic half-truth.

paradiddle (păr'ə-dĭd'əl) n. a basic drum roll.

paradigm (păr'ə-dīm) n. 1. an example or model. 2. an example of a conjugation or declension showing a word in all possible forms.

paragram (păr'ə-grăm) n. a pun, especially one made by changing the first letter of a word. *paragrammatist, n.*

paragraphia (păr-ə-grăf'ĭ-ə) n. aphasia in which the patient writes unintended letters or words (medicine).

paraleipsis (păr-ə-līp'sĭs) n. mentioning something by saying you won't mention it; *apophasis.*

paralian (păr-ā'lĭ-ən) n. someone who lives by the sea.

paralipomena (păr"ə-lĭ-pŏm'ən-ə) n.pl. deleted passages, or a supplement containing them.

paralipophobia (păr-ə-lī"pō-fō'bĭ-

ə) n. fear of responsibility.

parallelepiped (păr'ə-lĕl-ə-pī'pĕd) n. a six-sided prism with parallelogram faces. also *parallelepipedon.*

paralogic (păr-ə-lŏ'jĭk) adj. pertaining to the inability to think logically.

paramimia (păr-ə-mĭm'ĭ-ə) n. pathological misuse of gestures.

paramiographer (păr'ə-mĭ-ŏg'rə-fûr) n. a collector or writer of proverbs.

paranymph (păr'ə-nĭmf) n. 1. a bridesmaid or best man. 2. someone acting on another's behalf.

paraph (păr'əf) n. a flourish at the end of a signature, once used as a protection against forgery.

parapherna (păr-ə-fûr'nə) n. that part of a woman's property that remains legally hers after marriage.

paraphilemia (păr"ə-fĭl-ēm'ĭ-ə) n. love play. also *paizogony, sarmassation.*

parapraxis (păr-ə-prăks'ĭs) n. a memory lapse; a slip of the tongue; general clumsiness.

parasynesis (păr-ə-sĭn'ə-sĭs) n. corruption of words from a misunderstanding of their elements.

paratonic (păr-ə-tŏn'ĭk) adj. retarding movement or growth.

parbreak (pŏr'brāk) n. vomit. also *v.t.&i.*

parcener (pŏr'sən-ûr) n. a joint heir in an estate; a *coparcener.*

parenetic (păr-ə-nĕt'ĭk) adj. advisory, counseling.

parentate (păr-ĕn'tāt) v.i. to perform funeral rites for a relative.

parenteral (păr-ĕn'tər-əl) adj. occurring outside of or by another route than that of the intestines.

parepithymia (pă-rĕp"ĭ-thĭm'ĭ-ə) n. perverted cravings due to mental illness.

parerethesis (pàr-ē-rèth′ə-sĭs) n. abnormal excitement.

parergon (pàr-ûr′gŏn) n. 1. an embellishment; a decorative accessory. 2. an avocation.

pareunia (pàr-ōō′nĭ-ə) n. sexual intercourse.

parisology (pàr-ĭ-sŏl′ə-jē) n. deliberate ambiguity in use of words. words.

parnel (pòr′nĕl) n. a priest's mistress; a loose woman.

paronomasia (pàr″ə-nō-mā′zĭ-ə) n. punning; a pun.

paronymous (pàr-ŏn′ĭ-məs) adj. derived from a common source; conjugate.

parorexia (pàr-ō-rèks′ĭ-ə) n. perverted appetite; demanding strange foods.

parrhesia (pàr-ē′zĭ-ə) n. freedom of speech (in rhetoric).

parsec (pòr′sĕk) n. a unit of measure for interstellar space equal to 3.26 light years, or 19.2 trillion miles.

parterre (pòr-tèr′) n. 1. an ornamental and geometric arrangement of flower beds. 2. a building site. 3. the theater floor under the balcony.

partheniad (pòr-thē′nĭ-ăd) n. a poem in honor of a virgin.

parthenolatry (pòr-thē-nŏl′ə-trē) n. virgin worship; mariolatry.

parthenology (pòr-thē-nŏl′ə-jē) n. the medical study of virgins and virginity.

parthenophobia (pòr″thən-ō-fō′bĭ-ə) n. fear of virgins.

parturient (pòr-tyûr′ĭ-ənt) adj. pertaining to childbirth or parturition; about to produce an idea or discovery.

parturifacient (pòr-tyûr″ĭ-fā′shənt) adj. inducing childbith. -n. a

medicine for inducing parturition; an analgesic for labor pain.

parure (pàr-ōōr′) n. 1. peeling. 2. jewelry worn in groups.

parvanimity (pòr-vàn-ĭm′ĭ-tē) n. 1. pettiness; meanness. 2. a mean or petty person. opposite of magnanimity.

parvenu (pòr′və-nū) n. a pretentious snob of the nouveau riche. also aaj.

parvis (pòr′vĭs) n. 1. a courtyard. 2. a public brouhaha, so called from having been held in a church parvis.

parviscient (pòr-vĭsh′ənt) adj. uninformed.

paschal (pàs′kəl) adj. pertaining to Passover or Easter or their celebrations.

pascual (pàs′kū-əl) adj. growing in pastures. also pascuous.

pasigraphy (pàs-ĭg′rə-fē) n. a universal written language using signs and symbols instead of words.

pasilaly (pàs′ĭ-lā″lē) n. a universal language.

pasquinade (pàs-kwĭn-ād′) n. a malicious satire or lampoon, often in rhyme; a pasquil. -v.t. to lampoon or satirize. pasquinader, one who writes or collects pasquinades.

passacaglia (pŏs-ə-kŏl′yŏ) n. a stately old Italian or Spanish dance or its music.

passalorynchite (pàs″ə-lôr-ĭn′kĭt) n. a member of an early Christian sect who took a vow of perpetual silence.

passepartout (pàs-pòr-tōō′) n. 1. a master key. 2. a safeconduct or passport. 3. a mat or border used in framing pictures.

passim (pàs′ĭm) adv. throughout, frequently: used in footnotes to indicate recurrence of a word or phrase.

patavinity (păt-ə-vĭn'ĭ-tē) *n.* the use of local words or expressions; local pronunciation.

patchouli (pă-chōo'lē) *n.* an East Indian mint plant or its perfume.

patharmosis (păth-ȯr-mō'sĭs) *n.* mental adjustment to one's disease.

pathematic (păth-ə-măt'ĭk) *adj.* 1. pertaining to or caused by emotion. 2. pertaining to disease.

pathic (păth'ĭk) *n.* 1. a catamite. 2. a passive participator. -*adj.* passive; suffering.

pathocryptia (păth-ō-krĭp'tĭ-ə) *n.* unwillingness to believe in or talk about one's illness.

pathodixia (păth-ō-dĭks'ĭ-ə) *n.* talking to excess about one's illness and flaunting its signs.

pathognomy (pă-thŏg'nō-mē) *n.* 1. the study of emotions by their outward signs. 2. the science of diagnosis.

pathomimesis (păth"ō-mĭ-mē'sĭs) *n.* malingering.

patibulary (păt-ĭb'ū-lĕr"ē) *adj.* pertaining to the gallows or hanging.

patricentric (păt-rĭ-sĕn'trĭk) *adj.* gravitating toward or centered upon the father. see *matricentric*.

patrilineal (păt-rĭ-lĭn'ĭ-əl) *adj.* pertaining to male descent.

patrilocal (păt-rĭ-lō'kəl) *adj.* pertaining to a marriage in which the wife lives with her husband's relatives.

patripotestal (păt-rĭ-pō-tĕs"təl) *adj.* relating to paternal authority.

patroclinous (păt-rō-klī'nəs) *adj.* having characteristics inherited from the father.

patronomatology (păt"rō-nŏm-ə-tŏl'ə-jē) *n.* the study of patronymics and their origins.

patronymic (păt-rō-nĭm'ĭk) *n.* 1. paternal name with a suffix meaning "son of." 2. pertaining to the custom of children taking their father's name.

patten (păt'ən) *n.* 1. a wooden shoe or clog for muddy ground. 2. (pl.) horseshoes for muddy ground. 3. a skate or stilt. -*v.i.* to wear *pattens;* to skate.

patulous (păt'ū-ləs) *adj.* open, expanded, distended, spreading.

patzer (pŏt'sûr) *n.* a weak chess player.

pauciloquent (pô-sĭl'ō-kwənt) *adj.* speaking briefly.

pavis (păv'ĭs) *n.* a large shield of the Middle Ages. -*v.t.* to protect with a *pavis*.

pavonine (păv'ō-nīn) *adj.* pertaining to a peacock; iridescent; pertaining to *peacock blue*.

pawky (pô'kē) *adj.* cunning, shrewd, crafty (slang).

paynim (pā'nĭm) *n.* pagandom; a pagan or infidel, especially a Mohammedan.

peage (pā-ŏž') *n.* toll.

peccable (pĕk'ə-bəl) *adj.* liable to sin; susceptible to temptation; *peccant*.

peccant (pĕk'ənt) *adj.* 1. *peccable*. 2. liable to break certain social rules; incorrect. 3. inducing disease.

peccatophobia (pĕk"ə-tō-fō'bĭ-ə) *n.* fear of sinning or of having committed an imaginary crime. also *peccatiphobia*.

peckerwood (pĕk'ər-wŏod) *n.* a poor southern ASP or Anglo-Saxon Protestant (the woodpecker symbolizing whites in the South).

pecksniffian (pĕk-snĭf'ĭ-ən) *adj.* hypocritical, insincere, and gut-

màn; māde; lèt; bē; sĭp; wīne; hŏt; cōld; sôre; dùll; fūgue; bûrp; gŏŏd; fŏŏd; out; gèt; thin; *th*is; year; a*z*ure; ō'mən"; viN; fùr; Bach

less.

pecos (pā'kōs) *v.t.* to shoot a man and roll his body into the river.

pectinate (pĕk'tĭn-āt) *adj.* shaped like a comb; having teeth like a comb.

peculation (pĕk-ū-lā'shən) *n.* embezzlement.

pedality (pē-dăl'ĭ-tē) *n.* measuring by paces; going on foot.

pedantocracy (pĕd-ănt-ŏk'rə-sē) *n.* government by pedants.

pedetentous (pĕd-ē-tĕn'təs) *adj.* proceeding gradually or cautiously.

pediculophobia (pĕd-ĭk"ū-lō-fō'bĭ-ə) *n.* fear of lice.

pediluvium (pĕd-ĭ-lōō'vĭ-əm) *n.* a foot bath.

peditastellus (pĕd-ĭ-tăs'təl-əs) *n.* "a miserable, little infantryman" (Latin).

pedodontia (pē-dō-dŏn'shĭ-ə) *n.* pediatric dentistry.

pedology (pē-dŏl'ə-jē) *n.* soil study.

pedomancy (pĕd'ō-măn"sē) *n.* fortunetelling by the soles of the feet.

peen (pēn) *n.* the end of a hammer head opposite the striking face. also *pein, pean, pene, pane.*

peever (pē'vər) *n.* a stone used in hopscotch.

pegomancy (pĕg'ō-măn"sē) *n.* fortunetelling by seeing how bubbles rise in a fountain.

peirastic (pī-răs'tĭk) *adj.* experimental; ready to be tried.

pelagic (pĕl-ăj'ĭk) *adj.* pertaining to or living in the ocean.

pelargic (pē-lŏr'jĭk) *adj.* storklike.

pelf (pĕlf) *n.* 1. booty. 2. trash. 3. fur. 4. a good-for-nothing. -*v.t. &i.* to rob.

pelmatogram (pĕl-măt'ō-grăm) *n.* a footprint.

pelology (pĕl-ŏl'ə-jē) *n.* study of mud and its therapeutic applica-

tions.

pemmican (pĕm'ĭ-kən) *n.* 1. dried buffalo meat or venison. 2. condensed knowledge.

penates see *lares and penates.*

pendicle (pĕn'dĭ-kəl) *n.* 1. a hanging ornament. 2. a house and grounds of a larger estate; a Scottish *croft.*

penduline (pĕn'dū-lĭn) *adj.* pendulous, applied to birds that construct *penhiles,* or hanging nests.

penelopize (pĕn-ĕl'ō-pīz) *v.i.* to undo and redo to gain time (*Penelope* in Homer's *Odyssey*).

peniaphobia (pē'nĭ-ə-fō'bĭ-ə) *n.* fear of poverty.

peniatry (pē'nē-ăt"rē) *n.* branch of medicine dealing with prisoners.

penotherapy (pē-nō-thĕr'ə-pē) *n.* regulating prostitutes to control venereal disease.

pentacle (pĕn'tə-kəl) *n.* a five-pointed star with an inscribed pentagon.

pentad (pĕn'tăd) *n.* a period of five consecutive days or years.

pentapopemptic (pĕn"tə-pō-pĕmp'tĭk) *adj.* divorced five times.

penteteric (pĕn-tē-tĕr'ĭk) *adj.* recurring every five years.

pentheraphobia (pĕn"thər-ə-fō'bĭ-ə) *n.* fear or dislike of one's mother-in-law.

penumbra (pĕn-ŭm'brə) *n.* half-shadow.

peotomy (pē-ŏt'ə-mē) *n.* the surgical amputation of the penis.

percuss (pûr-kŭs') *v.t. &i.* to strike violently or smartly.

perduellion (pûr-dū-ĕl'yən) *n.* treason.

perdure (pûr-dyoōr') *v.i.* to continue to endure.

perendinate (pûr-ĕn'dĭn-āt) *v.t. &i.* to postpone until the next day; to postpone indefinitely.

perennate (pûr-ĕn'āt) *v.i.* to be perennial.

perflation (pûr-flā'shən) *n.* blowing through; ventilation; act of blowing through a space to expel accumulated secretions (medicine).

perfrication (pûr-frĭ-kā'shən) *n.* thorough rubbing.

perfuse (pûr-fūz') *v.t.* 1. to sprinkle with liquid or suffuse with light or color. 2. to pour over something.

pergameneous (pûr-gə-mē'nĭ-əs) *adj.* like parchment.

pergola (pûr'gō-lə) *n.* 1. an arbor or bower. 2. a colonnade supporting an open roof.

perhiemate (pûr-hī'ē-māt) *v.i.* to spend the winter.

peri (pē'rē) *n.* a beautiful, elfin person (Persian mythology).

periapt (pĕr'ĭ-ăpt) *n.* an amulet worn as protection from disease or harm.

perichareia (pĕr"ĭ-kŏ-rē'ə) *n.* excessive and violent rejoicing.

periclitation (pĕr-ĭk"lĭ-tā'shən) *n.* exposing to danger.

periegesis (pĕr"ē-ə-jē'sĭs) *n.* a description of an area.

perigraph (pĕr'ĭ-grăf) *n.* an inexact description or drawing; a tracing instrument for outlining bones.

peripatetic (pĕr"ĭ-pə-tĕt'ĭk) *adj.* 1. pertaining to walking or wandering. 2. pertaining to Aristotelian philosophy. 3. rambling speech.

peripety (pĕr-ĭp'ə-tē) *n.* a drama's dénouement; life's dénouement. also *peripeteia*, *peripetety*, *peripetia*.

periphrastic (pĕr-ĭ-frăs'tĭk) *adj.* pertaining to circumlocution; wordy.

peripteral (pĕr-ĭp'tûr-əl) *adj.* 1.

with columns on all sides. 2. pertaining to the motions of the air surrounding a moving body. also *peripterous*.

perischii (pĕr-ĭsh'ĭ-ī) *n.pl.* The inhabitants of the polar circles, so called because in summer their shadows form an oval.

perissopedics (pĕr-ĭs"ō-pē'dĭks) *n* pediatrics dealing with gifted children.

perissotomist (pĕr-ĭ-sŏt'əm-ĭst) *n* a knife-happy surgeon.

peristerophily (pē-rĭs"tûr-ŏf'ĭl-ē) *n* the breeding, care, and training of pigeons. *peristeronic*, *adj.*

peristrephic (pĕr-ĭ-strĕf'ĭk) *adj* turning around, rotatory; *peritropal.*

peristyle (pĕr'ĭ-stīl) *n.* 1. a colonnade surrounding a building or court. 2. the large inner court of a Roman house.

periwig (pĕr'ē-wĭg) *n.* a white pompadour-style wig of the eighteenth century. -*v.t.* to wear a *periwig.*

perjinkities (pûr-jĭnk'ĭ-tēz) *n.pl.* niceties (Scottish).

perlaceous (pûr-lā'shəs) *adj.* pearly.

perlustrate (pûr-lŭs'trāt) *v.t.* to review thoroughly; survey.

pernancy (pûr'nən-sē) *n.* a taking of rent or profit (law).

pernoctation (pûr-nŏk-tā'shən) *n.* a night-long vigil.

peroral (pûr-ôr'əl) *adj.* through the mouth.

perpend (pûr'pənd) *n.* a large stone acting as a wall. -*v.t.* to ponder carefully. -*v.i.* to concentrate, be attentive.

perqueer (pûr-kwîr') *adv.* by heart; perfectly. -*adj.* accurate. also *perqueir.*

perruquier (pĕr-ōō-kyā') *n.* a wig-maker. also *perukier.*

perseity (pûr-sē′ĭ-tē) *n.* independence or self-sufficiency.

persienne (pûr-syěn′) *n.* printed cotton or silk, originally made in Persia, later copied in France and England.

pertusion (pûr-too′żən) *n.* piercing or perforating; a perforation or hole.

pertussis (pûr-tŭs′ĭs) *n.* whooping cough.

peruke (pěr-ook′) *n.* a wig; periwig. *-v.t.* to wear a wig.

pervicacious (pûr-vĭ-kā′shəs) *adj.* extremely obstinate; willful.

pervulgate (pûr-vŭl′gāt) *v.t.* to publish. *pervulgation, n.*

perwitsky (pûr-wĭts′kē) *n.* a red, white, and black European skunk.

pesade (pěs-ād′) *n.* the rearing of a horse

pessary (pěs′ər-ē) *n.* 1. a support for the uterus worn in the vagina. 2. à vaginal suppository.

petalism (pět′əl-ĭz″əm) *n.* the custom in ancient Syracuse of banishing a dangerous citizen for five years.

petroglyph (pět′rō-glĭf) *n.* an ancient rock carving.

pettifogger (pět′ĭ-fŏg″ər) *n.* a mean, tricky, no-good lawyer. *pettifogulize, v.i.*

petulcous (pět-ŭl′kəs) *adj.* butting like a ram; offensively aggressive.

pfefferkuchen (pfěf′ûr-koo″kən) *n.* German gingerbread.

phaeochrous (fē-ŏk′rəs) *adj.* dark-skinned.

phagomania (făg-ō-mā′nĭ-ə) *n.* insanely hungry.

phalacrespia (făl-ə-krěs′pĭ-ə) *n.* aversion for baldness, or for bald men.

phalacrosis (făl-ə-krō′sĭs) *n.* baldness. *-syn. acomia, alopecia, atrichia, calvities.*

phallation (făl-ā′shən) *n.* movement of the penis in sexual intercourse.

phaneromania (făn″ər-ō-mā′nĭ-ə) *n.* a compulsion to pick at a skin growth or imperfection.

pharology (fă-rŏl′ə-jē) *n.* the science of signal lights and lighthouses.

phemic (fē′mĭk) *adj.* pertaining to speech.

phenakistoscope (fĕn-ə-kĭs′tō-skōp) *n.* a circular device with a series of figures seen through slits and viewed from a mirror, making the figures appear to move.

phenology (fē-nŏl′ə-jē) *n.* biological development affected by climate.

philalethe (fĭl′ə-lĕth) *n.* one who loves to forget.

philalethist (fĭl-ə-lē′thĭst) *n.* a truth-lover.

philauty (fĭl-ô′tē) *n.* self-love; selfishness. also *philautia.*

philematology (fĭl-ē″măt-ŏl′ə-jē) *n.* the study of kissing.

philematophobe (fĭl′ē-măt-ō-fōb″) *n.* a woman who dislikes kissing.

philiater (fĭl-ĭ-ā′tər) *n.* an amateur medical student.

philocalist (fĭl-ō′kə-lĭst) *n.* a lover of beauty.

philocomal (fĭl-ō′kə-məl) *adj.* pertaining to care of the hair.

philocubist (fĭl-ō′kū-bĭst) *n.* a lover of dice games.

philodox (fĭl′ō-dŏks) *n.* one who loves her own opinions; a dogmatist. *philodoxical, adj.*

philogastric (fĭl-ō-găs′trĭk) *adj.* greedy.

philomath (fĭl′ō-măth) *n.* a scholar;

---

măn; māde; lět; bē; sĭp; wīne; hŏt; cōld; sôre; dŭll; fūgue; bûrp; good; food; out; gět; thin; this; year; ażure; ō′mən″; viN; fûr; Bach a lover of learning, especially mathematics.

philonoist (fĭl-ŏn'ō-ĭst) *n.* a searcher for knowledge.

philopatridomania (fĭl-ō-păt"rĭ-dō-mā'nĭ-ə) *n.* fanatic desire to return home, as observed in war prisoners.

philophilosophos (fĭl"ō-fĭl-ŏs'ō-fəs) *adj.* fond of philosophers.

philophobia (fĭl-ō-fō'bĭ-ə) *n.* fear of falling in love or of being loved.

philopolemic (fĭl"ō-pō-lĕm'ĭk) *adj.* pertaining to love of argument or controversy.

philopornist (fĭl-ō-pôr'nĭst) *n.* a lover of prostitutes.

philoprogeneity (fĭl"ō-prō-jĕn-ē'ĭ-tē) *n.* love of offspring.

philosophastering (fĭl-ŏs"ō-făs'tər-ĭng) *adj.* pseudo-philosophizing.

philosophicopsychological (fĭl-ō-sŏf"ĭ-kō-sĭ"kō-lŏj'ĭ-kəl) *adj.* both philosophical and psychological.

philotherianism (fĭl-ō-thĭr'ĭ-ən-ĭz"əm) *n.* love of animals.

philoxenist (fĭl-ŏks'ən-ĭst) *n.* one who is happiest while entertaining strangers.

philtrum (fĭl'trəm) *n.* the vertical groove dividing the upper lip.

phlebotomize (flē-bŏt'əm-īz) *v.t. &i.* to bleed by opening a vein.

phlegmagogue (flĕg'mə-gŏg) *n.* a medicine supposed to expel phlegm.

phlogogenetic (flŏg"ō-jĕn-ĕt'ĭk) *adj.* causing inflammation.

phobophobia (fō-bō-fō'bĭ-ə) *n.* fear of phobias, or fear of fear itself.

phoebad (fē'băd) *n.* an inspired woman; a prophet (from those of Apollo at Delphi).

phoenixity (fē-nĭks'ĭ-tē) *n.* a model

of excellence; a paragon of beauty.

phon (fŏn) *n.* a unit for measuring sound.

phonasthenia (fō-nəs-thē'nĭ-ə) *n.* hoarseness.

phonogram (fō'nō-grăm) *n.* a character used to represent a word, syllable, or speech sound.

phonophobia (fō-nō-fō'bĭ-ə) *n.* fear of noise or voices; fear of speaking aloud.

phoresy (fôr'ə-sē) *n.* the life style of certain insects that ride on larger species waiting to gobble up their eggs.

photology (fō-tŏl'ō-jē) *n.* the science of light optics; *photics.*

photophilous (fō-tŏf'ĭl-əs) *adj.* light-loving; *photophilic.*

photophobe (fō'tō-fōb) *n.* an organ or organism that thrives in the dark or turns away from light.

phratry (frā'trē) *n.* 1. a clan. 2. a primitive tribe combining several totemic clans.

phreatic (frē-ăt'ĭk) *adj.* pertaining to a well or underground water.

phrontifugic (frŏnt-ĭ-fū'jĭk) *adj. &n.* relieving anxiety.

phrontistery (frŏn'tĭs-tĕr"ē) *n.* a place for study and contemplation.

phthartic (thŏr'tĭk) *adj.* deadly, destructive.

phthiriophobia (thĭ-rĭ"ō-fō'bĭ-ə) *n.* fear of lice.

phthisozoics (thĭ-sō-zō'ĭks) *n.* destroying harmful animals.

phycology (fī-kŏl'ə-jē) *n.* the science of seaweeds; *algology.*

phylactery (fĭl-ăk'tər-ē) *n.* 1. a box containing scriptural passages, worn by Jews during prayer. 2. any case for holy relics. 3. an amulet worn for protection. 4. something made for display. 5.

màn; māde; lĕt; bē; sĭp; wīne; hŏt; cōld; sôre; dŭll; fūgue; bûrp; gŏŏd; fŏŏd; out; gĕt; thin; this; year; aẑure; ō'mən"; viN; für; Bach

medieval version of cartoon dialogue omitting the balloons.

phyllomancy (fĭl'ō-măn"sē) n. fortunetelling with leaves.

phyloanalysis (fī"lō-ŏn-ăl'ĭ-sĭs) n. study of the psychology of society.

phylogeny (fī-lŏj'ən-ē) n. evolution of a race or related organisms (ontogeny is the evolution of the individual organism).

physagogue (fĭs'ə-gŏg) n.&adj. carminative, or medicine to induce farting.

physianthropy (fĭz-ĭ-ăn'thrō-pē) n. the study of human disease and related remedies.

physiolatry (fĭz-ĭ-ŏl'ə-trē) n. nature worship.

phytivorous (fī-tĭv'ôr-əs) adj. vegetable-eating.

piacular (pī-ăk'ū-lər) adj. requiring expiation; very bad, sinful.

piaffer (pyà'fər) n. a dance step for horses.

planteric (pē-ăn-tĕr'ĭk) n. fattening food. **piantic** (pē-ăn'tĭk) adj. fattened for slaughter.

piation (pī-ā'shən) n. atoning or expiating.

piblokto (pĭb-lŏk'tō) n. 1. a form of arctic rabies. 2. manic depression among Eskimo women.

pica (pī'kə) n. 1. the craving for strange foods. 2. one-sixth of an inch (printing).

picaroon (pĭk-ə-rōōn') n. a thief, pirate, or pirate ship. -v.i. to act like a pirate. -v.t. to pirate.

piccadill (pĭk'ə-dĭl) n. 1. a seventeenth-century collar for a décolleté dress. 2. a nineteenth-century wing collar for men. also piccadilly.

pickedevant (pĭk"ə-dē-vănt') n. à Van Dyke beard.

pickelhaube (pĭk'əl-hou"bə) n. the Prussian spiked helmet.

picklock (pĭk'lŏk) n. 1. a lock picker or lock-picking tool. also adj. 2. a fine grade of wool from merino sheep.

pickthank (pĭk'thănk) n. a flatterer or sycophant. -v.i. to curry favor. -v.t. to get by sycophancy.

picqueter (pĭk'ə-tûr') n. someone who bunches artificial flowers into a bouquet.

pidan (pē-dòn') n. Chinese duck eggs aged in brine.

pifferaro (pĭf-ər-ör'ō) n. a piffero player (the piffero being a cross between an oboe and a bagpipe).

pightle (pī'təl) n. a small field. also pightel.

pignorate (pĭg'nôr-āt) adj. pawned; pignoratitious. -v.t. to pawn or mortgage.

pilgarlic (pĭl-gàr'lĭk) n. a bald head that looks like peeled garlic.

pilikia (pē-lē-kē'ə) n. trouble (Hawaiian).

pililoo (pĭl-ē-lōō') interj.&n. a hunting cry of distress.

pilledow (pĭl'dou) n. a tonsured priest (peeled = bald + daw = blackbird).

pilliwinks (pĭl'ē-wĭnks) n.pl. an old instrument of torture for the thumbs and fingers.

piloerection (pī"lō-ē-rĕk'shən) n. hair standing on end.

pilon (pē-lōn') n. a kickback given customers who pay their bills.

pilose (pī'lōs) adj. hairy; covered with soft hair.

pilpul (pĭl'pōōl) n. an ingenious, hair-splitting, penetrating argument, especially in Jewish Talmudic study.

pimola (pĭm-ō'lə) n. an olive stuffed with sweet pepper; a stuffed olive.

pinacotheca (pĭn"ə-kō-thē'kə) n. a picture gallery.

màn; māde; lĕt; bē; sĭp; wīne; hŏt; cōld; sôre; dŭll; fūgue; bûrp; gōōd; fōōd; out; gĕt; thin; this; year; aẑure; ō'mən"; viN; für; Bach

pinag (pē-nŏg′) n. a temporary lake of flood water.

pinchback (pĭnch′bĕk) n. 1. imitation gold made from an alloy of copper and zinc. 2. something phony; a cheap imitation (from *Christopher Pinchbeck*, its discoverer, who died in 1732).

pinchem (pĭn′chəm) n. the blue European titmouse.

pinchpin (pĭnch′pĭn) n. 1. a married woman who insists on her rights. 2. a prostitute.

pinda (pĭn′də) n. 1. a ball of rice offered to Hindu ancestors. 2. the West Indian peanut.

Pindaric (pĭn-dăr′ĭk) adj. 1. pertaining to elaborate, irregular, or unrestrained poetry, like that of Greek poet, *Pindar*. 2. irregular or unrestrained. -n. pindaric poetry.

pinguedinous (pĭng-gwĕd′ĭn-əs) adj. fatty. *pinguid*, fatty and rich (applied to soil). *pinguescent*, adj. fattening.

pinxit (pĭnks′ĭt) "she [he] painted [it]": used after artist's signature (Latin).

piobaireachd (pē′ō-bĕr-ĕcht″) n. a traditional dirge, with variations, for the highland bagpipe. also *pibroch*.

pioupiou (pū-pū′) n. an infantryman (French slang).

piperitious (pĭp-ər-ĭsh′əs) adj. peppery.

pipient (pĭp′ē-ənt) adj. piping, chirping.

pipkin (pĭp′kĭn) n. a ceramic pot with a horizontal handle; a *piggin*, or wooden tub with a horizontal handle.

pipsissewa (pĭp-sĭs′ē-wò) n. an herb used as a diuretic.

pis-aller (pēs-ă-lā′) n. the last resort.

piscary (pĭs′kə-rē) n. 1. fishing privileges in another's waters. 2. a place for fishing.

piscatology (pĭs-kə-tŏl′ə-jē) n. science of fishing.

piscicapturist (pĭs″ĭ-kăp′chər-ĭst) n. a fisherman.

pismire (pĭs′mīr) n. an ant.

pismirism (pĭs′mīr-ĭz″əm) n. petty saving.

piss-proud (pĭs′proud) adj. having a false erection: said of an old man with a young wife.

pistic (pĭs′tĭk) adj. pure, genuine; pertaining to faith.

pistology (pĭs-tŏl′ə-jē) n. the study of faith.

pithecological (pĭth″ē-kō-lŏj′ĭ-kəl) adj. pertaining to the study of apes.

pithiatism (pĭth′ĭ-ə-tĭz″əm) n. forceful suggestion.

pizzle (pĭz′əl) n. a whip made of an animal's penis; the penis itself.

placophobia (plăk-ō-fō′bĭ-ə) n. fear of tombstones.

plangent (plăn′jənt) adj. sounding with loud reverberation.

plangorous (plăng′ər-əs) adj. wailing.

planiloquent (plăn-ĭl′ō-kwənt) adj. straight talking.

planiped (plăn′ĭ-pĕd) n. a barefoot person. -adj. barefoot.

planistethic (plăn-ĭs-tĕth′ĭk) adj. flat-chested.

planomania (plā-nō-mā′nĭ-ə) n. urge to live a bohemian life.

plantigrade (plănt′ĭ-grād) adj. walking on the soles of the feet, as bears and humans. opposite of *digitigrade*.

plantocracy (plănt-ŏk′rə-sē) n. government by planters; planters as a ruling class.

plastron (plăs′trŏn) n. 1. a metal breastplate. 2. the lower part of a turtle shell. 3. trim for the front of a woman's dress. 4. a man's starched shirt front.

plateresque (plăt-ûr-ĕsk') *adj.* like ornate silver work.

platitudinarian (plăt″ĭ-tōōd-ĭn-ĕr′ĭ-ən) *adj.&n.* full of platitudes; speaking platitudes.

plebicolist (plē-bĭk′ō-lĭst) *n.* someone who woos the common folk.

plegometer (plē-gŏm′ə-tûr) *n.* an instrument to measure and record the force of blows

pleionosis (plē-ŏn-ō′sĭs) *n.* exaggeration of one's own importance.

plenary (plē′nə-rē) *adj.* 1. entire, complete, absolute. 2. all present, as in a meeting. 3. having full powers.

pleniloquence (plē-nĭl′ō-kwəns) *n.* excessive talking.

pleonastic (plē-ō-năs′tĭk) *adj.* pertaining to oral or written repetitiousness.

pleonexia (plē-ō-nĕks′ĭ-ə) *n.* covetousness, avarice; mania for acquiring possessions.

plexiform (plĕks′ĭ-fôrm) *adj.* like a network; complicated.

plicate (plī′kăt) *adj.* folded like a fan.

plumassier (plōō-mŏs-yā′) *n.* someone who makes or sells ornamental feathers.

plumbeous (plŭm′bē-əs) *adj.* 1. like lead; leaden. 2. dull, heavy, stupid; *plumbean.*

plumbum (plŭm′bŭm) *n.* lead, symbol Pb., number eighty-two in the atomic series.

plumpers (plŭm′pərz) *n.pl.* padding for filling out sunken cheeks.

plutomania (plōō-tō-mā′nĭ-ə) *n.* mania for money.

pluviograph (plōō′vĭ-ō-grăf″) *n.* a self-registering rain gauge.

pluviophobia (plōō″vĭ-ō-fō′bĭ-ə) *n.* fear of rain or of being rained upon.

pneumonoultramicroscopicsilicovolcanokoniosis (nōō′mō-nō-ŭl″trə-mīk-rō-skŏp″ĭk-sĭl″ĭ-kō-vŏl-kā″nō-kō-nĭ-o′sĭs) *n.* pneumoconiosis caused by the inhalation of silicate or quartz dust.

pnigophobia (nī-gō-fō′bĭ-ə) *n.* fear of choking, as during sleep.

pochette (pō-shĕt′) *n.* 1. a thin transparent envelope for keeping stamps. 2. a small violin.

pococurante (pō′kō-kōō-rŏn′tā) *adj.* nonchalant, indifferent. *-n.* a nonchalant or indifferent person.

poculation (pŏk-ū-lā′shən) *n.* wine-bibbing.

poculiform (pŏk′ū-lĭ-fôrm″) *adj.* cup-shaped.

podobromhidrosis (pŏd″ō-brōm-hĭ-drō′sĭs) *n.* smelly feet.

poecilonymy (pē-sĭl-ŏn′ə-mē) *n.* the use of several names for one thing.

poger (pō′jûr) *n.* a passive male homosexual (hobo cant).

pogoniasis (pō-gən-ī′ə-sĭs) *n.* bearded: said of men and women. also *pogoniate, adj.*

pogonip (pŏg′ə-nĭp) *n.* an icy winter fog producing pneumonia when inhaled, peculiar to the Sierra Nevadas in the West.

pogonology (pō-gō-nŏl′ə-jē) *n.* a treatise on beards. *pogonotomy,* (-nŏt′ə-mē) *n.* cutting of the beard; shaving. *pogonotrophy, n.* beard-growing.

poiesis (poi-ē′sĭs) *n.* creation; creative power or ability.

poikilothermal (poi″kĭl-ō-thûr′məl) *adj.* cold-blooded; *poikilothermic, poikilothermous.*

poikilothymia (poi″kĭl-ō-thī′mĭ-ə)

n. extreme changes of mood.

poilu (pwò-lōō′) *n.* a man of great strength and courage (French = hairy man).

poitrel (poi′trəl) *n.* 1. a breastplate for man or beast. 2. a stomacher.

pokelocken (pōk′lō″kən) *n.* a bay or inlet; a marshy place.

polder (pōl′dər) *n.* land reclaimed from the sea.

poliosis (pòl-ĭ-ō′sĭs) *n.* premature graying of the hair.

pollage (pō′ləj) *n.* a poll tax; extortion.

pollard (pòl′ərd) *n.* 1. an animal that has lost its horns. 2. an Edwardian counterfeit coin. 3. a severely pruned tree. 4. coarse bran or wheat flour. *-v.t.* 1. to prune a tree. 2. to kill [rabbits] by feeding them poisoned grain.

pollaver (pòl-àv′ər) *n.* fawning behavior; gross flattery.

pollicitation (pòl-ĭs″ĭ-tā′shən) *n.* 1. an unaccepted offer. 2. a promise.

polyandrous (pòl-ĭ-àn′drəs) *adj.* having more than one husband or mate at a time.

polychrestic (pòl-ĭ-krĕs′tĭk) *adj.* useful for many reasons.

polyhistor (pòl-ĭ-hĭs′tôr) *n.* a universal scholar; a thoroughly educated person.

polylemma (pòl-ĭ-lĕm′ə) *n.* a dilemma with three or more equally undesirable solutions.

polylogy (pō-lĭl′ə-jē) *n.* wordiness.

polymetochia (pòl″ĭ-mē-tō′kĭ-ə) *n.* the use of many participles or participial phrases.

polymicrian (pòl-ĭ-mĭk′rĭ-ən) *adj.* compact.

polyphagia (pòl-ĭ-fā′jĭ-ə) *n.* excessive eating.

polyphyletic (pòl″ĭ-fī-lĕt′ĭk) *adj.* derived from more than one ancestor.

pombe (pòm′bā) *n.* a Tibetan chief.

pomology (pō-mòl′ə-jē) *n.* fruit growing.

ponent (pō′nənt) *adj.* western; occidental.

poniard (pòn′yərd) *n.* a thin dagger.

ponophobia (pòn-ō-fō′bĭ-ə) *n.* fear of overworking.

pontacq (pòn′tàk) *n.* a wine of southern France.

pontage (pòn′təj) *n.* a bridge toll.

pontificalibus (pòn-tĭf″ĭ-kàl′ĭ-bəs) *n.pl.* one's official uniform.

pont-levis (pòN-lĕ-vē′) *n.* a drawbridge.

pootly-nautch (pōōt′lē-nôch) *n.* a children's puppet show.

popekin (pōp′kĭn) *n.* a little pope (a term of contempt).

popinal (pòp′ĭn-əl) *adj.* pertaining to bars or restaurants.

popinary (pòp′ĭn-èr″ē) *n.* a frycook.

popination (pòp-ĭn-ā′shən) *n.* barhopping.

popoloco (pō-pō-lō′kō) *n.* one who speaks a strange or foreign language (Nahuatl).

poppa-stopper (pòp′ə-stòp″ər) *n.* 1. one who commits sexual acts with one's father. 2. an affectionate term. also *poppa-stoppa*, *poppa-loppa*.

poriomania (pôr″ĭ-ō-mā′nĭ-ə) *n.* wanderlust.

porlockian (pôr-lòk′ĭ-ən) *adj.* intrusive, interrupting (a man from *Porlock* wrecked Coleridge's train of thought during the writing of *Kubla Khan*).

pornerastic (pôr-nûr-às′tĭk) *adj.* licentious, lascivious, lewd, and horny.

pornocracy (pôr-nòk′rə-sē) *n.* government by prostitutes.

pornolagnia (pôr-nō-làg′nĭ-ə) *n.* desire for prostitutes.

---

porraceous (pôr-ā'shəs) *adj.* leek-green.

porrect (pôr-ĕkt') *v.t.* 1. to stretch out horizontally. 2. to present for examination (ecclesiastical law).

porte-cochère (pôrt-kō-shèr') *n.* a gateway big enough for cars to drive into the courtyard.

portmanteau (pôrt-mòn-tō') *n.* 1. a large suitcase. 2. a clothes rack; a hanger.

portmantologism (pôrt-măn-tòl'ə-jĭz"əm) *n.* a portmanteau, or blend word.

posada (pō-sò'dò) *n.* a hotel or inn (Spanish).

positron (pòz'ĭ-tròn) *n.* the positive electron, a subatomic particle.

posology (pō-sòl'ə-jē) *n.* the science of quantitative dosing; *dosology.*

postcibal (pōst-sī'bəl) *adj.* after dinner; *postprandial.*

postil (pòs'tĭl) *n.* 1. a marginal note. 2. a short homily on a scriptural passage; a collection of such.

postliminium (pōst-lĭm-ĭn'ĭ-əm) *n.* when a war prisoner returns to her own country and original status; the right by which captured enemy is returned.

postmenacmium (pōst-mèn-ăk'mĭ-əm) *n.* life after the menopause.

postpartum (pōst-pòr'təm) *n.* after childbirth. also *post.*

postprandial (pōst-prăn'dĭ-əl) *adj.* after dinner; *postcibal.*

postremogeniture (pòs-trē'mō-jèn'ĭ-tyûr) *n.* *ultimogeniture,* or the right of the youngest-born.

potagerie (pō-tòj-rē') *n.* garden vegetables and herbs; kitchen garden. also *potagery.*

potamic (pō-tàm'ĭk) *adj.* pertaining to rivers or river navigation.

potamophilous (pòt-ə-mòf'ĭl-əs) *adj.* river-loving.

potatory (pō'tə-tôr"ē) *adj.* pertaining to or addicted to drinking.

poteen (pō-tēn') *n.* moonshine. also *potheen.*

potichomania (pō"tĭ-shō-mā'nĭ-ə) *n.* the craze for imitating porcelain by coating the inside of glassware. *potichomanist, n.*

potomaniac (pō-tō-mā'nĭ-àk) *n.* an alcoholic.

potsherd (pòt'shûrd) *n.* a broken bit of crockery (*pot* + *shard*).

potvaliant (pòt'vàl"yənt) *adj.* courageous when drunk. -*n.* a potvaliant person. also *potvaliant.*

potwalloper (pòt'wòl"əp-ûr) *n.* 1. voting eligibility determined by one who boils (*wallops*) her own pot, or maintains her own household. 2. one who cleans pots; a sea cook.

pourboire (pōōr-bwòr') *n.* a tip. (French *pour* = for + *boire* = drinking).

pourparler (pōōr-pòr-lā') *n.* an informal conference (French *pour* = for + *parler* = to speak).

pouze (pōōz) *n.* refuse from cider-making.

pozzuolana. (pòts-wō-lòn'ò) *n.* 1. loosely compacted volcanic rock. 2. mortar made of lime and volcanic dust found near *Pozzuoli,* Italy. 3. any finely ground cement produced by mixing lime and volcanic ash.

pozzy-wallah (pò'zē-wòl"ə) *n.* a jam lover (British slang).

praetorian (prē-tôr'ĭ-ən) *adj.* 1. pertaining to the Roman *praetor* or magistrate, famed for political corruption. 2. pertaining to a Roman emperor's bodyguard.

pralltriller (prôl'trĭl"ər) *n.* an inverted mordent (music).

---

màn; māde; lèt; bē; sìp; wīne; hòt; cōld; sôre; dùll; fūgue; bûrp; gōōd; fōōd; out; gèt; thin; this; year; aźure; ō'mən"; viN; für; Bach

pranayama (prăn-ə-yò'mə) n. strenuous Yoga exercises and breath control.

pratal (prā'təl) adj. pertaining to, growing, or living in meadows. *pratincolous* (prà-tĭng'kō-ləs) adj. living in meadows.

pratiloma (prăt-ĭl-ō'mə) adv. not according to custom: said of Hindu marriages in which women marry men of a lower class.

pratityasamutpada (prăt-ēt″yə-sə-mōōt-pò'dò) n. the chain of causation (Hindu philosophy).

pravity (prăv'ĭ-tē) n. physical deformity.

praxiology (prăks-ē-òl'ə-jē) n. the study of human conduct. also *praxeology*.

preagonal (prē-àg'ən-əl) adj. just before death.

preantepenultimate (prē-àn″tē-pèn-ùl'tĭ-mət) n.&adj. fourth from last.

precant (prē'kənt) n. one who prays.

precibal (prē-sī'bəl) adj. before dinner; *preprandial*.

preconize (prē'kō-nīz) v.t. 1. to publish. 2. to commend publicly.

predacean (prē-dā'shən) n. a carnivorous animal.

predal (prē'dəl) adj. plundering, pillaging, predatory.

prehension (prē-hèn'shən) n. 1. seizing, grasping. 2. taking possession.

prejudicateness (prē-jōō'dĭ-kāt″nəs) n. the process of being decided beforehand; preconception; prejudice.

premenacmium (prē-mèn-àk'mĭ-əm) n. life before menstruation begins.

premial (prē'mĭ-əl) adj. like a reward.

premorse (prē-môrs') adj. ended abruptly, as if bitten off. -n. the blue scabious.

premundane (prē-mùn'dān) adj. existing before the creation of the world; *antemundane*.

prender (prèn'dər) n. the right of taking something without its being offered (law).

preominate (prē-òm'ĭn-āt) v.t. to prophesy by omens.

preprandial (prē-prăn'dĭ-əl) adj. before dinner; *precibal*.

prepuce (prē'pūs) n. the foreskin.

presbyophrenia (prèz″bē-ō-frē'nĭ-ə) n. female senility marked by loss of memory, disorientation.

prescind (prē-sĭnd') v.t. to separate in thought; to consider individually. -v.i. to abstract oneself. both with *from*.

prête-nom (prèt'nôm) n. one who lends her name.

preterient (prē-tĭr'ĭ-ənt) adj. transient.

preterist (prĕt'ûr-ĭst) n. someone whose main pleasure is in reliving the past. also adj.

pretermit (prē-tûr-mĭt') v.t. 1. to pass over; to neglect. 2. to interrupt or break off. *pretermission*, n.

preterpluperfect (prē″tûr-plōō-pûr'fèkt) adj. 1. past perfect, in grammar. 2. more than perfect (humorous).

priapean (prī-ə-pē'ən) adj. phallic. also *priapic*.

priapism (prī'ə-pĭz″əm) n. persistent and painful erection, usually the result of a disease.

prickmadam (prĭk'măd″əm) n. a low, spreading mosslike herb used in gardens. also *pricket*.

prickmedainty (prĭk-mē-dān'tē) adj. goody-goody. -n. a goody-goody person.

pridian (prĭd'ĭ-ən) adj. pertaining to

---

màn; māde; lèt; bē; sĭp; wīne; hòt; cōld; sôre; dùll; fūgue; bûrp; gōōd; fōōd; out; gèt; thin; this; year; aźure; ō'mən″; viN; fûr; Bach

the day before yesterday.

prie-dieu (prē-dyû′) *n.* a prayer desk.

primipara (prĭm-ĭp′ə-rə) *n.* a woman having her first child.

primogeniture (prī-mō-jĕn′ĭ-tyûr) *n.* state of being the first-born.

princeps (prĭn′sĕps) *adj.* first, original: used especially of a first edition. -*n.* one who is first, as the head of state.

princox (prĭn′kŏks) *n.* a conceited dandy; a fop, *coxcomb.*

Priscillianist (pris-ĭl′yən-ĭst) *n.* a follower of Priscillian, bishop of Avila; a *Montanist* or member of an ascetic Christian sect of the second century.

prisiadka (prēs-yŏd′kŏ) *n.* a Russian dance performed by men alternately extending a leg from a squatting position.

proa (prō′ə) *n.* a Malaysian sailing outrigger.

proamita (prō-ăm′ĭ-tə) *n.* a paternal great-aunt; your grandfather's sister.

probang (prō′băng) *n.* a thin rod with a sponge on the end, for removing obstructions from the esophagus.

probouleutic (prō-bōō-lōō′tĭk) *adj.* pertaining to preliminary deliberation.

procacious (prō-kā′shəs) *adj.* impudent; petulant.

proceleusmatic (prŏs″ē-lōōs-măt′ĭk) *adj.* 1. animating; encouraging. 2. composed of four short syllables.

procellous (prō-sĕl′əs) *adj.* stormy.

procerity (prō-sĕr′ĭ-tē) *n.* tallness; height.

prochnial (prŏk′nĭ-əl) *adj.* relating to submission or kneeling.

prochoos (prō′kō-ŏs) *n.* an old Greek vase containing water for preprandial hand-washing.

prochronism (prō′krō-nĭz″əm) *n.* the dating of an event before it occurs.

procrustean (prō-krŭs′tē-ən) *adj.* pertaining to the act of forcing submissiveness or conformity (from *Procrustes.* legendary Greek robber, who stretched or severed his victims' legs to fit his bed).

procryptic (prō-krĭp′tĭk) *adj.* camouflaged.

proctalgia (prŏk-tăl′jĭ-ə) *n.* a pain in the ass. also *rectalgia.*

procumbent (prō-kŭm′bənt) *adj.* lying or kneeling with face down; prostrate.

proditorious (prŏd-ĭ-tôr′ĭ-əs) *adj.* traitorous; prone to give away secrets.

prodromal (prŏd′rō-məl) *adj.* pertaining to first signs of a disease.

proedria (prō-ĕd′rĭ-ə) *n.* ancient Greek hospitality to visiting V.I.P's: front-row seats for sports and dramatic events.

proemial (prō-ē′mĭ-əl) *adj.* introductory, prefatory.

profectitious (prō-fĕk-tĭsh′əs) *adj.* pertaining to inherited property.

proficuous (prō-fĭk′ū-əs) *adj.* profitable, useful.

progenerate (prō-jĕn′ər-āt) *n.* a person with superior talent and intelligence. -*v.t.* to procreate. -*adj.* becoming superior to one's peers.

progeria (prō-jĭr′ĭ-ə) *n.* premature senility.

prognathous (prŏg′nə-thŭs) *adj.* having a protruding jaw.

projicient (prō-jĭsh′ənt) *adj.* helping an organism fit into its environment (psychology).

prolapse (prō′lăps) *n.* the collapse of an internal organ. -*v.i.* to fall

---

mǎn; māde; lĕt; bē; sĭp; wīne; hŏt; cōld; sôre; dŭll; fūgue; bûrp; gōōd; fōōd; out; gĕt; thin; this; year; ažure; ō′mən″; viN; fûr; Bach

or slip forward, down, or out.

prolegeron (prō-lèj'ər-òn) *n.* the childbearing period in a woman's life.

prolegomena (prō-lə-gòm'ən-ə) *n.pl.* preliminary remarks; long introductions.

prolepsis (prō-lèp'sĭs) *n.* anticipation.

proletaneous (prō-lə-tàn'ĭ-əs) *adj.* having many children.

prolicide (prō'lĭ-sīd) *n.* the killing of offspring.

prolusion (prō-lōō'żən) *n.* 1. a rehearsal, prelude. 2. an introductory essay.

pronken (pròng'kən) *v.i.* to move majestically; prance.

pronovalence (prō'nō-vàl'əns) *n.* ability to have sexual intercourse in a prone position only.

propaedeutics (prō-pē-dū'tĭks) *n.* preparatory instruction.

propale (prō-pāl') *v.t.* to disclose.

propugnation (prō-pŭg-nā'shən) *n.* means of defense; vindication.

proreption (prō-rèp'shən) *n.* a crawling forward.

prosonomasia (pròz"ō-nō-mā'zĭ-ə) *n.* use of a humorous modification of a person's name.

prosophobia (prō-sō-fō'bĭ-ə) *n.* fear of or aversion to progress.

prosopography (pròs-ō-pòg'rə-fē) *n.* facial or physical description.

prosopolepsy (prō-sō'pō-lèp"sē) *n.* judging people favorably from their looks.

prosopolethy (prō"zō-pō-lē'thē) *n.* inability to remember faces.

prosopopy (pròs'ō-pōp"ē) *n.* the personification of inanimate objects.

protasis (pròt'ə-sĭs) *n.* 1. a maxim. 2. an introduction to a play.

protean (prō'tē-ən) *adj.* infinitely variable; versatile.

protervity (prō-tûr'vĭ-tē) *n.* petulance.

prothalamion (prō-thə-lā'mĭ-òn) *n.* a wedding song.

prothonotary (prō-thòn'ō-tèr"ē) *n.* a legal or religious clerk.

protogenal (prō-tòj'ən-əl) *adj.* pertaining to primitive creatures.

protreptic (prō-trèp'tĭk) *adj.* persuasive; doctrinal.

provine (prō-vīn') *v.t.* to layer.

proxenete (pròks'ən-ēt) *n.* a marriage broker; a procurer.

pruritic (proōr-ĭt'ĭk) *adj.* pertaining to or producing itching without visible cause.

prushun (prŭsh'ən) *n.* a young boy who begs for a man; a male homosexual who lives with beggars.

psalmody (sàl'mō-dē) *n.* psalm-singing; psalms, collectively.

psammous (sàm'əs) *adj.* sandy.

psaphonic (sà-fòn'ĭk) *adj.* planning one's rise to fame.

pschutt (pshōot) *adj.* overly chic.

psellismophobia (sèl-ĭz"mō-fō'bĭ-ə) *n.* fear of stuttering.

psephology (sē-fòl'ə-jē) *n.* the study of elections. *psephologist,* *n.*

psephomancy (sē'fō-màn"sē) *n.* fortunetelling with pebbles.

pseudandry (sōō'dàn"drē) *n.* female use of a male pseudonym. see *pseudogyny.*

pseudautochiria (sōōd-ôt"ō-kī'rĭ-ə) *n.* murder disguised as suicide. see *pseudophonia.*

pseudepigraphous (sōō-də-pĭg'rə-fəs) *adj.* signed with a phony name.

pseudepisematic (sōō-èp"ĭ-sə-màt'ĭk) *adj.* an animal colored to look like its prey or its surroundings.

pseudoantidisestablishmentar-

ianism (soo͞o"dō-ăn-tē-dĭs"ĕs-tăb-lĭsh-mənt-ĕr'ĭ-ən-ĭz"əm) *n*. phony opposition to the withdrawal of state support from an established church.

pseudocyesis (soo͞o"dō-sī-ē'sĭs) *n*. false pregnancy, usually occurring in older, childless women.

pseudogyny (soo͞od-ŏj'ĭn-ē) *n*. male use of a female pseudonym. see *pseudandry*.

pseudologist (soo͞od-ŏl'ə-jĭst) *n*. a liar.

pseudomancy (soo͞o'dō-măn"sē) *n*. consciously fraudulent fortune-telling.

pseudomania (soo͞o-dō-mā'nĭ-ə) *n*. neurotic assumption of guilt by an innocent party.

pseudomnesia (soo͞o-dŏm-nē'zĭ-ə) *n*. memory for things that never happened.

pseudophonia (soo͞o-dō-fō'nĭ-ə) *n*. suicide disguised as murder. see *pseudautochiria*.

pseudorhombicuboctahedron (soo͞o"dō-rŏm"bĭ-kū"bŏk-tə-hē'drən) *n*. an Archimedean solid with twenty-six faces.

pseudothyrum (soo͞o-dō-thī'rùm) *n*. a private or secret entrance.

psilogy (sī-lŏl'ə-jē) *n*. empty talk.

psilosis (sī-lō'sĭs) *n*. the falling out of hair; depilation.

psilosopher (sī-lŏs'ō-fər) *n*. a superficial philosopher.

psilothrum (sī-lō'thrəm) *n*. a hair remover.

psithurism (sĭth'ə-rĭz"əm) *n*. a whispering sound, as of wind among leaves.

psittaceous (sī-tā'shəs) *adj*. parrotlike.

psomophagy (sō-mŏf'ə-jē) *n*. swallowing food without thorough chewing.

psychalgia (sī-kăl'jĭ-ə) *n*. mental anguish.

psychasthenia (sī-kăs-thē'nĭ-ə) *n*. neurotic lassitude, indecision; doubts, tics, and phobias.

psychrolusia (sī-krō-loo͞o'sĭ-ə) *n*. bathing in cold water.

psychrotherapy (sī-krō-thĕr'ə-pē) *n*. the use of cold in medical treatment.

psychurgy (sī'kûr-jē) *n*. mental energy.

psywar (sī'wôr) *n*. PSYchological WARfare.

ptarmic (tŏr'mĭk) *adj*. snot-promoting; *sternutatory, errhine*. -*n*. a substance that induces sneezing.

pteric (tĕr'ĭk) *adj*. pertaining to wings.

pteronophobia (tĕr-ō"nə-fō'bĭ-ə) *n*. fear of being tickled by feathers.

ptochocracy (tō-kŏk'rə-sē) *n*. government by the poor.

ptochogony (tō-kŏg'ən-ē) *n*. a system of producing beggars or poverty.

pucelage (pū'sə-lĭj) *n*. virginity.

pud (pùd) *n*. 1. a child's hand; an animal's forefoot (British slang). 2. the penis (U.S. slang).

pudency (pū'dən-sē) *n*. modesty; extreme prudishness. *pudent, pudic, pudical, adj*.

puericulture (pū'ər-ĭ-kŭl"chər) *n*. 1. bringing up children. 2. prenatal care.

puerperium (pū"ûr-pîr'ĭ-əm) *n*. childbirth; labor in childbirth.

pugil (pū'jĭl) *n*. a pinch that can be held between the thumb and the first two fingers.

puisne (pū'nē) *adj*. 1. later, subsequent. 2. feeble, unskilled. 3. junior; younger or inferior (law).

puissant (pū'ĭ-sənt) *adj*. powerful, potent, strong, masterful, authoritative.

puist (pūst) *adj.* in comfortable circumstances.

pukka (pŭk'ə) *adj.* 1. real, authentic. 2. superior. also *pucka.*

pule (pūl) *v.i.* to whine.

pulicous (pū'lĭ-kəs) *adj.* pertaining to or abounding with fleas.

pullulant (pŭl'ū-lənt) *adj.* sprouting or budding.

pultaceous (pŭl-tā'shəs) *adj.* pulpy; semifluid.

pulvil (pŭl'vĭl) *n.* 1. sachet powder. 2. snuff. *-v.t.* to put sachet powder on.

pulvinar (pŭl-vī'nər) *adj.* cushionlike. *-n.* a cushioned seat in bleachers.

punaluan (pōō-nə-lōō'ən) *adj.* group marriage in which like marries like (brothers wed sisters, etc.).

puncheon (pŭn'chən) *n.* 1. a dagger. 2. a barrel. 3. a carved stamp used by goldsmiths. 4. a split log with a smooth face. 5. a marble-working tool.

punctate (pŭnk'tāt) *adj.* 1. pointed. 2. spotted (medicine).

pundigrion (pŭn-dĭg'rĭ-ən) *n.* a pun.

pundonor (pōōn-dō-nôr') *n.* a point of honor (Spanish *punto de honor*).

puniceous (pū-nĭsh'əs) *adj.* bright red; purplish red.

punnology (pŭn-ŏl'ə-jē) *n.* punning.

punquetto (pŭnk-èt'ō) *n.* a prostitute.

pupillarity (pū-pĭl-ăr'ĭ-tē) *n.* the years before puberty.

purblind (pûr'blīnd) *adj.* 1. partly blind. 2. lacking insight or understanding.

purdah (pûr'də) *n.* a screen or its material for hiding women from the public (India).

purfle (pûr'fəl) *n.* an ornamental border or trim.

purlicue (pûr'lĭ-kū) *n.* 1. the space between the thumb and extended forefinger. 2. a curlicue at the end of a word.

purpresture (pûr-prĕs'chər) *n.* a private piece of public land.

purpuraceous (pûr-pū-rā'shəs) *adj.* purple. *purpurescent, adj.* purplish, or tinged with purple.

purseproud (pûrs'proud) *adj.* arrogant and haughtily proud of one's wealth.

pursiness (pûrs'ĭ-nĕs) *n.* vaingloriousness.

putage (pū'təj) *n.* prostitution. also *putanism.*

putative (pū'tə-tĭv) *adj.* supposed, alleged, reputed.

putrilage (pū'trĭ-ləj) *n.* that which is being putrefied. *putrilaginous, adj.*

putschist (pōōch'ĭst) *n.* one who participates in a popular uprising, or *putsch.*

putti (pōō'tē) *n.pl.* cupids in sculpture and painting.

puttock (pŭt'ək) *n.* 1. the European kite; the buzzard; the marsh harrier. 2. a greedy person; a sponger.

putz (pŭts) *n.* 1. a crèche. 2. the penis.

pygal (pī'gəl) *adj.* pertaining to the buttocks.

pygophilous (pī-gŏf'ĭl-əs) *adj.* buttock-loving.

pyknic (pĭk'nĭk) *adj.* short and stocky; *endomorphic* (pertaining to a body type).

pylon (pī'lŏn) *n.* 1. a truncated Egyptian pyramid serving as an entrance way. 2. an entrance monument. 3. a tower for supporting a long span of wire.

pyretic (pī-rĕt'ĭk) *adj.* pertaining to fever; *febrile. -n.* a remedy for fever.

pyriform (pǐr'ǐ-fôrm) *adj.* pear-shaped.

pyrography (pī-rŏg'rə-fē) *n.* creating designs by burning; the creation itself.

pyrolagnia (pī-rō-làg'nǐ-ə) *n.* sexual stimulation from watching fires.

pyromancy (pī'rō-màn"sē) *n.* fortunetelling with fire.

pyrrhonist (pǐr'ō-nǐst) *n.* a skeptic (from *Pyrrho*, a 365 B.C. Greek skeptic).

pyrrhotism (pǐr'ō-tǐz"əm) *n.* having red hair. *pyrrhotist, n.*

pysmatic (pǐz-màt'ǐk) *adj.* pertaining to questioning; always asking questions.

pythogenic (pī-thō-jĕn'ǐk) *adj.* coming from garbage.

pyx (pǐks) *n.* 1. the Host case or *ciborium.* 2. a ship's binnacle. *pyx chest,* a case for British coins being tested for weight and quality. also *v.t.*

qabbalah (kə-bôl′ö) *n.* 1. an occult interpretation of the Bible among certain Jews and medieval Christians. 2. occultism, mysticism. also *cabala, cabbala, cabbalah, kabala, kabbala, kabbalah, qabbala.*

qadi (kŏd′ē) *n.* a Moslem judge who administers religious law. also *cadi, kadi, kadhi, qazi.*

Qaraqalpaq (kŏr-ə-kŏl′păk) *n.* Turkish people of central Asia or their language. also *Karakalpak.*

qasida (kə-sē′dŏ) *n.* an Arabic poem.

qcepo (ksē′pō) *n.* a form of the parasitic disease, *leishmaniasis.*

qebhsnauf (kĕb′snouf) *n.* the hawk-headed son of Egyptian god, Horus.

qhythsontyd (kwĭth′sən-tĭd) *n.* obsolete form of *whitsuntide* (Whit Sunday, the seventh Sunday after Easter).

qintar (kĭn-tŏr′) *n.* money equaling 1/100 lek or 1/5000 U.S. dollar. also *qindar* (Albania).

qoph (kōf) *n.* the nineteenth letter of the Hebrew alphabet. also *koph, coph.*

qua (kwŏ) *adv.* as; in the capacity or role of. *-n.* 1. the night heron. see *quawk.* 2. quagmire.

quaa (kwŏ) *n.* a quagmire. also *qua, quaw.*

quab (kwŏb) *n.* 1. the eelpout or gudgeon; any similar small fish. 2. something immature or unfinished.

quackle (kwăk′əl) *v.i.* to choke or suffocate (slang).

quacksalver (kwăk′săl″vər) *n.* a charlatan, quack.

quaddle (kwŏd′əl) *v.i.* to grumble. *-n.* a grumbler (British dialect).

quadrable (kwŏd′rə-bəl) *adj.* that may be squared (mathematics).

quadragesimal (kwŏd-rə-jĕs′ĭ-məl) *adj.* 1. consisting of forty. 2. (cap.) pertaining to or used during Lent. *-n.* a forty-day fast; Lenten sermon or offering.

quadrennial (kwŏd-rĕn′ĭ-əl) *adj.* lasting four years; happening once every four years. *-n.* a four-year period; a four-year anniversary.

quadrifurcation (kwŏd″rĭ-fûr-kā′shən) *n.* separating or branching into four parts.

màn; māde; lèt; bē; sĭp; wīne; hŏt; cōld; sôre; dùll; fūgue; bûrp; gŏŏd; fōōd; out; gèt; thin; thìs; year; aźure; ō′mən″; viN; fûr; Bacĥ

quadrigamist (kwŏd-rĭg'ə-mĭst) *n.* someone who has married four times; someone with four husbands or wives at the same time.

quadrimum (kwŏd-rī'-mŭm) *n.* a four-year-old wine; an excellent wine, according to Horace (short for *quadrimum merum*).

quaedam (kwē'dăm) *n.* derogatory term for a woman.

Quaequae (kwā'kwā) *n.s.&pl.* a tribe of Hottentots.

quaesitum (kwē-sī'təm) *n.* 1. objective; end. 2. the true value of a quantity (mathematics).

quaestor (kwĕs'tôr) *n.* military or judiciary official of ancient Rome.

quaestuary (kwĕs'chōō-ĕr"ē) *adj.* done or performed for money. *-n.* someone who looks first to profit.

quagga (kwăg'ə) *n.* the wild ass of South Africa.

quaggle (kwăg'əl) *n.* a quivering, as of jelly.

quahog (kwô'hôg) *n.* a thick-shelled American or North Atlantic clam. *-v.i.* to dig for *quahogs*.

quaintise (kwān'tĭs) *n.* ingenuity, cunning; a trick or stratagem.

quakebuttock (kwāk'bŭt"ŏk) *n.* a coward.

qualtagh (kwŏl'tŏk) *n.* the first person seen after leaving the house (Isle of Man).

quannet (kwŏn'ət) *n.* a planelike file used in making combs.

quant (kwŏnt) *n.* a punting pole. *-v.t.&i.* to punt, or to be punted, with a *quant* (British).

quantulum (kwŏn'chōō-lùm) *n.* a small quantity.

quap (kwăp) *n.* 1. something which quakes or heaves, as soft ground. 2. a throb or palpitation, as of pain. *-v.i.* to heave or palpitate.

quaquaversal (kwā-kwə-vûr'səl) *adj.* turning or dipping in every direction; dipping from the center toward all points of the compass, as a dome. *-n.* a quaquaversal dome or ridge. *quaquaversally, adv.* (geology).

quar (kwôr) *v.t.&i.* to fill or block. *-v.i.* to curdle.

quardeel (kôr-dāl') *n.* a cask used by Dutch whalers. also *cardel*.

quarenden (kwôr'ən-dən) *n.* a deep-red apple.

quarentene (kwôr'ən-tēn) *n.* a furlong; a road.

quarl (kwôrl) *n.* a curved fire brick used to support melting pots for zinc. *-n.* a jellyfish. *-v.i.* to curdle.

quartan (kwôr'tăn) *adj.* happening every fourth day; pertaining to the fourth. *-n.* a fever that returns every fourth day. 2. a measure equaling one-fourth of another measure.

quarternight (kwôr'tər-nīt) *n.* halfway between sundown and midnight.

quarterpace (kwôr'tər-pās) *n.* a staircase platform where the stair turns at a right angle. see *halfpace*.

quartodeciman (kwôr-tō-dĕs'ĭ-mən) *n.* member of an early Christian sect who observed Passover.

quasihemidemisemiquaver (kwā"sī-hĕm-ē-dĕm"ē-sĕm-ē-kwā'vər) *n.* a 128th note, according to British musical notation. for other quavers, see *quaver*.

quatercentenary (kwā-tûr-sĕn'tən-ĕr'ē) *n.* a 400th anniversary.

quatercousin (kā'tər-kŭz"ən) *n.* a fourth cousin or distant relative; a close friend. also *catercousin*,

---

màn; māde; lĕt; bē; sĭp; wīne; hŏt; cōld; sôre; dùll; fūgue; bûrp; gŏŏd; fōŏd; out; gĕt; thin; thìs; year; aźure; ō'mən"; viN; fùr; Bach *katercousin.*

quaternary (kwăt-ûrn′ər-ē) *n.* 1. a group of four; the number four. 2. (cap.) the Quaternary period (geology: sometimes called the *Age of Man*).

quaternion (kwăt-ûrn′ĭ-ən) *n.* 1. a quaternary. 2. a quatrain. 3. a sheet of paper folded twice; a quire. 4. a word of four syllables; a *quadrisyllable*. 5. a factor which converts one vector into another (mathematics).

quatrayle (kwot′rāl) *n.* a great-great-great-grandfather.

quatrefoil (kăt′ər-foil) *n.* a flower or leaf with four lobes.

quatuorvirate (kwā-tōō-ôr′vĭ-rāt) *n.* an association of four men.

quaver (kwā′vər) *n.* an 8th note (British). see also.
  semiquaver = 16th
  demisemiquaver = 32nd
  hemidemisemiquaver = 64th
  quasihemidemisemiquaver = 128th.

quawk (kwôk) *n. & v.* 1. caw, screech. 2. the night heron. see *qua.*

queachy (kwē′chē) *adj.* 1. boggy, marshy. 2. bushy.

quean (kwēn) *n.* 1. a whore. 2. a young or unmarried woman. -*v.i.* to go around with *queans.*

Quechua (kěch′wô) *n.* the dominant Indian tribe of the Peruvian Inca empire; their language, also spoken by surrounding South American Indians.

qued (kwěd) *adj.* evil, bad. -*n.* evil; an evil person; the Devil.

queenite (kwēn′ĭt) *n.* one who supports or upholds a queen.

queenlet (kwēn′lèt) *n.* a petty queen.

queenright (kwēn′rīt) *adj.* having a queen bee in the hive.

queezmadam (kwēz′măd″əm) *n.* the *cuissemadam,* a French pear.

quelquechose (kĕl-kə-shōz) *n.* a mere trifle, *kickshaw* (which see).

quemado (kā-mŏ′dō) *n.* a burned district (past participle of Spanish *quemar* = to burn).

queme (kwēm) *adj.* pleasant, agreeable, suitable. -*v.t.&i.* to please, suit, satisfy.

quenelle (kěn-ĕl′) *n.* an entrée or stuffing made of minced chicken or veal, bread crumbs, and egg.

quercine (kwûr′sĭn) *adj.* pertaining to the oak.

querent (kwĭr′ənt) *n.* 1. someone who resorts to astrology. 2. a plaintiff. -*adj.* complaining.

querimony (kwěr′ĭ-mō″nē) *n.* a complaint.

quern (kwûrn) *n.* a spice grinder.

quetch (kwěch) *v.i.* 1. to move, twitch, shake. 2. to make a noise, break the silence (no clear-cut connection with Yiddish *kvetch*, which see).

quetzal (kět′səl) *n.* 1. a large red and green bird worshiped by the Aztecs, the male of which has a two-foot-long tail. 2. the national emblem of Guatemala, and the name of its currency.

Quetzalcoatl (kět″səl-kō-ŏt′əl) *n.* principal Aztec god, worshiped as the patron of arts and crafts; in art, he was often represented by the *quetzal* (see above).

quiapo (kē-ŏ′pō) *n.* the water lettuce.

quia-quia (kē″ŏ-kē′ŏ) *n.* the cigarfish.

quidam (kwī′dăm) *n.* an unknown person.

quiddity (kwĭd′ĭ-tē) *n.* the essence or nature of a thing. (that which answers the question, *quid est?* = what is it?) 2. a subtle distinction; cavil, quibble. 3. something intangible.

quidnunc (kwĭd′nŭnk) *n.* one who is curious to know everything that is going on; a gossip (Latin *quid nunc?* = what now?).

quiff (kwĭf) *n.* hair oiled and brushed away from the forehead.

quillback (kwĭl′băk) *n.* a small carp sucker of the Mississippi Valley or Chesapeake Bay.

quiller (kwĭl′ər) *n.* 1. a fledging. 2. a machine used in transferring yarn from spools to quills. 3. the operator of a *quiller* machine.

quillet (kwĭl′ət) *n.* 1. a small field; a narrow strip of land. 2. a subtle distinction.

quim (kwĭm) *n.* 1. queen. 2 the vagina (slang).

quincentennial (kwĭn-sĕn-tĕn′ĭ-əl) *adj.* pertaining to 500 years or a 500th anniversary. *-n.* a 500th anniversary; also *quincentenary*.

quincunx (kwĭn′kŭnks) *n.* a symmetrical arrangement of five objects: one at each corner and the fifth in the middle.

quindecennial (kwĭn-dē-sĕn′ĭ-əl) *adj.* pertaining to fifteen years or a fifteenth anniversary.

quink (kwĭnk) *n.* the common brant; also quink goose.

quinoa (kē-nō′ò) *n.* the pigweed of the South American Andes; its seeds are used as cereal.

quinquagesimal (kwĭn-kwò-jĕs′ĭ-məl) *adj.* consisting of fifty days; as, the *quinquagesimal* period between Easter and Pentecost. *Quinquagesima Sunday*, the Sunday before Lent.

quinquennial (kwĭn-kwĕn′ĭ-əl) *adj.* occurring every five years; lasting five years. *quinquennium*, *n.* a period of five years.

quinquertium (kwĭn-kwûr′shĭ-əm)

n. the pentathlon.

quinse (kwĭnz) *v.t.* to carve.

quinsy (kwĭn′zē) *n.* a severe inflammation of the throat or tonsils; *peritonsillar* abscess.

quintain (kwĭn′tĭn) *n.* something to be tilted at; the sport of tilting at a *quintain*. 2. a five-line stanza. *-v.i.* to tilt at a *quintain*.

quintessentialize (kwĭn-tĕs-èn′shəl-īz) *v.t.* to extract as a *quintessence;* to extract the *quintessence* of.

quinton (kàN-tôN′) *n.* a small five-stringed viol.

quipu (kē′pōō) *n.* an ancient Incan counting device.

quire (kwīr) *n.* 1. a set of folded sheets fitting one within another. 2. a collection of twenty-four sheets [of paper] of the same size. 3. a small book or pamphlet consisting of a *quire;* a work that might be contained in a *quire*. *-v.t.* to make into *quires*.

quirl (kwûrl) *n.* 1. a coil or curl. 2. a scraper for making butter curls. *-v.t.&i.* to coil, twist.

quirt (kwûrt) *n.* a South American riding whip. *-v.t.* to strike with a *quirt. -v.t.&i.* to block up [an opening].

quisby (kwĭz′bē) *adj.* bankrupt; down and out. *-n.* an idler (slang).

quisquilian (kwĭs-kwĭl′yən) *adj.* trashy. also *quisquiliary, quisquilious*.

quisquous (kwĭs′kəs) *adj.* perplexing. also *quiscos*.

qui vive (kē-vēv′) French version of "who goes there?" *to be on the qui vive* = to be on the alert.

quizzacious (kwĭz-ā′shəs) *adj.* bantering.

quo (kwō) *n.* something traded for something else.

quoc-ngu (kwòk′əng-gōō) *n.* the

Vietnamese alphabet.

quodlibet (kwŏd'lĭ-bĕt") *n.* 1. an improvised musical medley. 2. a debatable point; a scholastic dissertation on such a point. *quodlibetarian, n.* someone who writes *quodlibets.*

quoin (koin) *n.* 1. a cornerstone; keystone. 2. a wedge used to lock up type (printing). *-v.t.* 1. to provide with a cornerstone. 2. to wedge up with *quoins* (in printing).

quondam (kwŏn'dăm) *adj.* former, one-time. *adv.* formerly.

quonking (kwŏnk'ĭng) *n.* side-line chatter that disturbs a performer (slang).

quop (kwŏp) *v.i.* to throb.

quotennial (kwō-tĕn'ĭ-əl) *adj.* annual.

quoz (kwŏz) *n.* something ridiculous, absurd, or strange.

qursh (kōō'ərsh) *n.* 1. a monetary unit of Saudi Arabia equal to 1/22 *riyal.* 2. a coin representing one *qursh.*

qutb (kōō'dəb) *n.* an Islamic saint who has reached the highest degree of sanctity.

màn; māde; lĕt; bē; sĭp; wīne; hŏt; cōld; sôre; dŭll; fūgue; bûrp; gōōd; fōōd; out; gĕt; thin; this; year; azure; ō'mən"; viN; fūr; Bach

raash (rȯ-ȯsh') *n*. the electric cat-
fish.

rab (ràb) *n*. 1. master, teacher; a
Jewish title of respect. 2. a beater
used in mixing mortar.

rabat (ràb'ət) *n*. 1. a carpenter's
plane. 2. a polishing material of
potter's clay.

rabbinism (ràb'ĭn-ĭz″əm) *n*. 1. a
rabbinical expression or idiom. 2.
rabbinical doctrine.

rabiator (rā'bĭ-ā″tər) *n*. a violent
man.

rach (ràch) *n*. a hunting dog.

rackarock (ràk'ə-rȯk) *n*. an ex-
plosive.

rackrent (ràk'rènt) *n*. exorbitant
rent.

radicate (ràd'ĭ-kāt) *v.t.&i*. to plant
firmly; to establish solidly.

radiesthesia (rā″dĭ-eš-thē′zĭ-ə) *n*.
1. dowsing. 2. psychic healing
from unknown "rays."

radiolucent (rā″dĭ-ō-lōō'sənt) *adj*.
permeable to radiation.

radiopraxis (rā″dĭ-ō-pràks'ĭs) *n*.
the use of ultraviolet rays or x-
rays in medicine.

radioscopy (rā-dĭ-ȯs'kə-pē) *n*.
fluoroscopy; examination by x-
ray.

radix (rā'dĭks) *n*. 1. original source
or cause. 2. a plant root; a nerve
root. 3. the base number in a
number system (mathematical).

rafale (rȯ-fȯl') *n*. rapid bursts of
artillery fire from each gun of a
battery.

rafty (ràf'tē) *adj*. rancid; stale or
musty.

rahdar (rȯd'ȯr) *n*. toll collector in
India.

raisonné (rā-zō-nā') *adj*. logical;
arranged systematically.

raith (rāth) *n*. a quarter of a year
(Scottish).

rakehelly (ràk'hèl″ē) *adj*. dis-
solute, debauched.

rale (ròl) *n*. an abnormal respiratory sound heard in *auscultation*
(listening, with or without a
stethoscope).

rambooze (ràm-bōōz') *n*. wine and
sugar mixed with eggs and ale
(winter) or with milk and rose
water (summer).

ramdown (ràm'doun) *n*. a steep
section of logging road covered
with branches to inhibit sleds in
winter.

ramfeezled (răm-fē′zəld) *adj.* worn out, exhausted.

ramiferous (răm-ĭf′ər-əs) *adj.* bearing branches.

rammish (răm′ĭsh) *adj.* 1. lustful and horny. 2. rank-smelling or tasting. 3. violent, wild. *-v.i.* to rush about frenziedly.

rampick (răm′pĭk) *n.* 1. a tree whose top branches are dead. 2. a tree stump broken by the wind. *-adj.* pertaining to a *rampick*.

ranarium (răn-ĕr′ləm) *n.* a frog farm.

randan (răn′dăn) *adj.* noisy and disorderly. *-n.* 1. a three-person rowboat, one rower using short oars. 2. this kind of rowing. *-v.i.* to row in a *randan*.

randle (răn′dəl) *n.* a nonsensical poem recited by Irish schoolboys as an apology for farting at a friend.

ranivorous (răn-ĭv′ôr-əs) *adj.* frog-eating.

rantallion (răn-tăl′ĭ-ən) *n.* one whose scrotum is longer than his penis (British slang).

rantipole (răn′tĭ-pōl) *n.* 1. a wild, rambunctious young man. 2. a scolding, bad-tempered woman. *-v.i.* to act like a *rantipole*.

raphe (răf) *n.* a dice game.

rapparee (răp-ər-ē′) *n.* a seventeenth-century Irish armed robber; a hobo or drifter.

rappel (răp-ĕl′) *n.* 1. a way of descending a mountain using ropes. 2. a drum call to arms. 3. a rattlelike old musical instrument.

raptorial (răp-tôr′ĭ-əl) *adj.* 1. living on prey. 2. adapted for seizing prey. 3. pertaining to birds of prey. also *raptatorial*.

rareeshow (rĕr′ē-shō) *n.* a peep show; any cheap street show.

raskolniki (ròs-kôl′nyē-kē″) *n.pl.* dissenters from the Russian Orthodox church.

rasorial (rà-sôr′ĭ-əl) *adj.* habitually scratching the ground in search of food.

ratafee (răt-ə-fē′) *n.* 1. a fruit-flavored liqueur. 2. an almond liqueur from Danzig. 3. an almond cookie.

ratamacue (răt′ə-mə-kū″) *n.* a drum figure more difficult than the *paradiddle*.

rataplan (răt-ə-plăn′) *n.* the sound of a rapid drumbeat or a galloping horse. *-v.t.&i.* to beat a *rataplan* on something.

ratihabition (răt″ĭ-hà-bĭsh′ən) *n.* ratification, sanction.

ratoon (răt-ōōn′) *n.* second-year growth from a perennial plant. *-v.i.* to sprout from a previous year's root. *-v.t.* to cultivate using *ratoons*.

ratten (răt′ən) *v.t.&i.* to steal tools or machinery in order to force management to meet union demands (British).

raun (rôn) *n.* 1. fish eggs; roe. 2. a female herring or salmon.

rauwolfia (rou-wōōl′fĭ-ə) *n.* a tree whose root is the source of certain tranquilizers, such as *reserpine*.

ravening (răv′ən-ĭng) *adj.* greedy, voracious, preying.

razzia (răz′ĭ-ə) *n.* a sudden or plundering raid.

reable (rē-ā′bəl) *v.t.* to confirm, to legitimate.

Realpolitik (rā-ôl′pō-lĭt-ēk″) *n.* militarism.

rebarbative (rē-bôr′bə-tĭv) *adj.* repellent, repulsive, revolting, and altogether unattractive.

rebato (rû-bò′tō) *n.* 1. a woman's stiff collar worn high in back; a *piccadill*. 2. a wire framework to support the collar.

rebec (rē'bĕk) *n.* a three-stringed ancestor of the violin.

reboantic (rĕb-ō-ăn'tĭk) *adj.* reverberating. also *reboant.*

rebullition (rē-bū-lǐ'shən) *n.* renewed bubbling, boiling, or disturbance.

recadency (rē-kā'dən-sē) *n.* relapse.

recension (rē-sĕn'shən) *n.* scholarly editorial revision.

receptary (rĕs'əp-tĕr″ē) *adj.* accepted as fact but unproved. *-n.* 1. an unproved fact; a postulate. 2. a recipe collection.

réchauffé (rā-shō-fā') *n.* 1. leftovers. 2. something made from leftovers; hash or rehash.

recheat (rē-chēt') *n.* blast on the horn to call the hunting hounds.

reclivate (rĕk'lǐv-āt) *adj.* sigmoid; having an S-shaped shape.

recoct (rē-kŏkt') *v.t.* to recook; to redo, make over.

recrement (rĕk'rē-mənt) *n.* 1. waste product, impurity. 2. something secreted from the body, then reabsorbed.

recrudescence (rē-krōō-dĕs'əns) *n.* 1. renewal of a disease after remission. 2. reappearance of a wound or, figuratively, of something bad.

rectalgia (rĕk-tăl'jĭ-ə) *n.* a pain in the ass. also *proctalgia.*

rectigrade (rĕk'tĭ-grād) *adj.* moving in a straight line.

recto (rĕk'tō) *n.* a right-hand page, usually odd-numbered. *-adv.* on the right side. see *verso.*

rectopathic (rĕk-tō-păth'ĭk) *adj.* easily hurt emotionally.

rectrix (rĕk'trĭks) *n.* 1. a female ruler. 2. a bird's tail feather.

recubation (rĕk-ū-bā'shən) *n.* 1. lying down. 2. reclining while

dining in ancient Rome.

recumbentibus (rĕk-ŭm-bĕn'tĭ-bəs) *n.* a knockdown blow. also *recumbendibus.*

recusant (rĕk'ū-zənt) *adj.* dissenting; disestablishmentarian.

redargution (rĕd-ŏr-gū'shən) *n.* refutation.

reddition (rĕd-ĭ'shən) *n.* restoration; translation, explanation.

redhibition (rĕd-hĭ-bĭ'shən) *n.* the return of defective merchandise.

redingote (rĕd'ĭng-gōt) *n.* a long, full overcoat (from the French attempt to pronounce "riding coat").

redintegrate (rĕd-ĭn'tə-grāt) *v.t.* to renew, restore, recondition. *-v.i.* 1. to be renewed, restored. 2. to become reunited or reconciled.

redivivus (rĕd-ĭ-vī'vəs) *adj.* living again; revived.

redubber (rē-dŭb'ər) *n.* a buyer of stolen cloth who alters and resells it.

redux (rē'dŭks) *adj.* denoting renewed health after sickness.

reeve (rēv) *n.* 1. the female sandpiper. 2. an administrative official. 3. a cattle or poultry pen. 4. a foreman of a coal mine. 5. a string of onions. *-v.t.* to thread a rope through an opening; to pass through cautiously.

refection (rē-fĕk'shən) *n.* 1. food or drink; refreshment. 2. mental relief; satisfaction. 3. the giving or taking of meals. *-v.t.* to give *refection.*

refocillation (rē-fŏs″ĭ-lā'shən) *n.* revival, revitalization; refreshment.

refragable (rĕf'rə-gə-bəl) *adj.* capable of being refuted.

refrangible (rē-frăn'jĭ-bəl) *adj.* capable of being refracted. also *refringent.*

---

màn; māde; lĕt; bē; sĭp; wīne; hŏt; cōld; sôre; dŭll; fūgue; bûrp; gŏŏd; fōōd; out; gĕt; thin; ĭhis; year; aᴢure; ŏ'mən″; viN; fûr; Bach

refulgent (rē-fŭl'jənt) *adj.* radiant, brilliant, shining.

regrate (rē-grāt') *v.t.* 1. to buy in large quantities for profitable resale nearby. 2. to sell in this fashion. 3. to renovate by removing the outer layer (masonry).

reify (rē'ĭ-fī) *v.t.* to make real, to materialize.

relict (rē-lĭkt') *adj.* 1. widowed. 2. pertaining to a relic or survivor of a vanished species.

religate (rĕl'ĭ-gāt) *v.t.&i.* to tie together.

remanet (rĕm'ə-nĕt) *n.* 1. postponement of a case. 2. a parliamentary bill carried over to another session.

remeant (rē'mē-ənt) *adj.* returning.

remiped (rĕm'ĭ-pĕd) *adj.* with feet or legs used as oars: said of certain crustaceans and insects. *-n.* a *remiped* animal.

remolade (rā-mō-lŏd') *n.* 1. an ointment used in veterinary medicine. 2. a tangy sauce or salad dressing.

remontado (rā-môn-tŏ'dō) *n.* someone who has fled to the mountains; a person who has renounced civilization.

remontant (rē-mŏn'tənt) *adj.* flowering again: applied to roses which bloom more than once a season. *-n.* a *remontant* rose.

remplissage (rŏm-plē-sŏz') *n.* filling or padding used in music and literature (French *remplir* = to fill up).

remugient (rē-mū'jĭ-ənt) *adj.* rebellowing; roaring or shouting anew.

renable (rĕn'ə-bəl) *adj.* fluent, eloquent.

renard (rĕn'ərd) *n.* a fox; a sly or cunning person.

renascible (rē-nàs'ĭ-bəl) *adj.* capable of being reborn.

rencounter (rĕn-coun'tər) *v.t.&i.* 1. to have a hostile, sudden, or unexpected meeting. 2. to meet casually. *-n.* 1. a sudden or hostile meeting; a fight. 2. a contest or debate. 3. a casual encounter.

renidification (rē-nĭd"ĭ-fĭ-kā'shən) *n.* building another nest.

renifleur (rĕn'ĭ-flûr) *n.* one who gets sexual pleasure from body smells (sweat, urine, etc.).

renitency (rĕn'ĭ-tən-sē") *n.* resistance, reluctance.

rente (rŏnt) *n.* 1. annual income; annuity. 2. securities representing the French national debt; the interest paid on it.

rep (rĕp) *n.* 1. formerly, a dirty old woman, now, a dirty old man. 2. a transversely ribbed fabric also *repp.*

repand (rē-pănd') *adj.* having a wavy or undulating outline.

reparationist (rĕp-ər-ā'shən-ĭst) *n.* an abolitionist who believed in reparation to ex-slaves.

repartimiento (rā-pòr"tē-myĕn'tō) *n.* 1. a land grant together with its inhabitants, given to soldiers and priests by the Spanish conquistadores. 2. a tax assessment.

repertorium (rĕp-ər-tôr'ĭ-əm) *n.* an index, catalog, or collection.

repine (rē-pīn') *v.t.&i.* to complain, grumble, lament. *-n.* complaint, criticism.

repristinate (rē-prĭs'tĭ-nāt) *v.t.* to revive; to restore.

reptation (rĕp-tā'shən) *n.* 1. creeping, like a reptile. 2. a motion made by sliding two plane figures around each other (mathematics).

repugn (rē-pūn') *v.t.&i.* to oppose, resist, or repel.

repullulate (rē-pŭl'ū-lāt) *v.i.* to

---

sprout again; to recur, as a disease.

resile (rē-zīl') *v.i.* to recoil, retract; to return to its original position.

resipiscent (rès-ĭ-pĭs'ənt) *adj.* restored to sanity: learned from experience.

restaur (rès'tôr) *n.* the recourse insurers have against negligent or undue loss.

resupination (rē-sōō″pĭn-ā'shən) *n.* turning to an upside-down position.

resurrectionist (rĕz-ûr-ĕk'shən-ĭst) *n.* a body snatcher; a grave-robber.

ret (rĕt) *v.t.* 1. to soak or expose to moisture. 2. to rot. 3. to impute, ascribe.

retablo (rä-tò'blō) *n.* a painting of a saint in a Spanish or Mexican church.

retiary (rē'shĭ-èr″ē) *adj.* 1. netlike. 2. making a web to catch insects (as spiders do). 3. entangling.

reticulum (rē-tĭk'ū-lùm) *n.* 1. a net-like structure; a network. 2. the second stomach of ruminants (cattle, deer, etc.). also called a *honeycomb stomach.*

retrad (rē'trăd) *adv.* backward (anatomy).

retrochoir (rĕt'rō-kwīr) *n.* the space behind the altar or choir enclosure, used as a chapel or second choir enclosure.

retrocollic (rĕt-rō-kòl'ĭk) *adj.* pertaining to the back of the neck.

retrocopulation (rĕt″rō-kòp-ū-lā'shən) *n.* fornicating from behind.

retromancy (rĕt'rō-màn″sē) *n.* fortunetelling by things seen over one's shoulder.

retromingent (rĕt-rō-mĭn'jənt) *adj.* urinating backward. -*n.* a *retromingent* animal.

retrorse (rē-trôrs') *adj.* bent backward or downward.

retrousse' (rĕt-rōō-sā') *adj.* turned up, as a nose.

retroversion (rĕt-rō-vûr'żən) *n.* 1. looking back. 2. translation back into the original language.

rettery (rĕt'ər-ē) *n.* a place where flax is retted (soaked).

retund (rē-tŭnd') *v.t.* to blunt the edge of; to weaken.

reus (rē'əs) *n.* a defendant in a court trial.

revalescent (rĕv-əl-ĕs'ənt) *adj.* recovering from illness or injury.

revalorise (rē-vàl'ər-īz) *v.t.* to change money values after an inflation.

revehent (rĕv'ē-hènt) *adj.* carrying back.

revenant (rĕv'ən-ənt) *n.* 1. someone returning after a long absence. 2. a ghost. -*adj.* remembering something long forgotten.

revers (rə-vîr') *n.s.&pl.* a part folded back to show the inside; a piece put on to look this way.

reversicon (rē-vûrs'ĭ-kòn) *n.* a reversed dictionary listing the definitions as entries.

reverso (rē-vûr'sō) *n.* a left-hand page also *verso.* 2. a backhanded stroke in fencing.

rhabdomancy (răb'dō-màn″sē) *n.* fortunetelling by sticks or wands.

rhabdophobia (rà-dō-fō'bĭ-ə) *n.* fear of being punished or severely criticized.

rhadamanthine (răd-ə-màn'thĭn) *adj.* uncompromisingly just (from *Rhadamanthus,* a mythical Greek who was a thoroughly incorruptible judge).

rhapsodomancy (răp'sō-dō-màn″sē) *n.* fortunetelling with poetry.

---

mǎn; māde; lĕt; bē; sĭp; wīne; hòt; cōld; sôre; dùll; fūgue; bûrp; gōōd; fōōd; out; gĕt; thin; thĭs; year; aźure; ō'mən; viN; für; Bach

rhematic (rē-măt'ĭk) *adj.* 1. pertaining to word formation. 2. derived from verbs. 3. pertaining to early forms of expression.

rheology (rē-ŏl'ə-jē) *n.* the study of the flow of matter.

rhetor (rē'tər) *n.* 1. a teacher of rhetoric. 2. an orator. 3. a mere talker.

rhigosis (rĭ-gō'sĭs) *n.* sensation of cold *rhigotic, adj.*

rhinocerical (rī-nŏ-sĭr'ĭ-kəl) *adj.* 1. rhinoceroslike. 2. rich (slang).

rhinoplasty (rī'nō-plăs"tē) *n.* plastic surgery of the nose; *nasoplasty.*

rhipidate (rĭp'ĭ-dāt) *adj.* fan-shaped; *flabelliform.*

rhombicosidodecahedron (rŏm"bĭ-kō"sĭ-dō-děk"ə-hē'drən) *n.* an Archimedean solid with sixty-two faces.

rhombohedron (rŏm-bō-hē'drən) *n.* a parallelepiped whose faces are *rhombuses.*

rhomboid (rŏm'boid) *n.* a parallelogram with oblique angles and unequal adjacent sides.

rhombus (rŏm'bəs) *n.* an equilateral *rhomboid.*

rhonchisonant (rŏng'kĭ-sō"nənt) *adj.* snorting; snoring.

rhopalism (rō'pəl-ĭz"əm) *n.* a sentence or poem in which each word is one syllable longer than its predecessor.

rhusma (rŭs'mə) *n.* a depilatory used in tanning. also *rusma.*

rhyparography (rī-pär-ŏg'rə-fē) *n.* the painting of or writing on depressing, sordid, or demimonde subjects.

rhytiphobia (rī-tĭ-fō'bĭ-ə) *n.* fear of getting wrinkles.

rhytiscopia (rī-tĭ-skŏp'ĭ-ə) *n.* neurotic preoccupation with facial wrinkles.

riata (rē-ŏ'tō) *n.* a lariat.

ribroasting (rĭb'rōst"ĭng) *n.* a sound beating; a thrashing.

ricercare (rē-chěr-kò'rā) *n.* a fuguelike composition; an elaborate fugue.

rickettsialpox (rĭ-kěts'ĭ-əl-pŏks") *n.* an infectious disease transmitted by *rickettsia,* a microorganism infesting the ticks or fleas carried by mice. The first recorded case was in 1946 in New York.

rictus (rĭk'təs) *n.* a very wide mouth; a gaping mouth, as in terror.

rideau (rē-dō') *n.* a small mound or trench.

rident (rī'dənt) *adj.* laughing or broadly smiling *ridibund* (rĭd'ĭ-bŭnd) *adj.* prone to laughter.

ridgeling (rĭj'lĭng) *n.* half-castrated animal; a *monoball* or *cryptorchid* also *ridgel, ridgil, ridgling.*

ridotto (rĭ-dŏt'ō) *n.* 1. a masked ball or the place where it is held; an assembly hall. 2. an arrangement or abridgment of a piece of music from the full score.

rifacimento (rē-fò"chē-mèn'tō) *n.* 1. a renewing or reworking. 2. a literary or musical adaptation.

rigation (rĭ-gā'shən) *n.* the act of wetting or moistening.

rigescent (rĭ-jès'ənt) *adj.* growing stiff or numb.

rijksdaalder (rīks'dòl"dər) *n.* a former silver coin of Holland, equal to forty-eight stivers.

rimose (rī'mōs) *adj.* full of grooves, fissures, cracks, chinks, or clefts. also *rimulose.*

rincon (rēng-kòn') *n.* 1. a natural depression in rock. 2. a secluded retreat.

ringent (rĭn'jənt) *adj.* gaping, like

---

màn; māde; lĕt; bē; sĭp; wīne; hŏt; cōld; sôre; dŭll; fūgue; bûrp;
gŏŏd; fōōd; out; gĕt; thin; this; year; aźure; ō'mən"; viN; fûr; Bach

an open mouth. see *rictus*.

ringstreaked (ring'strēkt) *adj.* circularly streaked or marked.

riparian (rĭp-ĕr'ĭ-ən) *n.* someone living near water. *adj.* pertaining to or living near water also *riparial, riparious, ripicolous*.

ripieno (rē-pyä'nō) *adj.* supplementary, as a musician who plays only with others, never alone. *ripienist. n.*

riprap (rĭp'răp) *n.pl.* large rocks usually used to protect an embankment from erosion by waves.

riqq (rĭk) *n.* a tambourine without snares.

riroriro (rē'rō-rē'rō) *n.* the gray warbler of New Zealand.

risorgimento (rē-sôr'ji-mĕn'tō) *n.* 1. pre-renaissance classical revival of the fourteenth and fifteenth centuries. 2. a nineteenth-century Italian political movement.

risorial (rī-sôr'ĭ-əl) *adj.* pertaining to, causing, or producing laughter. see *rident*.

rissole (rē-sō-lā') *adj.* browned by frying in deep fat. *-n.* a meat- or fish-filled pastry; a jam or custard-filled pastry.

rive (rīv) *v.t.* 1. to tear apart violently; to split. 2. to plow. *-v.i.* 1. to be torn apart. 2. to burst, literally and figuratively. 3. to arrive or leave. *-n.* 1. a pull or tug; a rip. 2. a bite. 3. a shore or bank.

rivière (rēv-yèr') *n.* a multistringed necklace of diamonds or other precious stones.

rixation (rĭks-ā'shən) *n.* quarreling.

rixatrix (rĭks-ā'trĭks) *n.* a shrew or termagant; a scolding, nasty old woman.

robomb (rō'bŏm) *n.* robot bomb.

roborant (rŏb'ō-rənt) *adj.* strength-

ening. *-n.* a *roborant* drug; a tonic.

rocambole (rŏk'ăm-bōl) *n.* the Spanish or wild garlic.

rockoon (rŏk-ōōn') *n.* a small rocket carried high by a balloon and then fired.

rocta (rŏk'tə) *n.* a medieval violin-like instrument.

rodomontade (rŏd″ō-mŏn-tād') *n.* bragging, boasting. also *adj.* *-v.i.* to brag or boast.

roentgenology (rĕnt-gən-ŏl'ə-jē) *n.* the study of x-rays for diagnosis or therapy.

roinous (roin'əs) *adj.* mean, nasty, and contemptible.

roitelet (roi'tə-lĕt) *n.* a petty king.

roman à clef (rō-mŏN″ä-klā') *n.* a novel whose characters are actual people thinly disguised.

rood (rōōd) *n.* 1. a cross or crucifix. 2. a square measure equaling one fourth of an acre. 3. a linear measure equaling seven or eight yards (British and Scottish).

roorback (rōōr'băk) *n.* a dirty rumor used against a political opponent (from *Baron Roorback's Tour Through the Western and Southern States*, a fictional pamphlet of the 1840's.).

roque (rōk) *n.* a form of croquet played on a court with a border, sometimes faced with rubber, used as a cushion in bank shots.

roquelaure (rŏk'əl-ôr) *n.* a knee-length coat named after the *Duc de Roquelaure*, worn in the early eighteenth century.

roral (rôr'əl) *adj.* dewy *roric, adj.* pertaining to dew, *roriferous, adj.* generating dew *rorulent, adj.* covered with dew.

rosacea (rō-zā'sĭ-ə) *n.* a disease marked by a large red nose; whiskey-nose, not limited to

màn; māde; lèt; bē; sĭp; wīne; hŏt; cōld; sôre; dŭll; fūgue; bŭrp; gŏŏd; fōōd; out; gèt; thin; this; year; azure; ō'mən″; viN; fûr; Bach boozers.

rosinante (rŏz-ĭ-năn'tē) *n.* a worn-out nag (from *Bosinante.* Don Quixote's horse: bony, full of blemishes, but highly regarded by him).

rosland (rŏs'lənd) *n.* open land with low shrubs.

rosmarine (rŏz'mə-rēn) *n.* the walrus, once thought to climb rocks by its teeth to feed on dew.

rosolio (rō-zōl'yō) *n.* 1. a sweet Mediterranean liqueur of brandy and raisins; *rossolis.* 2. a sour black currant wine mentioned in Thackeray's *The Great Hoggarty Diamond.*

rosorial (rō-sôr'ĭ-əl) *adj.* 1. rubbish, waste. 2. the rough, exterior of bark.

rotche (rŏch) *n.* the small arctic auk.

roturier (rō-tōōr-yā') *n.* a medieval commoner who rented land.

rouleau (rōō-lō') *n.* 1. a roll of coins. 2. red corpuscles that look like a roll of coins when magnified. 3. *(pl.)* folds or pipings in dressmaking. 4. a bundle of sticks, or *fascines*, used in sieges.

rounceval (roun'sə-vəl) *adj.* 1. large or strong (from the huge bones found at *Roncesvalles*, France). -*n.* 1. anything huge. 2. a bad-mouthed old woman. 3. the marrowfat pea.

rovescio (rō-vĕsh'ō) *adj.* reversed.

rowen (rou'ən) *n.* 1. a field for cattle grazing, plowed late in autumn. 2. a second-growth crop; aftermath.

rowlyrag (rou'lē-răg) *n.* a dark gray stone.

rsi (rĭsh'ē) *n.* a Hindu mystic or mystical poet also *rishi.*

rta (rĭd'ə) *n.* Vedic principle of order and righteousness. also *rita.*

rubai (rōō-bŏ'ē) *n.* a Persian quatrain (from *rubaiyat*).

rubedinous (rōō-bĕd'ĭn-əs) *adj.* reddish; *rufescent.*

rubiginous (rōō-bĭj'ĭn-əs) *adj.* rust-colored, rusty.

rubineous (rōō-bĭn'ĭ-əs) *adj.* ruby-red also *rubious.*

rubric (rōōb'rĭk) *n.* 1. red chalk. 2. the title page, or other part of an old manuscript, printed in red. 3. red. 4. a chapter heading, once printed in red. 5. a class or category. -*adj.* marked in red; pertaining to rubric. -*v.t.* 1. to mark in red. 2. to arrange in a group or category.

ruck (rŭk) *n.* 1. a heap or pile. 2. a pack of horses behind the leaders. 3. a crowd of ordinary people or things. 4. a crease in cloth or paper. -*v.i.* 1. to sit, as a bird on eggs; to cower, squat. -*v.t.* to rake into a heap. -*v.t.&i.* to crease, often with *up.*

ructation (rŭk-tā'shən) *n.* belching.

ruction (rŭk'shən) *n.* a rough or noisy fight; an uproar.

rudas (rōō'dəs) *n.* an ugly foul-mouthed old hag; a beldam. -*adj.* coarse, foulmouthed.

rudesby (rōōdz'bē) *n.* a loud-mouthed ill-mannered boor.

ruelle (rōō-ĕl') *n.* 1. a select social gathering (from the French custom of entertaining special friends in one's bedroom). 2. the bedroom. 3. the space between the bed and the wall.

rugate (rōō'gāt) *adj.* wrinkled *rugulose* (rōō'gū-lōs) *adj.* having small wrinkles.

rumbelow (rŭm'bē-lō) *n.* 1. a refrain sung by rowing sailors. 2. a whore. 3. a carriage.

rumgumption (rŭm-gŭmp'shən) *n.* shrewdness.

---

măn; māde; lĕt; bē; sĭp; wīne; hŏt; cōld; sôre; dŭll; fūgue; bûrp; good; fōōd; out; gĕt; thin; this; year; aʒure; ō'mən"; viN; fũr; Bach

rummer (rùm'ər) *n.* a large wine glass.

runagate (rùn'ə-gāt) *n.* a good-for-nothing; a runaway, fugitive.

runcation (rùng-kā'shən) *n.* weeding.

runch (rùnch) *n.* the wild radish or jointed charlock.

runcible (rùn'sĭ-bəl) *adj.* sensuous [woman] *runcible spoon,* a fork with three tines, one of which is shaped like a spoon.

runic (rōō'nĭk) *adj.* pertaining to *runes* or alphabetical characters of third-century Germany. see *futhorc.* also pertaining to the spirit world or magic.

rupestrian (rōō-pès'trĭ-ən) *adj.* made of rock; inscribed on rock also *rupestral.*

rupicoline (rōō-pĭk'ō-līn) *adj.* living among or growing on rocks also *rupicolous, rupestrine.*

ruptuary (rùp'chōō-èr"ē) *n.* a commoner or plebeian.

rurigenous (rōōr-ĭj'ən-əs) *adj.* born in the country.

Russell's viper *n.* a brown and white venomous snake of Southeast Asia: the *daboia, jessur,* or *katuka.*

ruthful (rōōth'fəl) *adj.* pitiful, rueful, woeful, sad, sorrowful. *ruthfully, adv.*

rutilant (rōō'tĭ-lənt) *adj.* having a reddish glow; shining. *rutilate, v.i.* to shine.

ruttish (rùt'ĭsh) *adj.* horny, in heat.

ryot (rī'ət) *n.* an Indian peasant or farmer.

ryotwar (rī-ət-wòr') *n.* tax or rent paid directly to the government by farmers in India. also *adj.*

---

màn; māde; lèt; bē; sĭp; wīne; hòt; cōld; sôre; dùll; fūgue; bûrp; gŏŏd; fōōd; out; gèt; thin; t̄his; year; aẑure; ō'mən"; viN; für; Bach

sabbulonarium (săb″ū-lō-nĕr′ĭ-əm) *n.* a gravel pit; digging the gravel; the money paid for digging gravel.

sabulous (săb′ū-ləs) *adj.* sandy, gritty; *arenaceous.* also *sabulose.*

saburration (săb-ū-rā′shən) *n.* therapeutic sand-bathing; *arenation, ammotherapy.*

saccadic (săk-ăd′ĭk) *adj.* jerky, twitching.

sacchariferous (săk-ə-rĭf′ər-əs) *adj.* producing or containing sugar.

sacculate (săk′ū-lāt) *v.t.* to enclose.

sacerdotophrenia (săs″ər-dō-tə-frē′nĭ-ə) *n.* clerical stagefright.

sachem (sā′chəm) *n.* 1. an Indian chief. 2. the common kingbird, a fierce defender of its nest. 3. a government head or political leader. 4. an officer of the Tammany Society in New York. 5. a water pipe or hose. *sachemdom, n.* a sachem-led district.

sacheverell (săsh-ĕv′ər-əl) *n.* the blower of a coal stove (from *Sacheverell,* a cleric who was famous for "blowing the coals of dissension" in Queen Ann's reign).

sackbut (săk′bŭt) *n.* ancestor of the trombone.

sacramentarianism (săk″rə-mĕn-tĕr′ĭ-ən-ĭz″əm) *n.* belief that the sacraments have supernatural properties.

sacrarium (săk-rĕr′ĭ-əm) *n.* a shrine for keeping "sacred" objects.

sadda (săd′ə) *n.* a book of Zoroastrian writings.

sadiron (săd′ī″ərn) *n.* a flatiron.

sadr (sŏ′dər) *n.* 1. the lotus tree (Persian). 2. (cap.) a star in the constellation Cygni.

sagaciate (sə-gā′shĭ-āt) *v.i.* to thrive; to do well (slang).

sagamore (săg′ə-môr) *n.* a minor Algonquian chief.

sagaunash (sə-gôn′əsh) *n.* a white man (American Indian).

sagene (să-jēn′) *n.* a network or seine.

saginate (săj′ĭ-nāt) *v.t.* to fatten; pamper.

sagittate (săj′ĭ-tāt) *adj.* shaped like an arrowhead.

sagum (sā′gŭm) *n.* a Roman

soldier's cape, fastened and draped at the right shoulder.

salmagundi (sàl-mə-gùn'dē) *n.* 1. a dish of chopped meat and pickled herring, with oil, vinegar, pepper, and onions. 2. a heterogeneous mixture; medley, potpourri, mishmash.

salpinx (sàl'pìnks) *n.* 1. an ancient Greek trumpet. 2. the Eustachian or Fallopian tube.

salse (sòls) *n.* a mud volcano saturated with salts (Latin *salsus* = salted).

saltation (sàl-tā'shən) *n.* 1. a leap; jumpy dancing. 2. a spurting of arterial blood. 3. a sudden change. 4. a cultural mutation. *saltativeness, n.* capacity for jumping.

saltimbanco (sòl-tìm-bàng'kō) *n.* a mountebank, a quack. *saltimbankery, n.*

saltimbocca (sòl-tìm-bō'kò) *n.* veal pounded and rolled up with ham and cheese.

salubrious (sə-lōōb'rī-əs) *adj.* wholesome, healthy, and beneficial.

salutatorian (sàl-ōō"tə-tôr'ī-ən) *n.* the number two graduate who gives the "salutatory" address on graduation day.

salver (sàl'vər) *n.* 1. tray for presenting letters or calling cards. 2. a serving dish mounted on a pedestal. 3. one who *salves*, or cures.

salvific (sàl-vìf'ìk) *adj.* tending to help or promote safety.

sambuke (sàm'būk) *n.* an old, shrill harp; the sackbut, bagpipe, or hurdy-gurdy.

sammy (sàm'ē) *adj.* damp, clammy. *-n.* a U.S. soldier.

Samsam (sàm'sàm) *n.* a Malay-Siamese people.

sanability (sàn-ə-bìl'ì-tē) *n.* capability of being healed.

sanbenito (sàn-bèn-ē'tō) *n.* a black robe decorated with hellish figures worn by victims of the auto-da-fé.

sanctanimity (sànk-tə-nìm'ì-tē) *n.* mental "holiness."

sandik (sàn'dìk) *n.* the person who holds the child during the circumcision ceremony. also *sandek.*

sanemagogna (sàn"ə-mò-gôn'yò) *n.* Italian-American euphemism for the euphemistic "son-of-a-gun" (slang).

sangaree (sàng'gə-rē) *n.* a tropical drink of spiced and sweetened wine, brandy, and water.

sanglot (sòN-glō') *n.* a sobbing grace note inflicted upon us by singers.

sanguinivorous (sàng-gwìn-ìv'ôr-əs) *adj.* bloodsucking. also *sanguivorous.*

sanguisugous (sàng-swì-sōō'gəs) *adj.* bloodthirsty.

sannup (sàn'ûp) *n.* 1. a married male Indian, correlative of squaw. 2. an ordinary warrior.

sans-culottes (sòN-kü-lôt') *n.* a radical, a revolutionist, a Jacobin; literally: without breeches (a contemptuous term coined by French aristocrats for republicans who wore pants instead of the more stylish breeches).

sansei (sòn-sā') *n.* a child of Nisei parents.

sapfu (sàp'fōō) *n.* Surpassing All Previous Fuck-Ups (for more of the same, see *snafu.*)

sapidity (sàp-ìd'ì-tē) *n.* flavorful; tastiness.

sapient (sā'pì-ənt) *adj.* wise; discerning; now only used ironically.

saponaceous (sàp-ən-ā'shəs) *adj.*

---

màn; māde; lèt; bē; sìp; wīne; hòt; cōld; sòre; dùll; fūgue; bûrp; gŏŏd; fōōd; out; gèt; thin; thìs; year; aźure; ō'mən"; viN; für; Bach

1. soapy, slippery. 2. evasively ingratiating.

sapphism (săf'ĭz"əm) *n.* lesbianism.

saprogenic (săp-rō-jĕn'ĭk) *adj.* capable of producing decay; pertaining to, occurring, or produced in decaying matter; *saprogenous*.

saprophagus (săp-rŏf'ə-gəs) *adj.* eating decaying matter.

saprophilous (săp-rŏf'ĭl-əs) *adj.* thriving in decaying matter.

saprostomous (săp-rŏs'tō-məs) *adj.* having bad breath.

saraad (să-rŏd') *n.* a fine for injury payable in cattle (early Welsh law).

sarab (sò'rŏb) *n.* a mirage; deceit.

saran (sò'rən) *n.* a Hindu violin.

sarangousty (săr-ən-gōōs'tē) *n.* waterproof stucco.

sarcle (sòr'kəl) *n.* a hoe. -*v.t.* to weed.

sarcoid (sòr'koid) *n.* a skin disorder; a sarcomalike growth. -*adj.* skinlike.

sarcophagic (sòr-kō-făj'ĭk) *adj.* flesh-eating.

sard (sòrd) *n.* a deep orange-red chalcedony darker than carnelian.

sardanapalian (sòr"dăn-ə-pā'lĭ-ən) *adj.* luxuriously effeminate (like *Sardanapalus*, a Byron hero).

sardoodledum (sòr-dōō'dəl-dùm) *n.* stereotyped or unrealistic characterization in drama; staginess, melodrama.

sarmassation (sòr-măs-ā'shən) *n.* love play. also *paizogony*, *paraphilemia*.

sarmassophobe (sòr-măs'ə-fōb) *n.* a woman who dislikes love play.

sarwan (sòr-wòn') *n.* a camel driver.

satanophany (sā-tən-òf'ən-ē) *n.*

devil possession.

satisdiction (săt-ĭs-dĭk'shən) *n.* enough said.

satispassion (săt-ĭs-pà'shən) *n.* satisfactory suffering, according to theologists (Latin *satis pati* = to suffer enough).

satrapess (sā'trə-pĕs) *n.* a female *satrap*, or 1. ruler of an ancient Persian province. 2. despotic petty official.

saturnalian (săt-ər-nā'lĭ-ən) *adj.* riotous, unrestrained, wild, carousing, licentious.

satyagraha (sŭt'yə-grŭ"hə) *n.* Gandhian passive resistance.

saulie (sôl'ē) *n.* a hired mourner.

saurian (sôr'ĭ-ən) *adj.* any lizard-like reptile.

savate (să-vàt') *n.* fighting with the feet.

savssat (sòv'sòt) *n.* in the arctic, animals crowded around a hole in the ice.

saxatile (săks'ə-tĭl) *adj.* pertaining to rocks; *saxicoline*, *saxicolous*, and *saxigenous*.

saxify (săks'ĭ-fī) *v.t.* to turn into stone; to petrify.

sayyid (sò'yĭd) *n.* chief, prince; a Moslem title of honor. also *sayid*.

scacchic (skăk'ĭk) *adj.* pertaining to chess; chesslike.

scagliola (skōl-yō'lə) *n.* an imitation marble using gypsum, plaster, and glue. *scagliolist*, *n.* a scagliola artist.

scalar (skā'lər) *adj.* 1. ladderlike; *scalariform*. 2. pertaining to a number scale.

scaldabanco (skōl-dò-bòng'kō) *n.* a hotheaded debater; a fiery preacher.

scamander (skăm-àn'dûr) *v.i.* to wind, as a river (from the *Scamander* river in Asia Minor).

scamell (skăm'əl) *n.* the bar-tailed

godwit. also *scammel.*

scansorial (skăn-sôr'ĭ-əl) *adj.* pertaining to, capable of, or adapted for, climbing.

scantling (skănt'lĭng) *n.* 1. a model or rough draft. 2. measurement, size. 3. an abridgment. 4. a piece of lumber under eight inches wide, and from two to six inches thick. 5. a trestle. 6. the distance between a good shot and a miss in archery.

scaphism (skăf'ĭz"əm) *n.* an old Persian method of executing criminals by covering them with honey and letting the sun and the insects finish the job.

scaphoid (skăf'oid) *adj.* boat-shaped; *navicular.*

scapulimancy (skăp'ū-lĭ-măn"sē) *n.* fortunetelling by studying a charred or cracked shoulder blade.

scaramouch (skăr'ə-mōōsh) *n.* a cowardly buffoon (from *Scaramouch,* a character in Italian comedy). -*v.i.* to act in such a manner.

scarebabe (skĕr'bāb) *n.* something that scares a baby. also *adj.*

scarrow (skă'rō) *n.* a faint light, a shadow. -*v.i.* to shine faintly, as through a cloud.

scatch (skăch) *n.* a stilt, a crutch. 2. a kind of bridle bit.

scatomancy (skăt'ō-măn"sē) *n.* fortunetelling by studying feces.

scatophagus (skăt-ŏf'ə-gəs) *adj.* eating excrement.

scat-singing (skăt'sĭng"ĭng) *n.* meaningless syllables sung either when a singer forgets the words, or to imitate an instrument; "bop" talk.

scaturient (skăt-ōōr'ĭ-ənt) *adj.* gushing forth; effusive.

scaurous (skôr'əs) *adj.* with large ankles.

scend (sĕnd) *n.* 1. the upward movement of a boat in water. opposite of *pitch.* also *v.i.* 2. the lift of a wave.

scenography (sĕn-ŏg'rə-fē) *n.* the art of perspective.

schadenfreude (shŏ'dən-froi"də) *n.* enjoyment of others' misfortunes.

schatchen (shŏt'kən) *n.* a Jewish matchmaker.

schesis (skē'sĭs) *n.* mocking another's accent or manner.

schizothemia (skĭz-ō-thē'mĭ-ə) *n.* digression by a long reminiscence.

schlenter (shlĕn'tər) *adj.* imitation. -*n.* an imitation diamond (South Africa).

schnitz (schnĭts) *n.* cut-up and dried apples.

schnorrer (shnŏr'ər) *n.* a beggar or chiseler (Yiddish).

schoenabatist (skē-nŏb'ə-tĭst) *n.* a tightrope walker.

scholia (skō'lĭ-ə) *n.pl.* 1. marginal notes; explanatory comments, especially in classic texts by early grammarians. 2. explanatory notes inserted by the editors of Euclid's *Elements.* 3. wise sayings.

schrik (shrĭk) *n.* a sudden fright or panic.

schwa (shvȯ) *n.* the symbol: ə. for further explanation, see Pronunciation Guide.

scialytic (sī-ə-lĭt'ĭk) *adj.* dispersing shadows.

sciamachy (sī-ăm'ə-kē) *n.* fighting with a shadow, or with an imaginary enemy.

sciapodous (sī-ăp'ō-dəs) *adj.* having very large feet.

sciatheric (sī-ə-thĕr'ĭk) *adj.* pertaining to a sundial.

---

màn; māde; lĕt; bē; sĭp; wīne; hŏt; cōld; sôre; dŭll; fūgue; bŭrp; gŏŏd; fōōd; out; gĕt; thin; this; year; ażure; ō'mən"; viN; fūr; Bach

scibile (sĭb'ĭl-ē) *n.* something knowable.

scilicet (sĭl'ĭ-sĕt) *adv.* namely, to wit, that is to say (law).

sciolism (sī'ō-lĭz"əm) *n.* superficial knowledge without scholarship.

sciotheism (sī"ō-thē'ĭz"əm) *n.* belief that disembodied spirits are effective in human affairs.

scissile (sĭs'ĭl) *adj.* capable of being cut smoothly or split easily; *scissible.*

sclaff (sklŏf) *v.t.&i.* to hit the ground before hitting the golf ball. *-n.* such a golf stroke.

scobiform (skŏb'ĭ-fôrm) *adj.* like sawdust; *scobicular.*

scofflaw (skŏf'lô) *n.* one who scoffs at, hence, violates, the law, a term proposed during prohibition.

scolecophagous (skŏl-ē-kof'ə-gəs) *adj.* eating worms.

scolion (skō'lĭ-ŏn) *n.* an impromptu party song begun by one and continued by others.

scollardical (skŏl-ôr'dĭ-kəl) *adj.* a derogatory term for a scholar.

scoon (skōōn) *v.t.&i.* to skip across the water like a flat stone.

scopelism (skŏp'əl-ĭz"əm) *n.* 1. rockiness. 2. the scattering of stones on a field to hinder farming.

scopolagnia (skō-pō-lăg'nĭ-ə) *n.* the pleasure gained from voyeurism; *scoptophilia, scopophilia.*

scopophobia (skŏ-pō-fō'bĭ-ə) *n.* fear of being seen.

scorbutic (skôr-bū'tĭk) *adj.* pertaining to scurvy; sick with scurvy.

scordatura (skôr-dò-tōōr'ò) *n.* unusual tuning of a stringed instrument for some special effect.

scortation (skôr-tā'shən) *n.* fornication. *scortatory, adj.*

scotograph (skŏt'ō-grăf) *n.* an instrument for writing in the dark; an x-ray.

scotophobia (skō-tō-fō'bĭ-ə) *n.* fear of darkness.

scrannel (skrăn'əl) *adj.* 1. thin; weak. 2. harsh; unmelodious.

scree (skrē) *n.* a stone or heap of stones.

screed (skrēd) *n.* 1. a torn-off fragment. 2. a tirade or diatribe. 3. a drinking bout. 4. a tearing or scraping sound. 5. a tool drawn across fresh concrete to smooth it off. *-v.t.* 1. to rip. 2. to say glibly, especially with *away* or *off.* 3. to smooth off. *-v.i.* to make a round like ripping cloth; to rip.

screeve (skrēv) *v.i.* to ooze, leak. *-v.t.&i.* 1. to write [begging letters]. 2. to draw on a sidewalk for charity. *-n.* a begging letter or sidewalk drawing for charity. *screever, n.* (all slang).

scride (skrīd) *v.i.* to crawl on all fours.

scrimshaw (skrĭm'shô) *v.t.&i.* to engrave and color ivory or shell. *-n.* shell or ivory so ornamented. also *adj.*

scriniary (skrĭn'ē-èr"ē) *n.* a keeper of archives.

scripee (skrĭp-ē') *n.* someone who gets *land scrip,* entitling her to certain property.

scriptorium (skrĭp-tôr'ĭ-əm) *n.* monastery room for scribes.

scripturient (skrĭp-tyūr'ĭ-ənt) *adj.* having a passion for writing.

scrivello (skrĭv-èl'ō) *n.* an elephant's tusk.

scrobiculate (skrō-bĭk'ū-lāt) *adj.* with numerous shallow depressions; pitted.

scrofulous (skrŏf'ū-ləs) *adj.* 1. corrupt, degenerate. 2. pertaining to or afflicted with *scrofula.*

scroop (skrōŏp) *v.i.* to make a squeaking or grating sound. -*v.t.* to fix silk so that it will rustle. -*n.* the rustle of silk.

scrotiform (skrō'tĭ-fôrm) *adj.* pouch-shaped.

scrump (skrŭmp) *v.t.&i.* to shrivel. -*n.* anything shriveled or undersized.

scruto (skrōō'tō) *n.* a stage trap door.

scrying (skrī'ĭng) *n.* 1. crystal gazing. 2. hallucinating after staring at clear or bright objects.

scuddick (skŭd'ĭk) *n.* something small in size or value.

scuddy (skŭd'ē) *adj.* naked. -*n.* a naked child.

scumble (skŭm'bəl) *v.t.* to soften the lines or colors of a drawing by rubbing lightly with the finger. *scumbling.* *n.* the softened effect produced.

scurfy (skûrf'ē) *adj.* pertaining to or covered with dandruff (*scurf*).

scutiferous (skū-tĭf'ər-əs) *adj.* 1. carrying a shield. 2. covered with scales or horny plate like reptiles.

scybalum (sĭb'ə-lŭm) *n.* a hardened fecal mass.

Scylla (sĭl'ə) *n.* 1. a rock on the Italian coast opposite the whirlpool *Charybdis.* 2. a female monster who was a menace to seafarers (Greek and Roman mythology). *between Scylla and Charybdis* = between the devil and the deep blue sea.

sdrucciola (zdrōō'chō-lò) *n.* a three-syllable rhyme: copulate, populate.

sebaceous (sē-bā'shəs) *adj.* pertaining to or composed of fat; fatty.

sebastomania (sĕb-às"tō-mā'nĭ-ə) *n.* religious insanity.

sectary (sĕk'tər-ē) *n.* 1. a fanatic

disciple. 2. a Protestant nonformist. 3. a Shiite.

sectiuncle (sĕk'tĭ-ùng"kəl) *n.* an insignificant sect.

seculum (sĕk'ū-lùm) *n.* a long time; an era or generation; also *saeculum.*

secundation (sĕk-ùn-dā'shən). *n.* making prosperous.

secundogeniture (sĕk-ùn"dō-jĕn'ĭ-chər) *n.* 1. being the second born, especially among sons. 2. property inherited by the second son; this type of inheritance.

sedulous (sĕd'ū-ləs) *adj.* diligent, persistent, persevering.

seeksorrow (sēk'sòr"ō) *n.* a masochist.

seely (sē'lē) *adj.* blessed, happy, blissful, good, kind, innocent, harmless, weak, feeble, poor, wretched, frail, simple, timid, foolish, silly (to name a few).

seesee (sē'sē) *n.* the small sand-partridge of western Asia.

seiche (sāsh) *n.* rapid tidal rise in a large lake.

seinsemblers (sĕn-sòm-blā') *n.* falsies; also *colpomims.*

seity (sē'ĭ-tē) *n.* selfhood, individuality.

sejugate (sĕj'ōō-gāt) *v.t.* to unyoke, disconnect.

selcouth (sĕl'kōōth) *adj.* wondrous, miraculous. -*n.* a miracle.

selenian (sĕl-ē'nĭ-ən) *adj.* pertaining to the moon. *selenitic, adj.* influenced by or the moon.

selenography (sĕl-ən-òg'rə-fē) *n.* geography of the moon.

selvage (sĕl'vəj) *n.* 1. the finished edge of a woven fabric. 2. edge or border, literally or figuratively.

semasiology (sĕm-ā"sĭ-òl'ə-jē) *n.* semantics.

sematic (sĕm-àt'ĭk) *adj.* serving as a warning: said of certain animals' coloring.

semeiology (sĕm-ī-ŏl'ə-jē) *n.* 1. symptomatology. 2. the science of signs or sign language also *semiology*.

semese (sĕm-ēs') *adj.* half-eaten.

semidiurnal (sĕm″ī-dī-ûr′nəl) *adj.* pertaining to half a day; happening twice a day.

semiquaver (sĕm′ī-kwā″vər) *n.* a sixteenth note in Britain. see *quaver*, for the lot.

semiustulate (sĕm-ī-ŭs′tū-lāt) *adj.* half burned.

semordnilap (sĕm-ôrd′nĭ-làp) *n.* *reversal*, which semordnilap is for *palindromes*.

sempervirent (sĕm-pûr-vī′rənt) *adj.* evergreen.

sempiternal (sĕm-pī-tûr′nəl) *adj.* everlasting, eternal.

senary (sĕn′ər-ē) *n.* 1. six, sextuple. 2. using six as a base; involving six variables (mathematics).

senectitude (sĕn-ĕk′tĭ-tōōd) *n.* old age.

seneschal (sĕn′ə-shàl) *n.* 1. the chief steward of a medieval lord. 2. an administrative or judicial officer.

seneucia (sĕn-ōō′sī-ə) *n.* widowhood.

sennet (sĕn′ət) *n.* a trumpet call as an entrance or exit cue.

sensificatory (sĕn-sĭf′ĭk-ə-tôr″ē) *adj.* producing sensation; *sensific*.

sepicolous (sĕp-ĭk′ō-ləs) *adj.* living in hedges.

seppuku (sĕp-ōō′kōō) *n.* ritual suicide by disembowelment; *harakiri*.

septemplicate (sĕp-tĕm′plĭ-kāt) *n.* one of seven copies.

septentrionate (sĕp-tĕn′trĭ-ō-nāt″) *v.i.* to point north.

septimanarian (sĕp″tĭ-mǎn-ĕr′ĭ-ən) *n.* a monk on duty for a week.

septophobia (sĕp-tō-fō′bĭ-ə) *n.* fear of decaying matter.

sepulture (sĕp-ŭl′chər) *n.* 1. burial. 2. a sepulcher or grave. *-v.t.* to bury.

sequacious (sē-kwā′shəs) *adj.* 1. apt to follow; following. 2. malleable, pliant. 3. obsequious.

serac (sā-ràk′) *n.* part of a glacier left behind.

serendipitous (sĕr-ən-dĭp′ĭ-təs) *adj.* pertaining to the alleged ability to find a cloud's silver lining.

sereno (sĕr-ā′nō) *n.* a night watchman.

sericeous (sĕr-ĭ′shəs) *adj.* consisting of silk; silky. 2. having a silk-like or satiny luster.

sermocination (sûr-mŏs″ĭn-ā′shən) *n.* a speaker quickly answering her own question (rhetoric).

serotine (sĕr′ə-tīn) *adj.* flowering late. *-n.* the common European brown bat. *serotinous*, *adj.* blossoming later in the season than allied species.

serous (sīr′əs) *adj.* thin, watery; like serum; pertaining to serum.

serrurerie (sĕr-ōō″rə-rē′) *n.* highly wrought wrought iron.

sesquialteral (sĕs-kwĭ-ăl′tər-əl) *adj.* having a ratio of one to one and a half.

sesquipedalian (sĕs″kwĭ-pĕd-ā′lĭ-ən) *adj.* 1. measuring a foot and a half. 2. using long words. *-n.* 1. something that is a foot and a half long. 2. a long word. see *hippopotomonstrosesquipedalian*, a longer one.

setaceous (sē-tā′shəs) *adj.* bristly.

sevocation (sĕv-ō-kā′shən) *n.* a calling aside.

sferics (sfĕr′ĭks) *n.* 1. the study of electromagnetic radiation produced by natural phenomena. 2.

radio interference so produced. also *spherics, atmospherics.*

sfumato (sfōō-mȯ'tō) *adj.* painted with hazy outlines creating a misty quality.

sgabello (zgȯ-bèl'ō) *n.* an octagonal Italian Renaissance chair.

sgalag (zgȯ'làg) *n.pl.* former Scottish land-slaves.

sgraffito (zgrȯ-fēt'ō) *n.* 1. scratching a design in the outer glaze revealing a different color. 2. ceramics decorated this way.

shabash (shȯ'bȯsh) *interj.* well done, bravo (Persian).

shaconian (shā-kō'nĭ-ȯn) *n.* someone convinced that Bacon ghosted Shakespeare's plays.

shaftsbury (shàfts'bėr"ē) *n.* a gallon jug of wine.

shaganappy (shàg-ȯ-nàp'ē) *n.* rawhide cord or thread (Algonquian).

shagreen (shàg-rēn') *n.* 1. a kind of Russian green-dyed leather made to look pebbled. 2. sharkskin with a pebbly texture. 3. pebbled silk.

shahzadah (shȯ-zȯ'dȯ) *n.* son of a shah.

shamal (shȯm-ȯl') *n.* see *simoom.*

shaman (shȯ'mȯn) *n.* medicine man or witch doctor. *shamanism, n.* 1. spiritualism using shamans as mediums. 2. religious mania.

shamateur (shàm-ȯ-tûr') *n.* standard English (circa 1900) for a bogus tyro.

shapoo (shȯ'pōō) *n.* a wild mountain sheep of Tibet.

shardborn (shȯrd'bȯrn) *adj.* born in dung.

shaveling (shāv'lĭng) *n.* 1. a priest; hypocrite; *shorling.* 2. a stripling or youth.

shawabti (shȯ-wàb'tē) *n.* see *ushabti.*

shawm (shȯm) *n.* an obsolete oboe-like instrument.

shebeen (shē-bēn') *n.* a place where liquor is sold without a license.

shenk (shènk) *v.t.&i.* to pour someone a drink.

Sheol (shē'ōl) *n.* Hebrew hell, return from which it isn't possible.

sheriffwick (shèr'ĭf-wĭk) *n.* see *shrievalty.*

sherryvallies (shèr'ĭ-vàl"ēz) *n.pl.* chaps, leggings.

sheugh (shōōk) *v.t.* to dig ditches. *-n.* a ditch or gully. also *sheuch.*

shevvle (shèv'ȯl) *n.* euphemism for horse meat (French *cheval* = horse).

Shiite (shē'īt) *n.* a Persian Moslem sect who think Mohammed's son-in-law, Ali, was his rightful successor. *Shiitic, adj.*

shiko (shĭ-kō') *n.* position assumed before an alleged superior: kneeling, with joined hands and bowed head (Burma).

shillaber (shĭl'ȯ-bûr) *n.* a shill.

shillibeer (shĭl'ĭ-bĭr) *n.* a hearse with seats for mourners.

shilpit (shĭl'pĭt) *adj.* feeble, puny, worthless, insipid.

shinarump (shĭn-àr'ŭmp) *n.* petrified wood.

shintiyan (shĭn'tĭ-yàn) *n.* baggy pants for Moslem women.

shippo (shĭp'ō) *n.* Japanese cloisonné enamel.

shitepoke (shĭt'pōk) *n.* the green heron; the night heron; any heron.

shittim (shĭt'ĭm) *n.* wood from the *shittah* tree.

shode (shōd) *n.* 1. hair-parting. 2. top of the head.

shorling (shȯr'lĭng) *n.* 1. the skin of a shorn sheep. 2. someone with a shorn head; a monk, *shaveling.*

shote (shōt) *n.* a young hog; a

shoat.

shrievalty (shrĕv'əl-tē) *n.* the office or jurisdiction of a sheriff.

shriver (shrī'vər) *n.* confessor.

shroff (shrŏf) *n.* 1. a banker or moneychanger. 2. a bank expert who fixes coin values. *-v.t.&i.* to inspect coins.

shtchee (shchē) *n.* Russian cabbage soup. also *shchi, stchi.*

sialagogic (sī″ăl-ə-gŏj'ĭk) *adj.* promoting saliva flow.

sibship (sĭb'shĭp) *n.* relationship between siblings.

sibyline (sĭb'ĭl-īn) *adj.* prophetical, cryptic, occult.

sicarian (sĭk-ĕr'ĭ-ən) *n.* an assassin. *sicarious, adj.* murderous.

siccative (sĭk'ə-tĭv) *adj.* drying. *-n.* a drier. *siccity* (sĭk'sĭ-tē) *n.* dryness.

sicchasia (sĭk-ā'zĭ-ə) *n.* nausea.

sicchosism (sĭk'ō-sĭz″əm) *n.* morbid fastidiousness.

sicsac (sĭk'săk) *n.* the crocodile bird (Egypt).

sideration (sĭd-ər-ā'shən) *n.* 1. sudden and unexplainable sickness. 2. *erysipelas*, a skin disease. 3. the use of green manure.

sidereal (sī-dĭr'ĭ-əl) *adj.* 1. pertaining to stars; astral, stellar. 2. measured by means of stars.

siderodromophobia (sĭd-rŏd″rō-mō-fō'bĭ-ə) *n.* fear of train travel.

sideromancy (sĭd'ər-ō-măn″sē) *n.* 1. fortunetelling from looking at stars. 2. fortunetelling from watching burning straw.

sifflate (sĭf'ĭl-āt) *v.i.* to whisper.

sigillate (sĭj'ĭl-āt) *adj.* decorated with stamps or seals. *-v.t.* to seal.

sigla (sĭg'lə) *n.pl.* abbreviations, symbols, or shorthand in old manuscripts.

sigmate (sĭg'māt) *adj.* S or sigma-shaped; *sigmoid.* *-v.t.* to add a

sigma or S.

signaletics (sĭg-nəl-ĕt'ĭks) *n.* the use of *signalments:* description for identification by unusual markings or characteristics.

sikinnis (sĭk-ĭn'ĭs) *n.* an orgiastic dance of satyrs performed in Greek theater.

sile (sīl) *v.t.* 1. to conceal, deceive. 2. to filter. *-v.i.* 1. to flow or pour; to drip. 2. to subside. *-n.* 1. a strainer. 2. a beam. 3. a herring.

silentiary (sī-lĕn'shĭ-ĕr″ē) *n.* 1. someone appointed to keep peace and quiet. 2. someone sworn to keep state secrets secret.

sillabub (sĭl'ə-bŭb) *n.* 1. inconsequential puff; florid, inane language. 2. a dessert made mostly out of cream.

sillographer (sĭl-ŏg'rə-fər) *n.* a satirist.

simony (sĭm'ən-ē) *n.* traffic in religious offices, pardons, or prizes. *simoniac, n.* someone practicing simony (from *Simon Magus,* a first-century Samarian magician).

simoom (sĭm-ōōm') *n.* a hot, dry, dust-laden wind in Arabia and Syria. the *shamal* is another one. the *sirocco* and *solano* are hot, oppressive Mediterranean winds.

simous (sī'məs) *adj.* 1. having a snub nose. 2. concave.

simulacrum (sĭm-ū-lā'krəm) *n.* 1. an image. 2. a vague or shadowy vision.

sinapize (sĭn'ə-pīz) *v.t.* to sprinkle.

sinarquism (sĭn'ŏr-kĭz″əm) *n.* a Mexican counterrevolutionary movement that opposes communism, Pan-American labor unionism, and military conscription.

sinciput (sĭn'sĭ-pŭt) *n.* the forehead.

---

măn; māde; lĕt; bē; sĭp; wīne; hŏt; cōld; sôre; dŭll; fūgue; bûrp; gōōd; fōōd; out; gĕt; thin; this; year; ažure; ō'mən″; viN; fūr; Bach

singultus (sĭng-gŭl'təs) n. hiccup or hiccups. *singultous*, *adj*.

Sinicism (sĭn'ĭ-sĭz"əm) n. something Chinese.

sinistral (sĭn'ĭs-trəl) *adj*. 1. pertaining to the left. 2. left-handed. 3. illegitimate.

sipid (sĭp'ĭd) *adj*. tasty, flavorful.

sippet (sĭp'ət) n. 1. a small piece of toast soaked in milk or broth; a piece of toast as a garnish. 2. a piece or fragment.

sirenic (sī-rĕn'ĭk) *adj*. like a siren: fascinating and dangerous. also *sirenical*.

sirenomelia (sī"rən-ō-mē"lĭ-ə) n. a footless fetus with fused legs.

siriasis (sĭr-ī'ə-sĭs) n. sunstroke.

sirocco (sĭr-ŏ'kō) n. see *simoom*.

sirrah (sĭr'ə) n. a contemptuous term of address used to one's alleged inferiors.

siserara (sĭs-ûr-ĕr'ə) n. a severe blow or violent reproach.

sistle (sĭs'əl) *v.i.* to whistle with a hissing sound.

sisyphean (sĭs-ĭ-fē'ən) *adj*. like the labors of Sisyphus: unending.

sitology (sī-tŏl'ə-jē) n. dietetics.

sitophobia (sī-tō-fō'bĭ-ə) n. fear of eating.

sixmo (sĭks'mō) n. the size of a piece of paper cut six from a sheet; a page of this size.

sizar (sīz'ər) n. a Cambridge or Dublin University student who gets a college allowance.

sizzard (sĭz'ərd) n. heat with high humidity.

sjambok (shăm'bŏk) n. in South Africa, a heavy whip made of rhinoceros hide. *-v.t.* to whip with a *sjambok; sjamboking*.

skelp (skĕlp) n. 1. a push or slap. 2. heavy rain. *-v.t.* 1. to slap, beat, or kick. 2. to write or perform in a lively manner. *-v.i.* to walk briskly. *-adv*. quickly and violently; suddenly.

skewbald (skū'bôld) *adj*. [animals] marked by patches of white and one other color.

skiagraphy (skī-ăg'rə-fē) n. 1. projecting shadows. 2. making x-rays. 3. telling time by sundial.

skijoring (skē'jôr"ĭng) n. the pulling of a skier by a horse or car (Norway).

skink (skĭnk) n. 1. lizard. 2. drink; liquor. 3. beef hocks or beef hock soup. *-v.t.&i.* to pour liquor; to pour.

skive (skīv) *v.t.* to shave or pare. *-v.i.* to skim or dart. *-n.* a diamond wheel.

sklent (sklĕnt) *v.i.* to slander, lie; to glance sideways. *-n.* a lie, a side glance; slander.

skookum (skōō'kəm) *adj*. first-rate; the best (Chinook jargon).

skoptsy (skŏp'tsē) n. self-castration (from the *Skopts*, a Russian sect, who did it).

skybald (skī'bôld) n. a good-for-nothing; a worthless person, animal, or thing. also *skybal*.

skygodlin (skī'gŏd"lĭn) *adv*. diagonally.

slade (slād) n. 1. a small valley. 2. a cave. 3. a bog.

slampamp (slăm'pămp) n. medley, confusion.

slipslop (slĭp'slŏp) n. 1. malapropism. 2. poor food or drink. 3. inane talk, twaddle. 4. the sound made by walking in a loose slipper. *-v.i.* to make such a sound.

slobber-chops (slŏb'ər-chŏps) n. a child or animal that scatters its food (slang).

slojd (sloid) n. 1. skilled mechanical work. 2. a Swedish system of manual training.

sloom (slōōm) *v.i.* to doze. 2. to become weak; to decay. 3. to move sluggishly; to drift. *sloomy, adj.* sluggish.

slowcome (slō'kəm) *n.* a lazy person (slang).

slubber (slŭb'ər) *v.t.* 1. to stain, darken. 2. to botch. 3. to skim, with *over. -n.* 1. mire; slime. 2. a worker or machine that slubs textiles. 3. partly or badly twined thread.

slype (slīp) *n.* a narrow passage between the transept and the deanery in certain English cathedrals. *-v.t.* to sharpen.

smabbled (smăb'əld) *adj.* killed in battle. also *snabbled.*

smallclothes (smôl'klōthz) *n.pl.* 1. men's eighteenth-century knee breeches. 2. "small" clothes, such as underwear, handkerchiefs, etc.; *smalls.*

smaragdine (smàr-àg'din) *adj.* pertaining to emeralds; emerald-green.

smarmy (smòr'mē) *adj.* 1. over-polite, outrageously flattering; speaking obsequiously. 2. plastered-down [hair].

smatchet (smăch'ət) *n.* a small, nasty person or a nasty child.

smearcase (smîr'kās) *n.* cottage cheese.

smee (smē) *n.* the pintail duck, widgeon, pochard, or smew.

smeeth (smēth) *n.* mist, haze, powder. *-v.t.* to screen with mist.

smellfungus (smĕl'fŭng"gəs) *n.* a malcontent; a grumbler or fault-finder.

smich (smĭch) *n.* the stonechat.

smilet (smīl'ət) *n.* a little smile.

snaffle (snăf'əl) *n.* 1. a kind of bridle bit. 2. a slight restraint.

snafu (snà-fōō') *adj.&n.* Situation Normal: All Fucked-Up. *fubar,*

Fucked-Up Beyond All Recognition. *fubb,* Fucked-Up Beyond Belief. *fumtu,* Fucked-Up More Than Usual. *janfu,* Joint Army and Navy Fuck-Up. *sapfu,* Surpassing All Previous Fuck-Ups. *susfu,* Situation Unchanged: Still Fucked-Up. *tarfu,* Things Are *Really* Fucked-Up (all army slang).

snarleyyow (snòrl'ē-you) *n.* dog (slang).

snash (snăsh) *n.* abuse, insolence. *-v.i.* to talk insolently or abusively.

snast (snăst) *n.* a candlewick.

snath (snăth) *n.* a scythe handle; *snead.*

snathe (snāth) *v.t.* to prune, lop off.

sneckdraw (snĕk'drô) *n.* a sly person. *sneckdrawing, adj.* sly, crafty. *sneckdrawn, adj.* mean or stingy.

snickersnee (snĭk'ər-snē) *n.* a fight with knives; a knife.

snipsnapsnorum (snĭp-snăp-snôr'əm) *n.* a card game (from accompanying nonsense words spoken by the players).

snoach (snōch) *v.i.* to speak through the nose; to snuffle.

snod (snŏd) *adj.* trimmed; smooth; neat; cunning. *-v.t.* to make *snod.*

snollygoster (snŏl'ĭ-gòs"tər) *n.* a burgeoning politician with no platform, principles, or party preference.

snurge (snûrj) *v.i.* to avoid an unpopular job (British slang).

soceraphobia (sō"sər-ə-fō'bĭ-ə) *n.* fear or dislike of parents-in-law.

sociophobia (sō"shē-ō-fō'bĭ-ə) *n.* fear of friendship or society.

sockdolager (sŏk'dŏl"ə-jər) *n.* 1. a telling blow. 2. something unusually large or imposing.

sodality (sō-dăl'ĭ-tē) *n.* associa-

---

màn; māde; lèt; bē; sìp; wīne; hòt; cōld; sôre; dùll; fūgue; bûrp; gōōd; fōōd; out; gèt; thin; this; year; aźure; ō'mən"; viN; fûr; Bach

tion, union, fellowship.

solano (sō-lò'nō) *n.* see *simoom.*

solatium (sō-lā'shĭ-əm) *n.* anything that compensates for suffering or loss; an additional allowance.

solfatara (sōl-fə-tò'rə) *n.* a volcanic vent spitting up partly sulphurous gases.

solfeggio (sōl-fĕj'ō) *n.* sight-singing using sol-fa syllables.

solifidian (sōl-ə-fĭd'ĭ-ən) *n.* someone who believes that faith alone is sufficient for salvation.

solipsism (sŏl'ĭp-sĭz"əm) *n.* the theory that only the self is real and knowable.

solisequious (sŏl-ĭ-sē'kwĭ-əs) *adj.* following the sun.

solmization (sōl-mĭ-zā'shən) *n.* see *solfeggio.*

somatology (sōm-ə-tŏl'ə-jē) *n.* the comparative study of the structure, functions, and development of the human body.

somnifugous (sŏm-nĭf'ū-gəs) *adj.* driving away sleep.

somniloquacious (sŏm"nĭ-lō-kwā'shəs) *adj.* pertaining to talking in one's sleep.

somnipathy (sŏm-nĭp'ə-thē) *n.* hypnotic sleep.

sooterkin (sŏŏt'ər-kĭn) *n.* 1. an afterbirth allegedly produced by Dutch women from sitting over their stoves. 2. an abortive scheme. 3. an unsuccessful literary attempt. 4. a Dutchman.

sophomania (sŏf-ō-mā'nĭ-ə) *n.* delusion of exceptional intelligence.

sophophobia (sŏf-ō-fō'bĭ-ə) *n.* fear or dislike of learning.

sophrosyne (sō-frŏs'ĭn-ē) *n.* sober, sensible, prudent, and rational.

sorbile (sôr'bĭl) *adj.* drinkable.

sord (sôrd) *n.* a flock [of mallards].

sordor (sôr'dər) *n.* refuse, dregs.

sorner (sôr'nər) *n.* a sponger, idler, loafer, or beggar.

sororicide (sôr-ôr'ĭ-sīd) *n.* the killing of one's sister.

sortilege (sôr'tĭl-ĕj) *n.* witchcraft.

soss (sŏs) *interj.* a "come and get it!" call to animals. -*n.* slop. -*adv.* plump.

sotadic (sō-tăd'ĭk) *adj.* pertaining to the lewd, vulgar, and often palindromic verse of *Sotades* (276 B.C.). also *sotadean.*

soteriology (sō-tĭr"ĭ-ŏl'ə-jē) *n.* 1. the study of salvation by belief in the legendary Jesus Christ. 2. the science of hygiene.

sottise (sō-tēz') *n.* foolish behavior; stupidity.

soubrette (sŏŏ-brĕt') *n.* the role of a coquette or frivolous young woman; an actress in that role.

sough (sŭf) *n.* 1. a sighing sound, as of the wind. 2. a vague rumor. 3. a religious chant. 4. a swamp. -*v.i.* 1. to sigh, as the wind. 2. to breathe heavily. with *away*, to breathe one's last, to die. 3. to preach in a whining tone. -*v.t.* 1. to hum, to chant. 2. to dig a drainage ditch.

sous-entendu (sŏŏz"ðN-tðN-dū') *n.* something implied but not stated.

soutache (sŏŏ-tòsh') *n.* a kind of embroidery braid.

souterrain (sŏŏ-tèr-ān') *n.* an underground passage or chamber.

sovkhoz (sŏv'kôz) *n.* a Soviet state-owned farm paying wages to the workers. also *sovkhos, sovhoz.*

sowbelly (sou'bèl"ē) *n.* fat salt pork or bacon.

spadonism (spăd'ō-nĭz"əm) *n.* eunuchry.

spaneria (spăn-èr'ĭ-ə) *n.* scarcity of men.

---

măn; māde; lèt; bē; sĭp; wīne; hŏt; cōld; sôre; dùll; fügue; bûrp; gŏŏd; fŏŏd; out; gèt; thin; t̶his; yₑar; a̤zure; ō'mən"; viN; für; Bach

spanogyny (spăn-ŏj'ən-ē) *n.* scarcity of women.

spasmatomancy (spăz'mə-tō-măn"sē) *n.* fortunetelling by observing a twitching body.

spatchcock (spăch'kŏk) *n.* a bird split and grilled immediately after being killed. -*v.t.* 1. to prepare a bird like this. 2. to interpolate [a phrase], to add to by interpolation.

spatiate (spā'shǐ-āt) *v.i.* to stroll or ramble.

spatilomancy (spăt'ǐl-ō-măn"sē) *n.* fortunetelling by observing animal droppings.

spatrify (spăt'rǐ-fī) *v.t. &i.* to besmirch, befoul; to sully and spot.

spatulomancy (spăt'ū-lō-măn"sē) *n.* fortunetelling with a sheep's shoulder blade.

spawl (spôl) *n.* spit. -*v.t. &i.* to spit.

spearhouse (spîr'hous) *n.* a homosexual brothel (slang).

spectroheliokinematograph (spèk"trō-hē"lǐ-ō-kǐn'ə-măt-ō-grăf") *n.* a movie camera for taking pictures of the sun.

spectrophobia (spèk-trō-fō'bǐ-ə) *n.* fear of looking in a mirror.

specular (spèk'ū-lər) *adj.* pertaining to a *speculum*, or mirror; having a smooth, reflecting surface.

speleology (spēl-ē-ŏl'ə-jē) *n.* the scientific study of caves. *spelunker* (spēl-ŭnk'ər) *n.* one who explores and studies caves, a *speleologist*.

sperate (spîr'āt) *adj.* hoped for: said of a debt that may be repaid.

spermologer (spûrm-ŏl'ə-jûr) *n.* seed gatherer.

sphacelate (sfăs'əl-āt) *v.i.* to become gangrenous.

sphagnicolous (sfăg-nĭk'ō-ləs) *adj.*

growing among peat moss.

sphenographer (sfĕn-ŏg'rə-fûr) *n.* someone who deciphers cuneiform writing.

sphragistics (sfră-jĭs'tĭks) *n.* the science or history of seals or stamps.

sphygmic (sfĭg'mĭk) *adj.* pertaining to the pulse.

sphygmomanometer (sfĭg"mō-măn-ŏm'ə-tər) *n.* an instrument for measuring blood pressure.

spiegelschrift (shpē'gəl-shrĭft) *n.* mirror-writing. also *strephographia*.

spiloma (spī-lō'mə) *n.* a birthmark or mole.

spindrift (spĭn'drĭft) *n.* sea spray; *spoondrift*.

spintry (spĭn'trē) *n.* a male whore.

spiracle (spī'rə-kəl) *n.* a breathing hole; an air hole or vent also *spiraculum*.

spirated (spī'rāt"əd) *adj.* corkscrew-shaped.

spissated (spĭs'āt"əd) *adj.* thickened.

spizzerinctum (spĭz-ər-ĭnk'təm) *n.* 1. ambition; the will to succeed. 2. gimcrackery; cheap, vulgar decoration.

splacknuck (splăk'nŭk) *n.* a peculiar person or animal (from the character in Swift's *Gulliver's Travels*).

splanchnology (splănk-nŏl'ə-jē) *n.* the study of human internal organs.

splore (splôr) *n.* merrymaking, festivity; a carousal. -*v.i.* to frolic, carouse; to brag, boast.

spodogenous (spō-dŏj'ən-əs) *adj.* pertaining to or due to presence of waste matter.

spodomancy (spŏd'ō-măn"sē) *n.* fortunetelling with ashes.

spoffish (spŏf'ĭsh) *adj.* fussy;

---

măn; māde; lĕt; bē; sĭp; wīne; hŏt; cōld; sôre; dŭll; fūgue; bûrp; gŏŏd; fōōd; out; gĕt; thin; this; year; ażure; ō'mən"; viN; fûr; Bach

bustling (slang).

spoffokins (spŏf'ə-kĭnz) *n.* a whore pretending to be a wife.

spoliation (spō-lĭ-ā'shən) *n.* robbery; the authorized practice of robbing neutrals at sea in wartime.

spongology (spŏn-gŏl'ə-jē) *n.* the study of sponges.

sponsalia (spŏn-sā'lĭ-ə) *n.pl.* formal betrothal.

sporabola (spôr-ăb'ō-lə) *n.* the trajectory of a falling spore.

spoucher (spōōch'ər) *n.* a utensil for bailing water.

spousebreach (spous'brēch) *n.* adultery.

sprachgefühl (shprŏh'gə-fül) *n.* a talent for languages.

sprag (sprăg) *n.* 1. a piece of wood used as a prop. 2. a piece of wood put between the spokes of a wheel as a brake. -*v.t.* 1. to prop with a *sprag*. 2. to brake with a *sprag*. -*n.* a young codfish.

spraints (sprānts) *n.pl.* otter dung.

spumescent (spū-mĕs'ənt) *adj.* like foam; foaming.

spurcidical (spŭr-sĭd'ĭ-kəl) *adj.* foulmouthed.

sputative (spū'tə-tĭv) *adj.* apt to spit.

squabash (skwŏ-băsh') *v.t.* to crush by criticism. -*n.* a crushing blow. *squabasher, n.*

squabbish (skwŏb'ĭsh) *adj.* thick, fat, and heavy.

squaliform (skwŏl'ĭ-fôrm) *adj.* shaped like a shark.

squamaceous (skwăm-ā'shəs) *adj.* covered with scales, scaly; *squamous.*

squarson (skwôr'sən) *n.* a clergyman-landlord. *squarsonry, n. (squire + parson).*

squelette (skĕl-ĕt') *n.* a thin wood veneer used in making match-boxes.

squeteague (skē'tēg) *n.s.&pl.* the common weakfish.

squidgereen (skwĭj-ər-ēn') *n.* a short, insignificant person.

squirearchy (skwī'ər-ŏr"kē) *n.* 1. squires, collectively. 2. government by the English landed gentry, or squires.

squonk (skwônk) *n.* a mythical bird covered with warts and continually weeping in self-pity (slang).

sravaka (srŏv'kŏ) *n.* a direct disciple of Buddha.

sri (shrē) *adj.* fortunate, glorious, and holy also *shri, shree* (India).

ssu (sōō) *n.s.&pl.* a Chinese unit of weight equal to 1/100,000 *liang*; in general, 1/100,000.

stable-stand (stā'bəl-stănd) *n.* the stance of someone about to shoot a bow and arrow.

staboy (stăb-oi') *interj.* a cry for encouraging hunting dogs after their prey.

staffage (stŏ-fŏz') *n.* extras added to a painting or literary work; details, ornamentation, etc.

stagiary (stā'jĭ-ĕr"ē) *n.* a resident canon; a law student.

stagnicolous (stăg-nĭk'ō-ləs) *adj.* living in stagnant water.

stalko (stôl'kō) *n.* a poor man posing as a rich man.

stannary (stăn'ər-ē) *n.* a tin mine.

stasibasiphobia (stăs"ĭ-bā-sĭ-fō'bĭ-ə) *n.* fear of standing or walking.

stasis (stā'sĭs) *n.* stoppage of the flow of body fluids.

stasivalence (stăs-ĭ-vā'ləns) *n.* ability to have sexual intercourse only while standing.

stathmograph (stăth'mō-grăf) *n.* an instrument for measuring the speed of trains or projectiles.

staurolatry (stôr-ŏl'ə-trē) *n.* cross or crucifix-worship.

---

màn; māde; lĕt; bē; sĭp; wīne; hŏt; cōld; sôre; dŭll; fūgue; bûrp; gōōd; fōōd; out; gĕt; thin; this; year; azure; ŏ'mən"; viN; für; Bach

staurophobia (stôr-ō-fō'bĭ-ə) *n.* fear or dislike of the cross or crucifix.

steatopygia (stē"ăt-ə-pī'jĭ-ə) *n.* fatty-assedness. *steatopygous, adj.*

steganography (stĕg-ən-ŏg'rə-fē) *n.* cryptography.

stegmonth (stĕg'mŭnth) *n.* period of recuperation after childbirth.

stele (stē'lē) *n.* a decorated headstone or pillar.

stellated (stĕl'āt"əd) *adj.* starshaped; decorated with stars.

stellification (stĕl'ĭ-fĭ-kā'shən) *n.* glorification.

stellionate (stĕl'yən-āt) *n.* unauthorized resale of property; fraud, in general.

stenophobia (stĕn-ō-fō'bĭ-ə) *n.* fear of narrow things or places.

stenotic (stĕn-ŏt'ĭk) *adj.* pertaining to *stenosis,* a narrowing of body orifices.

stentorophonous (stĕn-tôr-ŏf'ən-əs) *adj.* having an abnormally loud voice.

stephane (stĕf'ən-ē) *n.* a headband, widest in the middle and narrowing toward the temples: often seen in statues of divinities.

stercoricolous (stûr-kôr-ĭk'ō-ləs) *adj.* living in dung.

sterculius (stûr-kū'lĭ-əs) *n.* the god of feces.

stereognosis (stĕr"ē-ŏg-nō'sĭs) *n.* learning the weight of a solid by handling it.

stereography (stĕr-ē-ŏg'rə-fē) *n.* the drawing of solids on a plane: a branch of solid geometry.

stereotypy (stĭr-ē-ŏt'ə-pē) *n.* monotonous repetition.

sterlet (stûr'lĕt) *n.* a small sturgeon of the Caspian Sea, noted for its fine caviar.

sternutation (stûrn-ū-tā'shən) *n.* sneezing.

sterquilinian (stûr-kwĭl-ĭn'ĭ-ən) *adj.* pertaining to a dunghill; filthy.

stertorous (stûr'tôr-əs) *adj.* characterized by loud breathing or snoring.

sthenia (sthē'nĭ-ə) *n.* strength or vigor.

sthenobulia (sthĕn-ō-bōō'lĭ-ə) *n.* strong will power.

sticcado (stĭ-kŏ'dō) *n.* a kind of xylophone.

stichomancy (stĭk'ō-mǎn"sē) *n.* fortunetelling by passages from books.

stickleback (stĭk'əl-bǎk) *n.* scaleless fish with two or more spines.

stigonomancy (stĭg'ō-mǎn"sē) *n.* fortunetelling by writing on tree bark.

stillatitious (stĭl-ə-tĭsh'əs) *adj.* falling in drops.

stilp (stĭlp) *v.i.* 1. to walk with stilts or crutches. 2. to take long strides. *stilpers, n.pl.* stilts or crutches.

stimulose (stĭm'ū-lōs) *adj.* having stinging hairs.

stipendiarian (stī-pĕn"dĭ-ĕr'ĭ-ən) *adj.* mercenary; performing services for a price.

stirious (stĭr'ĭ-əs) *adj.* like an icicle.

stirpiculture (stûrp'ĭ-kŭl"chər) *n.* animal eugenics.

stoa (stō'ə) *n.* a Greek portico.

stochastic (stō-kǎs'tĭk) *adj.* conjectural; conjectural expertise.

stola (stō'lə) *n.* a long robe worn by Roman women.

stomachous (stŭm'ə-kəs) *adj.* obstinate; angry.

stoopgallant (stōōp'gǎl"ənt) *adj.* humbling; ego-destroying.

stopcock (stŏp'kŏk) *n.* a pipe valve.

storge (stôr'jē) *n.* instinctive paren-

---

măn; māde; lĕt; bē; sĭp; wīne; hŏt; cōld; sôre; dŭll; fūgue; bûrp; gŏŏd; fōōd; out; gĕt; thin; this; year; ażure; ō'mən"; viN; fŭr; Bach tal affection among many animals.

storiology (stôr-ĭ-ŏl′ə-jē) *n.* study of folklore.

stot (stŏt) *n.* 1. a young horse. 2. a three-year-old castrated bull. -*n.&v.i.* 1. stumble, stagger. 2. bounce, rebound. 3. stammer.

stound (stound) *n.* 1. a short time, a moment. 2. season; occasion. -*v.i.* to stun; to astonish.

stoundmeal (stound′mēl) *adv.* from time to time, now and then; gradually.

strabismus (strà-bĭz′məs) *n.* squinting; *heterotropia.*

stramineous (stràm-ĭn′ĭ-əs) *adj.* strawlike; valueless.

stratephrenia (stràt-ə-frē′nĭ-ə) *n.* neurosis induced by military service.

strathspey (stràth′spā) *n.* a lively Scottish dance or its music.

stratocracy (stràt-ŏk′rə-sē) *n.* military government.

strepent (strĕp′ənt) *adj.* noisy, loud. also *streperous; strepitant.*

strephographia (strĕf-ō-gràf′ĭ-ə) *n.* mirror-writing. also *spiegel-schrift.*

strephonade (strĕf-ən-ād′) *n.* a love song.

strephosymbolia (strĕf″ō-sĭm-bō′lĭ-ə) *n.* a perceptual disorder in which objects appear reversed.

stridulous (strĭd′ū-ləs) *adj.* 1. making a creaking or squeaky sound. 2. pertaining to *stridor,* a whistling during respiratory blockage.

strigil (strĭj′ĭl) *n.* 1. an ancient Greek skin-scraper. 2. a curved Roman fluting.

strigine (strī′jĭn) *adj.* owlish.

strobic (strŏb′ĭk) *adj.* spinning like a top.

stromatology (strō-mə-tŏl′ə-jē) *n.* the history of stratified rock formation.

struthian (strōō′thĭ-ən) *adj.* like an ostrich, emu, cassowary, or moa.

stuboy (stōō′boi) *v.i.* to set a dog on a person (slang).

stufa (stōō′fə) *n.* a steam jet spouting from the ground.

stultiloquence (stŭl-tĭl′ō-kwəns) *n.* silly talk, babble.

stumpage (stŭmp′əj) *n.* the value of uncut timber; the right to cut it.

stupration (stōō-prā′shən) *n.* rape.

stupulose (stōōp′ū-lōs) *adj.* covered with fine short hairs.

sturm und drang (shtōōrm-ŏŏn-dròng′) storm and stress: applied to certain late eighteenth-century German literature that was trying to free itself from French influence.

stygian (stĭj′ĭ-ən) *adj.* pertaining to the river Styx: infernal and gloomy.

stygiophobia (stĭj″ĭ-ō-fō′bĭ-ə) *n.* fear of hell.

stylagalmaic (stīl″ə-gàl-mā′ĭk) *adj.* like a *caryatid*; full of *caryatids* (pillars shaped like women).

stylite (stī′līt) *n.* ascetics who lived on top of pillars. also called *pillarists.*

stylograph (stīl′ō-gràf) *n.* a fountain pen.

suant (sōō′ənt) *adj.* smooth, even, regular, steady, agreeable, placid, quiet, grave, or demure.

suaviation (swòv-ĭ-ā′shən) *n.* a love kiss.

suaviloquence (swòv-ĭl′ō-kwəns) *n.* bland or soothing, agreeable talk.

subacid (sŭb-às′ĭd) *adj.* slightly tart or biting.

subagitation (sŭb″àj-ĭ-tā′shən) *n.* copulation.

subaltern (sŭb-ôl′tərn) *adj.* second-string or fiddle (slang).

subarrhation (sŭb-ər-ā'shən) *n.* betrothal accomplished by the man's showering presents on his incipient bride.

subboreal (sŭb-ôr'ē-əl) *adj.* cold, but not freezing.

subderisorious (sŭb″dər-ĭs-ôr'ĭ-əs) *adj.* mildly ridiculing.

subdititious (sŭb-dĭ-tĭ'shəs) *adj.* secret substitution.

subdolous (sŭb'dō-ləs) *adj.* rather crafty or sly.

subfusc (sŭb-fŭsk') *adj.* a bit dark or dusky; *subfuscous.*

subhastation (sŭb-hăs-tā'shən) *n.* a public sale or auction.

subingression (sŭb-ĭn-grĕ'shən) *n.* a hidden entrance.

subintelligitur (sŭb″ĭn-təl-ĭj'ĭ-tər) *n.* a meaning implied but not stated.

subito (sōō'bē-tō) *adv.* suddenly (music).

suborn (sŭb-ôrn') *v.t.* 1. to hire, bribe, or urge someone to commit a crime. 2. to cause someone to commit perjury.

subrision (sŭb-rĭ'źən) *n.* smiling. *subrisive, subrisory, adj.*

subsannation (sŭb-săn-ā'shən) *n.* derision.

subsemifusa (sŭb″sĕm-ĭ-fū'sə) *n.* a thirty-second note, or *demisemiquaver* in medieval music.

substaquilate (sŭb-stăk'wĭl-āt) *v.t.* to defeat, overwhelm.

subsume (sŭb-sōōm') *v.t.* to enter something in a larger category.

subtegulaneous (sŭb″tĕg-ū-lā'nĭ-əs) *adj.* indoor.

subtend (sŭb-tĕnd') *v.t.* to extend under, or be opposite to.

subtrahend (sŭb'trə-hĕnd) *n.* the quantity to be subtracted.

sububeres (sŭb-ū'bər-ēz) *n.pl.* suckling children.

suburbicarian (sŭb-ûrb″ĭ-kĕr'ĭ-ən) *adj.* belonging to the suburbs.

subvention (sŭb-vĕn'shən) *n.* 1. aid and succor. 2. a grant or endowment.

succedaneum (sŭk″sə-dā'nē-əm) *n.* a substitute; a substitute remedy.

succes fou (sŭk-sā-fōō') *n.* a tremendous success.

succiferous (sŭk-sĭf'ər-əs) *adj.* producing sap.

succorance (sŭk'ər-əns) *n.* dependence.

succubus (sŭk'ū-bŭs) *n.* 1. a female goblin who seduces men in their sleep. 2. a lewd person; a whore.

succursal (sŭk-ûr'səl) *adj.* subsidiary, auxiliary.

sudarium (sōō-də-tôr'ĭ-əm) *n.* a sweat cloth or handkerchief, especially the one St. Veronica used to wipe the legendary Christ's face.

sudatorium (sōō-də-tôr'ĭ-əm) *n.* the sweating room in a bathhouse.

sudd (sŭd) *n.* 1. papyrus stems and aquatic grass that sometimes clog the White Nile, making it unnavigable. 2. a temporary dam.

suggilate (sŭg'jĭl-āt) *v.t.* to beat black and blue; to defame.

sui generis (sōō-ī-jĕn'ər-ĭs) unique; in a class by itself (Latin).

sullage (sŭl'əj) *n.* 1. sewage. 2. mud deposited by water.

summist (sŭm'ĭst) *n.* a philosopher who wrote *summas*, or treatises synthesizing or epitomizing whole areas of human knowledge.

sumpitan (sŭmp'ĭ-tăn) *n.* a blowgun used in Borneo to dispatch poisoned darts.

sumpsimus (sŭmp'sĭm-əs) *n.* a grammatically correct phrase substituted for a common error.

---

màn; māde; lĕt; bē; sĭp; wīne; hŏt; cōld; sôre; dŭll; fūgue; bûrp; gŏŏd; fōōd; out; gĕt; thin; thìs; year; aźure; ō'mən″; viN; für; Bach

sumpter (sŭmp'tər) *n.* a pack-
horse, its pack, or driver. *-adj.*
pertaining to baggage.

sumptuary (sŭmp'chŏō-ĕr"ē) *adj.*
pertaining to the limiting of certain expenditures.

sundowner (sŭn'doun"ər) *n.* 1. a
drink at sundown. 2. someone
with a secondary night job. 3. a
freeloader arriving at sundown.

suoid (sŏō'oid) *adj.* hoglike.

supellectile (sŏōp-əl-ĕk'tĭl) *adj.*
pertaining to furniture. *-n.* a piece
of furniture or apparatus.

superalimentation (sŏō"pər-ăl"ĭ-
mĕn-tā'shən) *n.* overfeeding: once
used as a remedy in certain
debilitating diseases.

superannuated (sŏō-pər-ăn'ū-
āt"əd) *adj.* 1. made obsolete; dis-
qualified because of old age. 2. re-
tired and pensioned because of
sickness or old age.

superbiate (sŏō-pûr'bĭ-āt) *v.t.* to
make arrogant or haughty. *superb-
ious, adj.*

**supercalifragilisticexpialidoc-
ious**(sŏō"pər-kàl-ĭ-fràj"ĭl-ĭs-tĭk-
eks"pē-àl-ĭ-dō'shəs) *adj.* atoning
for extreme and delicate beauty
while highly educable (*super* =
over + *cali* = beauty + *fragilistic*
= delicate + *expiali* = to atone
for + *docious* = educable).

supererogatory (sŏō"pər-ē-rŏg'ə-
tôr"ē) *adj.* superfluous; non-
essential.

superfetation (sŏō"pər-fē-tā'shən)
n. 1. conception during pregnancy. 2. the piling up of one growth
on another; cumulative development.

superlation (sŏō-pər-lā'shən) *n.*
glorification; *stellification.*

supernaculum (sŏō-pər-nàk'ū-
ləm) *n.* a liquor drunk to the last
drop; excellent booze.

supernal (sŏō-pûr'nəl) *adj.* coming
from above, sky-high; ethereal.

superseptuagenarian (sŏō"pər-
sèp"chŏō-ə-jèn-ĕr'ĭ-ən) *n.* someone over seventy.

supervacaneous (sŏō"pər-vàk-
ā"nē-əs) *adj.* needlessly added.

supinovalent (sŏō"pĭn-ō-vā'lənt)
adj. able to fornicate only while
supine.

suppalpation (sŭp-àl-pā'shən) *n.*
gaining affection by caressing.

suppedaneum (sŭp-ə-dā'nē-əm) *n.*
a foot support for crucifix victims.

sural (sŏōr'əl) *adj.* pertaining to the
calf of the leg.

surbate (sûr'bāt) *v.t.* to make or become footsore. *-n.* footsoreness.

surcingle (sûr'sĭng"gəl) *n.* a belt or
girdle for a horse or priest.

surculation (sûr-kū-lā'shən) *n.*
pruning; trimming.

surdity (sûr'dĭ-tē) *n.* deafness.

surrebutter (sûr-ē-bŭt'ər) *n.* plaintiff's reply to defendant's rebut-
tal.

susfu (sŏōs'fŏō) *adj.* Situation Unchanged: Still Fucked-Up (army
slang. for more, see *snafu.*)

suspercollate (sŭs-pər-kòl'āt) *v.t.*
to hang by the neck.

suspirious (sŭs-pĭr'ĭ-əs) *adj.*
breathing heavily; sighing.

susulike (sŏō'sŏō-lĭk) *adj.* pertaining to a blind platanistoid ceta-
cean about eight feet long with a
long snout; like a Ganges
dolphin.

susurration (sŏō-sûr-ā'shən) *n.* a
whispering or murmuring.

sutile (sū'tĭl) *adj.* sewn.

sutler (sŭt'lər) *n.* someone who
follows an army to sell the troops
provisions.

suttee (sŭ-tē') *n.* a Hindu widow
who cremates herself on her hus-

band's funeral pyre. also the practice of such cremation.

suzerainty (sōō'zər-ān"tē) *n.* the authority one state has over another.

swallet (swŏl'ət) *n.* an underground stream discovered by miners.

swan-upping (swŏn'ŭp"ĭng) *n.* the annual inspection and marking of the royal swans of the Thames.

swaraj (swə-rŏj') *n.* political independence; national self-government (India).

swartwouter (swôrt'wout"ər) *n.* an embezzler who flees.

sweetsop (swēt'sŏp) *n.* a tropical American tree or its fruit.

sweetwort (swēt'wûrt) *n.* a sweet *wort*, which see.

swelp (swělp) *n.* a perennial complainer (from "so help [me God]").

swillbowl (swĭl'bōl) *n.* a drunk.

syagush (syŏ'gōōsh) *n.* Persian-lamb fur; broadtail.

sybarite (sĭb'ər-īt) *n.* someone overly fond of luxury and pleasure.

sybilline (sĭb'ĭl-īn) *adj.* mysterious; like a prophet.

sycomancy (sī'kō-măn"sē) *n.* fortunetelling with figs.

symphoric (sĭm-fôr'ĭk) *adj.* accident prone.

symposiarch (sĭm-pō'zĭ-ŏrk) *n.* a master of ceremonies.

synallagmatic (sĭn"əl-ăg-măt'ĭk) *adj.* bilateral.

syncope (sĭng'kō-pē) *n.* fainting.

syncretism (sĭng'krə-tĭz"əm) *n.* 1. the union of conflicting religious beliefs. 2. uncritical acceptance of conflicting beliefs.

synecdoche (sĭn-ĕk'dō-kē) *n.* a figure of speech substituting a more general term for a less general one or vice versa.

synergism (sĭn'ər-jĭz"əm) *n.* working together.

synesthesia (sĭn-ĕs-thē'zĭ-ə) *n.* condition in which stimulus to one sense produces a reaction to another sense (attributing colors to sounds, for instance).

syngenesophobia (sĭn"jən-ĕs-ō-fō'bĭ-ə) *n.* fear or dislike of relatives.

synodite (sĭn'ə-dīt) *n.* friend or companion.

synomosy (sĭn-ŏm'ə-sē) *n.* a political association.

synonymicon (sĭn-ō-nĭm'ĭ-kŏn) *n.* a synonym dictionary.

syntomy (sĭn'tō-mē) *n.* brevity.

syntropic (sĭn-trŏp'ĭk) *adj.* 1. turning or pointing in the same direction. 2. pertaining to a well-balanced, socially mature personality; also *koinotropic.*

syrt (sûrt) *n.* quicksand.

syssitia (sĭ-sĭsh'ĭ-ə) *n.* the practice among some Spartans and Cretans of eating with the electorate for political expediency.

syzygy (sĭz'ĭ-jē) *n.* 1. a relation between the fundamental concomitants of one or more binary forms (mathematics). 2. the point of an orbit at which the planet is in conjunction or opposition (astronomy).

szopelka (sō-pèl'kə) *n.* a Russian oboe with a brass mouthpiece.

tabefy (tàb′ə-fī) *v.t.&i.* to waste away gradually.

tablature (tàb′lə-chər) *n.* 1. an old musical notation that showed how to produce the note rather than indicating its sound. 2. a painting on a tablet; a mental image from description or memory.

tache (tàch) *n.* a bad habit; a fault. *-v.t.* to mar one's reputation. *-n.* 1. a bond, tie. 2. an evaporating pan used in sugar making.

tachydidaxy (tàk′ĭ-dĭ-dàk″sē) *n.* fast teaching.

tachygraphy (tàk-ĭg′rə-fē) *n.* shorthand, stenography.

tachyphrasia (tàk-ĭ-frā′zĭ-ə) *n.* extremely fluent or voluble speech, sometimes indicating emotional disturbance. *tachylalia,* *n.* fast talking.

taeniafuge (tēn′ĭ-ə-fūj″) *n.* a medicine for expelling tapeworms.

talaria (tə-lèr′ĭ-ə) *n.pl.* the winged shoes worn by Mercury.

taligrade (tàl′ĭ-grād) *adj.* walking on the outer side of the foot, as does the great anteater.

talionic (tàl-ĭ-òn′ĭk) *adj.* pertaining to revenge in kind ("an eye for an eye . . . ").

tangantangan (tòng-òn-tòng′ôn) *n.* the castor-oil plant.

tangatanga (tăng-gə-tăng′gə) *n.* the Peruvian trinity of *Pachama, Virakotcha,* and *Mamakotcha.*

tangram (tàn′gràm) *n.* a square cut into seven pieces to be reassembled in different figures (Chinese toy).

taniwha (tòn′ē-hwò) *n.* a Maori monster.

tanquam (tàn′kwàm) *n.* someone educated enough to go to college.

tantivy (tàn-tĭv′ē) *adv.* quickly, headlong. *-adj.* fast. *-n.* 1. a fast ride. 2. a signal for "full speed ahead" in hunting.

taphephobia (tàf-ə-fō′bĭ-ə) *n.* fear of being buried alive; fear of cemeteries.

taphophilia (tàf-ō-fĭl′ĭ-ə) *n.* love of funerals.

tapinophobia (tàp″ĭn-ō-fō′bĭ-ə) *n.* fear of being contagious.

tapster (tàp′stər) *n.* a bartender.

tarantism (tàr′ən-tĭz″əm) *n.* dancing epidemic thought to have

---

been caused by a tarantula bite.

tarassis (tər-às'is) *n.* male hysteria.

tarbooshed (tòr'bōōsht) *adj.* wearing a *tarboosh*, or red felt Turkish hat.

tardigrade (tòr'dĭ-grād) *adj.* slow-moving, sluggish.

tare (tèr) *n.* 1. in weighing, the allowance made for the weight of the container. 2. the bitter vetch. 3. a counterweight. 4. soil clinging to sugar beets.

tarfu (tòr'fōō) *adj.* Things Are *Really* Fucked-Up (army slang, for more of the same, see *snafu*).

tarn (tòrn) *n.* a small mountain lake.

tarsiatura (tòr"sĭ-ə-tōōr'ə) *n.* a kind of mosaic woodwork. also *tarsia*.

tartuffish (tòr-tōōf'ĭsh) *adj.* pertaining to the pious hypocrisy of *Tartuffe*, the protagonist in Molière's play by the same name.

tath (tàth) *n.* cattle dung; grass growing near cattle dung. -*v.t.* to fertilize by pasturing cattle.

tathagatagarbha (tà-tö"gə-tà-gûr'bə) *n.* the eternal and absolute essence of all reality according to Buddhism.

tattogey (tàt'ə-jē) *n.* a user of loaded dice (British slang).

tauromachian (tòr-ō-mā'kĭ-ən) *adj.* pertaining to bullfights. -*n.* a bullfighter.

tautegorical (tôt-ə-gôr'ĭ-kəl) *adj.* saying the same thing with different words. opposite of *allegorical*.

tautoousious (tôt-ō-ou'sĭ-əs) *adj.* being absolutely the same.

taxonomy (tàks-òn'ə-mē) *n.* the science of classification.

technophobia (tèk-nō-fō'bĭ-ə) *n.* fear or dislike of arts and crafts.

tecnogonia (tèk-nō-gō'nĭ-ə) *n.* childbearing.

tectiform (tèk'tĭ-fôrm) *adj.* roof-like; used as a cover. -*n.* tent-shaped designs on paleolithic cave walls.

ted (tèd) *v.t.* 1. to put a serrated edge on. 2. to spread for drying. 3. to spread out, scatter, or to waste (figuratively).

tedesco (tèd-ès'kō) *adj.* Germanic, especially German influence on Italian art.

teetertail (tē'tər-tāl) *n.* the spotted sandpiper.

teetotum (tē-tō'təm) *n.* 1. a toplike toy. 2. a small thing or person. 3. something that spins like a top. -*v.i.* to spin like a top.

teknonymy (tèk-nòn'ĭ-mē) *n.* naming the parent after the child.

tektite (tèk'tīt) *n.* a greenish-brown glasslike stone thought to be meteoric.

telamnesia (tèl-àm-nē'žə) *n.* poor memory for events long past.

telamon (tèl'ə-mòn) *n.* a male *caryatid* (which see).

telarian (tèl-èr'ĭ-ən) *adj.* spinning a web. -*n.* a web-making spider.

telegenic (tèl-ə-jèn'ĭk) *adj.* suitable for televising.

telegnosis (tèl-èg-nō'sĭs) *n.* alleged occult knowledge of distant events.

telekinesis (tèl"ə-kĭn-ē'sĭs) *n.* in which objects seem to move by spiritualistic fiat.

teleology (tèl-ē-òl'ə-jē) *n.* the "fact" of design in nature.

teleophobia (tèl"ē-ō-fō'bĭ-ə) *n.* 1. fear of definite plans. 2. fear and dislike of religious ceremony.

telephanous (tèl-èf'ən-əs) *adj.* visible afar.

telepheme (tèl'ə-fēm) *n.* a telephone message.

telestich (tèl-ès'tĭk) *n.* a poem in which the consecutive final letters of the lines spell a name.

tellurian (těl-yûr'ĭ-ən) *adj*. pertaining to or characteristic of the earth. -*n*. someone who lives on earth.

telmatology (těl-mə-tŏl'ə-jē) *n*. the study of peat bogs.

temblor (těm-blôr') *n*. an earthquake.

temerarious (těm-ər-êr'ĭ-əs) *adj*. rash, headstrong, reckless.

tempean (těm-pē'ən) *adj*. beautiful and charming (from *Tempe*, a beautiful and charming Greek valley).

temulence (těm'ū-ləns) *n*. drunkenness.

tenebrific (těn-ə-brĭf'ĭk) *adj*. making *tenebrous*: dark or obscure.

tenesmic (těn-ěz'mĭk) *adj*. pertaining to *tenesmus*, a painful but ineffectual effort to urinate or defecate.

tentiginous (těn-tĭj'ĭn-əs) *adj*. 1. sensuous, lascivious. 2. stiff or strained.

tephramancy (těf'rə-măn″sē) *n*. fortunetelling with ashes from an altar.

tephrosis (těf-rō'sĭs) *n*. incineration.

tepidarium (těp-ĭ-děr'ĭ-əm) *n*. a warm room in a bath, halfway between the *frigidarium* and the *caldarium*.

teratology (těr-ə-tŏl'ə-jē) *n*. the study of monsters.

teratophobia (těr″ə-tō-fō'bĭ-ə) *n*. fear of bearing a deformed child.

teratoscopy (těr-ə-tŏs'kō-pē) *n*. fortunetelling with monsters.

terdiurnal (tûr-dī-ûr'nəl) *adj*. three times a day.

terebinthine (těr-ə-bĭn'thĭn) *adj*. pertaining to or consisting of turpentine. -*n*. turpentine.

terebration (těr-ə-brā'shən) *n*. boring or drilling.

tergiversation (tûr″jĭv-ər-sā'shən) *n*. abandoning a religion or cause; equivocation.

termagant (tûr'mə-gənt) *n*. a quarrelsome, scolding, loud woman; a virago. also *adj*.

termitarium (tûr-mĭ-těr'ĭ-əm) *n*. a termites' nest.

termor (tûr'mər) *n*. someone with an estate for a certain number of years (law).

terp (tûrp) *n*. a mound covering the site of a prehistoric settlement.

terpsichorean (tûrp″sĭ-kôr-ē'ən) *adj*. pertaining to dancing. -*n*. dancer.

terraculture (těr'ə-kŭl″chər) *n*. agriculture.

terraqueous (těr-ăk'wē-əs) *adj*. consisting of land and water; living in or extending over land and water.

tersion (tûr'shən) *n*. cleaning by rubbing.

tessaradecad (těs″ər-ə-děk'əd) *n*. a group of fourteen.

tessaraglot (těs'ər-ə-glŏt″) *n*. a person who speaks four languages. -*adj*. pertaining to or written in four languages.

tesselatted (těs'ə-lăt″əd) *adj*. made of glass or ceramic tiles arranged in mosaic patterns; marked like a checkerboard.

testaceous (těs-tā'shəs) *adj*. 1. pertaining to shells; having a hard shell. 2. ceramic. 3. brick-red or brownish-yellow.

testudineous (těs-tōō-dĭn'ē-əs) *adj*. slow, like a tortoise.

tête-bêche (tět-běsh') *adj*. pertaining to a pair of stamps, inverted in relation to each other (which may or may not be intentional).

tetnit (tět'nĭt) *n*. a child born of

---

màn; māde; lět; bē; sĭp; wīne; hŏt; cōld; sôre; dŭll; fūgue; bûrp; gōōd; fōōd; out; gět; thin; this; year; aźure; ō'mən″; viN; fūr; Bach elderly parents (slang).

tetragram (tĕt'rə-grăm) *n.* a word of four letters. 2. a quadrilateral.

Tetragrammation (tĕt-rə-grăm'ə-tŏn) *n.* YHWH (or variants with J and V substituted for Y and W), old Hebrew word for God, pronunciation of which is not known, but which probably sounded something like *Yahweh.*

tetralogy (tĕt-răl'ə-jē) *n.* 1. three tragedies and a comedy presented at the Dionysiac festival. 2. any series of four dramas or operas.

tetraskelion (tĕt-răs-kĕl'ĭ-ən) *n.* the swastika, or swastikalike figure.

tetricity (tĕt-rĭs'ĭ-tē) *n.* austerity, harshness, gloominess.

teutophobia (tōō-tō-fō'bĭ-ə) *n.* fear and dislike of Germans or German things.

textorial (tĕks-tôr'ĭ-əl) *adj.* pertaining to weaving.

thalassophobia (thə-lăs″ō-fō'bĭ-ə) *n.* fear of the sea.

thalassotherapy (thə-lăs″ō-thĕr'ə-pē) *n.* an ocean cruise as therapy.

thalian (thə-lī'ən) *adj.* pertaining to comedy; comic.

thalpotic (thăl-pŏt'ĭk) *adj.* pertaining to the sensation of warmth.

thalthan (tŏl'thən) *n.* a dilapidated cottage.

thanatism (thăn'ə-tĭz″əm) *n.* the belief in life before death, not after it.

thanatoid (thăn'ə-toid) *adj.* deathlike, deadly.

thanatomania (thăn″ə-tō-mā'nĭ-ə) *n.* suicidal mania; death by autosuggestion.

thanatophobia (thăn″ə-tō-fō'bĭ-ə) *n.* fear of death or of dying.

tharm (thŏrm) *n.* an intestine; the belly; catgut.

thaumaturgist (thôm'ə-tûr″jĭst) *n.*

a wonder-worker; a magician.

theanthropism (thē-ăn'thrō-pĭz″əm) *n.* attaching human traits to one's god; anthropomorphism.

thelymachy (thĕl-ĭm'ə-kē) *n.* a war of women.

thelyphthoric (thĕl-ĭf-thôr'ĭk) *adj.* that which corrupts women.

thelytokous (thĕl-ĭt'ō-kəs) *adj.* producing females only.

theologicophobia (thē-ō-lŏj″ĭ-kō-fō'bĭ-ə) *n.* fear and dislike of theology.

theologoumenon (thē″ō-lō-gōō'mən-ŏn) *n.* an epithet for The Almighty One.

theomachist (thē-ŏm'ə-kĭst) *n.* someone who opposes divinity.

theomicrist (thē-ŏm'ĭ-krĭst) *n.* someone who makes fun of Yahweh.

theophagy (thē-ŏf'ə-jē) *n.* the practice of ritual god-eating; communion.

theophobia (thē-ō-fō'bĭ-ə) *n.* fear or dislike of gods or religion.

therapistia (thĕr-ə-pĭs'tĭ-ə) *n.* a medical nonbeliever. see *iatrapistia.*

theriacal (thĕr-ī'ə-kəl) *adj.* medicinal. also *therial.*

therianthropic (thĕr″ĭ-ăn-thrŏp'ĭk) *adj.* combining human and animal form, as the centaur.

theriomancy (thĕr'ĭ-ō-măn″sē) *n.* fortunetelling by watching wild animals.

theriomimicry (thĕr″ĭ-ō-mĭm'ĭk-rē) *n.* imitation of animal behavior.

thermoplegia (thûr-mō-plē'jĭ-ə) *n.* sunstroke.

therology (thĕr-ŏl'ə-jē) *n.* mammalogy.

thersitical (thûr-sĭt'ĭ-kəl) *adj.* loudmouthed; scurrilous.

thesmothete (thĕs'mō-thĕt) *n.* a

lawgiver, a legislator.

thestreen (thĕs-trēn′) *adv.* last night.

thetical (thĕt′ĭ-kəl) *adj.* arbitrary; prescribed; laid down; positive.

theurgy (thē′ûr-jē) *n.* alleged supernatural intervention in earthly affairs.

thigging (thĭg′ĭng) *n.* begging or borrowing.

thimblerig (thĭm′bəl-rĭg) *n.* a gambler's sleight-of-hand game played with three small cups, shaped like thimbles, and a small ball or pea; the shell game.

thingus (thĭn′gŭs) *n.* in Saxon law, a thane, nobleman, knight, or freeman.

thirl (thûrl) *v.t.* 1. to pierce or perforate. 2. to make vibrate. 3. to enslave. -*v.i.* to pierce or vibrate. -*n.* a perforation or opening. -*adj.* gaunt, thin, shriveled.

thob (thŏb) *v.i.* to rationalize one's opinions or beliefs (from THink + Opinion + Believe).

thoke (thōk) *v.i.* to lie in bed; idle.

Thomist (tŏm′ĭst) *n.* a disciple of Thomas Aquinas or his philosophy.

thralldom (thrôl′dŭm) *n.* moral, mental, or physical servitude.

thrasonical (thră-sŏn′ĭ-kəl) *adj.* bragging, boastful.

thremmatology (thrĕm-ə-tŏl′ə-jē) *n.* the science of breeding.

threnody (thrĕn′ō-dē) *n.* a funeral song or dirge. -*v.t.* to lament in a dirge.

threpsology (thrĕp-sŏl′ə-jē) *n.* the science of nutrition.

threpterophilia (thrĕp″tər-ō-fĭl′ĭ-ə) *n.* a fondness for female nurses.

thrimble (thrĭm′bəl) *v.t.&i.* to handle in order to test quality; to hesitate, fumble; to squeeze.

thrion (thrē′ŏn) *n.* the fig-leaf garb

of Adam and Eve.

thropple (thrŏp′əl) *n.* the throat or windpipe. -*v.t.* to throttle.

thwaite (thwāt) *n.* forest land cleared and converted to tillage; a piece of land used as a meadow.

thwertnick (thwĕrt′nĭk) *n.* entertaining a sheriff for three nights, according to old English law.

thygatrilagnia (thī-găt″rĭ-lăg′nĭ-ə) *n.* a father's sexual love for his daughter.

tid (tĭd) *n.* 1. the right time or season. 2. mood. -*v.t.* to time. -*adj.* 1. affectionate; fond. 2. lively or silly.

tiddledies (tĭd′əl-dēz) *n.pl.* chunks of floating ice.

tiffin (tĭf′ĭn) *n.* a snack or light lunch.

tikolosh (tĭk′ō-lŏsh) *n.* a South African water elf.

tilikum (tĭl′ĭ-kəm) *n.pl.* Chinook term for Indian commoners.

timbal (tĭm′bəl) *n.* 1. the kettledrum. 2. the vibrating membrane in the shrilling organ of the cicada.

timbrology (tĭm-brŏl′ə-jē) *n.* the study of postage stamps; philately.

timoneer (tī-mən-ĭr′) *n.* helmsman.

timonism (tī′mən-ĭz″əm) *n.* misanthropy.

tinchel (tĭn′kəl) *n.* a ring formed by hunters to trap deer. also *tinchill.*

tinctorial (tĭnk-tôr′ĭ-əl) *adj.* pertaining to dyeing; coloring.

tinnitus (tĭn′ĭ-təs) *n.* a ringing or buzzing in the ears.

tintamarre (tĭn-tə-môr′) *n.* an uproar; a huge din.

tintinnabulation (tĭn″tĭn-ăb-ū-lā′shən) *n.* a ringing sound (from Poe's *The Bells*).

tirl (tûrl) *v.t.&i.* 1. to pluck a

string; to vibrate. 2. to peel. 3. to twirl. 4. to rattle. -*n.* 1. vibration. 2. something that revolves. 3. a rattle. 4. a drinking bout. 5. a fling at dancing.

tirocinium (tĭr-ō-sĭn'ĭ-əm) *n.* 1. a soldier's first battle. 2. a group of raw recruits.

tittup (tĭt'ŭp) *n.* lively or restless behavior. -*v.i.* to move in such a manner; to jump around.

titubation (tĭt-ū-bā'shən) *n.* a lurching staggering gait resulting from a spinal lesion.

tjaele (chä'lē) *n.* permafrost.

tjanting (chònt'ĭng) *n.* a Javanese tool for applying hot wax in batik work.

tlaco (tlŏ'kō) *n.* a small nineteenth-century Mexican coin worth one eighth of a *real* (Náhuatl).

tmema (tə-mē'mə) *n.* a section, piece, or segment.

tmesis (tə-mē'sĭs) *n.* the separation of a compound word by insertion of one or more words.

tnoyim (tən-ô'yĭm) *n.* a Jewish engagement party; marital agreements made there.

toatoa (tō'ə-tō"ə) *n.* a New Zealand tree with whorled branches.

tocology (tō-kŏl'ə-jē) *n.* obstetrics; midwifery.

tocophobia (tō-kō-fō'bĭ-ə) *n.* fear of pregnancy or childbirth.

toddick (tŏd'ĭk) *n.* a very small quantity.

toft (tôft) *n.* a building site.

togated (tō'gāt"əd) *adj.* wrapped in a toga; robed; dignified.

togue (tōg) *n.* the namaycush (probably from the Micmac or the Passamaquoddy).

tohubohu (tō'hōō-bō"hōō) *n.* chaos; confusion (Hebrew = formless).

toison (twȯ-zôN') *n.* lamb's wool.

tolly (tŏl'ē) *v.i.* to light candles after hours (British school slang).

tolutiloquence (tŏl-ū-tĭl'ō-kwəns) *n.* glib, fluent speech.

tomalley (tŏm'ăl"ē) *n.* lobster liver that turns green when boiled.

tombolo (tŏm'bə-lō) *n.* a sand bar or reef connecting an island to the mainland.

tomelet (tŏm'lət) *n.* a small book or tome.

tomentose (tō-mĕn'tōs) *adj.* covered with densely matted hair.

tomomania (tō-mō-mā'nĭ-ə) *n.* a mania for undergoing surgery.

tonguepad (tŭng'pàd) *v.t.&i.* to scold.

tongueshot (tŭng'shŏt) *n.* vocal range.

tonitrophobia (tŏn"ĭ-trō-fō'bĭ-ə) *n.* fear of thunder.

tonitruous (tō-nĭt'rōō-ùs) *adj.* thundering, exploding.

tonnish (tŏn'ĭsh) *adj.* fashionable, chic. also *tonish.*

tonsure (tŏn'shər) *v.t.* to shave the head.

tontine (tŏn'tēn) *n.* a group of beneficiaries who are each beneficiaries of the other, until the last survivor gets the lot.

toom (tōōm) *adj.* 1. empty. 2. stupid; empty-sounding. -*v.t.* to pour. -*n.* 1. a dumping ground. 2. leisure; spare time.

tootlish (tōōt'lĭsh) *adj.* childish; muttering, as an old man.

tophaceous (tō-fā'shəs) *adj.* sandy or gritty; rough.

topiary (tō'pĭ-èr"ē) *adj.* pertaining to tree pruning.

topinambou (tŏp-ĭn-ăm'bōō) *n.* the Jerusalem artichoke.

topolatry (tō-pŏl'ə-trē) *n.* worship of a place.

topomancy (tŏp'ō-màn"sē) *n.* fortunetelling by the contour of the

---

măn; māde; lĕt; bē; sĭp; wīne; hòt; cōld; sôre; dŭll; fūgue; bûrp; gōōd; fōōd; out; gĕt; thin; this; year; azure; ō'mən"; viN; für; Bach

land.

toponymics (tŏp-ō-nĭm′ĭks) *n.* the etymology of place names or place-derived family names.

topohobia (tŏp-ō-fō′bĭ-ə) *n.* fear of certain places.

topopolitan (tŏp-ō-pŏl′ĭ-tən) *adj.* limited to a certain area; opposed to *cosmopolitan.*

torcular (tôr′kū-lər) *n.* a wine press.

torii (tôr′ē-ē) *n.* a Japanese gateway.

toril (tôr-ēl′) *n.* a corral from which the bull enters the bullring.

torminous (tôr′mĭn-əs) *adj.* pertaining to or affected with acute, colicky pain.

torose (tôr′ōs) *adj.* muscular. also *tortulous, torulose.*

torpillage (tôr-pē-yŏz̧′) *n.* electric shock therapy.

torquated (tôrk′wät″əd) *adj.* having, wearing, or formed like a twisted chain.

torrefy (tôr′ə-fī) *v.t.* to dry or roast; to scorch.

torticollis (tôr-tĭ-kŏl′ĭs) *n.* wryneck; stiff neck.

tortious (tôr′shəs) *adj.* pertaining to a *tort:* a personal or civil wrong or injury.

toshence (tŏsh′əns) *n.* the youngest child; *torsh, tortience* (colloquial).

tossut (tŏs′ət) *n.* an igloo tunnel.

totipalmate (tō-tĭ-păl′māt) *adj.* web-footed.

totipotence (tō-tĭp′ō-təns) *n.* omnipotence.

tourbillion (to͞or-bĭl′yən) *n.* something which moves spirally: a whirlwind, vortex, or whirlpool; spiral fireworks.

tournure (to͞or-nyo͞or′) *n.* 1. graceful or elegant bearing; poise. 2. contour, outline. 3. expressiveness. 4. a bustle.

towdie (tou′dē) *n.* 1. a hen that hasn't laid. 2. a virgin Scottish lass.

toxophily (tŏks-ŏf′ĭl-ē) *n.* love of archery.

tractate (trăk′tāt) *n.* dissertation. *pl.* negotiations.

tractile (trăk′tĭl) *adj.* capable of being stretched out; ductile.

tragicomipastoral (trăj″ĭ-kŏm-ĭ-păs′tôr-əl) *adj.* pertaining to pastoral tragicomic poetry.

tragomaschalia (trăg″ō-măs-kăl′ĭ-ə) *n.* smelly armpits.

traiteur (trĕt-ûr′) *n.* a restaurateur.

tralatitiously (trăl-ə-tĭsh′əs-lē) *adv.* metaphorically; figuratively.

tramontane (trăm-ŏn′tān) *adj.* 1. coming from the other side of the mountains. 2. foreign, barbarous.

transfeminate (trănz-fĕm′ĭn-āt) *v.t.* to change from woman to man.

transfuge (trănz-fūj′) *n.* a deserter; an apostate.

transilient (trăn-sĭl′ĭ-ənt) *adj.* pertaining to abrupt changes.

transmogrify (trănz-mŏg′rĭ-fī) *v.t.* to change into a strange or absurd form. *transmogrification, n.*

transpadane (trăn′spə-dān) *adj.* north of the Po. opposite of *cispadane* (if you're in Rome).

transpontine (trănz-pŏn′tĭn) *adj.* 1. south of the Thames. 2. pertaining to tawdry theater once performed in London, south of the Thames.

transumption (trănz-ùmp′shən) *n.* a metaphor.

transuranic (trănz-yo͞or-ăn′ĭk) *adj.* having an atomic number greater than that of uranium, which is number ninety-two.

transvase (trănz-vās′) *v.t.* to pour out of one container into another.

trapezium (trăp-ēz′ĭ-om) *n.* a quadrilateral without parallel sides.

---

traulism (trôl'ĭz"əm) *n.* stuttering.

traumatophobia (trôm"ə-tō-fō-bĭ-ə) *n.* fear of injury.

travale (trǎ-vǎl') *n.* rubbing a tambourine with a wet thumb; the sound produced.

trave (trāv) *n.* 1. a crossbeam. 2. a frame to confine a restless horse while shoeing.

trebuchet (trĕb'ŏŏ-shĕt) *n.* 1. a stone-throwing machine of the Middle Ages. 2. a cucking stool. 3. a small scale.

trefoil (trē'foil) *n.* 1. a cloverleaf; any three-lobed flower or leaf. 2. a group of three closely related units.

tregetour (trĕj'ə-tûr) *n.* a magician or juggler.

treillage (trā'əj) *n.* latticework for supporting vines; an espalier or trellis.

tremellose (trĕm'əl-ōs) *adj.* gelatinous.

trencherman (trĕnch'ər-mən) *n.* 1. a hearty eater; a glutton. 2. a cook. 3. a freeloader.

trenchermate (trĕnch'ər-māt) *n.* an eating companion; a *messmate*.

trental (trĕn'təl) *n.* a series of thirty masses for the dead, celebrated once a day for thirty days.

trepan (trē-pǎn') *n.* 1. a cylindrical saw for perforating the skull, turned like a bit. 2. a heavy tool used in boring shafts. -*v.t.* 1. to perforate [the skull] in order to remove a piece of the bone. 2. to cut a disk out of.

trephine (trē-fīn') *n.* an improvement on the *trepan.* -*v.t.* to *trepan.*

tresayle (trĕs'īl) *n.* a grandfather's grandfather. 2. an heir's litigation to recover her *tresayle's* estate.

tret (trĕt) *n.* money back to buyers of goods damaged in transit.

tribadism (trĭb'əd-ĭz"əm) *n.* mutual genital-fondling between lesbians.

tricerion (trī-sĭr'ĭ-ən) *n.* a three-branched candlestick symbolizing the Trinity.

trichotillomania (trĭk"ō-tĭl-ō-mā'nĭ-ə) *n.* mania for pulling out one's hair. also *trichologia, carphology.*

triclinium (trī-klĭn'ĭ-əm) *n.* 1. a three-sided sectional couch for dining. 2. a dining room furnished with such a couch.

triheens (trī'hēnz) *n.* a pair of stockings with the feet cut out.

trilapse (trī'lǎps) *n.* a third downfall, *relapse* being the second.

trillibub (trĭl'ĭ-bŭb) *n.* a trifle.

trimenon (trī-mĕn'ən) *n.* a three-month period.

trimetrogon (trī-mĕt'rə-gŏn) *n.* a system of aerial mapping.

Trimurti (trĭm-ŏŏr'tē) *n.* the trinity of *Brahma* (the creator), *Vishnu* (the preserver), and *Siva* (the destroyer) in Hinduism.

trinkgeld (trĭnk'gĕlt) *n.* a tip. literally drink money.

triphibious (trī-fĭb'ĭ-əs) *adj.* capable of operating on land, sea, and air.

triplasian (trī-plā'žən) *adj.* three.

triptych (trĭp'tĭk) *n.* 1. a three-paneled picture or carving, sometimes used as an altarpiece. 2. a folding three-sectioned writing table.

triptyque (trēp'tēk) *n.* a customs pass for the temporary importation of a car.

tripudiary (trī-pū'dĭ-ĕr"ē) *adj.* pertaining to dancing.

triskadekaphobia (trĭs"kə-dĕk-ə-fō'bĭ-ə) *n.* fear of the number thirteen.

tristiloquy (trĭs-tĭl'ə-kwē) *n.* dull,

gloomy speech.

tritagonist (trī-tàg′ən-ĭst) *n.* third-ranked actor in ancient Greek plays.

tritavia (trĭt′ə-vē″ə) *n.* a great-grandmother's great-grand-mother.

tritavus (trĭt′ə-vŭs) *n.* a great-grandfather's great-grandfather.

triune (trī′ūn) *n.* three-in-one; a triad: used especially in reference to the Trinity of Christian legend.

Trknmli (tûrk′ən-mə-lē″) *n.* an extinct language of Asia Minor.

troat (trōt) *v.t.* to cry out like a rutting buck.

trochilics (trō-kĭl′ĭks) *n.* the science of rotary motion, or wheelwork.

trochlear (trŏk′lē-ər) *adj.* pulley-shaped; round and narrow in the middle, like a pulley wheel.

trochomancy (trŏk′ō-màn″sē) *n.* fortunetelling by wheel tracks.

troglodyte (trŏg′lō-dīt) *n.* 1. a cave dweller; like a cave dweller. 2. an anthropoid ape.

troilism (troil′ĭz″əm) *n.* sex à trois.

troke (trōk) *v.t.&i.* to barter; to negotiate. -*n.* a bargain or business deal.

trollylolly (trŏl′ē-lòl″ē) *n.* coarse lace.

trophic (trŏf′ĭk) *adj.* pertaining to nutrition.

tropoclastics (trō-pō-klàs′tĭks) *n.* the science of habit breaking.

tropodeics (trō-pō-dē′ĭks) *n.* the study of habit formation.

tropophilous (trō-pŏf′ĭl-əs) *adj.* adapted to seasonal changes of temperature or humidity.

tropophobia (trŏp-ō-fō′bĭ-ə) *n.* fear of making changes.

trucidation (trōō-sī-dā′shən) *n.* brutal slaughter.

truckle (trŭk′əl) *v.i.* to submit, knuckle under.

trutinate (trōō′tĭn-āt) *v.t.* to weigh, balance, consider. *trutination, n.*

truttaceous (trŭt-ā′shəs) *adj.* pertaining to a trout.

tsantsa (tsòn′tsə) *n.* a Jivaro shrunken head.

tsiology (tsĭ-ŏl′ə-jē) *n.* a dissertation on tea.

tsuba (tsōō′bə) *n.* the metal guard on a Japanese sword, often elaborately decorated.

tsunami (tsōō-nò′mē) *n.* a tidal wave caused by earthquakes or eruptions.

tsutsugamushi (tsōō-tsōō′gò-mōō″shē) *n.* a disease like Rocky Mountain spotted fever; also called Japanese river fever.

tubicinate (tū-bĭs′ĭn-āt) *v.i.* to play a trumpet.

tucket (tŭk′ət) *n.* a trumpet fanfare. -*n.* an unripe ear of Indian corn.

tucky (tŭk′ē) *n.* the common spatterdash.

tumbrel (tŭm′brəl) *n.* 1. a farmer's manure cart used for bringing victims to the guillotine. 2. a manure cart in general. 3. a cucking stool.

tumtum (tŭm′tŭm) *n.* a dogcart; a West Indian dish of boiled and beaten plantains. -*v.i.* to strum.

tumulate (tùm′ū-lāt) *v.t.* to entomb.

tupman (tŭp′mən) *n.* a ram breeder.

turbary (tûr′bə-rē) *n.* an easement to dig turf on another's land; the ground where turf is dug.

turbinate (tûr′bĭn-āt) *adj.* 1. shaped like a top. 2. spiraled, like some shells.

turdefy (tûrd′ə-fī) *v.t.* to turn into a turd.

turnverein (tûrn′və-rīn) *n.* a gymnastic club.

---

mān; māde; lĕt; bē; sĭp; wīne; hŏt; cōld; sôre; dŭll; fūgue; bûrp; gŏŏd; fōōd; out; gĕt; thin; this; year; aźure; ŏ′mən″; viN; fûr; Bach

turpitude (tûr'pĭ-tōōd) *n.* degeneracy, corruption, infamy, and depravity.

tussive (tŭs'ĭv) *adj.* pertaining to or caused by a cough.

tuzzimuzzy (tŭz'ē-mŭz"ē) *n.* a nosegay; the feather-hyacinth. *-adj.* rough or disheveled.

twaddleize (twŏd'əl-īz) *v.t.* to twaddle; to talk in a silly manner; to prattle, gabble.

twibil (twī'bĭl) *n.* a battle-ax with two cutting edges. also *twibill.*

twiddlepoop (twĭd'əl-pōōp) *n.* an effeminate-looking man.

twitchel (twĭch'əl) *n.* a path between hedges.

tychastics (tī-kàs'tĭks) *n.* science of industrial accidents.

tychism (tī'kĭz"əm) *n.* a theory of evolution which considers variation purely fortuitous.

tycolysis (tī-kŏl'ĭ-sĭs) *n.* accident prevention.

tyg (tĭg) *n.* a large ceramic seventeenth-century drinking mug with twelve handles.

typp (tĭp) *n.* the number of thousands of yards of yarn weighing one pound (Thousand Yards Per Pound).

typtology (tĭp-tŏl'ə-jē) *n.* the study of legendary spiritualistic "rappings."

tyromancy (tī'rō-màn"sē) *n.* fortunetelling by watching cheese coagulate.

tzigane (tsē-gŏn') *n.* a Hungarian gypsy.

U

uakari (wȯ-kȯr′ē) *n.* a kind of short-tailed monkey.

uayeb (wȯ-yèb′) *n.* the five days added at the end of each year to the Mayan calendar.

ubermensch (ū′bûr-mènsh) *n.* superman.

uberty (ū′bûr-tē) *n.* fruitfulness; plenty.

ubiety (ū-bī′ə-tē) *n.* placement, position, locale; being in a certain place.

udometer (ū-dòm′ə-tûr) *n.* a rain gauge.

ugglesome (ùg′əl-sŭm) *adj.* horrible, frightful.

ughten (ŭt′ən) *n.* morning twilight.

uglification (ùg″lĭ-fĭ-kā′shən) *n.* making ugly.

uhlan (ōō′lòn) *n.* a German cavalryman. also *ulan.*

uitlander (oit′lòn″dər) *n.* a foreigner (once used for Britons in South African colonies).

ukase (ū-kās′) *n.* any official decree or proclamation.

ulcuscule (ùl-kŭs′kūl) *n.* a little ulcer.

ulema (ōō-lə-mò′) *n.* a group of Moslem authorities on religion and law.

uletic (ū-lèt′ĭk) *adj.* pertaining to the gums.

uliginose (ū-lĭj′ĭn-ōs) *adj.* muddy, swampy; growing in muddy places.

ullage (ū′əj) *n.* 1. the empty part of a partially filled liquor container. 2. liquor dregs.

uloid (ū′loid) *adj.* scarlike.

ulotrichous (ū-lòt′rĭk-əs) *adj.* having woolly hair.

ulster (ùl′stûr) *n.* a long Irish coat, originally made in Belfast, Ulster.

ultimogeniture (ùl″tĭm-ō-jèn′ĭ-chər) *n.* a system in which inheritance goes to the youngest child.

ultion (ùl′shən) *n.* revenge.

ultraantidisestablishmentarianism (ùl-tro-ànt″ĭ-dĭz-ès-tàb″lĭsh-mènt-èr′ĭ-ən-ĭz″əm) *n. antidisestablishmentarianism,* only more so (coined by Mr. Gladstone during a political speech at Edinburgh).

ultracrepidarian (ùl″tro-krèp-ĭ-dèr′ĭ-ən) *adj.* overstepping one's boundaries; presumptuous.

---

màn; māde; lèt; bē; sĭp; wīne; hȯt; cōld; sȯre; dùll; fūgue; bûrp; gŏŏd; fōōd; out; gèt; thin; thĭs; year; aźure; ō′mən″; viN; fūr; Bach

ultrafidian (ŭl-trə-fĭd′ĭ-ən) *adj.* ultracredulous; extremely gullible.

ultraism (ŭl′trə-ĭz″əm) *n.* extremism, radicalism.

ultramontanism (ŭl-trə-mŏn′tən-ĭz″əm) *n.* advocacy of papal supremacy.

ultramundane (ŭl-trə-mŭn′dān) *adj.* lying beyond this world.

ultroneous (ŭl-trō′nē-əs) *adj.* 1. spontaneous. 2. pertaining to a witness who testifies voluntarily.

ulua (ōō-lōō′ə) *n.* a large Hawaiian fish.

ululate (ŭl′ū-lāt) *v.i.* to howl or wail.

umbrageous (ŭm-brā′jəs) *adj.* 1. shaded. 2. obscure. 3. jealous, angry, or suspicious.

umiak (ōō′mĭ-ăk) *n.* a thirty-foot-long Eskimo boat.

umzumbit (ŭm-zŭm′bĭt) *n.* a South African tree or its wood.

unasinous (ū-năs′ĭn-əs) *adj.* equally stupid.

unau (ōō-nou′) *n.* the two-toed sloth.

unbe (ŭn-bē′) *v.t.* to stop being.

unca (ŭng′kə) *n.* an eighth note.

uncial (ŭn′shĭ-əl) *adj.* 1. capital, as in letter. 2. a twelfth part, as in inch.

uncinate (ŭn′sĭn-āt) *adj.* hooked.

unco (ŭng′kō) *adj.* 1. strange, odd. 2. shy or awkward. 3. extraordinary. *-adv.* remarkably, extremely. *-n.* something new or strange.

undercroft (ŭn′dər-krôft) *n.* an underground chapel; an underground room.

underfong (ŭn′dər-fông) *v.t.* 1. to decide to do. 2. to trap.

underspurleather (ŭn-dər-spûr′lĕt″h″ər) *n.* an underling; also *understrapper.*

undinism (ŭn′dĭn-ĭz″əm) *n.* the association of water with erotic thoughts.

unguiculate (ŭng-gwĭk′ū-lāt) *adj.* with hooks, nails, or claws.

unhouselled (ŭn-hou′zəld) *adj.* without getting the sacrament.

unicity (ū-nĭs′ĭ-tē) *n.* uniqueness.

unigeniture (ū-nĭ-jĕn′ĭ-chər) *n.* being the only child.

unigravida (ū-nĭ-grăv′ĭ-də) *n.* a woman's first pregnancy.

unmew (ŭn-mū′) *v.t.* to free.

unnun (ŭn-nŭn′) *v.t.* to defrock a nun.

unparagoned (ŭn-păr′ə-gŏnd) *adj.* without equal; peerless.

unscorified (ŭn-skôr′ĭ-fīd) *adj.* not formed into drops.

unsonsy (ŭn-sŏn′sē) *adj.* causing unhappiness, misfortune; unpleasant.

untrowable (ŭn-trō′ə-bəl) *adj.* incredible.

unwemmed (ŭn-wĕmd′) *adj.* unblemished.

upaithric (ū-pīth′rĭk) *adj.* see *hypaethral.*

upanga (ōō-pŏng′gə) *n.* a nose-flute.

upasian (ū-pā′zĭ-ən) *adj.* as deadly as the *upas* tree, source of arrow poison.

upeygan (ōō-pā′gən) *n.* the black rhinoceros.

uppowoc (ŭp-ō′wŏk) *n.* tobacco (American Indian).

uranic (yōōr-ăn′ĭk) *adj.* 1. pertaining to the upper atmosphere. 2. celestial. 3. pertaining to, or containing, uranium. 4. relating to the palate.

uranism (yōōr′ən-ĭz″əm) *n.* male homosexuality.

uranography (yōōr-ən-ŏg′rə-fē) *n.* description of the sky and stars; making celestial maps.

uranophobia (yōōr″ən-ō-fō′bĭ-ə) *n.*

fear of heaven.

urbicolous (ûr-bĭk'ō-ləs) *adj.* living in the city.

urimancy (yûr'ĭ-măn"sē) *n.* fortunetelling with urine.

urolagnia (yûr-ō-lăg'nĭ-ə) *n.* sexual pleasure from urinating.

ursal (ûr'səl) *adj.* boorish or bearish. *-n.* the fur seal.

urticate (ûr'tĭ-kāt) *v.t.&i.* to sting with nettles; to beat with a whip.

urubu (ōō'rə-bōō) *n.* the black vulture.

ushabti (ū-shăb'tē) *n.* a mummylike figure entombed with mummy for certain farm chores required in the next world.

usquebaugh (ŭs'kwē-bô) *n.* Irish or Scotch whiskey.

ustion (ŭs'chən) *n.* cauterization.

usufruct (ū'zōō-frŭkt) *n.* the right to use another's property while not changing or harming it. *usufructuary*, *n.* someone who

does this.

utfangenethef (ōōt-făng'ən-ə-thēf") *n.* see *outfangthefī*.

utlesse (ŭt'lĕs) *n.* a prison break.

uturuncu (ōō-tōō-rōō'kōō) *n.* a sorcerer in the shape of a jaguar, according to Quechuan legend.

uvate (ū'vāt) *n.* grape jam.

uvid (ū'vĭd) *adj.* moist or wet.

uxoravalent (ŭks-ôr'ə-vā'lənt) *adj.* [men] able to score only extramaritally. see *uxorovalent*.

uxoricide (ŭks-ôr'ĭ-sīd) *n.* wifemurder.

uxorious (ŭks-ôr'ĭ-əs) *adj.* doting on a wife.

uxorium (ŭks-ôr'ĭ-əm) *n.* a bachelor tax.

uxorodespotism (ŭks-ôr"ō-dĕs'pō-tĭz"əm) *n.* wifely tyranny.

uxorovalent (ŭks-ôr"ō-vā'lənt) *adj.* able to score only with one's wife. see *uxoravalent*.

V

vaccary (văk′ər-ē) *n.* a dairy or cow pasture.

vaccimulgence (văk-ĭ-mŭl′jəns) *n.* cow milking.

vade mecum (vā-dē-mē′kəm) *n.* a favorite book carried everywhere (Latin = go with me).

vagient (vā′jĭ-ənt) *adj.* crying like a child.

vagitus (văj-ī′təs) *n.* cry of the newborn.

valetudinarianism (văl″ə-tōŏd-ĭn-ĕr′ĭ-ən-ĭz″əm) *n.* weak or sickly state; thinking only of one's illness.

valgus (văl′gəs) *adj.* bowlegged or knock-kneed.

vallate (văl′āt) *adj.* a hollow or crater with a rim around it.

valorization (văl″ər-ĭz-ā′shən) *n.* governmental price-fixing.

vancourier (văn-kŏŏr′ĭ-ər) *n.* an advance man.

vanillism (văn-ĭl′ĭz″əm) *n.* dermatitis from handling raw vanilla.

vaniloquence (văn-ĭl′ō-kwəns) *n.* vain and foolish talk.

vapulate (văp′ū-lāt) *v.t.&i.* to beat, whip.

vaquero (vŏ-kĕr′ō) *n.* a cowboy south of the border.

varietist (və-rī′ə-tĭst) *n.* 1. an unorthodox person. 2. someone who practices unorthodox sex.

variolation (văr″ĭ-ō-lā′shən) *n.* inoculation with smallpox virus, a medical procedure antedating vaccination.

variorum (vĕr-ĭ-ôr′əm) *adj.* 1. pertaining to a literary classic annotated by sundry contemporaries. 2. derived from various sources.

varsovienne (vŏr-sō-vyĕn′) *n.* a popular polka-like nineteenth-century ballroom dance or its music.

vastation (văs-tā′shən) *n.* purification through fire.

vaticide (văt′ĭ-sīd) *n.* murder of a prophet. *vaticinate, v.t.&i.* to prophesy. *vatic, adj.* prophetical.

vaticinal (văt-ĭs′ĭn-əl) *adj.* prophetic.

vecordious (vĕk-ôr′dĭ-əs) *adj.* senseless, insane, mad.

vectitation (vĕk-tĭ-tā′shən) *n.* carrying or being carried.

vector (vĕk′tər) *n.* 1. a disease carrier. 2. a line representing both

---

mǎn; māde; lĕt; bē; sĭp; wīne; hŏt; cōld; sôre; dŭll; fūgue; bûrp; gōŏd; fōŏd; out; gĕt; thin; this; year; azure; ō′mən″; viN; für; Bach

veery (vĭr'ē) *n.* the brown-and-white spotted thrush.

vega (vā'gə) *n.* a fertile meadow.

vegete (vĕj-ēt') *adj.* alive and flourishing.

velarium (vĕl-ĕr'ĭ-əm) *n.* an amphi-theater awning.

velitation (vĕl-ĭ-tā'shən) *n.* a petty fight; a skirmish.

velivolant (vĕl-ĭv'ō-lənt) *adj.* being under full sail.

velleity (vĕl-ē'ĭ-tē) *n.* slight or faint desire; inclination.

vellicate (vĕl'ĭ-kāt) *v.t.* to twitch, or cause to twitch; to tickle.

velouté (vĕl-ōō-tě') *n.* a white sauce.

velutinous (vĕl-ū'tĭn-əs) *adj.* velve-ty.

venatic (vē-nàt'ĭk) *adj.* pertaining to or fond of hunting.

venditation (vĕn-dĭ-tā'shən) *n.* dis-playing as if for sale.

vendue (vĕn-dū') *n.* a public auc-tion.

veneniferous (vĕn-ə-nĭf'ər-əs) *adj.* bearing or transmitting poison.

venireman (vĕn-ī'rē-màn) *n.* a juror.

vennootschap (vĕn-ōt'skòp) *n.* partnership.

ventoseness (vĕn-tōs'nəs) *n.* wind-iness; flatulence.

ventricumbent (vən-trĭ-kŭm'bənt) *adj.* lying face down; prone.

ventripotent (vĕn-trĭp'ō-tənt) *adj.* fat-bellied; gluttonous.

venust (vēn-ŭst') *adj.* Venuslike; beautiful and elegant.

verbicide (vûrb'ĭ-sīd) *n.* word-mur-der; mangling or perverting a word.

verbigeration (vûr-bĭj″ər-ā'shən) *n.* senseless reiteration of clichés.

verbophobia (vûr-bō-fō'bĭ-ə) *n.* fear and dislike of words.

verdigris (vûr'dĭ-grēs) *n.* 1. a blue or green paint, insecticide or fungicide. 2. a patina formed on metal by overexposure to sea air, or water.

verecund (vĕr'ə-kŭnd) *adj.* bash-ful, modest. *verecundity, n.*

veridical (vĕr-ĭd'ĭ-kəl) *adj.* real and truthful.

veriloquent (vĕr-ĭl'ō-kwənt) *adj.* speaking truthfully.

verism (vĕr'ĭz″əm) *n.* the theory that ugliness is valid in art and literature as long as it's true.

verjuice (vûr'jōōs) *n.* 1. crab-apple juice; sour grape juice. 2. sour-ness, in general.

vermeology (vûrm-ē-òl'ə-jē) *n.* the study of worms; *helminthology.*

vernalagnia (vûr-nəl-àg'nĭ-ə) *n.* spring fever.

vernality (vûr-nàl'ĭ-tē) *n.* being springlike; *vernal.*

vertex (vûr'tĕks) *n.* the highest point; summit, apex, zenith.

vertiginous (vûr-tĭj'ĭn-əs) *adj.* re-volving, dizzy; vacillating, un-stable, inconsistent; causing diz-ziness.

vervel (vûr'vəl) *n.* 1. a ring on a bird's leg for tying it to its perch. 2. a label tied to a hawk's leg. also *varvel.*

vesicate (vĕs'ĭ-kāt) *v.t.&i.* to blister.

vespertilian (vĕs-pûr-tĭl'ĭ-ən) *adj.* like a bat.

vespertine (vĕs'pûr-tĭn) *adj.* per-taining to or happening in the evening.

vespine (vĕs'pīn) *adj.* pertaining to wasps; *vespoid.*

vetitive (vĕt'ĭ-tĭv) *adj.* having or pertaining to the power of veto-ing; prohibiting.

vetust (vē-tùst') *adj.* old, ancient, antique.

viaggiatory (vĭ-ŏj′ə-tôr″ē) *adj.* on the move; traveling around.

viaticum (vī-ăt′ĭ-kŭm) *n.* 1. state expense account. 2. provisions for a trip. 3. communion given to someone dying.

viator (vī-ā′tər) *n.* a traveler.

vibratiunculation (vī-brā″shĭ-ŭnk-ū-lā′shən) *n.* a shudder; a slight vibration.

vicenary (vĭs′ən-ĕr″ē) *adj.* containing twenty or based on the number twenty; *vigesimal.*

vicereine (vīs′rān) *n.* the wife of a viceroy.

vicinage (vĭs′ĭn-əj) *n.* neighborhood, vicinity; the people of a certain neighborhood. *-adj.* neighboring, nearby.

vicissitudinary (vī-sĭs″ĭ-tōōd′ĭn-ĕr″ē) *adj.* pertaining to change, alteration, mutation.

videlicet (vĭd-ĕl′ĭ-sĕt) *adv.* to wit, namely, usually used in its abbreviated form: *viz.*

viduage (vĭj′ōō-əj) *n.* widowhood; widows. *viduous, adj.* widowed; bereaved.

vigesimation (vī-jĕs″ĭ-mā′shən) *n.* killing every twentieth person.

vilipend (vĭl′ĭ-pĕnd) *v.t.* to belittle, to disparage.

villanella (vĭl-ə-nĕl′ə) *n.* 1. an old rustic dance or its music. 2. an Italian part song, ancestor of the madrigal.

villeggiatura (vē-lĕj″ŏ-tōōr′ŏ) *n.* sojourn at a villa.

villein (vĭl′ən) *n.* a serf with limited freedom to conduct business.

vimineous (vĭm-ĭn′ĭ-əs) *adj.* pertaining to twigs; woven of pliant twigs.

vinaceous (vīn-ā′shəs) *adj.* like wine or grapes.

vinculate (vĭng′kū-lāt) *v.t.* to tie. *vinculation, n.*

vindemiate (vĭn-dē′mĭ-āt) *v.i.* to harvest fruit. *vindemial, adj.* pertaining to a vintage.

vinegarroon (vĭn″ə-gə-rōōn′) *n.* a scorpion of Mexico and the southwestern U.S.: so called from the smell it gives off when scared.

vinification (vĭn″ĭ-fĭ-kā′shən) *n.* the conversion of fruit juice into alcohol by fermentation.

vintry (vĭn′trē) *n.* a place where wine is sold or stored.

viparious (vī-pĕr′ĭ-əs) *adj.* life-renewing.

viraginity (vĭr-ə-jĭn′ĭ-tē) *n.* masculinity in a woman.

virago (vĭr-ā′gō) *n.* a termagant.

virason (vĭr-ŏ-sōn′) *n.* a sea breeze.

virgulate (vûr′gū-lāt) *adj.* rod-shaped.

virgule (vûr′gūl) *n.* the American slash/ or French comma.

viridarium (vĭr-ĭ-dĕr′ĭ-əm) *n.* a villa's garden.

viripotent (vĭr-ĭp′ō-tənt) *adj.* of a man: sexually mature.

virtu (vûr-tōō′) *n.* 1. enjoyment of the arts. 2. being rare or beautiful: interesting to a collector. 3. art curios or antiques, collectively.

virvestitism (vĭr-vĕs′tĭ-tĭz″əm) *n.* female preference for male clothes.

vitellus (vĭt-ĕl′əs) *n.* an egg yolk.

vitilitigate (vĭt-ĭ-lĭt′ĭ-gāt) *v.i.* to be particularly quarrelsome.

vitricophobia (vĭt″rĭ-kō-fō′bĭ-ə) *n.* fear of one's stepfather.

vituline (vĭt′ū-līn) *adj.* like a calf; pertaining to veal.

vivandière (vē-vòN-dyĕr′) *n.* a female *sutler*, which see.

vivarium (vī-vĕr′ĭ-əm) *n.* a barn or greenhouse for raising animals and plants indoors.

---

mǎn; māde; lĕt; bē; sĭp; wīne; hŏt; cōld; sôre; dŭll; fūgue; bûrp; gŏŏd; fōōd; out; gĕt; thin; t̶his; year; ażure; ō′mən″; viN; fûr; Bach

viviparous (vĭ-vĭp'ər-əs) *adj.* producing living young instead of eggs (*oviparous*).

vivisepulture (vĭv-ĭ-sĕp'əl-chər) *n.* live burial.

vlei (flā) *n.* a temporary lake; a swamp.

vocabulation (vō-kăb"ū-lā'shən) *n.* selection and use of words.

voidee (void'ē) *n.* a last-minute snack.

Volapuk (vō'lə-pūk) *n.* an international language invented by Johann Schleyer about 1879, based largely on English.

volery (vŏl'ər-ē) *n.* 1. a large bird cage; an aviary. 2 a flock of birds. 3. an airplane hangar.

volitation (vŏl-ĭ-tā'shən) *n.* flight; flying. *volation.*

volitient (vō-lĭsh'ənt) *adj.* exercising free will.

voltigeur (vŏl-tē-ẑûr') *n.* 1. a tumbler or gymnast. 2. a French sharpshooter.

volucrine (vŏl'ū-krĭn) *adj.* pertaining to birds.

volute (vō-lōōt') *adj.* rolled-up; spiraled.

vomiturition (vŏm"ĭ-chər-ĭ'shən) *n.* retching, ineffectual vomiting.

voortrekker (fōr'trĕk"ər) *n.* a pioneer (from the Boer's 1834 trek to the Transvaal).

voraginous (vôr-ăj'ĭn-əs) *adj.* devouring; *voracious.*

vorstellung (fōr'shtĕl-ōōng) *n.* a sensuous mental image.

vorticism (vôr'tĭ-sĭz"əm) *n.* post-impressionist art reflecting the machine age.

vortiginous (vôr-tĭj'ĭn-əs) *adj.* whirling around a center; vortical.

vraisemblance (vrĕ-sŏN-blŏNs') *n.* appearing to be true; likely, verisimilitude.

vrille (vrĭl) *n.* an aerobatic spinning nose dive. *-v.i.* to perform it.

vuggy (vŭg'ē) *adj.* pertaining to or abounding in *vuggs*: small rock cavities.

vulnerative (vŭl'nər-ā"tĭv) *adj.* wounding; *vulnific.*

vulpecular (vŭl-pĕk'ū-lər) *adj.* pertaining to young foxes; *vulpine.*

vulturine (vŭl'chər-ĭn) *adj.* pertaining to vultures.

W

wadget (wăj′ət) *n.* a bundle.

waffle (wŏf′əl) *n.* 1. a heartily disliked old person (U.S. slang). 2. nonsense; incessant talk. 3. the yapping of a small dog. *-v.i.* to talk nonsense; to talk incessantly (British slang).

waghalter (wăg′hŏl″tər) *n.* a rogue rascal, or knave.

wagwag (wăg′wăg) *n.* a watchmaker's polisher.

wainwright (wān′rīt) *n.* a maker and repairer of wagons; a *wagon-wright.*

waldgrave (wôld′grāv) *n.* keeper of the forests in old Germany.

wallaroo (wŏl-ər-ōō′) *n.* a kangaroo.

walla-walla (wŏ-lə-wŏ′lə) *n.pl.* theater slang for what extras say in mob scenes.

wallydrag (wăl′ē-drăg) *n.* the runt or youngest of the litter.

wally-gowdy (wă′lē-gō″dē) *n.* a precious jewel.

walm (wŏm) *v.i.* to seethe.

wamble (wŏm′bəl) *v.i.* 1. to feel nauseous. 2. to move unsteadily; to stagger; to writhe or shake. *-v.t.* to spin. *-n.* 1. stomach rumbling. 2. an irregular, staggering gait.

wamefu (wăm′fōō) *n.* a bellyful. also *wamefou, wameful.*

wampa (wŏm′pə) *n.* a hopeful starlet (from Western Associated Motion Picture Advertisers).

wampus (wŏm′pəs) *n.* a stupid, dull, loutish clod.

wamus (wô′məs) *n.* a cardigan or buttoned jacket.

wanderjahr (vŏn′dər-yŏr) *n.* a year of traveling before settling down. also *wanderyear.*

wanderoo (wŏn-dər-ōō′) *n.* the purple-faced Malabar monkey.

wanhope (wŏn′hōp) *n.* forlorn hope, despair, and delusion.

waniand (wā′nĭ-ənd) *n.* the waning moon, symbol of bad luck.

wanigan (wŏn′ĭ-gən) *n.* 1. a houseboat. 2. a lumber camp office.

wanion (wŏn′yən) *n.* a plague; a vengeance.

wantwit (wŏnt′wĭt) *n.* a fool. *-adj.* foolish, idiotic.

wapiti (wŏp′ĭ-tē) *n.* the American elk.

wappenschawing (wŏp′ən-shô″ĭng) *n.* a military review.

---

măn; māde; lĕt; bē; sĭp; wīne; hŏt; cōld; sôre; dŭll; fūgue; bûrp;
gŏŏd; fōōd; out; gĕt; thin; t̂his; year; aźure; ō′mən″; viN; fūr; Bach ′

wapperjawed (wŏp'ər-jôd) *adj.* having crooked jaws.

warmouth (wôr'mouth) *n.* the fresh-water sunfish of the eastern U.S.

watermanship (wô'tər-mən-shĭp") *n.* oarsmanship, particularly with regard to oar *blades*.

waveson (wāv'sən) *n.* goods floating after a shipwreck.

wawa (wǒ'wǒ) *n.* language, speech (Chinook).

waybill (wā'bĭl) *n.* 1. an itinerary. 2. a bill of lading. 3. identification for someone on relief.

wayzgoose (wāz'gōōs) *n.* a printers' annual holiday in Britain.

webster (wĕb'stər) *n.* a weaver.

wedbed (wĕd'bĕd) *n.* marriage bed.

wedbedrip (wĕd'bĕd"rĕp) *n.* a feudal law enjoining tenants to do *bedrip*, or a day's reaping, for their lord.

weftage (wĕft'əj) *n.* texture.

wegotism (wē'gō-tĭz"əm) *n.* excessive use of the editorial "we."

welkin (wĕl'kĭn) *n.* sky.

Weltanschauung (vĕlt'ŏn-shou"ŭng) *n.* philosophical world view.

wem (wĕm) *n.* stain, flaw, or scar.

wergild (wûr'gĭld) *n.* money paid by the killer's family to the family of the victim to avert a blood feud.

wether (wĕth'ər) *n.* a castrated ram.

whally (hwôl'ē) *adj.* having light-colored eyes.

whangdoodle (hwăng'dōō"dəl) *n.* a mythical bird that grieves continuously.

wharfinger (wôrf'ĭn-jər) *n.* the owner or manager of a wharf.

wheyface (hwā'fās) *n.* paleface.

whigmaleery (hwĭg-mə-lîr'ē) *n.* a knickknack or a geegaw; a whim.

whilom (hwī'ləm) *adv.* formerly, once. *-adj.* former.

whipjack (hwĭp'jăk) *n.* a beggar pretending to have been shipwrecked.

whirlygigs (hwûr'lē-gĭgz) *n.pl.* testicles.

whiskerino (hwĭsk-ər-ēn'ō) *n.* a beard-growing contest.

whisterpoop (hwĭst'ər-pōōp) *n.* see *whistersnefet*.

whistersnefet (hwĭst'ər-snĕf"ət) *n.* a hard blow; *whisterpoop*.

whurr (hwûr) *v.i.* saying the letter R noisily.

whurring (hwûr'ĭng) *n.* noise made by departing partridges.

widdifow (wĭd'ĭ-fōō) *n.* see *waghalter*.

wight (wīt) *n.* a person. *-adj.* brave and strong.

wilcox (wĭl'kŏks) *v.i.* to lie awake at night (slang).

wilcweme (wĭlk'wēm) *adj.* satisfied.

wilding (wīld'ĭng) *n.* 1. a crabapple tree or its fruit. 2. someone or something unorthodox.

windrow (wĭn'drō) *n.* 1. a row of racked-up, drying hay; other rows of things drying. 2. a furrow for planting sugar cane.

windsucker (wĭnd'sŭk"ər) *n.* 1. a carping critic. 2. a horse that chews its stable; a *cribbing* horse.

wingmanship (wĭng'mən-shĭp) *n.* flying skill.

winklehawk (wĭnk'əl-hôk) *n.* a rectangular hole in cloth.

winterkill (wĭn'tər-kĭl) *v.t. &i.* to die from exposure to winter weather.

withdrawingroom (wĭth-drô'ĭng-rōōm) *n.* drawing room; living-room; parlor.

withernam (wĭth'ər-nòm) *n.* taking one thing as reprisal for something else taken previously.

withershins (wĭth'ər-shĭnz) *adv.* contrary; against the grain.

---

mǎn; māde; lět; bē; sĭp; wīne; hŏt; cōld; sôre; dùll; fūgue; bûrp; gōōd; fōōd; out; gĕt; thin; this; year; azure; ō'mən"; viN; fūr; Bach

witzchoura (wǐ-chōōr'ə) *n.* a large-sleeved woman's cloak fashionable in the early nineteenth century.

witzelsucht (vǐts'əl-sōōkt) *n.* emotional state characterized by futile attempts at humor.

wlatsome (lŏt'sōōm) *adj.* loathsome.

wobbegong (wŏb'ə-gŏng) *n.* the carpet shark.

wombat (wŏm'bǎt) *n.* a burrowing Australian marsupial that looks like a small bear.

wommacky (wŏm'ə-kē) *adj.* weak and shaky as in convalescence.

wooer-bab (wōō'ər-bŏb) *n.* a garter tied below the knee as a lover's keepsake.

woofy (wōōf'ē) *adj.* dense texture.

woom (wōōm) *n.* beaver fur.

wootz (wōōts) *n.* oldest known steelmaking method; *wootz steel*; Indian steel.

worricow (wûr'ĭ-kōō) *n.* the devil, bogeyman.

wort (wûrt) *n.* fermenting malt, incipient beer; anything fermenting.

woundy (wōōn'dē) *adj.* excessive. *-adv.* excessively.

wowf (wōōf) *adj.* crazy, wild, extreme.

wowser (wou'zər) *n.* a pecksniffian puritan.

wuntee (wŭn'tē) *n.* a lone old buffalo bull.

wyliecoat (wī'lē-kōt) *n.* a warm undershirt or slip.

wyvern (wĭv'ərn) *n.* a two-legged dragon with a snake on its ass (heraldry).

Xanthippe (zăn-tǐp′ē) *n.* Socrates' wife, noted for her bad temper.

xanthochroid (zăn′thō-kroid) *adj.* having blond hair and a light complexion.

xanthocyanopsia (zăn″thō-sī-ə-ŏp′sǐ-ə) *n.* form of color blindness in which only yellows and blues are seen.

xanthoderm (zăn′thō-dûrm) *n.* yellow-skinned race.

xanthodont (zăn′thō-dŏnt) *n.* a person with yellowish teeth.

xanthomelanous (zăn-thō-mĕl′ən-əs) *adj.* pertaining to those races with an olive or yellow complexion and black hair.

xassafrassed (zăs′ə-frăst) *adj.* pregnant (slang).

xat (zŏt) *n.* a carved post in front of certain North American Indian homes.

xebec (zē′bĕk) *n.* a lateen-rigged, three-masted ship.

xenagogue (zĕn′ə-gŏg) *n.* a guide.

xenagogy (zĕn′ə-gŏ″jē) *n.* a guidebook.

xenapistia (zĕn-ə-pīs′tǐ-ə) *n.* extreme distrust of strangers.

xenium (zē′nǐ-əm) *n.* 1. a present given to a guest. 2. in the Middle Ages, a compulsory gift to church or state.

xenobombulate (zē-nō-bŏm′bū-lāt) *v.i.* to malinger (slang).

xenodochium (zĕn-ō-dō′kǐ-əm) *n.* a home for the disabled and friendless.

xenodochy (zĕn-ŏd′ə-kē) *n.* hospitality. *xenial* (zē′nǐ-əl) *adj.* pertaining to hospitality.

xenoepist (zĕn-ō′ə-pǐst) *n.* someone who speaks with a foreign accent.

xenogenesis (zĕn-ō-jĕn′ə-sǐs) *n.* the imagined reproduction of an organism totally unlike its parent.

xenomancy (zē′nō-măn″sē) *n.* fortunetelling by studying the first stranger that appears.

xenomania (zĕn-ō-mā′nǐ-ə) *n.* a mania for foreign customs, traditions, manners, etc.

xenophobia (zĕn-ō-fō′bǐ-ə) *n.* fear of strangers or foreigners.

xeres (zĕr′ĕs) *n.* sherry.

xerga (ksä′gò) *n.* a saddle blanket.

---

xeromyron (zĭr-ŏm′ĭ-rŏn) *n.* solid ointment.

xeronisus (zĭr-ŏn′ĭ-səs) *n.* inability to reach orgasm.

xerophagy (zĭr-ŏf′ə-jē) *n.* a strict religious fast.

xerophilous (zĭr-ŏf′ĭl-əs) *adj.* drought-resistant, as desert plants.

xerophobous (zĭr-ŏf′ə-bəs) *adj.* unable to withstand drought.

xerotic (zĭr-ŏt′ĭk) *adj.* dry.

xertz (zûrts) *v.t.&i.* to swallow quickly (slang).

xibalba (hē-bŏl′bŏ) *n.* the Mayan Hades.

xiphoid (zĭf′oid) *adj.* shaped like a sword.

xiphopagus (zĭf-ŏp′ə-gəs) *n.* twins joined at the abdomen.

xiphosuran (zĭf-ō-sŏŏr′ən) *adj.* pertaining to the American king crab.

Xiuhtecutli (hē″ŏŏ-tā-kŏŏt′lē) *n.* the Aztec fire god.

xylanthrax (zī-lăn′thrăks) *n.* charcoal.

xylem (zī′ləm) *n.* woody plant fiber.

xyloglyphy (zī-lŏg′lĭ-fē) *n.* artistic wood carving.

xylography (zī-lŏg′rə-fē) *n.* 1. wood engraving. 2. color-printing on wood.

xylomancy (zī′lō-măn″sē) *n.* fortunetelling with pieces of wood.

xylophobia (zī-lō-fō′bĭ-ə) *n.* fear of wooden objects; fear of forests.

xylophonist (zī-lŏf′ən-ĭst) *n.* a patient who annoys others with frequent and noisy farts (slang).

xylopolist (zī-lŏp′əl-ĭst) *n.* a dealer in wooden objects.

xyresic (zī-rĕs′ĭk) *adj.* razor-sharp.

xyster (zĭs′tər) *n.* a surgical instrument for scraping bone.

xystus (zĭs′təs) *n.* an indoor porch for exercising in winter.

Y

yaffle (yǎf'əl) *n.* 1. an armload. 2. the green woodpecker.

yahoo (yò'hōō) *n.* a boor or a hayseed (Swift's *Gulliver's Travels*).

yahoomanity (yò-hōō-mǎn'ĭ-tē) *n.* people en masse.

Yahwism (yò'wĭz"əm) *n.* 1. Yahweh or God-worship. 2. using the name, Yahweh.

yair (yèr) *n.* an enclosure for catching salmon.

Yajnavalkya (yŭj-nə-vŭlk'yə) *n.* a classic fifth-century Hindu lawbook.

yakalo (yăk'ə-lō) *n.* a cross between a yak and a cattalo.

yang (yŏng) *n.* the good (and, you might guess, male) half of the Chinese twins *yin and yang.*

yapok (yă-pŏk') *n.* the water opossum.

yardang (yŏr'dŏng) *n.* a ridge carved by wind erosion.

yardwand (yŏrd'wŏnd) *n.* a yardstick.

yarely (yèr'lē) *adv.* avidly; readily.

yarmouth (yŏr'məth). *adj.* insane (slang).

yarwhelp (yŏr'hwĕlp) *n.* the bartailed godwit.

yashmak (yŏsh'mŏk) *n.* a veil worn by Moslem women in public.

yataghan (yăt'ə-găn) *n.* a long curved Turkish knife.

yati (yăt'ē) *n.* a Hindu ascetic.

yatter (yăt'ər) *n.&v.i.* chatter and clatter.

yaud (yŏd) *n.* the overworked mare.

yauld (yŏd) *adj.* strong, wide-eyed, and bushy-tailed.

yaw (yô) *v.t.&i.* to deviate from one's course, both literally and figuratively.

yaya (yŏ'yə) *n.* any of several Central American trees.

Yazoo (yăz'ōō) *n.* an Indian tribe formerly living on the Yazoo River in Mississippi.

yclad (ĭ-klăd') *adj.* clothed, clad.

yclept (ĭ-klĕpt') *adj.* called, named.

ydromancy (ĭd'rō-măn"sē) *n.* fortunetelling with water.

yean (yēn) *v.t.&i.* to give birth; to *ean.*

yeanling (yēn'lĭng) *n.* a lamb or kid; an *eanling.* *-adj.* newborn; young.

yeara (yā-ŏr'ə) *n.* West Coast poison oak.

yearock (yĭr'ək) *n.* a one-year-old

---

mǎn; mǎde; lĕt; bē; sĭp; wīne; hŏt́; cōld; sôre; dŭll; fūgue; bûrp; gŏŏd; fŏŏd; out; gĕt; thin; t́his; year; ažure; ō'mən"; viN; fūr; Bach

hen.

yed (yĕd) *n. & v.i.* lie or quarrel.

yede (yĕd) *v.i.* to go; proceed.

yeld (yĕld) *adj.* not old enough to procreate; giving no milk.

yeowoman (yō′wŏōm″ən) *n.* wife of a yeoman.

yeply (yĕp′lē) *adv.* craftily; eagerly.

yepsen (yĕp′sən) *n.* cupping the hands; the amount cupped hands can hold.

yerba (yĕr′bə) *n.* an herb or plant.

yerga (yûr′gə) *n.* coarse material used for horse blankets.

yesterfang (yĕs′tər-făng) *n.* what was taken yesterday, or some time ago.

yestreen (yĕs-trēn′) *n. & adv.* last night.

yetlin (yĕt′lĭn) *n.* cast iron; a small iron pot.

yette (yĕt) *v.t.* to concede.

yeuk (ūk) *n. & v.t.* itch. *yeuky, adj.* itching. *yeukiness, n.*

yeuling (ū′lĭng) *n.* walking around fruit trees praying for a good crop.

yex (yĕks) *n.* hiccup, cough. also *yox, yux. -v.i.* to hiccup or cough.

yhte (ĭh′tə) *n.* possession.

yill-caup (yĭl′kôp) *n.* an ale cup or mug.

yirn (yûrn) *n.* to whine or pout.

yiver (yĭv′ər) *adj.* eager; greedy.

ylahayll (ĭl-ə-hāl′) *interj.* bad luck to you! (obs.).

ylang-ylang (ē′lŏng-ē″lŏng) *n.* a tropical Asian tree or its perfume.

ylespil (ĭl′əs-pēl) *n.* the hedgehog.

ynambu (ē-nŏm-bōō′) *n.* a large Brazilian tinamou, or bird.

yokefellow (yōk′fĕl″ō) *n.* a spouse, close friend, or partner; a *yokemate.*

younker (yŭnk′ər) *n.* 1. a young man. 2. a junior ship's officer.

youward (ū′wərd) *adj.* toward you.

yperite (ēp′ər-īt) *n.* mustard gas.

ypsiliform (ĭp-sĭl′ĭ-fôrm) *adj.* upsilon-shaped. also *ypsiloid.*

Yquem (ē-kĕm′) *n.* a fine French sauterne from *Chateau Yquem.*

yuga (yōōg′ə) *n.* one of the four ages of the world, according to the Hindus.

yurt (yōōrt) *n.* a portable tent used by Siberian nomads.

yuzluk (yōōz′lōōk) *n.* a former Turkish coin equal to one hundred paras or two and a half piasters.

---

mǎn; mōde; lĕt; bē; sĭp; wīne; hŏt; cōld; sôre; dŭll; fūgue; bûrp; gŏŏd; fōōd; out; gĕt; thin; t̵his; year; az̵ure; ō′mən″; ·viN; für; Bach

zabti (zŭb'tē) *adj.* seized or confiscated by the government (India).

zakusky (zŏ-kōōs'kē) *n.pl.* hors d'oeuvres (U.S.S.R.).

zapateado (zŏ"pŏ-tĕ-ŏ'dō) *n.* a Spanish tap dance.

zaptiah (zŭp-tē'ə) *n.* a Turkish cop.

zareba (zŏ-rē'bə) *n.* a stockade of thorn bushes; a fortified camp.

zarf (zŏrf) *n.* a cuplike holder for handling hot coffee cups (Arabia).

zarzuela (zŏr-zwä'lŏ) *n.* a seventeenth-century musical play or operetta, ancestor of opera.

zax (zăks) *n.* a tool for trimming roofing slates.

zebrula (zē'brŏŏ-lə) *n.* a cross between a male zebra and a female horse.

zebu (zē'bōō) *n.* a tame bovine with a hump (the white male is sacred to Hindus).

zebub (zē'bŭb) *n.* the *zimb*, which see.

zedland (zĕd'lənd) *n.* the English counties of Devonshire, Dorsetshire, and Somersetshire, where Z replaces S in colloquial speech.

zeekoe (zā'kŏŏ) *n.* the hippopotamus.

zeitgeist (tsīt'gīst) *n.* the general intellectual, moral, and cultural level of an era.

zelotypia (zĕl-ō-tīp'ĭ-ə) *n.* intense, extreme zeal.

zemmi (zĕm'ē) *n.* the great mole rat. also *zemni*.

zenana (zĕn-ö'nə) *n.* 1. a harem or seraglio. 2. a thin, striped material for women's clothes.

zendikite (zĕn-dē'kīt) *n.* an Arab atheist or unbeliever; a *zindiq*.

zenography (zē-nŏg'rə-fē) *n.* the study or description of Jupiter's surface.

zenzizenzizenzic (zĕn"zĭ-zĕn-zĭ-zĕn'zĭk) *n.* the eighth power of a number.

zephyry (zĕf'ĭr-ē) *adj.* like a soft, gentle wind.

zetetic (zĕt-ĕt'ĭk) *adj.* asking; questioning.

zho (zō) *n.* see *dzo*.

zibeb (zĭ-bĕb') *n.* a raisin.

zibeline (zĭb'əl-īn) *adj.* pertaining to sable.

zigeuner (tsĭ-goi'nûr) *n.* a gypsy.

ziggurat (zĭg'ər-ăt) *n.* a Babylonian pyramidlike temple.

---

măn; māde; lĕt; bē; sĭp; wīne; hŏt; cōld; sôre; dùll; fûgue; bûrp; gŏŏd; fōōd; out; gĕt; thin; thĭs; year; aźure; ō'mən"; viN; fūr; Bach

ziim (tsē'ĭm) *n.pl.* wild animals (Hebrew).

zilch (zĭlch) *n.* anyone whose name is not known (slang).

zimb (zĭmb) *n.* the Ethiopian fly.

zimentwater (zĭm'ənt-wôt″ər) *n.* copper-polluted water found in copper mines.

zimme (zĭm'ə) *n.* a gem.

zimmerwaldian (tsĭm″ər-vŏl-dē'ən) *n.* a proponent of internationalism as a way to prevent war. also *adj.* (from the International Socialist Congress, 1916, in Zimmerwald, Switzerland).

zimmi (zĭm'ē) *n.* a Christian or Jew in a Moslem country who is specially taxed.

zincography (zĭnk-ŏg'rə-fē) *n.* printing with zinc plates.

zindiq (zĭn-dēk') *n.* an Arab heretic or infidel; a *zendikite.*

zingaresca (tsēng-gŏ-räs'kə) *n.* a gypsy song, dance, or music.

Zmudz (żmōōj) *n.* a Lithuanian dialect.

zneesy (znē'sē) *adj.* freezing, frosty. also *znuzy.*

zoanthropy (zō-ăn'thrə-pē) *n.* insanity in which a patient believes she's an animal.

zobo (zō'bō) *n.* a cross between the zebu and the yak.

zoetic (zō-ĕt'ĭk) *adj.* pertaining to life.

zoiatrics (zō-ĭ-ăt'rĭks) *n.* veterinary medicine.

zoilism (zō'ĭl-ĭz″əm) *n.* nagging criticism.

zomotherapy (zō-mō-thĕr'ə-pē) *n.* treating tuberculosis with a raw meat diet.

zonda (sōn'də) *n.* a hot wind of the Argentine pampas.

zondek (zŏn'dĕk) *n.* a pregnancy test (slang).

zonesthesia (zōn-ĕs-thē'żə) *n.* the feeling of wearing a tight girdle.

zoodynamics (zō″ō-dī-năm'ĭks) *n.* animal physiology.

zooerastia (zō″ō-ē-răs'tĭ-ə) *n.* sexual intercourse with an animal.

zoolite (zō'ō-līt) *n.* an animal fossil.

zoomorphism (zō-ō-môr'fĭz″əm) *n.* 1. the representation of gods in animal form. 2. using animals in art.

zoopery (zō-ŏp'ər-ē) *n.* experimentation on primitive animals. *zooperist, n.*

zoophobia (zō-ō-fō'bĭ-ə) *n.* fear of animals.

zoopraxiscope (zō-ō-prăks'ĭ-skōp) *n.* an early type of motion-picture projector.

zoopsychologist (zō″ō-sī-kŏl'ə-jĭst) *n.* an animal psychologist.

zootechny (zō'ō-tĕk″nē) *n.* scientific animal breeding.

zootomy (zō-ŏt'ə-mē) *n.* animal anatomy.

zoozoo (zōō'zōō) *n.* the ringdove.

zoppo (tsô'pô) *adj.* musically syncopated.

zorillo (sôr-ē'yō) *n.* a skunk.

zortzico (zôr-sē'kō) *n.* a Basque song or dance in five/eight time.

zoster (zŏs'tər) *n.* a girdle.

zubr (zōō'bər) *n.* the *aurochs,* ancestor of modern cattle.

zucchetto (tsōō-kĕt'ō) *n.* a Catholic yarmulke: white for the pope, red for the cardinal, purple for the bishop, and black for the rest.

zuche (zōōsh) *n.* a tree stump.

zugzwang (zōōgz'vòng) *n.* in chess, when any move weakens the position.

zumbooruk (zŭm-bōō'rŭk) *n.* a small cannon fired from the back of a camel.

zuurveldt (zōōr'vĕlt) *n.* a tract of land covered with coarse grass.

---

màn; māde; lèt; bē; sǐp; wīne; hòt; cōld; sôre; dùll; fūgue; bûrp; gōōd; fōōd; out; gèt; thin; t̄his; year; aźure; ō'mən″; viN; fūr; Bach

zwetschenwasser (tsvĕch'ən-vôs"ər) *n.* plum brandy.

zygal (zī'gəl) *adj.* H-shaped.

zygomancy (zī'gō-măn"sē) *n.* fortunetelling with weights.

zymology (zī-mŏl'ə-jē) *n.* the science of fermentation. *zymurgy* (zī'mûr-jē) *n.* the chemistry of fermentation in wine- or beer-making.

zymotic (zī-mŏt'ĭk) *adj.* 1. pertaining to fermentation. 2. pertaining to or causing infectious disease.

zythepsary (zī-thĕp'sə-rē) *n.* a brewery.

zythum (zī'thəm) *n.* beer in ancient Egypt.

zyxomma (zĭks-ŏm'ə) *n.* an Indian dragonfly.

zyzzogeton (zĭz-ə-jē'tən) *n.* South American leafhoppers with tuberculate pronota and grooved tibiae.

zzxjoanw (zĭks-jō'ən) *n.* a Maori drum.

---

mån; māde; lĕt; bē; sĭp; wīne; hŏt; cōld; sôre; dŭll; fūgue; bûrp; gōōd; fōōd; out; gĕt; thin; this; year; aźure; ō'mən"; viN; fūr; Bach

BIBLIOGRAPHY

The following are source books which were thoroughly culled from *aasvogel* to *zzxjoanx:*

The Abecedarian Book by Charles W. Ferguson; Little, Brown and Company, Boston and Toronto, 1964.

Acronyms Dictionary; Gale Research Company, Detroit, Michigan, 1960.

Americanisms: The English of the New World by M. Schele De Vere; Charles Scribner and Company, New York, 1872.

The American Language by H.L. Mencken; Alfred A. Knopf, New York, 1937.

The American Language, Supplement I by H.L. Mencken; Alfred A. Knopf, New York, 1945.

The American Language, Supplement II by H.L. Mencken; Alfred A. Knopf, New York, New York, 1948.

The American Thesaurus of Slang, second edition, by Lester V. Berry and Melvin Van Den Bark; Thomas Y. Crowell Company, New York, 1956.

The Anatomy of Dirty Words by Edward Sagarin; Lyle Stuart, Publisher, New York, 1962.

Beginnings of American English by Mitford M. Mathews; University of Chicago Press, Chicago, 1931, 1963.

Beyond Language by Dmitri A. Borgmann; Charles Scribner's Sons, New York, 1967.

Black's Law Dictionary, fourth edition, by Henry Campbell Black; West Publishing Company, St. Paul, Minnesota, 1951.

Chamber's Technical Dictionary, third edition, edited by C.F. Tweney and L.E.C. Hughes; The Macmillan Company, New York, 1965.

A Compendious Dictionary of the English Language by Noah Webster; Crown Publishers, Inc., New York, 1970 (first edition, 1806).

Computer Dictionary and Handbook by Charles Sippl; Howard W. Sams and Company, Inc.; Bobbs-Merrill Company, Inc., Indianapolis and New York, 1966.

Construction Dictionary: A Handbook of Construction Terms and Tables; published by the National Association of Women in Construction, Ch. 98, Phoenix, Arizona, 1966.

The Devil's Dictionary by Ambrose Bierce; World Publishing Company, New York, 1942.

Dictionary of Afro-American Slang by Clarence Major; International-al Publishers, New York, 1970.

Dictionary of Americanisms on Historical Principles by Mitford M. Mathews; University of Chicago Press, Chicago, 1951.

Dictionary of American Slang by Harold Wentworth and Stuart Berg Flexnon; Thomas Y. Crowell Company, New York, 1960.

A Dictionary of American Underworld Lingo by Hyman E. Goldin, Frank O'Leary, and Morris Lipsius; Citadel Press, New York, 1950, 1962.

A Dictionary of Buckish Slang, University Wit, and Pickpocket Eloquence by (for the most part) Frances Grose; C. Chappel, London, 1811; Digest Books, Illinois, 1971.

A Dictionary of Building by John S. Scott; Penguin Books, Great Britain, 1964.

Dictionary of Civil Engineering by Rolt Hammond; Philosophical Library, New York and Great Britain, 1965.

Dictionary of Classical Antiquities by Oskar Seyffert; World Publishing Company, Cleveland and New York, 1956.

A Dictionary of Difficult Words by Robert Hill; Philosophical Library, New York, 1959.

Dictionary of Early English by Joseph T. Shipley; Littlefield, Adams and Company, New Jersey, 1963.

Dictionary of Foreign Phrases and Abbreviations by Kevin Guinagh; Pocket Books, New York, 1965.

A Dictionary of Geography, third edition, by W.G. Moore; Penguin Books, Great Britain, 1963.

Dictionary of Medical Slang and Related Esoteric Expressions by J.E. Schmidt; Charles C Thomas, Springfield, Illinois, 1959.

A Dictionary of Music by Robert Illing; Penguin Books, Great Britain, 1950.

Dictionary of Psychiatry and Psychology by William H. Kupper, M.D.; Colt Press, New Jersey, 1953.

A Dictionary of Science by E.B. Uvarov and D.R. Chapman; Penguin Books, Great Britain, 1951.

A Dictionary of Slang and Unconventional English, fourth edition, by Éric Partridge; Routledge and Kegan Paul, Ltd., London, 1950.

Dictionary of Word Origins by Joseph T. Shipley, Littlefield, Adams and Company, Ames, Iowa, 1959.

Dictionary of World Literature by Joseph T. Shipley; Philosophical Library, New York, 1943.

The Evolution of the English Language (formerly titled *Modern English in the Making*) by George H. McKnight; Dover Publications, Inc., New York, 1968 (first edition, 1928).

The Gift of Language by Margaret Schlauch; Dover Publications, Inc., New York, 1942, 1955.

Growth and Structure of the English Language by Otto Jespersen; Doubleday and Company, New York, 1905, 1955.

Harbrace Guide to Dictionaries by Wilson, Hendrickson and Taylor; Harcourt, Brace and World, Inc., New York and Burlingame, 1963.

Horsefeathers and Other Curious Words by Charles Earle Funk; Harper and Brothers, New York, 1958.

I Give You My Word and *Say the Word* by Ivor Brown; E.P. Dutton and Company, New York, 1964.

Illusions and Delusions of the Supernatural and the Occult by D.H. Rawcliffe; Dover Publications, New York, 1959.

A Jazz Lexicon by Robert S. Gold; Alfred A. Knopf, New York, 1964.

Johnson's Dictionary, A Modern Selection by E.L. McAdam, Jr., and George Milne; Pantheon Books, New York, 1963.

Language in America by Charlton Laird; The World Publishing Company, New York and Cleveland, 1970.

Language on Vacation by Dmitri A. Borgmann; Charles Scribner's Sons, New York, 1965.

Mathematics Dictionary by Glenn James and Robert James; D. Van Nostrand Company, Inc., New York and New Jersey, 1949.

The Merck Manual of Diagnosis and Therapy, tenth edition; Merck and Company, Inc., Rahway, New Jersey, 1961.

Oddities and Curiosities of Words and Literature by C.C. Bombaugh, edited by Martin Gardner; Dover Publications, New York, 1961.

The Oxford Universal Dictionary on Historical Principles, third edition, edited by C.T. Onions; Oxford, 1955.

Reversicon, A Medical Word Finder by J.E. Schmidt; Charles C Thomas, Springfield, Illinois, 1958.

Short Dictionary of Classical Word Origins by Harry E. Wedeck; Philosophical Library, New York, 1957.

A Short Dictionary of Mathematics by C.H. McDowell; Littlefield, Adams and Company, New Jersey, 1962.

Sisson's Word and Expression Locater by A.F. Sisson; Parker Publishing Company, Inc., New York, 1969.

Some Curios From a Word-Collector's Cabinet by A. Smythe Palmer; E.P. Dutton and Company, New York.

The Unabridged Crossword Puzzle Word Finder by A.F. Sisson; Doubleday and Company, Inc., New York, 1963.

University Pronouncing Dictionary of Troublesome Words by Frank O. Colby; Thomas Y. Crowell Company, New York, 1950.

Unusual Words and How They Came About by Edwin Radford; Philosophical Library, New York, 1946.

Van Nostrand's Scientific Encyclopedia, third edition; D. Van Nostrand Company, New Jersey, 1958.

Walker's Critical Pronouncing Dictionary and Expositor of the English Language abridged by the Reverend Thomas Smith; H. and E. Phinney, Cooperstown, New York, 1845.

Webster's Twentieth Century Dictionary, unabridged, second edition; World Publishers, New York, 1961.

A Word in Your Ear and *Just Another Word* by Ivor Brown; E.P. Dutton and Company, New York, 1963.

Word People by Nancy Sorel; American Heritage Press, New York, 1970.

Words Ancient and Modern by Ernest Weekley; Dover Publications, Inc., New York, 1946, 1965.

Words and Their Ways in English Speech by James Greenough and George Kittredge; Beacon Press, Boston, 1900, 1962.

Words, Words and Words About Dictionaries by Jack C. Gray; Chandler Publishing Company, San Francisco, 1963.

Word Ways, The Journal of Recreational Linguistics, sixteen issues: from Vol. I, No. 1 through Vol. IV, No. 4 (1968-1972), A. Ross Eckler, editor; New Jersey.

World of Mathematics by James R.

Newman; Simon and Schuster, New York, 1956.

The following books were consulted for definitions, pronunciations, new-word lists, etc.:

The American College Dictionary; Random House, New York, 1962.

The American Heritage Dictionary of the English Language; Houghton Mifflin Company and The American Heritage Publishing Company, Inc., New York, 1969.

The Century Dictionary, William Dwight Whitney, editor; The Century Company, New York, 1889.

The Comprehensive Word Guide by Norman Lewis; Doubleday and Company, New York, 1958.

A Dictionary of American-English Usage by Margaret Nicholson (based on Fowler's *Modern English Usage*); Oxford University Press, New York, 1957.

Dorland's Illustrated Medical Dictionary, 24th edition; W. B. Saunders Company, Philadelphia and London, 1965.

Funk & Wagnalls New Standard Dictionary of the English Language, unabridged; Funk & Wagnalls Company, New York, 1941.

Funk & Wagnalls Standard College Dictionary; Funk & Wagnalls Company, New York, 1963.

The Oxford Dictionary of English Etymology, edited by C.T. Onions; Oxford University Press, New York, 1966.

Oxford English Dictionary (A New English Dictionary on Historical Principles); Oxford, 1888-1928; *Supplement and Bibliography;* Oxford, 1933.

A Pronouncing Dictionary of American English by Kenyon and Knott; G. & C. Merriam Company, Springfield, Massachusetts, 1944.

Psychiatric Dictionary, third edition, by Leland E. Hinsie, M.D., and Robert Jean Campbell, M.D.; Oxford University Press, New York, 1960.

The Random House Dictionary of the English Language, Jess Stein, editor; Random House, New York, 1966.

Thorndike-Barnhart Comprehensive Desk Dictionary; Doubleday and Company, New York, 1957.

Webster's New International Dictionary, first edition, unabridged; G. & C. Merriam Company, Springfield, Mass., 1881.

Webster's New International Dictionary, second edition, unabridged; G. & C. Merriam Company, Springfield, Massachusetts, 1934.

Webster's New International Dictionary, third edition, unabridged; G. & C. Merriam Company, Springfield, Massachusetts, 1961.

Webster's New World Dictionary, college edition; World Publishing Company, Cleveland and New York, 1960.

medieval French battle cry. 2. a memorial stone pile.

mool (mōōl) *n.* 1. dry earth. 2. a grave *-v.t.* to bury. *-v.i.* to crumble.

moonglade (mōōn'glād) *n.* moonlight reflected on water.

moonwort (mōōn'wûrt) *n.* 1. a fern. 2. an herb called honesty. 2. a Canary Island bush.

moorup (mōō-rōōp') *n.s.&pl.* a cassoway with rather small, fat legs.

mopus (mō'pəs) *n.* 1. a small coin. 2. money, usually in *pl.* (-puses).

mora (môr'ə) *n.* 1. an unwarranted legal delay. 2. a hardwood tree of Guiana and Trinidad. 3. a division of the Spartan army. 4. a wicker footstool. 5. dishonor. 6. a finger game. *-adj.* cheap.

moraine (môr-ān') *n.* an accumulation of earth, stones, etc., deposited by a glacier.

morbidezza (môr-bē-dèts'ə) *n.* 1. the subtle, delicate, and lifelike handling of skin texture in painting and sculpture. 2. a musical direction calling for extreme delicacy.

morbific (môr-bĭf'ĭk) *adj.* causing disease.

morbillous (môr-bĭl'əs) *adj.* measly; pertaining to measles.

morcellate (môr'sèl-āt) *v.t.* to divide into small pieces.

mordacious (môr-dā'shəs) *adj.* biting, acrid, caustic.

mordant (môr'dànt) *adj.* 1. mordacious. 2. burning, corrosive. *-n.* 1. a jeweled metal plate at the end of a belt. 2. any corroding substance used in etching. 3. metal glue.

mordent (môr'dènt) *n.* a musical ornament executed as a quick alternation between a principal tone and an auxiliary one a half or whole step below.

morepork (môr'pórk) *n.* the New Zealand owl or the Tasmanian nightjar.

moreta (môr-èt'ə) *n.* a salad with garlic.

morganatic (môr-gən-ăt'Ĭk) *adj.* pertaining to marriage between an aristocratic male and untitled female in which she and their issue acquire neither rank nor property.

morganize (môr'gən-īz) *v.t.* to kidnap in order to prevent a security leak (from William *Morgan,* who was snatched by the Masons in 1826).

morigerous (môr-ĭj'ər-əs) *adj.* obedient, obsequious.

morology (môr-ŏl'ə-jē) *n.* nonsense, foolishness.

morosis (môr-ō'sĭs) *n.* imbecility.

morpheme (môr'fēm) *n.* a word or word part broken down to its basic element.

morphology (môr-fŏl'ə-jē) *n.* 1. the branch of biology dealing with the form and structure of plants and animals. 2. the science of language form and structure. 3. any science of forms and their variations (philosophy). *morphic, morphologic, morphological, adj.*

morphous (môr'fəs) *adj.* having a definite form.

morpunkee (môr-pŭng'kē) *n.* a long, paddle-powered Indian barge.

morris (môr'Ĭs) *n.* 1. an old English dance in which the performers played the parts of folklore characters. 2. a Moorish dance performed by a castanet-clacking man. 3. a larval conger eel. *-v.t.* to dance. *-v.i.* to depart, leave.

morro (môr'ō) *n.* a round hill or

màn; māde; lèt; bē; sĭp; wīne; hòt; cōld; sôre; dùll; fūgue; bûrp; gōōd; fōōd; out; gèt; thin; t̵his; year; a̵zure; ō'mən"; viN; fûr; Bach

point of land.

morsure (môr'shər) *n.* biting; a bite.

mort (môrt) *n.* 1. death. 2. a trumpet blast announcing the death of animals in the hunt. 3. skin removed , from diseased sheep. 4. an iron coffin to discourage body snatchers. 5. a large quantity. 6. a three-year-old salmon. 7. pork fat.

mortling (môrt'lĭng) *n.* wool taken from a dead sheep.

mortmain (môrt'mān) *n.* permanent ownership of real estate by institutions (French *mort* = dead + *main* = hand).

mortpay (môrt'pā) *n. deadpay:* 1. continued pay dishonestly drawn for soldiers and sailors now discharged or dead. 2. someone in whose name the pay is drawn.

mortress (môr'très) *n.* a strange dish; hodgepodge.

mos (mŏs) *n.* the singular of *mores.*

mossback (môs'băk) *n.* a conservative (slang).

motatorious (mō-tə-tôr'ĭ-əs) *adj.* constantly active.

motile (mō'tĭl) *adj.* moving spontaneously, as certain microorganisms. *-n.* a person whose mental imagery consists mainly of her own body's movements.

motitation (mō-tĭ-tā'shən) *n.* a quivering movement.

mouchard (mōō-shôr') *n.* a police spy.

moue (mōō) *n.* pout

moulage (mōō-lŏž') *n.* 1. the making of plastic molds of objects to be used in evidence. 2. the mold itself (criminology).

mouthfriend (mouth'frĕnd) *n.* a false friend.

mouton (mōō'tŏn) *n.* a prison spy.

moxibustion (mŏks'ĭ-bŭs"chən) *n.*

cauterization with *moxa,* a cottony material burned on the skin.

mpret (əm-prĕt') *n.* the title of the ruler of Albania (in the bad old days).

msasa (əm-sŏ'sŏ) *n.* the *Brachystegia* tree of Southern Rhodesia.

mubble-fubbles (mŭb'əl-fŭb"əlz) *n.pl.* a fit of depression.

mucilaginous (mū-sĭl-àj'ĭn-əs) *adj.* viscid, sticky. also *mucid* and *muculent.*

muckender (mŭk'ĕnd"ər) *n.* a dirty handkerchief (dialect).

mucker (mŭk'ər) *n.* 1. a muddy pratfall. 2. a gloomy person. 3. a stableboy. 4. a muck-digger. 5. a low-down uncouth boorish lout. *-v.i.* 1. to make a mess or failure of. 2. to be lowdown, uncouth, or boorish. *-v.t.* to hoard.

muckibus (mŭk'ĭ-bəs) *adj.* drunk (slang).

muckmidden (mŭk'mĭd"ən) *n.* a dunghill.

muezzin (mōō-ĕz'ĭn) *n.* a Mohammedan town crier who exhorts the pious to their prayers.

muglent (mū'jĭ-ənt) *adj.* bellowing.

mugwump (mŭg'wŭmp) *n.* 1. an ex-Republican; a political independent. 2. a chronic party critic. 3. a "big" man; a chief (Algonquian *mugquomp* = a chief).

mujtahid (mōōj-tŏ'hĭd) *n.* a Moslem Shiite who excels in law and theology.

mukkus (mŭk'əs) *n.* a dull, stupid person (slang).

mulada (mōō-lò'dŏ) *n.* a mule herd. herd.

mulct (mŭlkt) *n.* 1. a fine or penalty. 2. a blemish.

muleteer (mū-lə-tĭr') *n.* one who drives mules; a *mule skinner.*

muliebrity (mū-lĭ-ĕb'rĭ-tē) *n.* 1. assumption of female character-

---

istics by a male. 2. femininity.

mulierose (mū″lĭ-ĕr-ōs″) *adj.* extremely fond of women.

mullah (mŏŏl′ə) *n.* a learned teacher or expounder of the laws and dogmas of Islam.

mulligatawny (mŭl″ĭ-gə-tôn′ē) *n.* a strong East Indian curried soup.

mulligrubs (mŭl′ĭ-grŭbz) *n.pl.* 1. abdominal pain; colic. 2. the "blues." 3. the *hellgrammite*, a larval insect.

mullock (mŭl′ək) *n.* rubbish, dirt.

mulse (mŭls) *n.* wine boiled and mixed with honey.

multanimous (mŭl-tăn′ĭ-məs) *adj.* mentally multifaceted.

multigravida (mŭl-tĭ-grăv′ĭ-də) *n.* a woman who has been pregnant more than once.

multiloquent (mŭl-tĭl′ō-kwənt) *adj.* loquacious, gabby.

multiversant (mŭl-tĭ-vûr′sənt) *adj.* infinitely variable.

mumblecrust (mŭm′bəl-krŭst) *n.* a toothless person; a beggar.

mumpish (mŭmp′ĭsh) *adj.* sullen or sulky.

mumpsimus (mŭmp′sĭ-məs) *n.* 1. an unswerving bigot. 2. a prejudice adhered to regardless of evidence.

mumruffin (mŭm′rŭf″ĭn) *n.* the long-tailed titmouse.

Munchausenism (mŭn-chô′zən-ĭz″əm) *n.* telling fantastic adventure stories as did Baron Karl Friedrich Hieronymus von *Münchausen*.

mundificant (mŭn-dĭf′ĭ-kənt) *adj.* having cleansing and healing properties. *-n.* a salve with these properties.

mundivagant (mŭn-dĭv′ə-gənt) *n.* wandering over the world.

mundungus (mŭn-dŭng′gəs) *n.* 1. garbage. 2. stinky tobacco.

mungo (mŭng′gō) *n.* 1. one who retrieves valuables from garbage (slang). 2. the mung bean. 3. the mongoose. 4. an herb used as a snake charm in India. 5. reclaimed wool.

muniment (mū′nĭ-mənt) *n.* 1. documentary evidence of ownership. 2. a means of protection.

murdrum (mûr′drəm) *n.* homicide.

murenger (myûr′ən-jûr) *n.* one in charge of the town wall and its upkeep.

muricate (myûr′ĭ-kāt) *adj.* formed with sharp points; prickly.

muriphobia (myûr-ĭ-fō′bĭ-ə) *n.* fear of mice.

murrey (mûr′ē) *n.&adj.* dark red.

musard (mū′zərd) *n.* an absent-minded dreamer, or fool.

muscovado (mŭs-kō-vā′dō) *n.* sugar from cane.

mush-faker (mŭsh′fāk″ər) *n.* a Mr. Fixit, especially of umbrellas (hobo slang).

muskimoot (mŭs′kĭ-mōōt) *n.* a sack for holding pelts.

musnud (mŭs′nŭd) *n.* a thronelike dais; a seat of honor.

mussitation (mŭs-ĭ-tā′shən) *n.* muttering.

mutsuddy (mōōt′sŭd″ē) *n.* a native clerk (Anglo-Indian).

muzhik (mōō-zēk′) *n.* a Russian peasant.

mycophagy (mī-kŏf′ə-jē) *n.* the eating of fungi or mushrooms.

mycterism (mĭk′tər-ĭz″əm) *n.* sneering; derision.

mykiss (mī′kĭs) *n.* the Kamchatka salmon; the cutthroat trout.

mymy (mī′mī) *n.* 1. an aboriginal hut. 2. a bed. also *miamia* (Australian).

myomancy (mī′ō-măn″sē) *n.* fortunetelling by watching mice.

myoxine (mī-ŏks′ĭn) *adj.* pertain-

---

mǎn; māde; lĕt; bē; sĭp; wīne; hŏt; cōld; sôre; dŭll; fūgue; bûrp; gŏŏd; fōŏd; out; gĕt; thin; thĭs; year; ażure; ŏ′mən″; viN; fūr; Bach

ing to the dormouse.

myriadigamous (mǐr″ǐ-ə-dǐg′ə-məs) *adj.* pertaining to someone who marries all kinds.

myriologue (mǐr′ǐ-ō-lôg″) *n.* a Greek funeral song sung and composed by the girl friend of the departed.

myriotheism (mǐr′ǐ-ō-thē″ǐz-əm) *n.* polytheism.

myrmecoidy (mûr′mē-koid″ē) *n.* the mimicking of ants by other insects.

myrmecology (mûr-mē-kŏl′ə-jē) *n.* the scientific study of ants.

myrmidon (mûr′mǐ-dŏn) *n.* a blindly loyal, though unscrupulous, factotum.

mysophobia (mī-sō-fō′bǐ-ə) *n.* fear of dirt or contamination; having a compulsion to wash one's hands. see *molysmophobia.*

mystacial (mǐs-tā′shǐ-əl) *adj.* like a mustache: said of a patch on the lower jaw of a woodpecker. also *mustachial, mystacal, mystacine, mystacinous.*

mytacism (mī′tə-sǐz″əm) *n.* using the letter M incorrectly or to an extreme.

mythomania (mǐth-ō-mā′nǐ-ə) *n.* compulsively telling lies and believing them.

màn; māde; lèt; bē; sǐp; wīne; hòt; cōld; sôre; dùll; fūgue; bûrp; gŏŏd; fōōd; out; gèt; thin; thìs; year; ażure; ō′mən″; viN; für; Bach